The Ramayana

The Ramayana

A New Retelling of Valmiki's Ancient Epic—Complete and Comprehensive

Linda Egenes
Kumuda Reddy

A TarcherPerigee Book

tarcherperigee

An imprint of Penguin Random House LLC
375 Hudson Street
New York, New York 10014

Library of Congress Cataloging-in-Publication Data

Names: Egenes, Linda, author. | Reddy, Kumuda, author. | Våalmåiki. Råamåayaòna.
Title: The Ramayana : a new retelling of Valmiki's ancient epic—complete and comprehensive / Linda Egenes, Kumuda Reddy.
Description: New York : TarcherPerigee, 2016. | Series: Tarcher cornerstone editions
Identifiers: LCCN 2016012659 | ISBN 9780143111801 (paperback)
Subjects: LCSH: Våalmåiki. Råamåayaòna—Adaptations. | BISAC: RELIGION / Hinduism / Sacred Writings. | PHILOSOPHY / Hindu. | BODY, MIND & SPIRIT / Meditation.
Classification: LCC BL1139.25 .E54 2016 | DDC 294.5/92204521—dc23

Printed in the United States of America
ScoutAutomatedPrintCode

Book design by Katy Riegel

For Maharishi Mahesh Yogi,

in gratitude

यावत्स्थास्यन्ति गिरयः सरितश्च महीतले ।
तावद्रामायणकथा लोकेषु प्रचरिष्यति ॥

So long as mountains and rivers
have their place on the face of the earth,
the story of the Rāmāyaṇa will be told in the world.

—Bāla Kāṇda 2.36

Contents

Introduction

The great epic known as the Rāmāyaṇa may be one of the most generative pieces of literature ever written. The sixteenth-century saint and reteller of the Rāmāyaṇa, Tulsīdās, effused:

Rām incarnates in countless ways.
And there are tens of millions of Rāmāyaṇas.

The Rāmāyaṇa has an extraordinary tradition of re-creating itself, and through this process it has appeared in many different forms and media. Whether chanted in Sanskrit or expressed in the literary traditions of the vast range of South Asian languages; whether appearing in the dim light of Indonesian shadow puppet plays or celebrated ritually in an all-night Kachuk dance; or whether decorating the royal palace in Thailand in miles of bas-relief or moving audiences in the many dance dramas in both classical and folk traditions, the sheer number of Rāmāyaṇa tellings over the last several thousand years has been nothing short of astonishing.[1]

Continuing this tradition, there is always room for one more retelling of the Rāmāyaṇa, especially when it captures the essence of the

1 Richman, Paula, ed. *Many Ramayanas.* "Three Hundred Ramayanas: Five Examples and Three Thoughts on Translation," Ramanujan, A.K. (Berkeley: University of California Press, 1991), 22–49.

original, as reflected in this new retelling by Linda Egenes and Kumuda Reddy. Their abridged adaptation, with its direct and simple style, using rhythmic prose rather than poetic meter, has captured the essence of the original with a purity and simplicity that is true to Vālmīki's original intent, yet is moving and touching to the heart in a very modern sense.

For those not familiar with the Rāmāyaṇa, it has been described as the original epic quest—comparable to the Bible, *Star Wars*, and *Romeo and Juliet* all rolled into one. Revered today by over one billion people worldwide as the most sacred of stories, the Rāmāyaṇa not only has its roots as the national treasure of India and Southeast Asia, but has emerged as one of the great classics of world literature. The Rāmāyaṇa is the "ayana" (journey) of one of the most illustrious of epic heroes—Rāma.

Cognized by the illustrious sage Vālmīki, the Rāmāyaṇa was originally chanted in Sanskrit, the language of the Vedic civilization of ancient India. The date of the composition of the Rāmāyaṇa cannot be fixed, since in the tradition of Vedic knowledge, the literature was handed down orally for thousands of years, singer to singer, generation after generation. Whenever he actually wrote down his cognition, Vālmīki—considered the first poet—captured the Rāmāyaṇa in poetry of unsurpassed dramatic power and richness in over 24,000 couplet verses, or shlokas, making it one of the longest epic poems ever written. Of the many branches of the Sanskrit literature, the Rāmāyaṇa belongs to the Itihāsa branch, which also contains its longer companion epic, the Mahābhārata.

The Rāmāyaṇa is the epic adventure of the enlightened hero Rāma and his quest to purify the world of ignorance and negativity. Along the way, Rāma is united with his wife Sītā; encounters separation from his beloved; and finally overcomes these challenges by destroying the forces of darkness and transforming the world. Throughout this journey, the themes of love and *Dharma* intertwine in an exquisite archetypal play that deepens the story at every turn.

There is a saying, "That which lasts longest is closest to the truth." By this measure, the Rāmāyaṇa holds a unique position in the field of world literature. Both in terms of its lasting impact over time, as well as its influence across many cultures, the Rāmāyaṇa has maintained a universal appeal that has reverberated across millennia. In addition to its revered status throughout the East, the Rāmāyaṇa has also had a seminal impact on Western mythic traditions and popular cultures. Many of the themes recurrent in Western myths and fairy tales, such as the "exile to the forest" or the "evil stepmother," originated in the Rāmāyaṇa. George Lucas was himself strongly influenced by the Rāmāyaṇa as he created the original *Star Wars*. Unlike many of the archaic epics lost in obscurity, the Rāmāyaṇa has remained a vital living tradition, propagating throughout the world in its myriad forms.

How has the Rāmāyaṇa maintained this universal appeal? The secret of the Rāmāyaṇa lies in its depth, within which is embedded a comprehensive, multileveled mythic structure—layer upon layer of understanding and meaning. These layers move from the most outward, surface level to the deepest and most refined levels—inexorably propelling the beholder to dive in toward the source.

Before we proceed, I would like to clarify the use of the term "myth." Some individuals and scholars still treat the word "myth" as signifying a fanciful tale from the distant past. Many people in the field now use the word "myth" as the multicultural expression popularized by Joseph Campbell, who defines myth as the underlying archetypal "blueprint" of a culture—the wellspring of unseen values and deeply held world pictures that shape the behavior of the individual and the entire society. I propose to take the concept of myth to an even deeper level: that the Rāmāyaṇa transcends the scholarly and popular use of myth and is the fundamental structure of life itself. It is the concrete expression of abstract principles of knowledge (Veda), much like human physiology is the expression of its underlying DNA. The Rāmāyaṇa is the living expression of the Veda.

Let us explore these nested Chinese boxes of meaning and structure that make up the Rāmāyaṇa. The outer level of the story of the Rāmāyaṇa reveals the field of changing mores and customs within a civilization. The virtuous Rāma and the other characters embody ideal levels of behavior that become guidelines for all to emulate. A deeper level of the Rāmāyaṇa is the level of the heroic quest and heroic life, describing the transformation of the characters within the stages of their heroic journeys. It corresponds to the heroic action that the hero must undertake for the benefit of the society as a whole. This level is seen in Arthurian legends, the Grail myth, or in the *Odyssey*.

A still deeper level is that of the gods and goddesses, describing life as it was close to the beginning of creation. This level personifies the elemental forces of nature and is seen in the creation myths from various cultures or in Genesis. Deeper still is the fourth, almost transcendental level of myth—a level so powerful and all-encompassing that it could only be seen as an expression of the divine intelligence itself that has created nature in the first place. This level reveals the very mechanics of creation, which synthesize all the elemental forces of nature into a more all-encompassing wholeness. The Rāmāyaṇa knits together all these levels in a profound, comprehensive structure.

But what enthralls us so much that we cannot resist moving through these various levels of meaning and depth as we journey through the Rāmāyaṇa? Throughout his journey, Rāma encounters an extraordinary "līlā" (divine play) of opposing forces—apparently irreconcilable opposites—that must be overcome until his ultimate victory. This is the very essence of the myth-making process—the process whereby opposing forces are transcended to a deeper level of synthesis. A classic example of this is seen in the Rāmāyaṇa's companion epic, the Mahābhārata. The Mahābhārata portrays a great war in which Arjuna, the most respected archer of his time, is torn between his duty to oppose evil and his inability to kill members of his own family who oppose righteousness. Standing in that state of suspension, he must transcend to a deeper level of synthesis to encompass these irreconcilable values. The reader who identifies with Arjuna in this case must also transcend to a more comprehensive worldview and embrace these values within himself.

As our expanded sense of self unfolds in this process, we find a corresponding expansion in our sense of Dharma. Dharma is the force of evolution, the invincible force of life that flows through all created things. Dharma is also personal—as in, how do I create the smoothest, most evolutionary path for my own life? At every step of the way, the expansion of our individual consciousness yields a more comprehensive vision of what is most significant both for our evolution and for the evolution of life as a whole.

Now we can see how these themes extend throughout the Rāmāyaṇa. Great epics such as the Rāmāyaṇa and the Mahābhārata take us into this sacred world of archetypal depth where all these opposing values are magnified in the extreme. As we journey into the Rāmāyaṇa, for example, we become Rāma's father, King Dasharatha, who is torn between the love of his son and his duty to uphold his word. He wishes to crown his universally-loved eldest son as his heir apparent, but in the past he has promised Rāma's stepmother Kaikeyī two boons, and she now demands that her son, Bharata, be crowned and Rāma be exiled to the forest for fourteen years.

As the saga continues, we are also Rāma, who has just fought a cataclysmic battle to recover his cherished wife, Sītā, who was abducted by the king of the demons, Rāvaṇa. Even though he knows in his heart that Sītā is pure, he must banish his precious wife from the kingdom to satisfy the doubts of the people that their king has reunited with a woman who may have been corrupted by living in a demon's household for almost a year. In both these situations, we feel a tremendous pull of emotion played out in the tug between our heart and mind. Herein lies the secret of the Rāmāyaṇa. The story is so vast, profound, and multilayered, it contains virtually every expression of relationship in the play and display of life. As we follow its epic journey, we also explore every swing of emotion in this field—from the depths of despair to supreme ecstasy, and everything in between. Again and again we encounter its apparently irreconcilable values, and our consciousness expands in the process. Simultaneously, the Rāmāyaṇa spurs us to follow this unfolding process—discriminating finer and finer values of Dharma until we ultimately experience the fullest expression of what Dharma can truly be.

What makes the Rāmāyaṇa unique is this internal dynamic, which provides a pathway whose exploration appears to have no end to its depth. Other great epics display deepening values of Dharma through this play of opposites, so what makes the Rāmāyaṇa so different? This may have to do with the expansive qualities that Rāma embodies. Rāma not only displays the exemplary virtues of many heroes, but his capacity for enlightenment moves the story toward much deeper waters. Rāma commands a sphere of influence that administers all of nature—his mission being to rid the entire world of ignorance. This breadth of scope appears unique among the heroic pantheon. Rāma is a divine being born as a man, fully integrated in heart and mind, and united with his Self. In Hindi there is a saying, *Rām Brahm paramārath rūpā*—"Rāma is Brahman, Totality."

We now begin to glimpse the profound parallels within our own consciousness. The endpoint of Rāma's journey is nothing less than the eternal story of All That Is (Totality) and its relationship with our Self. The great Vedic sage Maharishi Mahesh Yogi describes this relationship:

> Rām is the embodiment of pure spirituality, of pure Being—Totality in its absolute unity. All activity in the universe is orderly because of that eternal law of life, the administration of Rām, which establishes and maintains harmony in all relationships; which harmonizes everything with every other thing in the universe.[2]

This selection underscores why the experience of the Rāmāyaṇa should yield such profound results. If Rāma embodies all the diverse relationships in the universe, then the study of his story is essentially the study of our Self and our evolving relationship with creation. In this view, the impulses of the Rāmāyaṇa are the structures of our own consciousness, our own Self. All the characters of the Rāmāyaṇa are aspects of our own nature, playing out all its possibilities and tendencies. The vanquishing of ignorance and the reestablishment of Rāma's realm, for example, are actually the "inner" drama within our own Self as we grow in enlightenment. The tapestry that the Rāmāyaṇa weaves embraces both the entire fabric of nature and the dynamics of our own nature.

There is a scientific basis for this profound connection between Rāma's journey and our own evolution. Dr. Tony Nader, a medical doctor and physiologist by training, conducted highly original research that found a stunning correlation between the form and function of our physiology and all these details of the story of the Rāmāyaṇa (*Rāmāyaṇ in Human Physiology*).[3] This may be hard to fathom, but this timeless saga appears to be a "script of our nature," continually unfolding our brain and body, and acting as a template for the growth of our full potential as human beings.

Let us now return to resolve our earlier dilemma. We are now Rāma, who, after banishing Sītā, grieves deeply at his loss when Sītā asks Divine Mother to return home and is then swallowed up by the earth. Rāma is inconsolable, but then the Creator himself (Brahmā) reminds Rāma of his divine origins. Brahmā is able to shift Rāma's whole perception by reminding him that his separation from Sītā is only a flicker in the vast

---

2 Maharishi Mahesh Yogi. *Rām, Rāmāyaṇa, Rām Līlā, Rām Rāj*. (Holland: Maharishi Vedic University Press, 1992), 10.

3 Nader, Tony, MD, PhD. *Rāmāyaṇ in Human Physiology: Discovery of the Eternal Reality of the Rāmāyaṇ in the Structure and Function of Human Physiology* (Fairfield, IA: Maharishi University of Management Press, 2012).

span of eternity. Rāma transcends and realizes that he will be "momentarily" reunited with his consort Lakshmī (Sītā) when he returns to heaven. Are not we all like Rāma, forgetting our divine nature in grieving over our own "momentary losses"?

The reestablishment of the wholeness of life, inside and out, seems to be Rāma's odyssey (or, shall we say, Rāmāyaṇa) as well as our own. Rāma's quest, and our identification with his journey, inevitably expands to cosmic dimensions, since the "ayana" of the Rāmāyaṇa is a Sanskrit term that signifies a cosmic journey, like a planet revolving around the sun, or a solar system moving around the center of the galaxy. So our journey has also come full circle.

This introduction may have given a glimpse of the evolutionary potential for a dive into the deep well of the Rāmāyaṇa. We have explored two movements in this process. First, the deep container of the Rāmāyaṇa enables us to plumb vertically into its depths, inspiring and reinspiring us with its many layers of meaning. The display of great contrasting values and their seemingly irreconcilable opposites challenges us to expand our personal framework and shift to a deeper level of synthesis within ourselves to embrace this play of opposites. In the process, we have learned to align our individual nature (or Dharma) with all of nature. Thus the Rāmāyaṇa serves as the ultimate dramatic vehicle by enlivening the deepest values of life. This is why audiences are eternally touched by it.

Simultaneously, the Rāmāyaṇa expands horizontally, through cultures and societies, diversifying itself through its array of forms and styles of adaptation.

It spreads, ceaselessly, various,
one and many at once.

Thus when Kampan, a twelfth-century adapter of the Rāmāyaṇa for South India, poetically described this quality of the Rāmāyaṇa, he seemed to cognize the Sanskrit expression from the Bhagavad-Gītā: *prakṛitiṁ svām avashtabhya vishṛijāmi punaḥ punaḥ*—"Curving back on my own nature, I create again and again." This expression has been used to describe the creative process of nature itself, as it generates the universe through its own internal dynamics. The Rāmāyaṇa seems to hold a similar dynamic in its ability to also "curve back on itself to create again and again."

The Rāmāyaṇa is like that iconic Indian image of the banyan tree, with its roots going deep while its boughs spread in a huge, enveloping canopy. You are invited to enjoy the shade of one of these beautiful new boughs in the Egenes/Reddy rendition, which contains the capability to blossom and inspire both the "unity of the one" and the rich diversity of the "many at once." Enjoy your adventure.

—Michael Sternfeld

Prologue

The Qualities of Rāma

Of all the sages in ancient India, Vālmīki was the most learned in the Vedic literature. Having purified his mind through long meditations, he was established in the Self and eloquent in speech.

One day Vālmīki was meditating in his quiet *āshram*, nestled in a vast and silent forest between the River Gangā and the River Tamasā. Suddenly, his own illustrious teacher, Sage Nārada, appeared to him. Nārada was not only a learned sage, but a divine musician who enchanted mortal and celestial alike with his melodies.

"Do you have a question?" asked Nārada quietly.

Vālmīki smiled, for he did, indeed, have a question to ask Sage Nārada, who could see the past, present, and future with equal clarity.

"Is there such a thing as a perfect person?" asked Vālmīki. "Is there anyone in this world with all the heroic qualities—who is dutiful, truthful, kind to all, learned, patient, free of envy, slow to anger, handsome as a god, and who can vanquish all foes? Does such a person exist?"

Now Nārada was smiling. "There is such a man who embodies all of these rare qualities and more. His name is Rāma, and he comes from the family of Ikshvāku. Let me tell you about him." Nārada said:

Rāma has controlled his mind.
Radiant, powerful, and resolute,
wise, eloquent, and glorious—

he can easily destroy his enemies.
With broad shoulders, a neck like a conch, and a prominent chin,
he has long arms, reaching to his knees.
His head is noble, his limbs well-proportioned,
his complexion like the blue lotus.
Of medium stature,
his eyes large and his chest broad,
filled with splendor, with auspicious marks adorning his body,
he is courageous and skilled in the science of warfare.

The personification of integrity,
he helps those who seek him out.
Ever mindful of the good in others,
he is generous and keeps his word.
Pure and devoted to truth, he is adept at attaining samādhi,
transcendental bliss.

With a pleasing disposition,
Rāma inspires virtue in others.
With a perfect memory,
he knows the essential nature of the Veda.
As rivers flow to the ocean,
so the virtuous are devoted to Rāma.

Rāma is delightful to gaze upon, like the full moon,
mighty, like the ocean;
firmly established in silence, like the Himālaya.
Like the earth, he is patient
and devoted to the welfare of all.

Then Nārada told Vālmīki the story of Rāma, how he was born to King Dasharatha and was an obedient son. How he married the beautiful and faithful Sītā. How he was to be crowned king, but through no fault of his own was instead banished to the forest for fourteen years. How he and Sītā traveled in dense jungles, and Rāma fought the evil demons, called *rākshasas*, who were the enemies of all that is good and pure on earth. How Sītā was abducted by Rāvaṇa, the king of the rākshasas. How Rāma fought and conquered Rāvaṇa, freeing the world from evil. How he was crowned king of Ayodhyā. Nārada said:

In the reign of Rāma, everyone was happy, prosperous, and virtuous.
No parents witnessed the early death of their children,
no women were left widows, and all women were devoted to their husbands.
There was no danger of violent storms, nor fear of drowning or fire.
None starved nor fell sick; no one was a thief.
Granaries overflowed with food, treasuries with gold.
Everyone in the kingdom of Rāma was wealthy, happy, and devoted to Rāma.
Rāma himself bestowed untold riches on the sages
and established royal dynasties of immense wealth under his reign.
He led the people in following their duties and, after ten thousand years,
ascended to Brahma Loka, the highest heaven.

"Indeed," said Nārada, "anyone who hears the story of Rāma is freed of all sin, will live a long life, and will be honored in heaven along with all his children and grandchildren."

The wise Vālmīki listened to the words of Nārada and was filled with joy and wonder.

Later that day, Nārada returned to the heavenly realms, and Vālmīki strolled quietly to the nearby River Tamasā to bathe. After a refreshing dip, he wandered in the forest, enjoying the joyful call of birds, the play of light filtering through dense trees, and the soft moss under his feet. As he walked, his mind was filled with devotion to Shrī Rāma, the one man who embodied all that is good.

A bird broke into a lovely song. Looking up, Vālmīki spotted a pair of beautiful red-crested *krauncha* birds high in a tree. The sage noticed that the birds called tenderly to each other. If one flew to a tree, the other followed. They were never apart even for a moment, for they delighted in each other's company.

Vālmīki smiled at the birds swooping and darting through the trees. He did not realize that another was watching too, a hunter looking for game. Suddenly, just as the male bird spread his wings to please his mate, an arrow pierced him, and he tumbled from the tree. Seeing her beloved mate lying on the ground, the female bird cried out in grief again and again.

Vālmīki felt his own heart contract with the pain of the bereaved bird. How cruel to separate this happy pair! Turning to the hunter, he burst out:

> *O hunter, having slain this bird enjoying with its mate,*
> *may you never find rest, may you never find peace.*

Vālmīki was silent for a long time, reflecting upon his own words. Then he said aloud, "Moved by compassion for this bird, I have spoken a Sanskrit verse in perfect poetic meter, which could be sung with the *vīṇā*. Let this meter be called *shloka*, because it has arisen from my sadness, *shoka*."

Vālmīki returned to his āshram and started the evening's lesson with his disciples. But his mind kept returning to the suffering of the bird, the hapless hunter whom he had cursed, and the perfect verses he had so spontaneously uttered. As he was pondering these strange events, a golden light filled the room, and to his astonishment, Brahmā, the Creator, appeared to him.

"It was I who inspired you to recite that verse," said Brahmā. "And it will only bring you glory, so there is no more need to worry that you cursed the hunter. Now you will compose a poem of the story of Rāma. To help you with your task, I will bestow a boon upon you. You will be able to see the events of Rāma's life unfolding. You will be able to see into the minds of Rāma, Sītā, and Lakshmaṇa. You will know all that happens and will tell the world the truth in your epic poem. So long as mountains and rivers have their place on the face of the earth, the story of the Rāmāyaṇa will be told in the world." Having said these words and blessed the exalted sage, Brahmā faded from view.

At first, no one moved, so awed were Vālmīki and his disciples by the unexpected visit. As his disciples murmured in excited whispers about the great honor conferred on their guru, it occurred to Vālmīki that the entire poem should be composed in the same shloka meter as the lines he had uttered earlier that day.

Retiring to his hut, Vālmīki sipped water to purify himself, and with his mind and heart devoted to God, he closed his eyes. The sage Vālmīki sank deep into meditation and, with the power of insight given to him by Brahmā, began to see the entire life of Rāma unfolding before him like a river flowing. He saw it as clearly as one sees a fruit in the palm of the hand. What he saw, he composed into the beautiful, timeless poem of the Rāmāyaṇa, known as the first poem (*ādikavya*).

The Rāmāyaṇa is the story told by the wise and enlightened Vālmīki, who, filled with wonder, celebrated the deeds of the hero Rāma.

मा निषाद प्रतिष्ठां त्वमगमः शाश्वतीः समाः ।
यत्क्रौञ्चमिथुनादेकमवधीः काममोहितम् ॥

O hunter, having slain this bird enjoying with its mate,
may you never find rest, may you never find peace.

—Bāla Kāṇda 2.15

ONE

Bāla Kāṇḍa

Childhood

Chapter 1

King Dasharatha's Joy

O Ayodhyā!
Architects designed you
to be beautiful,
gracious, and strong.
Untouched by enemies,
invincible behind towering gates
with a wide moat circling your waist,
your brave and noble warriors
could find their target through sound alone.

O Ayodhyā, delight to the senses!
Melodies of poets, singers, and musicians
echoed through your markets
where merchants from faraway kingdoms
traded their wares in peace.
Trumpets, bugles, flutes, conches, and gongs
sweetened the air with music.

Mansions lined your wide, straight streets,
their high-arched porches streaming
with flags and banners,
ringed by gardens

of sweet-smelling flowers.
An array of palaces adorned you
like a string of pearls,
their walls set with precious gems
and their high domes towering
like mountain peaks.
Mango groves and
tall trees girded your edges like a sash.

The chanting of sages and pandits
learned in the four Vedas
blessed your people,
who shimmered with gold
and jeweled ornaments
like the sun.
Truthful, brave, and contented,
no one lived in poverty,
and all lived happily with their families.
Elephants, camels, horses, cattle, and mules
lightened the work.
Rice was plentiful
and the water pure.

Your generous and truth-loving people
lived long lives,
revered by their children and grandchildren.
Like great sages,
they were pure and chaste,
clear-minded, self-controlled,
and only did what was right.
All your people were blessed
with beauty and riches.
And all these noble people of Ayodhyā
were devoted to their noble king, Dasharatha.

King Dasharatha waited alone inside his private chambers. It was spring, the ninth day of the pleasing lunar month of Chaitra. A light breeze carried the sweet scent of jasmine blossoms through the open windows, but the king did not notice. His mind was absorbed in thoughts of his three cherished queens, who at this moment were about to give birth.

How many years had he waited to be blessed with an heir? How many hours had he prayed for healthy offspring? And now, the fulfillment of his heart's desire was only moments away. As King Dasharatha reflected on his long and celebrated life, the past, glorious as it had been, seemed like the darkness of night compared to the joy he glimpsed ahead.

The king stepped onto his verandah. From there, he could see the golden rooftops of the city below, beyond that the holy River Sarayu, and beyond that the fertile fields of his beloved country of Kosala, which stretched as far as the rays of the sun. Since the beginning of time, King Dasharatha's family, of the glorious and peaceful dynasty of Ikshvāku, had ruled Kosala from the capital city of Ayodhyā. Founded by Manu, the father of Ikshvāku, king of the solar dynasty, the fabled city of Ayodhyā was celebrated throughout the three worlds.

As King Dasharatha thought of the virtuous people of Ayodhyā, he was grateful that they deemed him worthy to rule. For the king was humble in his greatness. Learned in the Vedas, truthful and pious, he had never broken his word. He had performed many *yagyas*, ceremonies to create balance in nature, and always gave generously to the pandits, saints, and wise men of the kingdom. His name, Dasharatha, meant "strong as ten chariots," a title he had earned long ago, while helping the *Devas*, the divine forces of nature, achieve victory over the *asuras*, the negative forces of nature. Celebrated on earth and in heaven, King Dasharatha was loved and revered by all.

Standing on his verandah, King Dasharatha reflected on his long rule, the years when Kosala had lived peacefully with its neighboring kingdoms and increased its wealth many times.

Like the sun surrounded by brilliant rays, King Dasharatha was surrounded by eight wise ministers, who practiced right conduct with their families and friends, never speaking a word in anger. They were known for their honesty, courage, and friendliness.

Versed in economics, they kept the kingdom's treasuries full without unduly taxing the people. Experts in defense, they made friends with the neighboring kingdoms. Skilled in lawmaking, they governed all with justice, levying fines on wrongdoers, but never more than the person could afford.

King Dasharatha also relied on the judgment of spiritual advisors, wise *Ṛishis*, headed by the radiant Vasishtha. Supported by benevolent ministers and enlightened sages, celebrated as the ocean of truth, King Dasharatha had no equal among all the monarchs on earth.

In all the years of his long rule, the king had known only one sorrow: even though he had ruled with wisdom and had conducted many yagyas, he had not been blessed with an heir. The grief of reaching old age without a son had weighed heavily on him, like a grinding stone on wheat chaff. Knowing that the illustrious line of the Ikshvākus would not continue, Dasharatha and his three wives were not able to fully enjoy the wealth and glory of their kingdom.

But that was behind him now, for on this very day his three queens would give birth to his children.

King Dasharatha felt the cool spring breeze and stepped back inside his palace, drawing the curtains over the doors. His chief minister, Sumantra, waited inside. Ghee lamps cast a warm glow over Sumantra's shining garments.

"O Sumantra," said King Dasharatha with a smile. "How delightful to have your company as I await glad tidings. After all, it was you who helped me reach this happy state."

Sumantra, who was the minister of the household and the king's most trusted ally and friend, smiled as he bowed low to King Dasharatha. "It was not I who helped you, but Destiny herself," he said humbly. He took a seat across from his esteemed monarch, whom he had served during King Dasharatha's entire rule.

The king smiled at Sumantra, but soon was lost again in his thoughts. As old friends, they fell into a comfortable silence, content just to be in each other's company at such a moment.

King Dasharatha thought back six seasons, to the moment when he realized that he could no longer bear to live without an heir. On that day he had called the sage Vasishtha and all of his wise advisors to the court.

"O honored sages," he said, "I have walked the path of virtue, and yet I have not been fortunate enough to produce an heir. With your blessings, it is my desire to conduct a special yagya, and by so doing I wish to gain a son."

"Glory to King Dasharatha!" the ministers exclaimed. "Success to King Dasharatha! Your wish is now our desire."

Later that day Sumantra asked for a private audience with King Dasharatha.

"O gracious king," said Sumantra, bowing low. "There is an ancient story that came to my mind as you spoke today. I think it will help you obtain a son."

"Then by all means, tell me, trustworthy Sumantra," said Dasharatha, his eyes shining with love.

"Many years ago I heard a prophecy about our kingdom. Sanatkumāra, the sage of eternal youth, predicted that a certain young ascetic called Ṛishyashṛinga would marry the daughter of King Romapāda in order to end a drought in his kingdom. After that, the story predicted, the esteemed Ṛishyashṛinga would travel to Ayodhyā and perform a yagya, and as a result, King Dasharatha would gain four sons of untold valor, who would become the glory of the Ikshvākus."

Sumantra paused for a moment. Then he said, "Just today, word reached us that King Romapāda's daughter has recently married the pure-souled sage named Ṛishyashṛinga, and their marriage did, indeed, end the drought in their kingdom."

King Dasharatha's face lit up.

"O fearless king," Sumantra advised, "do not delay. Invite Ṛishyashṛinga here to conduct your yagya and thereby obtain your sons."

Taking his trusted minister's words to heart, King Dasharatha first sought the blessing of the holy Vasishtha. Having received the sage's blessing, King Dasharatha, the most powerful ruler on earth, set out the next day to the domain of King Romapāda with his wives and ministers. As they neared that virtuous king's domain, they passed fertile fields and lush gardens, and noticed that the rivers ran with ample waters now that the drought was ended there.

He spent a week being entertained in the opulent palace of his friend King Romapāda, where the young sage Ṛishyashṛinga sat beside his father-in-law like a blazing fire. On the seventh day, King Dasharatha shared with King Romapāda the reason for his visit, and humbly requested that the king's lovely daughter Shantā and the wise Ṛishyashṛinga return to Ayodhyā with him.

When King Romapāda consented, King Dasharatha faced the young sage with his palms pressed together in a sign of respect, said, "O holy one, I beseech you to fulfill my desire for an heir, just as you have ended the drought for King Romapāda."

Sage Ṛishyashṛinga said, "Do not fear, O noble king. Four courageous sons will be born to continue your line."

Thus the luminous Ṛishyashṛinga and his wide-eyed bride, Shantā, traveled to Ayodhyā with King Dasharatha. There, in due time, Ṛishyashṛinga began the powerful *Ashvamedha Yagya*, the ceremony of the horse, which lasted more than a year and was attended by all the kings of the land.

After the flawless completion of the Ashvamedha Yagya, which is difficult even for the greatest monarch to achieve, King Dasharatha radiated purity and light. Sage Ṛishyashṛinga, in the silence of his meditations, knew what to do next. He said to Dasharatha, "I will now perform a certain yagya from the *Atharva Veda* to enable you to attain an heir."

WHILE THE YAGYA was taking place, while King Dasharatha and Queen Kausalyā, his first queen, were pouring ghee on the ceremonial fire, a secret meeting of the celestials was taking place in heaven.

It seemed that Rāvaṇa, a demon who terrorized the earth, could not be defeated even by Indra, the king of the divine Devas. Rāvaṇa and his rākshasa armies wreaked havoc on the people and even desecrated the yagyas of holy men, spreading fear in all three worlds.

All of the Devas and the celestial musicians called *Gandharvas* had gathered together to ask Brahmā, the Creator, to save them from this dangerous tormentor.

"O revered Brahmā," said Indra, bowing low, "it is because of your boon that Rāvaṇa is so powerful. He destroys all good, all truth in the world. He and his warriors make the heavens and the earth tremble."

Everyone knew that at one time Rāvaṇa had engaged in difficult austerities and had mastered the four Vedas. Pleased with his devotion, Brahmā had granted him any boon he desired. "May I never be destroyed by Devas, Gandharvas, *yakshas*, or rākshasas," Rāvaṇa begged. And Brahmā had granted him his wish.

That was why even Indra, the king of the Devas, could not defeat Rāvaṇa in battle. Rāvaṇa and his armies had even entered the gates of heaven and scattered the Devas to the four ends of the earth.

Now Brahmā, the Creator, seated on his lotus flower, clearly remembered the boon that he had bestowed on Rāvaṇa. Rāvaṇa was, in fact, his great-grandson. But Rāvaṇa was also the son of a rākshasa woman and had followed in her ways of evil. Rāvaṇa was terrifying to look at, with ten heads and twenty powerful arms. He had become the king of Lankā, the sumptuous city of the rākshasas far to the south. There he enjoyed boundless wealth, entertainments, and luxury. Yet it was not enough. He wanted to rule over heaven and earth.

Brahmā knew all of this, but he also knew a secret. "In his arrogance," Brahmā told the assembly quietly, "Rāvaṇa did not ask to be invulnerable to mankind. He thought that man was not significant enough to hurt him. This blind pride is Rāvaṇa's weak point, for he will surely be destroyed by a mere man."

At this the celestial Devas and Gandharvas joyfully cried out praises to Brahmā. Then, placing their palms together in respect, they turned and bowed to the immortal Vishṇu, the Maintainer of the Universe. He rested on a golden couch, his skin blue as a summer sky, his face radiant and peaceful.

"Revered Lord Vishṇu, we entreat you to hear our prayers," cried the Devas after bowing to him in reverence. "Today the noble King Dasharatha is conducting a ceremony to beget four sons. His three queens are chaste and virtuous, beyond reproach. O most compassionate one, we entreat you, let yourself be born as King Dasharatha's son! This monster Rāvaṇa has destroyed all good in the world. The way of Dharma, of truth, has never been in greater danger. Cruelty reigns on earth while he still lives. Be born as Dasharatha's son and destroy him!"

The ever-compassionate Lord Vishṇu, whose desire was to maintain the balance of good and evil in the world, reassured the Devas. "So be it," he said, raising his right hand to bless them. "I will take birth in the world of men and destroy this enemy of truth."

MEANWHILE, BACK ON earth, the blameless Ṛishyashṛinga, having conducted the yagya without flaw, poured a final offering of ghee on the ceremonial fire. A radiant being emerged from the flames. It was Agni, the lord of fire. Shining like the sun, he wore robes of red, the color of his flaming hair. His skin shimmered like burnished copper, and his eyes blazed like yellow sapphires.

Agni stepped out of the flames holding a golden container with a silver lid, filled with a mixture of milk, rice, and sugar called *pāyasa*. He handed the sacred vessel to King Dasharatha, who bowed with reverence. "Take this pāyasa, prepared by the Devas. Give this fruit of your yagya to your three queens, who will bear sons in due time."

Having delivered the pāyasa, Agni melted into the flames. Dasharatha offered half of the pāyasa to the pious Queen Kausalyā, who was his first wife. He offered half of what remained to Queen Sumitrā, and half of what remained of that to his youngest queen, Kaikeyī. That still left a tiny portion, and that he gave to Queen Sumitrā, who then had two portions. The queens felt blessed to eat the auspicious pāyasa, the fruit of King Dasharatha's yagya.

In a few months, the three queens basked in carefree happiness as they prepared for the birth of their children. The children that they carried were so pure that the wombs of the three queens were said to glow like the sun. The halls of the palace were filled with laughter and delight, and the entire kingdom lived in happiness, hearts swelling in joyful anticipation of the long-awaited births of King Dasharatha's sons.

As King Dasharatha sat with his trusted friend Sumantra, remembering the blissful months since Sage Ṛishyashṛinga's yagya, he fell into a sweet slumber. Sumantra slipped away, leaving his beloved monarch to his dreams.

कोसलो नाम मुदितः स्फीतो जनपदो महान् ।
निविष्टः सरयूतीरे प्रभूतधनधान्यवान् ॥
अयोध्या नाम नगरी तत्रासील्लोकविश्रुता ।

There was a great country by the name of Kosala
on the bank of the River Sarayu.
It was joyful and prosperous, filled with riches and an abundance of grains.
There stood the city of Ayodhyā, famed throughout the world.

—*Bāla Kāṇḍa 5.5–6*

CHAPTER 2

The Birth of Rāma

When stars are auspicious
rising in the eastern sky,
when planets are exalted,
radiating good fortune and peace to all,
when the moon is full,
shining in happy union with the benefic planet Guru,
then will I come to bless the earth.

Running footsteps roused King Dasharatha from his slumber. Queen Kausalyā's personal servant burst into the room. "My lord, the First Queen has given birth to a son!"

King Dasharatha's face flooded with light. He cried, "Praise to Lord Vishṇu!" and loaded the girl with strings of jewels that lay heaped on his royal divan. "For your good tidings!"

Before long a hunched, white-haired woman hobbled into the room as fast as her age would allow. She was Mantharā, the personal attendant of his favorite wife, Kaikeyī.

The old woman cried, "Sire, Queen Kaikeyī has given birth to a son!" Mantharā's eyes were overflowing with tears of joy, for her adored Kaikeyī, whose own birth she had attended, was now a mother herself.

Before Mantharā could hobble away, laden with the gold and jewels King Dasharatha had showered upon her, she met two of Queen Sumitrā's attendants who were running into the king's chambers. Breathlessly the young girls said in unison, "Queen Sumitrā has given birth to *two* sons!"

King Dasharatha could not contain his happiness. After rewarding Queen Sumitrā's young attendants with necklaces of precious gems for their happy news, he bestowed lavish gifts upon Sage Ṛishyashṛinga and the other Brahmins, teachers, scholars, and holy men of the city. He prepared lavish feasts and declared a holiday for all. He gave away gold and cows.

As for the good people of Ayodhyā, they too were overwhelmed with happiness. After so many years of longing for an heir to the crown, now their kingdom was blessed with not one, but four princes. The people adorned their homes with bright banners and garlands of sweet-smelling flowers. They prepared their best dishes. Dancers twirled and musicians sang outside the palace gates for the joy of the royal family and the common people alike. King Dasharatha generously rewarded his servants with gifts and threw strands of precious gems to the performers below his windows.

And in the heavens, the Devas themselves celebrated the birth of Lord Vishṇu on earth with the divine melodies of Gandharvas and the dancing of divine nymphs called *apsarās*. To show their joy, they showered flower petals on King Dasharatha's palace.

The three queens were overcome with happiness, having become the adoring mothers of precious sons at long last. On the tenth day following their births, the family preceptor, the irreproachable Vasishtha, flawlessly performed the *nāmakaraṇa*, the naming ceremony, and bestowed the names of the boys at the auspicious moment, according to the precepts of the scriptures.

"O fortunate king, your cherished firstborn, son of Queen Kausalyā, born under all auspicious signs and stars, will be called 'Rāma,'" said Vasishtha. "Throughout his life he will be the upholder of Dharma, of Natural Law."

The shining Rāma was indeed born at the moment when all the stars and planets were in the most auspicious position in the long span of time extending thousands of years before and thousands of years after. In the ninth lunar day, the *nakshatra* (auspicious star cluster) *Punarvasu* was rising in the eastern sky, and five *grahas* (planets) were in exaltation—*Sūrya* (Sun), *Mangala* (Mars), *Shani* (Saturn), *Guru* (Jupiter), and *Shukra* (Venus). Three *rāshis* (signs of the zodiac)—*Mesha* (Aries), *Mīna* (Pisces), and *Tulā* (Libra)—were aspected by auspicious grahas. The moon formed a most happy union with the benefic graha Guru in the rising sign of *Karka* (Cancer).

Other signs pointed to a divine birth. Adorned with auspicious marks befitting one who was the embodiment of Lord Vishṇu, the baby Rāma had long arms, rose-colored lips, lustrous skin, and a voice that resounded like a gong. Basking in the sinless Kausalyā's lap, he enhanced her beauty as the moon enhances the glory of the ocean.

As the pandits chanted and incense sweetened the air, Vasishtha said to King Dasharatha, "Your second-born, son of Queen Kaikeyī, born under the auspicious nakshatra *Pushya* and the sign of *Mīna*, the fish, shall be called 'Bharata.' He will be the essence of heroism, duty, and grace." Kaikeyī beamed and clasped the baby Bharata to her heart in joy.

"And the radiant twins born to Queen Sumitrā under the star of *Āshleshā*, the serpent, shall be called 'Lakshmaṇa' and 'Shatrughna,'" said Vasishtha. Sumitrā, her arms enfolding her baby sons, felt her eyes fill with tears of pride and wonder.

Vasishtha completed the ceremony, proclaiming, "These four sons, born with all good qualities, will be radiant and handsome, upholders of Dharma. They will surpass even their father in brilliance and will be cherished for generations to come as the glory of the illustrious Ikshvāku line!"

From that day, King Dasharatha lived as if in a happy dream. The palace was filled with the laughter of the three queens and the prattle of the royal babes. The king delighted in the sound of tiny feet pattering over marble floors, and he would rush from the court to the private chambers each day to join his family. Toys made of silk, gold, and precious gems now filled the king's palace, and children's games filled the king's days. Nothing could cloud King Dasharatha's happiness. His three queens were entranced by the four radiant children, caring for all the sons equally, and the four boys called all three "Mother."

King Dasharatha loved each of his four sons dearly, although of the four, he was most attached to Rāma. As Rāma grew, King Dasharatha's devotion also grew in intensity. He could not imagine how he had once lived without his beloved son by his side.

Rāma returned his father's love with filial devotion. He was happiest when he was serving his father, the king. Nothing was more important to him.

At the same time, Rāma was so full of compassion that everyone he met felt that he loved them most. He was affectionately called "Rāmachandra" by the people of Ayodhyā because he was like *Chandra*, the full moon—his face ever glowing in a sweet smile, his words soft and loving, his actions without fail bringing delight to others. His own mother, Kausalyā, who was the essence of virtue, was filled with pride to have such a son. And the playful and affectionate Kaikeyī, who loved her own son, Bharata, beyond imagination, loved Rāma with the same intensity.

Rāma was like a second father to his younger brothers. They were so devoted to him that they never questioned his role as leader. All the brothers treated one another with respect and love.

Yet of the three younger ones, Lakshmaṇa was most devoted to Rāma and was ever happy to serve him. In turn, Rāma was extremely fond of Lakshmaṇa. The two boys slept side by side, and when Rāma was offered rice or milk or other food, he would not eat unless Lakshmaṇa did too. Whenever Rāma left the palace to hunt, Lakshmaṇa followed, his bow ready to defend Rāma. Lakshmaṇa was a second Rāma, like his shadow.

In the same way, there was a special friendship between Bharata and Shatrughna. And so the four boys grew in harmony and happiness, serving their parents and each other.

When they reached the age of nine, the boys began their education in the four Vedas. Their family guru, Vasishtha, taught them to practice meditation and to follow the path of Dharma, of right action, toward their parents, teachers, holy men, king, and subjects. To prepare for their roles as future leaders of their people, they learned the Vedic sciences of economics, politics, and diplomacy. They became expert marksmen, skilled in archery, and were fully trained as warrior-princes. They learned how to ride elephants and horses and became skilled at driving a chariot.

The four brothers grew to be strong, handsome, virtuous, brave, intelligent, courteous, and humble. They learned to honor the sacred rituals and rites, to honor their parents and teachers, and to honor their ancestors. In every way, they brought joy to the king.

King Dasharatha lacked nothing in his life now that he had his four illustrious sons to light his days. He gave even more generously to the holy men of his kingdom and loved nothing more than to show his kindness to all.

AND SO THE years passed, and the boys grew into young men. One day, when his four sons had reached the age of sixteen, King Dasharatha called his ministers and sages together. His sons were grown and it was time to find brides for them. He had just started to speak when the royal gatekeeper unexpectedly entered the room.

"Your Royal Majesty," announced the gatekeeper. "The renowned sage Vishvāmitra has graced us with his presence!"

King Dasharatha felt his face flush with excitement. How auspicious that the great Ṛishi had called at the very moment he was beginning arrangements for Rāma's marriage.

"I shall greet him myself," announced the good King Dasharatha. Followed by his ministers in a trail of golden silk, he made his way to the front gate of the palace.

King Dasharatha greeted the revered Ṛishi with hands folded and then touched his feet. He offered him water and a seat, and then he himself washed the holy man's feet. He circled the Ṛishi's head with a ghee lamp. After these traditional greetings, King Dasharatha led the sage to his court, presenting him with refreshments of fruit and cooling drinks. Then Vishvāmitra inquired after the welfare of the kingdom, the state of the royal treasury, and the prosperity of the king's subjects, friends, relatives, and sages.

"O most holy one," said King Dasharatha, his face glowing with reverence and happiness, "you have truly blessed us with your presence. The glory of the Ikshvākus is increased many times by the dust of your feet. Surely there must be some way I can serve you further. Whatever is your wish, I will surely be honored to fulfill it myself." With these pleasing and humble words, King Dasharatha paid homage to the celebrated teacher.

Smiling in return, Vishvāmitra said, "There is indeed a way that you can help me, most virtuous king, and by helping me you will ensure the way of truth for all good men on earth. For I am in need of someone to guard my āshram while I perform a difficult yagya. My hermitage in the forest is unprotected from evil rākshasas. The hideous demons wait until the ceremony is almost finished and then swoop down from the skies to scatter unspeakable filth, even bones and blood, over the sacred place—snuffing out the sacred fire. Because it is prohibited to express anger or even speak while performing the yagya, I cannot stop them with my yogic power."

King Dasharatha leaned forward eagerly. Old man that he was, the thought of a battle still excited him. Born and bred as a warrior, he had never been defeated.

"My armies and I will leave this day for your āshram," said the gracious king. "We will surely defend your hermitage from these outrageous acts."

Vishvāmitra smiled. "It is not you, nor your armies, that I seek. Lend me your son Rāma for a few months. Rāma will kill these bloodthirsty monsters and will return to you unharmed."

King Dasharatha could not believe his ears. How could this learned sage think that his treasured son could face such terrifying foes?

"O revered sage," said King Dasharatha, his voice trembling, "I have promised to fulfill your every desire. But surely there is some mistake. Rāma is yet of a tender age and is as dear to me as my own heart. I could not live a day without him by my side. How could I go on living, knowing that I sent him to his death? Take me, I am old but experienced in battle. Take my kingdom's many armies. I pray to you, release me from this ill-timed promise."

Unmoved by King Dasharatha's plea, Vishvāmitra's face darkened with rage. Vasishtha and the other sages glanced at each other uneasily, for Vishvāmitra's hot temper was well known.

"So, you are not the king I thought you were." The powerful Vishvāmitra raised his voice so all could hear. "First you promise me anything, then you retract the promise. Keep your son Rāma and keep your promises. They mean nothing to me now."

Faced with the prospect of breaking his word and disgracing the age-old tradition of his race, King Dasharatha slumped in his chair. He could not possibly live without Rāma, even for an hour. How could he send his cherished son to his death? Why was the sage holding him to his unlucky promise? All the happiness of the past sixteen years seemed to be slipping away as a dream dissolves into a nightmare. The good king, paralyzed by indecision, fell into a faint, unable to break his promise and unable to give his cherished son to Vishvāmitra.

In the heavens the gods trembled, for they knew that in his wrath, Vishvāmitra could wreak havoc on the hapless king.

विप्रयुक्तो हि रामेण मुहूर्तमपि नोत्सहे ।

Separated from Rāma I cannot live even for an hour.

—Bāla Kāṇḍa 20.8

Chapter 3

Rāma Conquers the Rākshasas and Receives Celestial Weapons

No one dared speak in the court of King Dasharatha. Vishvāmitra, who was once a famous warrior, was as renowned for his wrath as for his immense spiritual power. The gods in heaven shuddered, for even they would not be able to stop him from reducing the good King Dasharatha to ashes.

Only Vasishtha, who possessed equanimity acquired through long meditations, was not afraid. In the silence that followed Vishvāmitra's angry words, the atmosphere tense as the sky between bursts of lightning, Vasishtha roused Dasharatha from his swoon with nourishing words.

"Dear King," he said, "remember who you are. Never in the long line of Ikshvākus has a monarch broken his word. You have promised Vishvāmitra to fulfill any desire; it is only fitting that you keep your word. Brahmaṛishi Vishvāmitra is asceticism incarnate; he is supreme virtue personified. He is not asking you to do anything that will harm you or your son Rāma. On the contrary, the holy Vishvāmitra could destroy the rākshasas all by himself. It is for Rāma's sake alone that he is asking this. He knows Rāma's strength, and he knows that Rāma will be in no danger. This will only bring greater glory to Rāma. Rise up, O king of kings! Do not fear. All will be well."

These encouraging words revived King Dasharatha as the gentle rain revives the parched desert. Braced by Vasishtha's clear discourse, he remembered his duty. Confident that his trusted preceptor, the blameless

Vasishtha, foresaw no harm for Rāma, King Dasharatha called Rāma to his side, along with Lakshmaṇa, for the two were inseparable.

"O Rāma," said King Dasharatha, gazing at his sons tenderly. "Brahmaṛishi Vishvāmitra wishes you and your brother Lakshmaṇa to accompany him on a journey. Obey him as you would your own father, and serve him as you would your own preceptor, Vasishtha. Please him in every way, and bring glory to yourself and the entire line of the Ikshvākus."

"Yes, Father," said Rāma. "As you wish."

With the blessings of their father, mother, and guru, Rāma and his brother Lakshmaṇa, only sixteen years old, gathered their bows and arrows and set off with the great sage Vishvāmitra on a journey to his āshram. As they left, the wind wafted sweet breezes, full with the scent of vanilla blossoms, and the gods showered flower petals on their path. Drums and conches hailed their auspicious departure.

After walking south of the capital, the three came to the banks of the River Sarayu.

"Beloved child," said the warrior-sage Vishvāmitra to Rāma, "purify yourself in the waters and then I will teach you the Science of *Bala* and *Atibala* (strength and that which surpasses strength)."

The brilliant and pure Rāma and the faithful Lakshmaṇa purified themselves by bathing in the river. When they were ready to receive the teaching of warfare, Vishvāmitra said to Rāma,

Neither hunger nor thirst will be known to you,
nor fever, fatigue, old age.
Wedded to grace, beauty, skill,
learning, intelligence, and eloquence,
you will grow in imperishable glory
in all fields of life.
Know bala and atibala,
nourish them with deep meditation.
Enjoy the fruits of your virtue,
O immortal hero.

Imbued with the supreme energy of this ancient knowledge, shining like the sun in autumn, the radiant Rāma shed even greater brilliance all around.

After resting in the āshram of the sage Kama, Vishvāmitra, followed by the pure and radiant Rāma and his loyal brother Lakshmaṇa, crossed the River Sarayu and faced a desolate forest.

"Great Sage," said Rāma with his compassionate smile, "this wood is dark and sinister. Rather than the happy call of mating birds, the frightening roar of beasts echoes through it. What caused this forest to be overgrown with thorns and twisted, leafless trees?"

"Beloved Rāma," said Vishvāmitra, "long ago two prosperous cities were built here by the Devas. But then an evil demoness was born nearby. Her name is Tātakā. Possessed of the strength of a thousand elephants, she allows no one to pass through here unharmed. She has made uninhabitable this place, once a garden of the gods.

"Tātakā lives only five miles from here," he continued. "To pass through these Tātakā Woods alive, you must slay her. You will incur no sin by ridding the world of this oppressive and monstrous evil."

Rāma listened carefully, and with a free heart he bowed to Vishvāmitra. "O most compassionate Ṛishi, as my father has instructed me to follow your command, I will kill the evil Tātakā and bring happiness to the people of this forest."

Then the all-powerful Rāma lifted his bow and plucked its string. Like a clap of thunder, the sound of Rāma's bow reverberated through the forest and struck the ears of Tātakā, who stood at the far end of the forest. Enraged, she ran toward them.

Gigantic and monstrously ugly, as wide as five elephants, she towered over the giant wild jack trees of the forest. Her mouth was as big as a cave, her teeth cracked and broken. Her eyes were slits of blind fury.

Most young men would have taken one look and fled in fear. But the steadfast Rāma was filled with righteous anger. "See how she strikes terror in the hearts of good people," Rāma said to Lakshmaṇa. "She is a master of the evil arts. Still, she is a woman, so I will not kill her."

As Rāma spoke, the terrifying monster of cavernous mouth and red tongue rushed at the boys, howling.

"Jai Rāma!" Vishvāmitra shouted. "Victory to Rāma of the illustrious house of Raghu!"

Bearing down on them like a tornado, the demoness Tātakā churned clouds of dust that blinded Rāma and Lakshmaṇa. Showers of rocks rained on the brothers. But these only increased the wrath of Rāma and glanced off his strong body as the rain glides off a rock.

Seeing that her weapons were useless, the demoness used her powers of black magic to disappear. Yet her invisibility didn't prevent her from hurling bigger and bigger boulders on Rāma and Lakshmaṇa.

"Enough," called out Vishvāmitra. "O compassionate Rāma, if you spare her life, she will continue to rain down evil on my sacred yagyas. For the sake of the sages of the forest, now is the time to kill her. Night is creeping upon us, and her powers will increase with the onset of darkness." He pointed to the spot where the invisible creature was hiding, as he could see her with his divine sight.

The obedient Rāma shot a barrage of lightning-quick arrows at the spot where Vishvāmitra pointed. Pierced by Rāma's arrows, the terrible Tātakā became visible again and rushed at the boys with a roar. Rāma shot a single, swift arrow through her heart.

Like clouds giving way to thunder, the evil monster's body crashed to the earth. From the heavens, the voices of Indra and the other Devas cried out, "Well done, O Rāma!"

And to Vishvāmitra they cried, "May prosperity shower upon thee, O fortunate sage. Honor these youths for freeing the forest of evil. Offer Rāma and his brother celestial weapons of all kinds, for these two are destined for great things."

Overflowing with happiness, Vishvāmitra clasped the head of the youthful warrior and blessed him.

And as they rejoiced in victory, the dreadful Tātakā Woods suddenly sighed with the soft breath of spring. A moment later the trees burst into delicate blossoms, birds caroled cheerful songs, and young deer leapt playfully on forest paths.

There the three spent the night, resting under the canopy of the blossoming magnolia tree. As the sun set, the two princes massaged the feet of their teacher. Then they, too, lay down, the starry night enfolding them like a blanket. There they slept, lulled by the lapping of the river, nourished by the praise of Vishvāmitra.

DAWN WASHED THE new sky with delicate hues when Vishvāmitra awakened Rāma.

The two young men bathed in the holy river and sat at Vishvāmitra's feet.

"O Rāma of fearless heart, I am pleased with your valor," said Vishvāmitra. "Now I will bestow upon you the celestial weapons." He gestured for Rāma to sit beside him.

"Know this," said Vishvāmitra. "Divine weapons are made powerful by the silence of your mind, the purity of your heart, and the strength of your spirit. Only by virtue of sacred mantras (Vedic sounds) will these weapons hit their mark. Go deep within your mind and receive from me the celestial disc of Vishṇu, the spear of Shiva and the thunderbolt of Indra."

Facing east, seated on *kusha* grass, the holy sage closed his eyes and whispered the mantras to Rāma, who repeated them with eyes closed. A different missile appeared each time Rāma repeated another mantra. In this way, Vishvāmitra bestowed on Rāma hundreds of weapons of all the Devas, which he himself had received from Lord Shiva as a reward for his great purity of heart and mind, earned through years of meditation. After Rāma received the weapons, Sage Vishvāmitra bestowed them on Lakshmaṇa in the same way.

Later that day, his quiver bursting with powerful weapons unknown on earth, the illustrious Rāma followed the great sage Vishvāmitra on the path through the forest, with Lakshmaṇa close behind him. From afar, the sensitive Rāma spotted a peaceful place ahead, which emanated a profound silence.

"O revered Ṛishi," asked Rāma respectfully, "is this your quiet refuge, which you wish us to protect? I feel the breath of serenity emanating from it like perfume, but I also see the dark cloud hanging over it. Please show us the ceremonial place where you conduct the yagyas, and we will destroy the evil obstructions to your holy acts today!"

Pleased by Rāma's eagerness to fulfill his duties, the sage wasted no time in preparing for the yagya. After a night's rest, and the morning ablutions and prayers, he and his disciples seated themselves by the ceremonial fire at the auspicious moment.

Rāma asked quietly, "At what time during the yagya will the rākshasas attack? We must be prepared."

The disciples were cheered in their hearts that the intelligent Rāma wished to help them. The eldest disciple answered, "O esteemed prince, the rākshasas could attack at any moment during the six days and nights of the sacrifice. During this time, the holy sage Vishvāmitra will be bound by a vow of silence."

Soon Vishvāmitra began the yagya with offerings of ghee and rice. His disciples joined him in chanting sacred mantras and pouring ghee on the yagya fire.

The brave princes kept watch for five days and nights without closing their eyes even for a moment. They scanned the sky repeatedly, looking for any intrusion. Finally, on the dawn of the sixth day, Rāma said to Lakshmaṇa, "Today they will come!"

At that moment the ceremonial fire blazed higher, as if in agreement, illuminating heaps of orange marigolds, golden bowls of liquid ghee, and the glowing faces of the holy men gathered around.

Suddenly the sky turned dark and threatening, and a thunderous chaos of shouting, screaming, and laughing filled the air. Showers of bones and blood rained on the golden altar and nearly extinguished the fire.

Rāma and Lakshmaṇa, filled with righteous anger, drew their formidable weapons. "I will scatter these evil creatures like the wind," said Rāma. After invoking the sacred mantra, he let loose the celestial weapon of Manu. It struck Mārīcha, the most powerful of the demons present, and hurled him one hundred *yojanas* into the sea.

"Mārīcha has only been stunned, but the others I will not spare," said Rāma. His eyes blazing with power, he seized the Agni weapon and, after invoking the mantra, hurled it at the other rākshasas. Without flinching, Rāma and Lakshmaṇa expertly fired the celestial weapons bestowed upon them by Vishvāmitra and destroyed the entire army of murderous demons.

Then just as suddenly as the tumult had started, all was silent. The happy song of birds once again filled the forest. Peace pervaded the āshram and washed away the darkness as the sages completed their yagya. They chanted the Veda and ladled ghee on the fire, uttering "*svāhā*" (hail).

After the yagya, the sages gathered around the youthful brothers. "Glory to Rāma!" they cried. "Glory to Lakshmaṇa! May happiness be yours!"

At last the holy men were freed from the evil cloud of destruction. No more would creatures of darkness spoil their sacred acts. No more would rākshasas extinguish their sacred fires. No longer would they be hindered in bringing peace to all.

"O Rāma," said Vishvāmitra, "you have brought glory to your father and the entire Ikshvāku line. Tomorrow I will take you on another journey, to the fabled kingdom of Janaka, the philosopher-king, who is conducting a special contest. There you will find the rare and magical bow of Shiva, bestowed upon the worthy King Janaka by the Devas. No one has been able to lift this colossal bow—neither Deva, nor asura, nor rākshasa, nor man. A great competition among monarchs is going on as we speak, to see who will raise the great bow above his head in victory. I believe you are worthy to try."

The obedient Rāma, his heart filled with joyful anticipation, bowed to Vishvāmitra. That night, as they rested in the peaceful hermitage, the brave Rāma and Lakshmaṇa smiled, having accomplished their purpose, and dreamed of the journey to come.

अथ तां रजनीं तत्र कृतार्थौ रामलक्ष्मणौ ।
ऊषतुर्मुदितौ वीरौ प्रहृष्टेनान्तरात्मना ॥

That night, as they rested in the peaceful hermitage,
the brave Rāma and Lakshmaṇa smiled, having accomplished
their purpose, and dreamed of the journey to come.

—Bāla Kāṇḍa 31.1

Chapter 4

Rāma Frees Ahalyā

The next morning, the two princes, the sage, and his disciples set out on their journey. While before the two brothers had walked silently through the forest with the great Ṛishi Vishvāmitra, now they were part of a long train of a hundred bullock carts. As the wagons lumbered past tall trees and cool streams, the āshram's birds, cows, deer, and antelope followed them. After a few leagues, the compassionate Vishvāmitra implored the gentle animals to return home, where they would be safe.

The travelers continued on their pleasant journey, stopping to bathe in the River Shoṇa when the sun sank near the horizon. There the sage and his disciples performed their evening meditations and sacred rites as darkness gathered round. Later, after the two resplendent princes massaged the feet of the perfected sage, he told them stories of their illustrious ancestors.

The second day, as they approached King Janaka's city of Mithilā, the holy men cried "Wonderful! Wonderful!" for they could see the graceful outline of the city, her buildings artfully painted in radiant colors.

The party camped for the evening in a woods outside the city. Rāma and Lakshmaṇa went exploring. They came upon an abandoned āshram, its crumbling walls overgrown with vines. There was something eerie about this silent place where the chants of pandits once filled the air, and without entering they returned to their camp.

Later that evening, after he and Lakshmaṇa massaged the feet of Vishvāmitra, Rāma asked, "O revered sage, tell us the story of that deserted hermitage. Who lived there? Why did they leave?"

"The great ascetic Gautama lived there with his wife, Ahalyā, who was famed for her beauty," said Vishvāmitra. "She was so radiant that Indra came down from heaven to see her."

Rāma listened with wonder as the sage Vishvāmitra told the following story.

One morning, while the holy Gautama was bathing in the river, Indra disguised himself as Gautama and approached the lovely Ahalyā as if he were her husband. Ahalyā knew that he was Indra in disguise, but out of curiosity, she yielded to his embrace. Afterward, she panicked and urged him to leave. "O God of a thousand eyes, go now quickly. Do not reveal yourself to Gautama!" she cried.

But as fate would have it, just as Indra hurried away, he nearly collided with the powerful sage Gautama, who was returning home after bathing in the river. Seeing Indra trembling with fear, disguised in Gautama's own body, that bull among sages swelled with rage. "O perverse one," he cursed. "To repay you for this forbidden act, may you never have children!"

To Ahalyā, he said, "O betrayer of truth! You have not used your beauty to enhance your spirit. May you turn invisible, so none can enjoy your beauty, and exist here alone for thousands of years."

No longer desiring to remain in his tainted āshram, Gautama prepared to retire to the pure air of the Himālayas. As he was leaving, Gautama took pity on his wife, who was dear to his heart, and softened his curse. "When the compassionate Rāma walks these grounds, you will return to your beautiful form and offer him hospitality. Then your sin will be absolved."

"And so, dear son," concluded Vishvāmitra, "go to the āshram tomorrow and liberate the virtuous Ahalyā."

The next morning, Rāma, Lakshmaṇa, and Vishvāmitra rose early and quietly entered the hermitage that had been abandoned by Gautama so long ago. There they were greeted by the shining Ahalyā, who became visible the moment she set eyes on Rāma. She had grown even more brilliant from her many years of silence.

Falling at the feet of Rāma, her eyes brimming with tears of gratitude, Ahalyā paid homage to her liberator with hands folded in respect. True to Gautama's prophecy, she offered Rāma and Lakshmaṇa hospitality, water to drink and fruit to eat. She met them with the traditional greeting, circling their heads with the light of a ghee lamp, paying them every reverence, as was traditional for guests at the āshram.

At that moment, the sky filled with the sounds of tinkling chimes, gongs, and the melodies of Gandharvas strumming their lyres. "Wonderful! Wonderful!" called the Devas. They rained rose petals on the wife of Gautama, who at long last had been restored to her exalted state.

As Rāma, Lakshmaṇa, and Vishvāmitra left the āshram, they saw Gautama descending from the Himālayas in a celestial chariot to take Ahalyā to heaven. The sage Gautama blessed Rāma and showered him with blessings for freeing his cherished wife.

Now that the prophecy had been fulfilled, the time had come to enter the city of Mithilā. The two princes and Vishvāmitra's disciples walked behind the orange-robed sage along wide boulevards, past gaily painted mansions inhabited by prosperous and virtuous citizens and adorned with flowers, gold, and precious gems.

The essence of youth and beauty, bronzed and muscular, intelligent and modest, the brothers dazzled the eyes of the people. Their golden quivers filled with celestial weapons, they walked like gods in the beautiful city.

Soon they came to a *yagyashālā*, the hall that King Janaka had built for a great yagya. Thousands of pandits from kingdoms all around had gathered there, and as Vishvāmitra and the two princes approached, many holy men hurried forth to pay obeisance to the renowned sage.

A few moments later, King Janaka himself arrived to welcome the highly esteemed Vishvāmitra. Like Dasharatha, King Janaka was a wise and virtuous king. He was respected throughout the world not only for his knowledge of the Veda, but for living an enlightened state of life. He enjoyed all that was desirable—wealth, honor, fame, and glory. Once childless, King Janaka had a special daughter, Sītā, whom he loved more than life itself.

The philosopher-king Janaka greeted Vishvāmitra and the two princes with the traditional greeting, circling their heads with the flame of a ghee lamp, and invited them to reside in the palace as his guests.

As soon as they arrived at the palace and were seated in a place of honor, King Janaka asked, his face alight with joy, "Who are these two resplendent warriors, who walk like lions among men and shine like the immortals themselves?"

And so the praiseworthy Vishvāmitra told the wise King Janaka of the brave deeds of Rāma and Lakshmaṇa—how they vanquished the demoness Tātakā, restored peace to Vishvāmitra's āshram, and freed Ahalyā from her curse.

King Janaka, the embodiment of goodness, gazed with affection and wonder at the two radiant princes. His heart quivered with an auspicious premonition. Surely these young men would bring him good fortune.

He said to Vishvāmitra, "With your arrival, I am already enjoying the fruits of the yagya. I feel that you have come here with the intention of blessing me. Please tell me what I can do to make you happy."

"I have brought these princes to see the great bow of Shiva," replied Vishvāmitra. "They are skilled archers and wish to gaze upon the most famous bow in the world."

King Janaka nodded and said, "I will tell these young men the story of the bow. One day I was preparing a field for a yagya. As I ploughed the first furrow, accompanied by sages and ministers, suddenly I stopped. For there at the tip of the blade a beautiful baby girl clutched handfuls of earth and playfully threw them at her kicking feet.

"The queen and I felt that this baby was divine, because she was the daughter of Mother Earth. We named her Sītā, which means 'furrow.' I have loved and cherished this daughter, born of the soil. She is sweet, compassionate, intelligent, and beautiful beyond words. Like Lakshmī herself, she is no ordinary mortal.

"When it came time for her to marry, I decided that Sītā must be matched with one worthy of her divine nature. I wanted her to marry a hero among men, one who had been tested in battle and could protect and cherish her. That is why I have called a special *svayaṁvara* for Sītā.

"Now you know that in a typical svayaṁvara, the royal bride chooses her own husband among the eligible princes present. But for Sītā, I proposed a test to separate the worthy from the unworthy. I announced that Sītā would marry the man who could string the immense bow of Shiva, which my ancestor received in eons past as a gift from the Devas.

"Hundreds of princes have come from far and wide to string the bow. Yet not one has succeeded in lifting it even one inch, because through its divine properties the bow assumes the weight of the *karma* of the person who touches it. Now I despair that a man does not exist who is worthy of Sītā."

The king bowed his head to hide his emotion, for he dearly loved his daughter Sītā and was pained by the thought that she might never marry.

"These youths are warriors," said Vishvāmitra quietly. "They are anxious to see this famous bow. Bring it to them."

Rāma and Lakshmaṇa exchanged glances. So it was to attend the divine Sītā's svayaṁvara that they had traveled so far.

अथ मे कृषतः क्षेत्रं लाङ्गलादुत्थिता ततः ।
क्षेत्रं शोधयता लब्ध्वा नाम्ना सीतेति विश्रुता ॥

As I ploughed the land set apart for the sacred ritual,
there arose from the course of the plough a baby girl,
who became known by the name of Sītā.

—Bāla Kāṇḍa 66.13–14

CHAPTER 5

The Winning of Sītā

The bride sits on her velvet throne.
Her red sārī is heavy with gold,
drawn 'round her jasmine-plaited hair.
It hides her smooth brow,
shining with rubies and pearls,
and her large eyes
turned within.

Her jeweled feet rest in rose petals.
Garlands twine a canopy above
the narrow-waisted,
the envy of maidens,
King Janaka's daughter.

Mithilā's bravest princes
gather at her feet.
The bronzed arms
of two hundred heroes
flex with pride and glory.
Who will lift Shiva's bow
and claim her?

She smiles at none.
Her veiled eyes do not reveal
her secret desire.

Twenty thousand blow their conches and ring their bells
when the first man bends to lift the bow
glittering in the morning sun.
But when the evening star rises above
the dim embers of the sinking orb,
the bow lies in the dust still,
unmoved, and none dare whisper.

Then the golden Prince of Ayodhyā
enters the city of Sītā.
Her breath soaks inward,
collected in a quiet pool,
and the air hangs heavy
over the earth standing still.

In one swinging motion Rāma raises the bow,
bends the ends of infinity,
and cracks the waiting silence.
Her eyes, still inward, see the sun.

"Heave, ho!" The shouts of five hundred men filled the air as they dragged the immense bow of Shiva, mounted on a golden carriage with eight wheels, through the streets of Mithilā. Inch by inch, straining against the ropes, they made their way to the palace. Hundreds followed them, ringing bells and blowing conches. Others watched from their windows high above the street, tossing flower petals on the bow and its carriage.*

"The Prince of Ayodhyā will try his hand at the bow!" As word spread through the city, tides of people flowed toward the palace. No one wanted to miss this stirring event.

"He is merely a boy," lamented one aged lady, with a sigh. "How will he possibly succeed where grown men and even the gods have failed? How can a youth pick up a weight greater than Mount Mandara?" She watched the bow inching through the street below her window.

"But have you seen him?" asked her granddaughter, as she cast rose petals out the window and watched them float down to the bow. "He and his brother are like gods! As the sun warms heaven and earth, so these brothers will bless our kingdom."

Hidden in her chambers, Sītā heard from her attendants that people were gathering to see the handsome prince lift the bow. She fixed her heart on Rāma and knew he was her beloved. With tears of devotion Sītā implored the Devas, "Be gracious unto me, O Devas! Lighten the weight of the bow! Be kind to me! It is for this day that I have often prayed to you."

At last the bow reached the palace, where King Janaka and Vishvāmitra waited. As Rāma stepped forward like a young lion to see the famous bow, the assembly fell silent as the night.

Covered in mounds of orange, red, and yellow flower petals, even its golden cabinet seemed to emit a radiance, a power from its legendary past. As Rāma gently lifted the lid and peered at the giant bow, the fragrance of sandalwood paste filled the room.

While Rāma gazed at the immense and ancient bow, Lakshmaṇa, filled with excitement, pounded the ground with his foot and roared,

---

* Although we have primarily based our retelling on Vālmīki's Rāmāyaṇa, the marriage of Rāma and Sītā described in this chapter, and the great leap of Hanumān described in chapter 32, contain elements from the *Rāma Charita Mānasa* (*The Lake of the Deeds of Rāma*), the devotional epic poem based on the *Rāmāyaṇa* and composed in Hindi dialect by Tulsīdās, the sixteenth century sage and scholar.

"Earth be stable! Waters be stable! Directions be stable! Hold on to your breath, for Rāma will break the ends of infinity!"

He would have continued, to the amazement of all, except an amused glance from Rāma told him that was enough.

Rāma humbly bowed to the bow and then to Vishvāmitra. He said, "O revered one, with your permission I would like to lift this bow and string it."

Vishvāmitra nodded. Powerful as an elephant, Rāma stepped close to the sacred weapon. Then in one fluid motion, Rāma lifted the bow and strung it, bending the ends together with such force that it broke in two with a clap of thunder.

The earth shook, and the people fell to the ground in terror. Only King Janaka, Vishvāmitra, Rāma, and Lakshmaṇa remained standing, calmly waiting in silence while the forces of nature churned around them.

"Wonderful! Wonderful!" shouted the celestial Ṛishis, Devas, and Gandharvas, who watched from the heavens above. Brahmā praised Rāma and celestial nymphs danced in the sky. They showered wreaths of flowers on the radiant Rāma and cried, "Rāma has broken the bow!" The sweet sounds of celestial bells soothed the air like a healing balm, and soon the people were exulting, "Jai Rāma! Jai Shrī Rāma!"

Lakshmaṇa, filled with pride, gazed upon his brother like a rabbit at the full moon. Sītā, still in her chamber, felt her soul fill with rapture. In her mind's eye, she placed the white garland, cherished in her heart, upon the breast of her lord.

When silence once again stole over the crowd, King Janaka spoke to Vishvāmitra with his heart overflowing with gratitude. "Now I know that you have, indeed, come to Mithilā to bless me. This Rāma is surely a god among men. That such a youth could lift this mighty bow when others could not even budge it! Surely, my dear daughter Sītā is fortunate to become his bride. I have promised her to the man who could string the bow, and now I offer her in marriage to the radiant Rāma, who is her match in virtue. With your permission, O Vishvāmitra, I will inform Rāma's father of these wonderful events and invite him here."

"So be it," proclaimed Vishvāmitra, his voice lifting in happiness. "Send the messengers without delay."

And so King Janaka instructed his royal messengers to leave that very moment and travel to Ayodhyā with all haste. The messengers departed at once, delighted to carry the news.

King Dasharatha stood at the doorway to his verandah, gazing fondly upon the city of Ayodhyā below. How celestial it looked, with the setting sun glancing off golden rooftops. His thoughts, as always, went to Rāma, who had been away for several weeks now. Was his son safe? When would the king see him again? It was this same familiar doorway where the king stood sixteen years earlier, waiting to hear of Rāma's birth.

Suddenly his chief minister, Sumantra, entered the king's chamber. "Your Majesty, messengers have come with tidings from King Janaka of Mithilā. They have traveled for three days to receive an audience."

King Dasharatha hastened to his court. There his eight ministers and the kingdom's holy sages, headed by Vasishtha, were already assembled.

"O King Dasharatha," the messengers announced from the center of the court, "King Janaka of Videha sends good tidings concerning your son Rāma, who is now with Vishvāmitra and Lakshmaṇa in the royal city of Mithilā." Everyone in the hall held their breath as the messengers began to tell the king of all the wondrous events of the last few days.

Hearing their words, King Dasharatha's eyes filled with tears. At the news of the coming union between his handsome son and the beautiful daughter of King Janaka, the entire assembly shook with delight, like peacocks at the sound of an approaching rain. They realized that Vishvāmitra had, indeed, brought blessings to the king's sons when he led the boys away from their home.

King Dasharatha first addressed Vasishtha: "With your blessings, revered sage, we will leave at once for Mithilā."

The wise Vasishtha replied, "O most fortunate king, for a wise man such as yourself the world is full of happiness. As rivers freely flow into the sea without being asked, so joy flows unbidden to your virtuous soul. Prepare the marriage procession!"

The sky streaked crimson with dawn when King Dasharatha and the royal entourage departed for Mithilā. The king swayed in his royal palanquin, led by Vasishtha and other sages and followed by hundreds of elephants and chariots heavy with gifts of jewels and gold. They slowly made their way to Mithilā, where their beloved Prince Rāma waited.

King Janaka himself greeted King Dasharatha at the gates to the city, accompanied by servants offering baskets of gifts and golden platters of cake and fruit. What a sight for the gods—the historic meeting of these two enlightened monarchs. It was difficult to determine which could surpass the other in virtue, compassion, and wealth. They were the supreme rulers of their time.

"O king of kings," said King Janaka, "by accepting my daughter as your son's wife, you have fulfilled my vow. I am forever in your debt." He fell at King Dasharatha's feet, honoring him with the traditional greeting.

"Nay, nay, it is I who am in your debt," said King Dasharatha, raising King Janaka with his own hands. "You have blessed our family by offering the divine Sītā as Rāma's wife. We are truly fortunate."

And so the two kings greeted each other with both humility and respect. The royal family of King Dasharatha was given a palace to live in, furnished with red and gold silken carpets and comforts of every kind. There Rāma and Lakshmaṇa were reunited with their father, who tenderly embraced them again and again as they told him of the happenings of the past weeks.

In the ensuing days King Janaka made plans for the wedding, which was to take place on a most auspicious day. One evening King Janaka's bards sang with great joy, telling the story of the king's ancestors. Then King Dasharatha's bards did the same. In this way, the two families who were to be united learned the full glory of one another's heritage.

When the bards fell silent, King Janaka said to King Dasharatha, "Just as Sītā will become the wife of Rāma, let my younger daughter, Ūrmilā, become the wife of your younger son Lakshmaṇa."

"I will accept your daughter Ūrmilā as my own daughter," said King Dasharatha, his heart swelling with happiness. "She will grace our home with light."

Then Vishvāmitra addressed the two kings, "O most auspicious rulers, hear my suggestion. Let the two beautiful and virtuous daughters of King Janaka's brother wed Bharata and Shatrughna. In this way these two illustrious houses will forever be bound together."

King Dasharatha could not contain his joy. Such a glorious beginning for his four sons! The next day he rose early and bestowed a generous gift to the Brahmins of the land: one hundred thousand cows with gilded horns for each son. The four hundred thousand cows each came with a calf, were in excellent health, and gave abundant milk.

Finally, the auspicious day set by the Vedic astrologers arrived. The Prince of Ayodhyā and the Princess of Mithilā, as well as Rāma's brothers and their brides, were to be married at the hour of *Vijaya* (victory)—at sunset, as the cows were returning from the pastures.

As the time approached, conches and drums sounded, joyous songs of women filled the air, and pandits chanted the sacred Vedic hymns. Flowers floated from the heavens, gracing Rāma and his noble brothers, who rode to the pavilion on white horses. As they took their seats near the sacred fires, the people tossed gold coins to wish the princes prosperity.

Vishvāmitra, Vasishtha, and other famed Ṛishis were seated in places of honor. King Dasharatha and King Janaka greeted each other with ceremonial words of praise, then took their seats.

At the auspicious moment, Sītā entered the hall, circled by her friends and handmaids as the moon is circled by a ring of light. Sītā walked like a young deer, her pure and simple beauty unsurpassed. Upon seeing her, it is said that the god of love forgot his duties and bowed to her in the innermost recesses of his heart.

Rāma's eyes flashed upon Sītā's divine beauty and grace, and his heart was filled with love. Her clear eyes sparkled like the ocean in the moonlight. Her forehead was adorned with a pearl, as well as gold and rubies, her hair bound with garlands of jasmine. Her sārī was woven with golden thread and shimmered around her like a luminous cloud. Rāma's eyes forgot to blink as he drank in the loveliness of her sweet face, like a bee drawing in honey from a lotus.

Like the goddess Lakshmī walking on lotus flowers, Sītā slowly made her way to Rāma's side. She gazed at her prince. His dark forehead was wide, the center adorned with a red *tilaka* mark. His eyes were bright, his hair curly, and his arms strong, like the trunks of young elephants. Filled with love, she received him into her heart through her eyes and then shyly closed her eyelids to hold him captive there.

"This is my dearest daughter Sītā," said King Janaka to Rāma. "Take her hand. Now she will walk the path of Dharma with you. May you live long together in fulfillment." Then King Janaka washed the feet of the prince with water and honey.

Smiling with recognition, as if greeting a long-lost friend, Rāma took Sītā's hand. They circled the fire as the pandits chanted, first with Rāma leading, then with Sītā leading. Rāma applied red powder to the part in Sītā's hair, and together they took the seven steps, making a vow at each step. Watching them seated side by side, everyone said that Rāma and Sītā were like heaven and earth, like Vishṇu and Lakshmī. Sītā kept her eyes downcast, gazing at her beloved's reflection in the golden sapphire of her ring.

Then Bharata wedded the beautiful Māṇdavī, Lakshmaṇa the lovely

Ūrmilā, and Shatrughna the incomparable Shrutakīrti. Thus the four sons of King Dasharatha led their four brides around the auspicious fire, and the two celebrated dynasties of King Dasharatha and King Janaka were united.

QUITE SOME TIME after the wedding, the four brothers and their brides prepared to leave for their home in Ayodhyā. King Janaka accompanied them partway, and then after a tearful farewell to his adored daughters and nieces, he returned to Mithilā, consoled by the knowledge that they would be loved and cared for by their new family.

The royal procession lumbered along slowly, laden with a multitude of gifts from the brides' fathers. King Janaka and his brother had given them a hundred thousand cows, plus hundreds of chests of gold, silver, pearls, and precious gems. Sītā, shy to be with her husband, rode in her covered palanquin amidst flower petals and sweets, listening to the tinkle of bells and the rumble of elephants. As the evening darkness came each day, and the air cooled, she dreamed of her life in Ayodhyā with her beloved prince.

When they finally arrived at the celebrated city of Ayodhyā, the four brides were welcomed as cherished daughters by King Dasharatha's three queens. After a warm celebration by the people of Ayodhyā, all four couples settled happily into their new life together.

Rāma and Sītā delighted in each other's presence. Sītā was a happy and devoted wife, smiling before she spoke, steadfast in her love for Rāma. She shone like a goddess in charm and beauty, and knew every detail hidden in the heart of Shrī Rāma. Rāma was equally devoted to her and made it his aim to fulfill her every desire. Giving to each other, they created a perfect and happy union. In this way ten years passed in happiness, as they lived an ideal life together in the legendary city of Ayodhyā.

तस्य भूयो विशेषेण मैथिली जनकात्मजा ।
देवताभिः समा रूपे सीता श्रीरिव रूपिणी ॥

Sītā, the princess of Mithilā and daughter of King Janaka,
who shone like a goddess in charm and beauty,
knew every detail hidden in the heart of Shrī Rāma.

—Bāla Kāṇda 77.28

End of Bāla Kāṇda

TWO

Ayodhyā Kāṇda

The City of Ayodhyā

Chapter 6

King Dasharatha Plans the Coronation of Rāma

King Dasharatha said,
"Rāma has never told a lie.
He speaks sweetly
and affectionately to all.
He never says a harsh word,
and no one speaks harshly to him.

"Rāma reveres his teachers
and has learned the four Vedas.
He is the most skilled archer on earth
and master of the arts of warfare.
Undefeated in battle,
he plays the vīṇā and flute
like a Gandharva.

"Skilled in reading character,
Rāma is able to fathom
a heart at a single glance.
He is never surprised by an enemy.
Nor does he speak of his achievements,
but keeps them secret.
He is humble,

drawing attention
to others' good deeds and qualities,
never his own.

"Rāma is highly intelligent,
free of disease, handsome, and strong.
He knows how to amass wealth
and distribute it fairly.
He is thrifty or liberal
as the occasion demands.

"Rāma never speaks or acts
against Dharma,
nor can he even bear
to hear another do so.
He is gifted at uttering
the right words at the right time,
always acting in accord
with his surroundings.
The ultimate aim of Rāma
is to defend good and destroy evil."

"Ah, Sumantra," said King Dasharatha. "Please sit down." The king had called his dear friend and trusted minister for a private conference. The two friends sat together and talked for some time.

After sharing memories of their long friendship, the king raised a new subject. "As you know, I am well into my old age."

The king paused a moment, thinking about his four sons. Having been blessed with their birth when he was already quite old, he held all his sons dear to his heart, even more than his own self. He thought first of Bharata, who was away visiting his maternal grandfather, King Ashvapati, the father of Queen Kaikeyī. King Dasharatha thought also of Shatrughna, who could never be parted from Bharata, and so had accompanied him to the kingdom of Kekaya. There the two brothers and their wives enjoyed the affections lavished on them by their grandfather and uncle. The king's attention dwelled fondly on Lakshmaṇa, ever devoted to Rāma, and his brother's equal in strength and valor.

As King Dasharatha's thoughts turned to Rāma, his heart expanded even more. For although he truly cherished all his sons, he loved Rāma most of all. Perhaps this was because Rāma's many virtues inspired him, or because Rāma always served him and thought of the king's desires before his own. But King Dasharatha's deep love for his firstborn son was not limited to one cause or another.

Sumantra waited quietly.

"I was just thinking how Rāma has all of my virtues and many more," said the king at last. "Rāma loves the people of Ayodhyā and is adored by them. He is compassionate, patient, and caring. It would be impossible to find a person in this kingdom who does not respect and honor him. Just one look at his sweet and affectionate face, full and charming as the moon, is enough to erase all cares."

Once again King Dasharatha paused. "My friend," he said. "Not only am I very old, but I have been told by the sages that the planetary configurations are not good. Some kind of calamity is waiting to befall me, probably my own death."

"O Your Majesty," cried Sumantra, "may it not be so!" His eyes filled with tears. He could not bear to think of being parted from his dear friend and sovereign.

But the king was resolute. "I wish you to call all the ministers of the court together, as well as my subjects. For in my heart I have only one desire—to see my virtuous son Rāma take the throne during my lifetime. Only then will the kingdom be secure."

Sumantra's face now beamed in relief. "That is an excellent idea, Your Majesty. Your son Rāma will rule the kingdom with glory. And with him on the throne, you can rest more and prolong your life. Today I will begin inviting your subjects for a royal assembly."

"Yes, so be it," said the king. "For I must see what the people think. Also invite the rulers from nearby kingdoms."

As they planned the list of rulers to invite, the obedient Sumantra asked, "Shall we invite the king of Kekaya, where your son Bharata is staying? And shall we invite King Janaka of Mithilā, father of Sītā?"

"They live so far away," said King Dasharatha. "We cannot wait for them to arrive. Let them hear about it in due time."

Two days later, the royal guests had arrived and were seated in the great hall according to their rank. Also present were the king's eight ministers, his spiritual advisors, headed by Vasishtha, and the people of Ayodhyā. The entire assembly buzzed excitedly, wondering why the magnanimous King Dasharatha had called them together.

At last the aged king entered the grand hall and seated himself on his golden throne. In a voice strong and sure, he began to tell the people of his plan.

"As you may know, I am feeling the consequences of age. For many years I have watched over this kingdom with all my strength, not minding my own desires. Now I am weary. It is my desire that my eldest son, Rāma, most worthy among men, be installed as the king. Thus the glorious line of Ikshvākus will be preserved."

When their revered king finished speaking, the hall erupted in shouts of approval, like the roar of an earthquake.

"Your Majesty," said the head minister, "there is no one among us who would not feel gladness at the sight of Rāmachandra on the throne. You have served us long and well. It is now our desire to see your highly esteemed son riding on the royal elephant, shaded by the canopy of the *rājā*!"

Again a roar of approval swept the crowd. The king was happy beyond words, but still he wanted to be sure he was following the will of the people. "I have served you long and faithfully. Yet you wish to see my son replace me on the throne? Is it that I have erred in some way or neglected my duties?"

"Your Majesty," said the minister. "That is hardly the case. Let the people themselves explain why they wish Rāma to serve as our leader."

"Rāma is dear to us because he is noble and good," said one man, who stood with hands folded in respect. "He is truthful; he makes truth his religion. He will never swerve from the path of Dharma."

"He is as charming as the full moon," said another. "Like the earth in patience, in wisdom he is like Bṛihaspati, the spiritual preceptor of the Devas. He is ever ready to forgive another's faults. His intellect is as sharp as a sword. He is as brave as Indra, the king of the Devas."

"He is ever ready to do even the most common man a favor," yet another said, "and he is never angry. He is in control of his senses."

Other voices chimed in, from different parts of the hall.

"He speaks lovingly to everyone at all times. He stops us on the street and asks after our welfare, as well as that of our wives, children, and servants."

"He always smiles and his face is radiant and pleasing to look upon. His skin is tinted blue like that of Lord Nārāyaṇa, and his strength, dignity, and radiance are unsurpassed."

"Rāma sees only good in everyone," a young man offered, "yet he is not afraid to fight evil. Always victorious, he is the greatest archer on earth, the most skilled in battle, the most knowledgeable in warfare. He rides an elephant, a horse, a chariot with ease."

And so the people went on and on, never tiring of praising Rāma.

Finally, the voice of an older man carried clearly throughout the hall. "He is always respectful to elders," he said. "He has learned the wisdom of the Veda, and he lives it. He will be an ideal ruler. Please, O revered king, crown him at the earliest possible date!"

King Dasharatha's eyes filled with tears of gratitude, seeing how much the people loved his virtuous son Rāma.

"So be it," said the king, at last satisfied that it was the people's will for Rāma to be crowned king. "Let your desires be fulfilled. Let Rāma's coronation be set for the earliest possible date."

With this, the assembly surged with joy, cheering again and again, "Jai Shrī Rāma! Jai Shrī Rāma!"

As the hall finally grew quiet again, the king addressed Vasishtha, "O venerated one, will you take care of the arrangements, to be sure that we follow the ancient traditions of our glorious house of Ikshvāku?"

Vasishtha immediately called the king's ministers to him and gave each a different task. He said, "Let us begin decorating the city today. Adorn the doorways of the palace with garlands, flags, and banners, and let the pleasant scents of incense fill every street and every home. Sprinkle the royal pathways with pure water and flower petals. Call the royal musicians and dancers to the palace hall. Set out blossoms, fruits, and delicacies in lavish trays. Prepare food to satisfy one hundred thousand Brahmins and holy ones. Spare no effort to honor our prince!"

Satisfied that the preparations were under way, the good King Dasharatha asked Sumantra to bring Rāma to the palace.

Very soon, King Dasharatha saw Rāma approaching. Rāma shone bright as the full moon on a cloudless night.

As was his custom, Rāma approached his father with humility. With palms folded together in reverence, he bowed low and touched his father's feet. The kindly king, the happiest of fathers, raised Rāma from the floor and embraced him warmly. For King Dasharatha, looking at

Rāma was like looking in a mirror, for the king rejoiced to see his beloved son, even as one would rejoice to see himself.

"O Rāma," said the king, "you are the noble son of my most noble wife, the virtuous Kausalyā. With your many exalted qualities, you have endeared yourself to the people. It is their will that tomorrow, when the auspicious star cluster *Pushya* is on the horizon, you will become their king. Spend the night fasting with your faithful consort Sītā. Follow all of Vasishtha's directions exactly. Be prepared to accept the rites of rulership tomorrow."

Ever willing to please his father, Rāma again bowed humbly and said, "As you wish, dear Father."

Then King Dasharatha invited Rāma to sit down with him. "In my affection I wish to give you advice for ruling the people, even though you already possess all the virtues necessary to become a great king.

"Do not be guided by lust or anger, in your public or private life. Ever humble, keep your senses under control and shun all vices. Store up your granaries and arsenals.

"Use the direct means of rule, by inviting petitions from your subjects, making tours of the kingdom to see the state of affairs firsthand, hearing the people's complaints and judging their cases. Use also the indirect means of rule, relying on a network of emissaries to ascertain the condition and loyalty of your own people, and the strength and intentions of neighboring kingdoms.

"Make yourself loved by the people. Rule the kingdom in a way that wins the good wishes and devotion of your subjects. Conduct yourself with your mind fully subdued.

"Such a ruler, who protects his kingdom and the very earth with his nurturing care, is a joy to his friends and all the people, and the nectar of immortality to the Devas."

After taking leave of his father, Rāma walked directly to see his mother, the virtuous Kausalyā. Her palace rose before him like the white peak of a cloud. There the pious Queen Kausalyā waited with Queen Sumitrā by her side. Sītā and Lakshmaṇa joined the two queens there, having already heard the good tidings.

"Surely I gave birth to you under an auspicious star," said Kausalyā with tears of joy in her eyes as she embraced her son. "Today the gods have answered my prayers. May you live long, O Rāma, and conquer all your enemies."

Having received his mother's blessings, Rāma turned next to Lakshmaṇa. "O brother, rule the kingdom with me. You are my other half, and only with you by my side can I enjoy the pleasures and fruits of being a king."

And so Rāma took leave of his two mothers and his brother, and returned home with his radiant wife, Sītā, to begin preparations for the coronation.

THAT VERY DAY, the people of Ayodhyā began to decorate the city. Soon festive banners fluttered from every temple, mansion, and terrace. Lotus petals covered the roads, and the perfume of incense wafted through the air. Lining the streets were torches as large as trees, lighting the way at nightfall.

Having adorned the city, citizens dressed in fine jewelry and rainbow colors of silk poured into the streets to rejoice. On every street corner, bards and minstrels entertained with songs of celebration. Dancers and actors performed for the delighted crowds. Like an underground stream nourishing all the festivities, the chanting of the Veda echoed throughout the city. Their hearts swelling with joy and excitement like the rising tide of the sea, the people of Ayodhyā played like waves on the ocean.

Among all the subjects of King Dasharatha, there was only one who was unhappy. If anyone had looked up to the lofty peaks of Queen Kaikeyī's palace late that afternoon, they would have seen a dark figure huddled on one of the upper balconies. Like a shadow over the moon, she darkened the brilliant festivities of Rāma's coronation.

Her name was Mantharā, the old and hunchbacked servant of Queen Kaikeyī. Seeing the exultation of the people, she slammed the terrace door and ran as quickly as she could to bring her mistress disturbing news.

तं पश्यमानो नृपतिस्तुतोष प्रियमात्मजम् ।

The king rejoiced to see his beloved son,
even as one would rejoice to see himself.

—Ayodhyā Kāṇḍa 3.37

Chapter 7

The Betrayal

How dare Mantharā speak
such traitorous words?
May her teeth break
into a thousand pieces.
May she fall into the fire of her own fury
and be consumed in the jaws of the earth.

How dare Kaikeyī betray her favorite son?
Like the graceful flowering vine
that hides a viper's sting,
like sweet-smelling nightshade,
she snares the virtuous king
with fatal beauty.
Let her be stung by her own venom
rather than hurt the benevolent Rāma.
Yet she, too, follows the designs of the gods.

Mantharā was Queen Kaikeyī's trusted servant, having served the queen's parents even before Kaikeyī was born. It was Mantharā who had accompanied the young queen to her new home in Ayodhyā many years before. It was Mantharā who rejoiced when her queen became the favorite of King Dasharatha.

And it was Mantharā who attended Queen Kaikeyī when, after long years of waiting, she gave birth to the faithful Bharata. With her hunched back and deeply wrinkled face, Mantharā was not beautiful to look upon. But she had proven her loyalty to the family over many decades, and was the queen's tie to her ancestral home. If anything, Mantharā was loyal to a fault—although until now, she had not revealed her selfish ambitions.

Now, on the eve of Rāma's coronation, Mantharā burst into Queen Kaikeyī's private apartments and woke her with a violent shake, shouting, "O my innocent lady, how can you sleep when your destruction is at hand?" At first, the lovely queen feared that a misfortune had fallen on her most trusted servant.

"What is troubling you, dear Mantharā?" asked the queen in concerned tones. "Please, tell me what has caused you to feel so distressed."

Mantharā's mind churned with dark thoughts and malicious schemes. "O heart of my heart, I am frightened for your welfare," she said. "Here your husband calls you his favorite, but he schemes to undermine you. Like a snake, he sent Bharata away to visit your father so he can craftily install Rāma as king. The coronation takes place tomorrow, while Bharata is away. Act quickly, innocent one, to stop this devious act, and save yourself and your son from destruction!"

"Rāma is being crowned tomorrow?" Queen Kaikeyī asked. Her voice lifted in happiness. Living a protected life in her inner chambers, she relied on others to tell her the news of the court. She rose quickly from her bed and gave the angry old woman a large, precious blue sapphire.

"For your good news, take this, O faithful one," exclaimed the queen, her face shining. "Rāma will be a just and noble king. He will bring happiness to all. These tidings fill me with ecstasy. Have I not loved Rāma as my own son? Rāma will make a splendid king." She sank on her couch, smoothing the luxurious velvet with her hands and repeating over and over in a happy dream, "My Rāma will be king."

Mantharā began to moan and threw herself on the floor. She flung the blue sapphire across the room.

"O beautiful lady, I am in the pit of despair. The fire of grief consumes me, for with Bharata's destruction comes your destruction, and also my own. Once Rāma is installed, his mother, Kausalyā, will rid herself of her rivals. You will become a slave, and your son Bharata will be nothing but a mere servant to Rāma. The women of Rāma's household are rejoicing today. The women of your household should be weeping, for they will be ruined."

The innocent Kaikeyī laughed. "How can you say such things about Rāma? He is the eldest son, and it is his birthright to become king. Besides, everyone knows that he is compassionate, just, honest, kind, loyal, and faithful to Dharma. He will protect his brothers like a father. After ruling for a hundred years, he will surely turn the throne over to Bharata. As for his mother, the pious Kausalyā, she has always been kind to me. Why are you so distressed, dear Mantharā, when this joyous event will bring immeasurable delight to all?"

These soothing and sensible words only increased Mantharā's fury. She sighed deeply and moaned. "These words of yours afflict me, because you are unaware of the ocean of sorrow that awaits you. Rāma will become king and his son will succeed him, not your Bharata. Thus it has been since time immemorial. Rāma will start his own dynasty. He will never harm Lakshmaṇa, as the love and trust between Rāma and Lakshmaṇa are known the world over. But once in power, without doubt he will banish the younger sons, Bharata and Shatrughna, or put them to death."

At the thought of Bharata being killed, a searing pain struck Queen Kaikeyī's heart. As if a veil had fallen over her eyes, she started to see truth in Mantharā's false and destructive words.

Seeing her queen weakening, Mantharā drove her wedge in deeper, again and again spewing ugly lies. "It is Bharata who will suffer. He is Rāma's rival. All this wealth, all this luxury, all the favors of King Dasharatha cannot save you from being abandoned once Rāma is king. You will be penniless and die a beggar. Be wise and save yourself from perishing!"

Gradually, over the next hour, the words of the malevolent Mantharā wormed their way into Kaikeyī's emotions, finally finding their target. Kaikeyī's face flushed with terror at the thought of being humiliated and abandoned. After all, she had always been the favorite, ever since she came to the court. Her heart pounded and she clawed the royal couch with her nails.

"But what can I do to save Bharata?" she cried out. She rose from the couch and staggered to the window. Her inner chambers faced a courtyard, so she could not hear the people of Ayodhyā joyfully preparing for Rāma's coronation. The sound of her own pulse pounded in her ears like storm waves crashing on the rocks. Overcome with fear, she sank back onto the royal cushions. "The coronation will surely happen tomorrow," she moaned.

"O lovely one, listen to my plan," said the vengeful Mantharā. "Many years ago, didn't you save King Dasharatha's life in the conflict between the Devas and the asuras? When your lord fainted from battle wounds, was it not you who seized the reins of the chariot and bore him to safety? In gratitude, did he not grant you two boons?"

Kaikeyī started to smile. "But I never used them!"

"Exactly. Now is the time to ask for your boons. Ask first for Rāma's coronation to be stopped and for Bharata to be installed as king. Then ask King Dasharatha to exile Rāma to the forest for fourteen years. During those long years, the people will forget Rāma and will come to love Bharata. Thus your son will enjoy a lasting and prosperous reign."

Kaikeyī was now completely in the grip of Mantharā's twisted mind. "Yes," she said, her fingers distractedly wringing her sārī. "I see that only your plan will save me now."

"Once the water has run out of the pond, it does no good to build a dam," intoned Mantharā. "Go now to the chamber of anger, O lotus-eyed beauty. Cast off your jewels and silks. Wait for your lord there. When he sees you filled with grief, he will do anything in his power to please you."

Like a colt being led down the wrong path, Kaikeyī, filled with anger and fear, did what the old woman told her. For the first time in her life, she entered the chamber of anger. Shedding her silk and gold sārī, she replaced it with a soiled, plain garment. She removed her jewels and flung them on the floor. She lay on the ground moaning, her hair loose and ragged. There was only one thought in her mind: to save herself and her son from destruction.

Mantharā followed her into the chamber to give her a last bit of poisonous advice. "The king will offer you jewels, a kingdom, wealth of all kinds, anything to save his precious Rāma. But you must remember that if Rāma is crowned tomorrow, that will be the end for you and Bharata!"

Then the wicked woman, satisfied that she had infected Kaikeyī with her evil plans, crept away to await the queen in her private apartments.

Like a viper ready to strike, Queen Kaikeyī lay in wait for the king.

"I HAVE NOT yet told Kaikeyī of the festivities," King Dasharatha thought as he made his way to his favorite wife's palace that evening. He had spent the day making the final arrangements for Rāma's coronation, and now he wanted to rest and rejoice.

Inside Kaikeyī's palace, he was greeted by the calls of peacocks, cranes, and swans, intertwined with the melodies of *vīṇā*, flute, and drum. Flowering vines shaded the verandah, and the fragrant blossoms of magnolia and mango trees scented the air. Fruit hung heavy on trees, reflected in clear pools lined with flowers. Scattered throughout the garden, benches of ivory, gold, and silver awaited visitors, who were served sweet drinks and other refreshments.

As he entered Kaikeyī's inner apartments, the king knew immediately that something was wrong. For the first time in their long marriage, Kaikeyī was not waiting for him on her luxurious couch. Shaken, he called out for her in distress.

With head bowed low, trembling with the weight of her words, a humble servant whispered, "Your Majesty, the queen has entered the chamber of anger."

The king could barely believe his ears. What could be wrong with his tenderhearted queen, whom he loved more than life itself? He ran quickly to the chamber of wrath. There on the hard floor lay his precious Kaikeyī, her ornaments and clothing scattered about her like a creeper torn from a tree. The sight of his cherished wife suffering was too much for the aged king, who fell to the floor beside her like a leaf crumpling in the wind.

"O darling one, who has caused you to lie like a fawn separated from its mother? Whosoever has done you an injustice, speak the name and they shall be punished. Indeed, in my love for you I am unable to refuse you anything. I and the entire kingdom are here to fulfill your every desire, even if it costs me my life. Rise and tell me what troubles you, and I will end your troubles, just as the sun dispels the morning mist."

Kaikeyī, completely entangled in Mantharā's deadly web, answered these loving words with cunning ones. "My Lord, no one has insulted me. But I have a wish that I want you to grant me. If you first promise to fulfill it, then I will tell you what it is."

The king smiled tenderly and stroked her hair. "You who are dearer to me than all save Rāma, you must know that I will do anything to please you. In the name of Rāma himself, that tiger among men, I promise to fulfill your wish."

Now the devious queen had heard the words she wanted to hear, for she knew her husband would never go back on his word. In his blind and passionate love, he fell into her trap like a fly caught in a spider's web.

"You have promised in the name of Rāma to fulfill my wish. I call on the gods, the sun, the moon, the planets and all that is sacred on this earth to witness your promise."

"Of course, my lovely one," said King Dasharatha, perplexed by her tone.

"You will recall that many years ago I saved your life on the battlefield. At that time you offered me two boons. Now I wish to claim those boons."

"Anything you wish is yours," said King Dasharatha, who was now seated at her feet.

Untouched by her husband's gentle words, under the influence of the vengeful Mantharā, Kaikeyī stood over the king, and in a harsh voice uttered the words that would shatter her husband's life.

"First, I wish you to stop the coronation of Rāma and crown Bharata instead. For the second boon, I wish you to banish Rāma to the dreaded Daṇḍaka Forest. There he will remain for fourteen years. These are my wishes, and let all that is sacred in this world hold you true to your word, for it is said that nothing is more important than keeping a vow."

These words were so cruel and unexpected that at first the king felt paralyzed, his heart so filled with pain he could barely move. "Am I awake or am I caught in a nightmare?" he wondered. Then his mind collapsed under the weight of Kaikeyī's heartless words, and he fainted on the floor at her feet.

When he came to his senses, he remembered the queen's request and trembled. The one he loved had become his enemy, and he felt like a doe beside a lion.

"Shame to you!" he cried out. "How can you harm Rāmachandra, who is blameless? He has treated you with love and tenderness; indeed he has shown you more affection than your own son! You have always said that Rāma is as dear to you as Bharata. Why do you wish to kill me and destroy my dynasty?"

Again and again the king pleaded with her. But he was unable to undo what Mantharā had done.

Hardening her heart, the obstinate queen lifted her chin and said with flashing eyes, "If you refuse to keep your promise to me, what kind of king will you be? Your ancestors gave up their lives to keep their promises. What will the future generations think of you? I swear that I will not rest until Bharata is king and Rāma banished to the forest."

Seeing that Kaikeyī could not be moved, the king again fell to the floor, like a tree uprooted. His mind thrashed about wildly. Weeping, he begged her to change her mind.

"How can I live without my son? Do not inflict this curse upon me and my beloved Rāma, who has never uttered a harsh word to any person and who will never say a word of protest to me. If I say, 'Go to the forest,' he will only say, 'So be it.'"

Now beseeching Kaikeyī on his knees, Dasharatha tried to touch her feet.

The scornful queen recoiled from him. The king lay on the floor, groaning like a madman.

बालं द्वितीयं वचनं पुत्रो मां प्रतिभाषितुम् ।
स वनं प्रव्रजेत्युक्तो बाढमित्येवक्ष्यति ॥

Rāma will never say a word of protest to me.
If I say, "Go to the forest," he will only say, "So be it."

—Ayodhyā Kāṇda 12.85

Chapter 8

On the Coronation Day

On the coronation day
flags and flowers adorn Rāma's palace.
Garlands of sapphire drape the gracefully arched windows.
Sandalwood and aloe perfume its walls.

Cries of peacocks pierce the air.
Cranes stretch their legs in quiet, shaded pools.
Birds flit through gardens
in melodies of light.
Spotted deer gaze in sweet surprise
at golden statues and tall alabaster columns.

Like the sea swelling in waves,
the palace surges with happy, festive friends
gathered to honor their beloved Rāma.

Gifts of gold and silk they bring
on rainbow-covered elephants, horses, and chariots.
Rising like a billowing cloud to the heavens,
the palace of Rāma sings.

Sumantra was happy. He had spent his entire life serving his friend and king, yet he could not remember a day as fortunate as this. For today Rāma would be crowned king. Sumantra smiled as his chariot stopped again and again to make way for the stream of visitors crowding the streets, even as the dawn rose over the city. Colorful banners and garlands of flowers welcomed the guests on the royal highway. At every street corner, tables laden with lavish sweets and refreshing drinks provided refreshment. Merchants sold silks, gold ornaments, and fine goods of all kinds. Bonfires of sandalwood and aloe lit the morning sky.

Sumantra made his way to Rāma's palace to deliver a message from King Dasharatha: Rāma was to come to the palace immediately. Actually, Sumantra remembered, it was Queen Kaikeyī who had ordered that Rāma be summoned.

Earlier that morning, Sumantra had entered the king's palace singing songs of praise and happiness. "Wake up, O glorious emperor," he sang. "Today the sun shines brighter, today the birds sing louder, today the people rejoice, for today your eldest son will be crowned king. All the people have gathered, and the revered Vasishtha and the wise pandits are ready. They have spread the sacred kusha grass over the coronation site, have collected in golden vessels the waters from the sacred Gangā and the seven seas. Honey, curds, butter, roasted grain, flowers, and fresh milk have been set out. The guests are waiting, the canopy has been raised, orchestras and singers are assembled to entertain the crowds. Rise and perform your happy duty, O most excellent among kings!"

It was strange, remembered Sumantra, how the king looked as if he hadn't slept all night, and his eyes were red, as if he'd been weeping. And when King Dasharatha cried out, "O Sumantra, your happy words tear at my heart," Sumantra did not know what to think.

But Queen Kaikeyī had quickly stepped forward to explain the king's disheveled state. "O Sumantra, His Majesty has not slept well because he is so excited about Rāma's coronation. He wishes for you to bring Rāma here without delay."

"How can I do this unless the king himself commands me?" asked the ever-faithful Sumantra.

"Yes, Sumantra, bring my dearest son Rāma to me as quickly as possible," Dasharatha whispered.

Sumantra bowed deeply and left the palace, reassured that all was well. Apparently the king wished to see Rāma once more before the coronation began.

Now at last, Sumantra reached Rāma's palace and made his way through the multitude of friends and well-wishers arriving on richly decorated horses, elephants, and chariots. Everyone recognized Sumantra as the king's most trusted minister, and Rāma's guards showed him the greatest respect, escorting him quickly to Rāma's private quarters.

There Sumantra beheld Rāma, dressed in heavy silk robes, seated on a golden couch like a god, smeared with rare sandalwood paste. At his side sat the beautiful Sītā, like the moon in close orbit to the planet Jupiter. He knew the royal couple had spent the night fasting and the early morning performing sacred rites in preparation for this day.

"O Rāma," said Sumantra, "your father, the king, and your mother, Queen Kaikeyī, desire to see you."

Rāma rose lightly and bade Sītā goodbye. "No doubt there is some happy addition to the coronation ceremony that my mother and father wish to discuss with me. Would you like to rest here with your devoted attendants until I return?"

Sītā smiled. She said, "Today your father will crown you king, and I will bow down before you. May the four directions—north, south, east, and west—bless you. May you rule long and happily as emperor of this world."

As he stepped out of his private chambers with Sumantra, Rāma was greeted by his brother Lakshmaṇa, who was in the habit of waiting there to serve him. Rāma's heart swelled with joy as they slowly made their way to the royal chariot through the throng. Like the sun moving across the sky, the two resplendent princes journeyed to the palace of their father in Rāma's golden chariot.

As they drove to his father's palace, crowds on all sides called out, "Jai Rāma! Jai Shrī Rāma!" and mounted their horses and elephants to follow their beloved Rāma in a parade. Trumpets blared in jubilation, the bards sang Rāma's praises, and graceful ladies showered handfuls of flower petals from their balconies onto the princes below.

"Surely we are the most fortunate people on earth, to deserve such a king as Rāma," said one.

"Ayodhyā has only fortune and happiness to look forward to," said another.

"With Rāma as king, we will live a heavenly life," was the joyful expression of a third.

Others called blessings to Rāma. "May your rule be long and prosperous, and may you exceed your ancestors in glory!"

Rāma smiled as he passed by, his heart gladdened by the happiness of the people. The tumult of the crowd did not touch his serene inner nature. Ever the same, he looked on all his people with love and compassion.

Yet even Rāma felt his happiness drain away when he saw King Dasharatha. He knew immediately that his father was in distress, crumpled like an autumn leaf on his throne, tears streaming from his eyes. Queen Kaikeyī stood over him like a guard.

As was customary, Rāma bowed low to his father, touching his feet. His father did not even greet him.

"Dear Father," said Rāma in his quiet, soft voice. "What has happened to strike you down like a mighty oak felled in the forest? Have I done something to displease you? If so, just tell me and I will remedy the wrong."

On hearing his devoted son's voice, King Dasharatha moaned, "O Rāma!"

Alarmed, Rāma turned to Queen Kaikeyī. "What is troubling my dear father? Is he ill?"

Queen Kaikeyī answered in a harsh voice, "There is nothing wrong with your father that you cannot fix, O Rāma."

"Speak the words and I will do it," said the tenderhearted Rāma.

The shameless Queen Kaikeyī said, "In order to honor his word, your father has promised me two boons. The first is that my son Bharata should be crowned king instead of you. The second is that you should leave today to dwell in the forest for fourteen years."

Rāma was not in the least ruffled by these severe words. "If that is what my father wishes, then so be it," said Rāma. "My only desire is to fulfill my father's desires. For him, I will willingly don the robes of an ascetic. My brother Bharata must be summoned at once. Let him come here tomorrow to care for my father and rule the kingdom."

The hardhearted Queen Kaikeyī, still not satisfied, pressed him further. "It is important that you leave immediately. Your father must abstain from food and drink until his promise is fulfilled."

"Then so be it," said Rāma in pleasant tones. "I will leave today. My only concern is for my father. Promise me that you will take care of him and bring Bharata here to serve him."

With his radiance undimmed, Rāma bowed low to his father. Circling his father in a clockwise direction, he left the chamber, followed by Lakshmaṇa, whose eyes flashed with the fire of wrath. Pausing to enter the coronation hall, Rāma reverently bowed to the sacred milk, ghee, and other items that were intended for his coronation ceremony, and left the palace without looking back.

Like a yogi with no thought for his personal happiness, Rāma sent away his bewildered chariot driver and friends, and made his way on foot to his mother Kausalyā's palace, followed by Lakshmaṇa, who was nobly fighting back tears. To those who gazed upon his face, Rāma appeared unchanged. He smiled as serenely as when he had arrived at the palace, expecting to be crowned king.

Passing through the gate, he greeted the happy crowds with respect and joy. No one suspected that he had just been cruelly deprived of his kingdom. By Rāma's smile, ever contented, no one could know that he would soon be setting out alone into the wild forest, without an ounce of the gold and riches that were once his.

Rāma entered his mother's palace, which as always was filled with the smell of incense and the chanting of pandits. He knew that she had spent the previous days fasting and performing sacred rites for his success as king. Her face, pale from fasting, brightened when she saw him, and she ran to greet him. Rāma bowed low and touched the feet of his mother, but she did not wish him to bow to her, and drew him to her in a loving embrace. He kissed her on the forehead.

"I have waited so long for this moment," said the pious Kausalyā, who normally dressed in simple silk but today wore a festive sārī embroidered with gold and precious gems. "Surely all the gods and the four directions are smiling on me. My heart is filled with happiness."

"Ah, dear Mother, there has been a change of plans," said Rāma quietly as he took a seat beside his aged mother. He held her hand and spoke as gently as he could. "I have come to receive your blessings. Today I will not be crowned king, but will retire to the Daṇḍaka Forest for fourteen years. There I will eat the roots and fruits of the ascetic, and spend my time fasting and meditating with the holy saints who dwell there. My father, in an ancient promise to Mother Kaikeyī, has asked me to do this, so that Bharata can be installed in my place. While I am happy to uphold my father's honor and pleased to fulfill Mother Kaikeyī's desire, I am concerned for your welfare and also for my beloved Sītā and Lakshmaṇa, who serve me so faithfully."

All color drained from the noble queen's face and she fainted. Rāma caught her and held her in his arms until she woke up. It pained his heart to see his tender mother, so unaccustomed to hardship, in a state of distress.

When she recovered, the normally serene queen burst out, "How can I accept this slight from Kaikeyī? All these years I have waited for this day, when you would be king. How can the gods, whom I have petitioned daily on your behalf, treat me with such indifference?"

Then the fiery Lakshmaṇa stepped forward. His whole life, his very breath, he had spent in serving the radiant hero Rāma. To see Mother Kausalyā crying, to see Rāma dealt such an outrageous injustice, was more than he could bear, for he was devoted to Rāma with every cell of his being.

"This wicked deed of Mother Kaikeyī must not be heeded!" His nostrils flared and he hissed like a fire spitting sparks. "Surely our father's mind is touched by old age. How else could he banish the sinless Rāma, who does not take offense even if someone directs anger at him, but is patient and compassionate to all? He is adored by the people, who have dreamed all their lives of being ruled by him. Let us ignore this wicked plot and go ahead with the coronation. I will vanquish all who oppose us!"

To prove his point, the impetuous Lakshmaṇa, so young and handsome, drew an imaginary bow. If the situation were not so grave, Rāma would have smiled at Lakshmaṇa's passion. Instead he spoke gently but firmly.

"All my life I have lived to serve my father and the path of truth. How can I abandon him in his old age? How can I let him go to his death in dishonor? No, I must uphold his honor and fulfill his promise to Mother Kaikeyī."

He went on, "Surely there are forces at work here that we cannot see. Surely Mother Kaikeyī, who has always loved me, would not be banishing me and bringing such grief to my poor parents if this idea of hers were not part of a larger design, whose purpose is hidden from us now. Our only hope is to follow our Dharma. We cannot waste our time now, blaming those who play a part in this grand design.

"As for myself, I could not live another instant if I thought I were bringing dishonor to my father and our ancestors. Only bloodshed and suffering would result from disobeying my father now."

With compassion and respect, Rāma wiped away Lakshmaṇa's tears with the edge of his golden robe.

Then he tenderly addressed his mother, "I know this separation is not easy to bear. But you are a noble lady, known far and wide for your virtue and purity. I have come here today to receive your blessings, so that I may leave for the forest with a light heart."

Queen Kausalyā, seeing Rāma's fortitude and equanimity, gathered her emotions like a seamstress gathering her embroidery threads at the end of a day.

"Then I will follow you. Take me into the forest with you, to care for you. I have no life here without you. Surely I must be a hardhearted woman, or my heart would already be broken. Grant me this one wish, O Rāma." Again, she gave in to her sadness and cried, her body shaking.

Even when faced with his mother's entreaties, his own heart heavy with her grief, Rāma did not falter. "O Mother, just as I must follow my Dharma, so must we all. My father needs you. He has been betrayed by Mother Kaikeyī, who is temporarily blinded by the gods. It is your duty to serve my father, as it is every married woman's highest duty to serve her husband, especially in great need."

The virtuous Kausalyā, brought to her senses by Rāma's words, wiped her tears and said, "I shall do as you say, my noble son. For you are the embodiment of Dharma."

Rallying about her son as a crowd rallies about a hero, she smeared sandalwood paste on his forehead and sprinkled rice on his head. Then, in a gesture of maternal love, she drew him to her breast and kissed the top of his head.

Smiling bravely despite her anguish, the virtuous Kausalyā said, "Just as I waited long years for your auspicious birth, so I will wait these fourteen years for your return. On that day I will be born anew. On that day I will live again. Until then, I will pray for you daily, my son. May only fortune and wisdom meet you; may you be blessed by all the Devas." One by one, she invoked Gaṇesha, Lakshmī, Kṛishṇa, Vishṇu, and all the Devas she worshipped every day, who resided like familiar friends in her devoted heart.

"Follow in the footsteps of your noble ancestors, and may you surpass them in glory. You are my love and my life." With these words, her heart breaking, the high-minded Queen Kausalyā set aside her own desires and gave her blessings to her son.

कैकेय्याः प्रतिपत्तिर्हि कथं स्यान्मम वेदने ।
यदि तस्या न भावोऽयं कृतान्तविहितो भवेत् ॥

Surely Kaikeyī would not be banishing me
if this idea of hers were not part of a larger design.

—Ayodhyā Kāṇda 22.16

CHAPTER 9

Rāma Prepares for Exile

SĪTĀ WAITED, WONDERING what could be keeping Rāma. Wasn't the auspicious hour for the coronation fast approaching? Wasn't it time for him to receive the royal oblation of holy water, honey, and curds, his eyes shielded by the royal umbrella, his attendants fanning him with the hair of one hundred yak tails?

As soon as Rāma entered the room, Sītā asked softly, "My dear, what has happened? Isn't it time for the bards to be singing your praises as you mount the royal elephant, towering like a lofty mountain?"

Rāma related the strange turn of events. "It is the way of Dharma for a son to honor the words of his father and his mother, so I must obey," said Rāma. "The wise say that there is nothing in the three worlds that cannot be won by honoring father, mother, and guru."

Hearing of her husband's exile, Sītā did not fall to the floor in a faint. Nor did she smolder with anger like the faithful Lakshmaṇa. Instead, she immediately began preparing in her mind for a fourteen-year journey through the forest. For in temperament and valor, she was an equal match for the heroic Rāma. Like Rāma, she cared not for her own happiness, but lived to serve others.

"I will go with you, my lord," she said simply.

Rāma embraced her affectionately and said, "My sweet Sītā, a forest is no place for your tender feet to tread. You are a noble lady, versed in the ways of Dharma. While I am away, you must start the day with fasting and prayers. Honor my father Dasharatha, for he is old and ill. Each day, comfort my mothers Kausalyā and Sumitrā, who are filled with grief. Treat my brothers Bharata and Shatrughna with respect and affection, as you would your brothers or sons. Never speak my praises in the presence of Bharata, for nothing displeases a king more than hearing others lauded in front of him. Always serve him as your ruler and do nothing to displease him, for the powerful love those who fulfill their wishes."

At the thought of being separated from Rāma, Sītā's heart contracted. "My mother and father have taught me to serve my husband and to stay with him always, whether he is a ruler in a palace or a poor forest dweller. You yourself have taught me that a wife shares the destiny of her husband. This is her joy and her duty. For a devoted wife, there is no worse punishment than being separated from her husband. Grant my prayer and let me come with you, O Lord."

"O Sītā," said Rāma, taking her hands in his. "One as tender as you cannot possibly know how dangerous the Daṇḍaka Forest is. There the wind howls at night. There the monstrous rākshasas and fierce beasts attack the innocent. There the only foods to eat are roots and fruits scavenged during the day. I could never risk your life in this way."

As tears streamed down her face, Sītā continued to entreat Rāma. "Many years ago, Vedic astrologers told me that I would spend time in the forest, meeting the sages and saints who dwell there. Do you not remember how many times I have asked you to take me to the forest? I am longing to accompany you now. With you by my side, I will be happy. With you by my side, I will be free from harm. With you by my side, I will sleep peacefully at night and sport playfully in the day in honey-scented woodlands and lotus waters. I will befriend the deer and the swan. Without you, I will be like the moon without the sun to light it. Without you, the jewels of the palace will be like heavy stones around my neck."

Still Rāma refused to consent. Finally, the thought of separation becoming too real, the lovely Sītā grew agitated and sprang to her feet. She taunted her beloved husband, "Surely my father did not know that you were so cowardly, or he would never have given my hand to you at the sacred fire! How can the world say you are as resplendent as the sun? I have never cast my thoughts to another man. Ever devoted to you, I cannot endure even an hour of separation. How could I live in grief for ten plus four years of sorrow?"

With this she wailed piteously, exhausted with crying. Like a rose petal falling, she collapsed in his arms.

At last Rāma revealed his true thoughts, clasping her to his heart. "O Sītā, I would not bring you unhappiness even for all the rewards of heaven. I did not wish to subject you to the hardships of the Daṇdaka Forest, even though I am surely capable of protecting you from them. But since you have shown me that you are not only destined but determined to follow me into the forest, I would not be separated from you for all the riches on earth. I only needed to know the strength of your feelings, O precious daughter of Janaka, dearest to my heart."

At his words, Sītā embraced him tenderly.

"Now, my lotus-eyed lady, prepare to give away your jewels, your silken clothes, and your golden housewares to the wives of the ascetics and the poor," said Rāma. "For you will be needing none of these in the forest."

Sītā, her cheerful mood restored, began making one pile of golden sārīs and another of glittering gold and jeweled ornaments. Like a bride opening gifts at her wedding, she prepared to give away her life's possessions, for she was happy to become a forest dweller if it meant being with Rāma.

All this time Lakshmaṇa, who always followed his brother Rāma like a shadow, had remained silent, though his face was also drenched with tears. Now he approached his brother, folding his hands in respect. His words burst forth like water from a dam. "Only one thing will appease my quaking heart," said Lakshmaṇa. "Let me follow you, as I have always done."

Rāma, his heart filled with love for his younger brother, gave many reasons for Lakshmaṇa to stay. But Lakshmaṇa persisted, saying, "Since our birth, I have never been separated from you even for a day. How could I part from you for fourteen years?"

Rāma consoled him, saying, "If you come with me, then who will care for our mothers Kausalyā and Sumitrā, who will grieve inconsolably without your company? And surely someone must look after their interests when Bharata is king, for he may be blinded by his mother's ambition and may slight them. Serving your elders is your duty."

The valiant Lakshmaṇa, whose love for Rāma arose from the core of his being, was himself a persuasive speaker. His face radiating with love, he said, "You can ask Shatrughna to care for Mother Kausalyā and Mother Sumitrā. Surely there is no loss of Dharma if I serve you."

When Rāma didn't raise an objection, Lakshmaṇa continued, "With my bow and arrow, I will walk before you, clearing the way of all harm. With my basket and trowel, I will search the countryside for roots and fruits to sustain you. Each night I will watch over you and Sītā while you sleep."

Rāma smiled broadly, for in truth he could not imagine living without the faithful Lakshmaṇa by his side.

"Then come with me, dear Lakshmaṇa! Go at once to Vasishtha's house and bring the celestial bows and quivers, filled with arrows, bestowed on us by Vishvāmitra. We will need them in the dreaded Daṇḍaka Forest."

Lakshmaṇa smiled, his heart light for the first time that day. He quickly left to do Rāma's bidding.

Later, after Lakshmaṇa returned from his sad goodbye to his beloved wife, Rāma said, "Ask Suyagya, son of the noble Vasishtha and leader of the Brahmins, to come here. Then call all of the holy men who will guide the kingdom while I am away."

Next Rāma summoned the royal treasurer and instructed him, "Bring all that belongs to me." Shimmering gold and jewels were heaped in a mountainous pile. The immeasurable wealth Rāma had won through acts of valor lay before him.

After the virtuous Suyagya and his wife arrived, they stood by while Rāma and Sītā bowed low to show respect. Rāma bestowed upon Suyagya gold bracelets, necklaces, earrings, precious gems, an elephant, and one thousand gold pieces. To Suyagya's wife, Sītā gave pearls, gold bracelets, precious gems, intricately woven tapestries, and a luxurious couch with silk coverlets embroidered in gold thread. The Brahmin and his wife thanked them, their faces bright with tears.

Throughout the long morning, Rāma and Sītā gave away all of their jewels, ornaments, clothing, cows, horses, and gold pieces. They gave to holy sages, students of the Veda, their friends, the elderly, and the poor. Rāma distributed gold, jewels, and thousands of cows to one elderly minister, who had long served the royal family. He heaped gold and jewels on his servants, who were moved to tears by his generosity. He did not forget any who had served him or were in need.

By the end of the morning, Rāma's immense wealth was gone.

न देवि बत दुःखेन स्वर्गमप्यभिरोचये ।

O Sītā, I would not bring you unhappiness even for all the rewards of heaven.

—Ayodhyā Kāṇḍa 30.27

Chapter 10

Rāma Is Exiled

See how tender his age,
he whose lips have never spoken angry words,
even when falsely accused.
The great-souled one, our guide and protector,
shares our joys and our sorrows.

See how Sītā sheds no tears,
for she is happy
following her lord wherever he goes.

See how Lakshmaṇa enters the forest
as a child enters a room full of sweets,
eager to serve his soft-spoken brother.

O see how King Dasharatha runs after his son,
arms outstretched like the blind.
The blameless Kausalyā
cries out like a cow for her calf.

All because of one
whose heart is black ice.
Surely our king must be senseless,
or mad,
to fall under her sway.
Why else would he allow Ayodhyā's song
to slip away?

It was a sad and subdued crowd who watched Rāma, Sītā, and Lakshmaṇa walk to King Dasharatha's palace, bereft of jewels, chariot, and riches. Their radiance undimmed, they were followed by servants carrying their weapons, flashing in the sun.

People were still pouring into the streets for the coronation, but having heard the devastating news they now hoped to glimpse Rāma before he was gone.

"To think he who never went anywhere without his charioteer to drive him and attendants to serve him is now treading in the dust," said a white-haired woman, her eyes filled with tears.

"And our lotus-eyed Sītā, even the birds flying overhead never before saw her face," said another. "Now she walks through the streets like a common woman, exposed to the stares of all."

"Surely our king has lost his senses," said a man who tried to prop up a festive banner, now dragging in the street.

"How can we live without Rāma to warm our days?" asked a young man.

Here and there a murmuring began: "Let us follow Rāma to the forest."

"Yes, we will follow Rāma!" cried the people. "Let Kaikeyī be left with the wind howling through empty rooms."

Like a river gathering speed as it nears the ocean, the people of Ayodhyā surged through the streets, following the royal couple and the faithful Lakshmaṇa. So great was their love for Rāma, the loyal townspeople abandoned their palaces, gardens, and riches without a glance behind. Standing outside the palace gates, they patiently waited while

Rāma, Sītā, and Lakshmaṇa entered the palace to receive their father's blessings for the journey.

Inside the royal chambers, the three saw Dasharatha lying on his couch, surrounded by his wives, who were crying inconsolably. All except Kaikeyī, that is, who stood defiantly at the head of his bed, her hands clasped at one hip.

As Rāma and Sītā approached the king, their palms folded together in reverence, King Dasharatha struggled to rise from his couch and greet them. His eyes red from tears, his face drawn and pale, limbs shaking and lips trembling with the effort of forming words, he looked years older. Kausalyā tried to help him, but he fell to the floor, overwhelmed by emotion.

Rāma caught his father in his arms and helped him back to his couch. "O Rāma," the king cried plaintively, "take away my throne by force. I am the one who should be banished."

Smiling sweetly, his face as full as the moon, Rāma spoke words as soothing as the fragrance of jasmine. "O Father," said Rāma, "may you rule this earth for another hundred years. The throne is not for me. I have given my word to dwell in the forest and have come to receive your blessings, along with Sītā and Lakshmaṇa, who wish to accompany me."

The king said piteously, "I see that you are determined to uphold my ill-fated vow, because it is impossible for you to stray from the path of righteousness. Go with a peaceful heart, for you have won the blessings of all lovers of truth. But please, do not leave today. I cannot bear it. Stay one more night with your mother and me."

"Dear Father," said the gentle Rāma, "surely it is better to cut short this unhappy day. Why prolong your grief when nothing can be changed? I am happy to fulfill your vow, so your name will always be honored among the truthful. In this way the fourteen years will pass quickly, and your pledge will be fulfilled."

For a moment, nothing could be heard but the wrenching sobs of King Dasharatha's wives, who looked upon Rāma as their favorite son.

Then even the serene Sumantra burst into tears. Seeing the anguish of his friend, the king, the faithful charioteer turned to Kaikeyī.

"Don't you see that you have destroyed our beloved king, for he cannot live without Rāma?" Sumantra asked her. "The people will follow Rāma to the forest and leave Bharata with an empty kingdom. You will be reviled for all eternity for this evil deed. Stop now. Come to your senses. O, why doesn't the earth open its jaws and swallow you, why doesn't the sun burn you to ashes for this unforgivable act?"

Kaikeyī stood staring straight ahead, her face and heart like granite.

At that point the king rallied his will and said, "Sumantra, you must send riches, bedding, and comforts with Rāma. Send armies to protect him. Send his favorite friends to keep him company. Send hunters to catch his food. Send the strongest fighters to slay the dangerous tigers and bears. Let him pass the fourteen years in comfort, visiting the holy spots of the forest."

Like a sleeping volcano suddenly revealing its hidden fire, Kaikeyī erupted in fury. "Do you believe even for a moment that Bharata would accept a kingdom without its riches, its armies, its people?"

"For shame!" cried King Dasharatha. "How can you continue on this evil plan?" The servants looked down, never having heard angry words spoken in this family before. Kaikeyī, however, only flung more angry words.

Rāma soothed her, saying respectfully, "O Mother, do not fear. I will keep the king's promise and Bharata shall keep the kingdom with all its riches."

Turning to his father, he said, "Dear Father, I care nothing for wealth or power. I live only to fulfill your desires. What good would gold do me in the forest? No, I will tread lightly there, living at peace with the humble creatures and sages alike. All I need is tree bark for clothing and a shovel and basket for digging roots."

With those words, Kaikeyī handed the illustrious Rāma and the faithful Lakshmaṇa rough garments woven from the inner fibers of tree bark. "Wear these," she commanded coldly. The two brothers shed their royal silken robes and donned the humble clothing of ascetics, their splendor undiminished by the change of attire. But when the shameless Kaikeyī handed the rough garments to the delicate Sītā, women and men alike cried out with loud sobs.

Holding up the coarse tree-bark robe, Sītā looked puzzled. "How do I wear this?" she asked. Rāma quickly came to her aid, draping the ascetic's garb over her silken sārī.

With that, Vasishtha had to speak out. "O Kaikeyī, are you determined to ruin your family's name? Now that Sītā has decided to follow Rāma, unwilling to leave his side, then all of Ayodhyā will also follow Rāma. You will see, even Bharata and Shatrughna will don bark clothing, as they, too, are lovers of Rāma. Even the birds and deer will follow him. There is no kingdom without Rāma."

Vasishtha gestured to the unrefined garments that Sītā wore. "Let Sītā forever be adorned as befits the wife of the king. These are not for her to wear."

Even with these words from the holy Vasishtha, Queen Kaikeyī refused to relent. Those present, sobbing openly now, turned to King Dasharatha and said, "Shame to you!"

Stung by these words, the king roused himself. Railing at Kaikeyī, he said, "This was not part of my vow. Surely you have no grudge against the pure-hearted Sītā, with her delightful and gentle ways. So devoted to Rāma that she will follow him even into the dangerous forest, must she also wear these coarse garments?"

The king mustered his strength and said, "Sumantra, bring rare and costly jewels and silken sārīs for Sītā, to last all her years in the forest."

When Sumantra returned, Sītā took off the bark-cloth robes and adorned herself with resplendent jewels, gladdening the hearts of all.

Sensing the time for departure was near, Rāma begged his father, "Comfort and cherish my mother, who today has sustained a terrible blow, being separated from her only son. Known throughout the world for her virtues, she does not blame you, but grief may cause her life to slip away."

Then Sītā, steadfast in her devotion to Rāma, bowed to her mother-in-law. Overcome with emotion, the flawless Kausalyā praised Sītā. "Blessed is the wife who stays by her husband even when misfortune overtakes him. Faithful wives who are virtuous, who follow the teachings of their elders, hold their husband sacred. I know you will never forget to honor Rāma as your lord, even though he is dressed in bark instead of gold."

"Your teaching of Dharma is not lost on me," said Sītā, folding her hands in love and respect. "I will surely follow the path you have laid out. Please trust that I will always live my life just as my parents and guru have instructed me."

Sītā smiled at Rāma's mother and continued, "I could no more be separated from Dharma than the moonlight from the moon. Just as the wood is inseparable from the tree, so a woman's happiness is inseparable from her husband. Even her mother, father, or children cannot give the happiness that the husband gives—to the wife he is the giver of all. I feel only respect and honor for my husband, for indeed, the wife finds God in her spouse."

Hearing these simple words of Sītā's, Kausalyā was filled with joy, and her tears flowed in both happiness and sorrow.

Then Rāma, his hands folded in devotion, his heart set in the path of Dharma, walked reverently around his mother. Facing her, he spoke words of courage. "Mother, you must not give way to grief. My father needs you at this desolate hour. Let the fourteen years pass quickly, like a long winter's sleep. You will see me return here once again, accompanied by friends." He did the same for Sumitrā and Kaikeyī.

Next Rāma addressed both his stepmothers together. "If ever I have spoken harshly to you, if ever in my childish ignorance I have caused you harm, please forgive me now and give me your blessings for my journey." With these humble words from the blameless Rāma, Sumitrā could contain her feelings no longer and wailed with immeasurable grief.

Rāma now took his leave from his father, circling once around him.

Then Lakshmaṇa bowed in reverence, first to his mother Kausalyā, and then to his birth mother, Sumitrā, who embraced him through her tears. "You have my blessings to follow your brother to the forest, even though my heart is deeply tied to you," she said. "Serve him faithfully, as you are accustomed. Rāma is your refuge. To serve your elders is the highest Dharma; now you must look upon Rāma as your father and Sītā as your mother. Go and be happy."

Thus taking leave of their father, their mothers, and their beloved servants, Rāma and Sītā slowly walked through the palace, with Lakshmaṇa following. At the palace gate, Sītā, glittering like a thousand stars, stepped lightly into the gold chariot, happy to be at Rāma's side.

With Sumantra driving, the chariot rolled slowly through the crowds of soldiers, sages, and common people. The laments of the people hung in the air like a thick fog. Women wailed. Dogs howled. Men shouted, "Slow down, slow down, slow down!" Clinging to the sides of the chariot, young and old alike begged to see Rāma's face one last time. All around, people cried out in distress.

Hearing the cries of the people, the aged king staggered to the road, followed by his wives. "Rāma," he cried after the chariot. "Rāma." Tears streaming down his face, he held out his arms like a beggar. "Stop, I beg you, stop!"

Seeing his father crying out piteously, his mother trailing behind with faltering steps, Rāma said urgently, "Speed up!" Sumantra hesitated, not knowing whether to follow the orders of his king or those of Rāma. "If the king reprimands you when you return, tell him that I did not want to prolong his misery," said Rāma.

And so the chariot left the grieving king and his wives behind. Queen Kausalyā, her eyes blinded by tears, cried out, "O Rāma! O Sītā! O Lakshmaṇa!" again and again.

The king stumbled after the chariot until a minister gently said, "One must not follow too far the guest he desires to return home." Nodding in acquiescence to these words of tradition, the elderly king stopped. Bent over with grief, he stared helplessly as Rāma's chariot rolled out of sight. The citizens of Ayodhyā roiled around the chariot like a river around a boulder, determined to follow Rāma to the forest.

An eerie silence stole over the city, the only sounds the sobbing of the bereft monarch and his wives. Still the king remained there, his hands outstretched to the cloud of dust gradually disappearing on the horizon.

Then it was over. The brokenhearted king stood staring at the tracks left by Rāma's chariot until a wind swept them into oblivion. He fell to the ground in a swoon.

धर्माद्विचलितुं नाहमलं चन्द्रादिव प्रभा ।

I could no more be separated from Dharma
than the moonlight from the moon.

—Ayodhyā Kāṇḍa 39.28

CHAPTER II

The People Follow Rāma

Rāma is a sun to the sun,
fire to burn all fires,
law to lawgivers,
and a God to the gods.

The essence of all life,
he imparts grace to the graceful

and diverts fear from the fearless.
To him can come no harm.

The night breezes caress
the noble one to sleep.
Mangoes drop from the trees,
a willing offering to a pure being.
The sun softens its heated rays
and the moon embraces him like a mother.
Rāma is a tiger among men
whom none can defeat.

Though Ayodhyā mourns his departure
like an orphaned child,
Rāma walks with happiness, resplendent with light.
Before him strides the invincible Lakshmaṇa,
keeper of swords and celestial weapons.
Between the two brothers Sītā steps lightly,
shining with grace and beauty.

When King Dasharatha fell, the queens rushed to his side, raising him up. The king's eyes fluttered and opened. The first person he saw was Kaikeyī, who had once been his favorite.

Raising his face to the sky, he declared with force, "Never again will my eyes rest upon you. Before all the gods and the sun, I renounce the vows that I made, the hand that I held, as I led you around the sacred fire. All that is mine is no longer yours; what is yours is no longer mine. For you have shunned Dharma and have chosen a path merely for material gain."

Then he turned to Kausalyā. His energy spent, he said weakly, "O Mother of Rāma, take me to your palace. I cannot bear to stay anywhere else." The heartbroken queen, herself barely able to stand, led the king away, his face dark as an eclipse of the sun.

The palace echoed hollowly without the two princes and the adored Sītā. The king lay on Kausalyā's couch, tormented by thoughts of Rāma and Lakshmaṇa sleeping in the dust and Sītā stepping on thorns. He slept fitfully. At midnight, he called out to Kausalyā, "Let me feel your loving touch. My sight, which followed Rāma, has not returned. I fear I am blind."

The good Queen Kausalyā, sunk in her own dark thoughts, roused herself to comfort the king. After he fell once again into a fitful slumber, Kausalyā, overcome with sadness and fatigue, gave way to her feelings. "My precious son, that tiger among men, has been ripped from my arms. Who knows what plight Rāma is facing this very minute? How can I live, when grief burns me as the sun scorches the desert?"

Sumitrā heard Kausalyā crying. Steadfast in Dharma and charming of speech, she comforted the devout and pure Kausalyā with words straight from her heart.

"You know more than anyone that this son of yours is no ordinary man. All good qualities adorn him like ornaments on a bride. Your son, who is endowed with all the attributes of an ideal ruler, renounced his own kingdom for the sake of his high-souled father. What can be the reason for mourning such a noble deed? His brother Lakshmaṇa, in his compassionate service to Rāma, will also be honored throughout time as an exalted soul. Sītā, who has given up all comfort and luxury to follow her husband, will evermore be held highest among women.

"The gods shower blessings on those who uphold Dharma," Sumitrā went on. "What harm can come to these lovers of truth? The time will pass quickly, and soon Rāma of the blue complexion will return to Ayodhyā, and you will shed tears of joy like a cloud sprinkling the earth below."

With these sweet, healing words of Sumitrā, Queen Kausalyā felt heartened, and her grief left her like a bad dream at daybreak.

Meanwhile, far from the palace, Rāma's chariot rolled ahead, followed by the men of Ayodhyā, who could not bear to lose sight of their beloved prince. Over and over they begged him to turn back. When they reached the gates of the city, Rāma turned and spoke to them from the chariot, his eyes filled with the love of a father for his children.

"I have renounced the kingdom as my father wished. Now it is for the people of Ayodhyā, who have always lavished love and affection on me, to direct that loyalty to Bharata. Though young in years he is old in wisdom. He will rule the kingdom with prudence and gentle strength. The king's wishes must be carried out, and then he will have no reason to grieve."

The more Rāma remained true to his Dharma, the more the people felt attached to him. He now ordered the chariot to go on—yet no one turned back when it hurtled forward. Even the pandits of the kingdom, who were old, wise, and powerful through years of reciting the Veda, followed him.

Struggling to keep up, they called to the horses, "Slow down, noble ones! We know you can hear us, for you have sharp ears. Bring your master, the lover of truth, back to Ayodhyā. Otherwise, with our bodies covered with dust, our hair white as a swan, we will leave our wives and families to follow the one who is steadfast in Dharma. Even the trees are beckoning him to return; even the birds cry out to hold him."

When Rāma saw these venerable and respected sages falling behind, he compassionately ordered Sumantra to stop. Stepping from the chariot, he continued on foot with Sītā and Lakshmaṇa. In this way the holy men could keep up.

Finally, at the end of an exhausting day, the procession reached the River Tamasā. There Sumantra let the horses roll in the grasses and graze. After the evening ablutions, he and Lakshmaṇa prepared a bed of boughs for Rāma and his wife.

While Rāma and Sītā and the people of Ayodhyā slept under the starry sky, Lakshmaṇa stood watch, and Sumantra kept him company. To pass the long hours of the night, Lakshmaṇa expounded on Rāma's virtues while Sumantra listened.

In the early hours of the morning, long before dawn, Rāma awoke. Seeing the men of Ayodhyā still sleeping, he whispered to Lakshmaṇa, "Let us leave now, so these good men can return to their warm beds and their families. After all, it is the Dharma of a prince to save the people from hardships, not to create difficulties for them."

Without making a sound, Sumantra hitched the horses to the chariot and took his place in front. Driving Rāma, Sītā, and Lakshmaṇa, Sumantra carefully pulled away from the encampment and crossed the River Tamasā in the darkness, the spokes of the wheels churning the high waters.

Once on the other bank, Rāma said, "Travel north to begin the journey in an auspicious direction. Then switch back, so the people cannot trace us."

On Sumantra drove, on through the night. At daybreak, after his morning meditation and prayers, Rāma ordered Sumantra to press on—on beyond the fertile rolling hills of Kosala, tucked into the earth like the folds of a mother's apron. On across the Gomatī and other rivers the chariot forged ahead.

When the people awoke at dawn and found that Rāma had disappeared, they lamented, "O cursed sleep, we have lost him!" In vain they tried to trace his tracks, and in the end returned home, dejected and weeping.

When they reached Ayodhyā, their wives, whose love for Rāma was like a mother for a son, chastised their husbands. "What use was it returning without him?"

The loss was so great that the whole city of Ayodhyā plunged into mourning. No women cooked food, no men decorated their shops; all were overcome with memories of the happiness they had once enjoyed and thoughts of future glories blighted. Ayodhyā was like a star whose light had been snuffed by the clouds, a vast ocean whose waters had shrunk to a puddle.

As they rolled on through the countryside, Rāma chatted with Sumantra, trying not to hear the laments of the people in villages they passed, who followed him as the people of Ayodhyā had done. Finally they reached the farthest boundary of Kosala.

Here Rāma motioned to Sumantra to pause. Before going into exile, he wished to honor one last time the kingdom of his birth—a kingdom rich in grain, precious gems, and gold. A kingdom lush with gardens and mango orchards, with cows crowding its pastures, and the chanting of sacred texts reverberating in its homes. Long free from fear of attack, its people were prosperous and contented.

Rāma bowed reverently with folded hands and spoke to the country folk who had followed him from the nearby village. "You have proven your love and devotion, but now you must return to your homes and your work."

Facing the direction of his birthplace, he vowed, "May the gods bless you, fair city of Ayodhyā. When my exile in the forest is over, and I have fulfilled the vow of my father, I shall see you again, O Ayodhyā, together with my father and mother." Then the chariot surged forward, and Ayodhyā slipped out of sight as the sun slips below the horizon at day's end.

Beyond the boundaries of Kosala kingdom, the chariot at last came to rest at the sacred Gangā, the River Ganges, winding its way to the sea. Ancient āshrams adorned its shores, its waters purifying all sin. Called the "Stream of Golden Lotuses" by the gods in heaven, the stream swirled like a dancer in one place and drifted graceful as a swan in the next. Birds flitted in bursts of light on its shores. Elephants drank its waters like nectar, flowering trees dropped their petals in obeisance, and fishes shining like jewels flashed through its waves.

Taking in this delightful scene, Rāma's heart suddenly felt lighter. As he was about to dip in the purifying waters, he saw a group of tribal men approaching, wearing decorative paint and simple clothing of bark and feathers.

Rāma smiled broadly. He immediately recognized his dear friend Guha, the king of the Nishāda tribe, who ruled this region of dense forest on the edge of the kingdom of Kosala. Guha had been like a brother to Rāma when they studied together in Vasishtha's āshram.

Greeting Rāma with folded hands, the humble Guha said with devotion, "O dear Rāma, my kingdom is now your kingdom. Please, rest here in our comfortable beds and nourish yourselves with delicious food, which I have brought. As long as you wish, let this be your home, and let all that you see be yours."

Rāma embraced Guha fondly in his strong arms and asked after his friend's family. "It is a delight to visit you here," he said. "But as you must have heard, I have vowed to become an ascetic, so I cannot accept your gifts of food and bedding. My father's horses, though, will surely appreciate grass and water."

Rāma walked to the river to bathe, drinking only a little water brought to him by Lakshmaṇa, fasting as he had been taught to do upon reaching a holy place.

The tireless Lakshmaṇa again prepared a bed of boughs, this time under a flowering *ingudī* tree, and then took up his watch over Sītā and Rāma as they slept. Distressed to see the loyal Lakshmaṇa forgoing sleep, Guha said, "Please, you must rest on a comfortable bed. Let those of us who are accustomed to sleeping in the forest watch over Rāma during the night."

Then the brave Lakshmaṇa gave way to his emotions, weeping like an elephant in pain. "How can I rest when the pride of Ayodhyā, whose birth was accompanied by all auspicious signs, sleeps on the ground with the blameless Sītā? At this moment, our revered father is surely dying of grief."

Guha, agitated beyond bearing, consoled the loyal Lakshmaṇa with inspiring words and stories, and so passed the night.

The next morning, Rāma said to Lakshmaṇa, "Hear the cry of peacocks in the woodland and the dark-feathered *kokila* bird. See how the dawn streaks the sky. Today we will cross Mother Gangā. Dear brother, ask our loyal friend Guha to supply a boat to ferry us over."

Delighted to be of service to his beloved friend Rāma, Guha delivered a splendid boat and boatmen to guide it. As Rāma, Sītā, and Lakshmaṇa prepared to board, Sumantra knew that he would not be following them. The faithful minister could not bear the parting. His eyes flooding with tears, he entreated, "What are your wishes?"

Gently Rāma touched the aged minister's shoulder with his right hand and said, "You have served me well, but now you must return home to serve the king with all devotion, as you always have. For now we leave the chariot and our belongings behind and enter the forest on foot."

Sumantra gave way to his grief and sobbed, for he had never imagined that he could be separated from Rāma. "You will earn great merit for following your father's wishes and entering the forest like a commoner," he said. "But the rest of us will pine away without you. What will we do, now that we are subject to Kaikeyī's desires?"

Rāma comforted him by saying gently, "In the long line of Ikshvākus, no one has served our family as well as you. Now I am depending on you to help my father bear his sorrow. He is old and fraught with suffering; he needs you to support and guide him. Kindly return home with messages of love and respect for my father and mothers."

Still Sumantra could not reconcile his heart to this painful separation. "Please do not think me disrespectful, for today I speak not as a servant, but with my heart and soul. How can I return with an empty chariot to Ayodhyā, where the people thirst for your return as men thirst for water in a drought? You, who always treat your servants with love, cannot abandon one who wishes to serve you."

Rāma, who felt sympathy for those who assisted him, finally said, "I know that by attending to my father for so long, you have become intensely devoted to me. Perhaps it will help you to know that there is a reason for my request. When Mother Kaikeyī sees the empty chariot, she will know without a doubt that her wishes are being fulfilled, and will not suspect the truthful king of deception."

Sumantra reluctantly accepted the wisdom of Rāma's words. Having blessed Sumantra and taken his leave, Rāma now asked Guha to bring him the milky sap of the banyan tree. Seated on the ground, Rāma and Lakshmaṇa smeared their hair with sap and tied it in a knot at the top of their heads. Speaking the sacred vows of ascetics, dressed in bark-cloth robes and matted locks, Rāma and Lakshmaṇa glowed like two ancient Ṛishis.

The knower of Dharma thanked his gracious host Guha and embraced him fondly. Without looking back, the three boarded the boat, Lakshmaṇa entering first to help Sītā. After rinsing his mouth with water, Rāma offered salutations to the holy river and prayed for a safe crossing. At the midpoint, the boat stopped as Sītā sang a prayer to the holy Gangā.

O Mother Gangā, grant your son a safe journey.
After fourteen years, may he return safely, and then,
O Devī, in thanksgiving will I perform a yagya to you.
O lady of a thousand lotuses, consort of the ocean king,
to you I bow down,
to you I offer adoration.
When the mighty-armed Rāma returns and regains his empire,
a hundred thousand cows will I give away,
a thousand vessels of gold
to please you.
I will worship all the gods who adorn your shores,
visit all the sacred āshrams
when Rāma, his brother, and I
touch your shore once more,
delivered from exile.

Guided across by the devoted boatman, they reached the far shore of the Gangā, where their life in the forest would begin.

निवृत्तवनवासस्त्वामनृणो जगतीपतेः ।
पुनर्द्रक्ष्यामि मात्रा च पित्रा च सह संगतः ॥

When the period of my exile in the forest is over,
and I have fulfilled the vow of my father,
I shall see you again, O Ayodhyā, together with my father and mother.

—*Ayodhyā Kāṇda 50.3*

Chapter 12

Life on Chitrakūta Mountain

High on Chitrakūta Mountain
Rāma said to Sītā,
"See, my beloved, how this mountain shimmers
in ribbons of gold, silver, emerald,
and traces of stars.
Flocks of birds light on its peaks
like a cloud.
Herds of deer leap through mango groves.
Leopard, hyena, and bear
frolic under rose-apple blossoms.

"See how the trees never lose their bloom
in this enchanted place
and bow down to offer us jackfruit and mango.
The wind carries sweet fragrances
of the flowering champa tree
and trills of birds.

"In the moonlight healing herbs
glow like flames.
Sages with matted locks
salute Sūrya, the sun Deva, each morning,

and those of disciplined vows
perform their oblations each evening
as the setting sun tints its waters gold.

"Bathe with me in this river
three times a day,
for it is the refuge of the sinless.
My lovely one, bathe in the Mandākinī,
with its carpets of red and white lotuses,
and escape all fatigue.

"Imagine these wild beasts
are the citizens of Ayodhyā,
and the mountain is the city,
with its peaks of palaces brushing the sky.
Imagine this river is the Sarayu, passing
by our distant home.

"As for me, I find this perpetual spring of Chitrakūta
even more pleasing than that fabled city.
Neither loss of kingdom nor loss of friends troubles me.
With you here to give happiness,
with Lakshmaṇa here to serve me,
I cling to the discipline of forest life
and drink the nectar of this river
to honor my promise to my father."

After offering his blessings to the faithful boatman, Rāma surveyed the narrow path leading into the heart of the forest. Though he still felt the light and pure air of the River Gangā, he noticed that the woods here seemed denser and wilder than those they had left on the other shore. Vines choked the trees, the forest canopy so thick that sunlight barely reached the ground.

"Lakshmaṇa," Rāma said, "together we must shield Sītā from the perils of this uninhabited forest. It is, after all, the duty of warriors to protect others. If you walk first and I walk last, with Sītā in between us, she will be safe from dangers all around. We must keep watch without fail, for Sītā's safety depends solely on us."

And that is the way they would walk for the next thirteen years.

Later, Rāma, Sītā, and Lakshmaṇa took rest under a tree, and the three prepared to spend their first night in the forest there. Freed from the company of his subjects for the first time, Rāma at last unburdened his heart to his brother as Sītā slept. Stretched on the earth, Rāma said, "The nights must weigh on our father like a shadow, and I fear he is sleeping badly. What if Kaikeyī goads and taunts my mother and yours? Without sons to defend their interests, what will become of those women? Lakshmaṇa, you must return home at once to defend them from Kaikeyī."

Lakshmaṇa waited until his brother ran out of words. Then that able-bodied warrior said comfortingly, "O Rāma, it is true that our family and the people of Ayodhyā are bereft without you. But you must not lament, for Sītā and I also depend on you. Without you, we are like fish without an ocean. I do not wish to leave you, even to see my own father and mother—even to see heaven, if it is far from you."

Cheered by Lakshmaṇa's tender words, his heart relieved from its acute pressure, Rāma fell asleep without fear or distress, like a lion in his mountain kingdom.

The next day the three walked along the river, hoping to find the confluence of the Rivers Gangā and Yamunā. They walked through pleasant flowering groves, admiring the views. By the time the sun reached its zenith, they spotted the smoke of an āshram fire and quickened their pace.

Coming to a clearing, they saw before them the āshram of the famed Ṛishi Bharadvāja, who lived at the meeting point of the two holy rivers. The sage sat before his hut, and they approached reverently, bowing to him and introducing themselves.

"I have been expecting you," said Bharadvāja simply. "I have heard of your unjust banishment and how the faithful Sītā and the lionhearted Lakshmaṇa followed you to the forest."

After offering them water to bathe their feet, he gave them *madhuparka*, a traditional offering of yogurt, clarified butter, honey, and coconut milk. Then he served them foods and drinks made from roots and berries, gathered in the forest. Versed in Dharma, the holy Bharadvāja revived his guests with pleasing food and generous hospitality.

"You are welcome to stay here as long as you like," said Bharadvāja. "Why not make your forest home here with me?"

"Thank you, revered sage," said Rāma, "but if we stay here, we will be close neighbors with Ayodhyā. I am afraid the people would seek us out. Do you know of a secluded place farther away that would be safe for Sītā?"

The sage smiled. "I know of just the place. Chitrakūta is a holy mountain, with lush vegetation, grassy clearings, and high waterfalls. It abounds in roots, berries, and honey. Peacocks and songbirds sing sweet melodies, deer leap and play, and streams sparkle with the splashing of elephants. Holy sages fill its caves, and it is said that as long as a man sees the peaks of Chitrakūta Mountain, he will devote himself to virtue and will not set his mind on misdeeds." Sītā glanced at Rāma and smiled. It sounded like the perfect place.

After spending the night at the peaceful āshram, the three forest dwellers thanked the holy sage again and again for his kindness, and set out on their long walk to Chitrakūta Mountain. Only now their hearts were lighter.

When it came time to cross the sacred River Yamunā, known as the daughter of the sun, the two strong-armed brothers hewed wood and bamboo and built a raft. Lakshmaṇa fashioned a comfortable seat of rattan reeds for Sītā and adorned it with auspicious rose-apple blossoms. Tenderly Rāma gathered the bashful Sītā and settled her on the seat. Seated on her flower and bamboo throne, radiating beauty and light, Sītā floated like a forest queen on her barge, attended by the two princes.

Rāma and Lakshmaṇa rowed swiftly across the streaming river, pausing midway for Sītā to sing a prayer. When they reached the other side, the blameless Sītā, friend to all living beings, cried in delight, "There is the banyan tree that Sage Bharadvāja told me about! He said to pray for my heart's desires there."

Sītā circled the ancient tree, long revered by saints. Bowing low before it, she prayed, "Glory to you, Mother of the Forest. May my husband return home safely, and may we live to see Mother Kausalyā, Mother Sumitrā, and Mother Kaikeyī once again."

As he watched his beloved Sītā with tender affection, Rāma said to Lakshmaṇa, "Be sure to gather any flowers that Sītā would like along the way."

Enchanted by the herons and swans frolicking in the sacred waters of the Yamunā, Sītā pointed to trees and songbirds that were new to her.

Rāma, who knew the forest, taught her their names. Lakshmaṇa gallantly stopped to pick flowers that caught her eye, and soon a garland of blossoms adorned her neck.

In this happy way Sītā walked in a leisurely fashion toward their new home.

The next day, as they drew near Chitrakūta Mountain, Rāma felt more and more joyful. "See how the trees are illuminated with blossoms, now that winter is past," he said to Sītā. "See the mango trees, filled with crowds of monkeys, branches bowing low with their offerings of fruit. We can live here and eat these fruits."

Rāma gestured toward the sky. "Lakshmaṇa, see the giant honeycombs dripping from every tree. See how the lofty peak of Chitrakūta Mountain touches the heavens. We will settle in this holy place, in the company of high-minded sages, on a level spot populated with trees, entertained by melodies of birds and trumpeting of elephants. We will be happy here."

When they at last reached the mountain, the three royal travelers came upon the āshram of the high-souled sage Vālmīki, who would many years later compose the Rāmāyaṇa. As befitted a knower of Dharma, Vālmīki greeted them by circling their heads with a ghee lamp. After eating the food offered by the sage, they took their leave with gratitude and respect.

After walking deep into the forest once more, Rāma wasted no time. "Lakshmaṇa, gather the materials for building our home. My heart longs to live here." Immediately, the mighty-armed warrior Lakshmaṇa hewed logs of many different trees and built a strong hut with a leaf-woven roof.

"The hour is auspicious," said Rāma. "Let us perform the ceremonies for blessing a home." After taking his bath in the River Mandākinī, the pure and illustrious Rāma performed the rites, reciting the sacred mantras to bring happiness and blessings from nature. Rāma, Sītā, and Lakshmaṇa entered together and began to dwell quietly in the forest.

Their minds deep in silence, living in harmony with the wild birds and beasts, gathering nuts and fruits to eat, the three wanderers made their home on Chitrakūta, between the pure waters of the River Maṇdākinī and the tall peaks of the mountain. Flower petals covered their path, honey sweetened their food, and the river quenched their thirst. Charmed by the forest and his dear Sītā, buoyed by Lakshmaṇa's companionship,

Rāma's days were infused with joy. Soon he forgot the sadness of leaving Ayodhyā and lived happily as before.

यावता चित्रकूटस्य नरः शृङ्गाण्यवेक्षते ।
कल्याणानि समाधत्ते न पापे कुरुते मनः ॥

As long as a man sees the peaks of Chitrakūta Mountain,
he will devote himself to virtue and will not set his mind on misdeeds.

—Ayodhyā Kāṇḍa 54.30

Chapter 13

The Death of King Dasharatha

In a land without a ruler
clouds no longer bless the earth with rain,
farmers harvest no grains,
and no sons obey their fathers.

In a land without a ruler
no one plants shade trees or flower beds
or builds a palace.
Armies cease to march
and the lawless rule.
Merchants neglect
to travel with their wares
to distant cities.

In a land without a ruler
young women abandon evening pleasure gardens,
the wealthy lock their doors at night,
fields no longer yield bounty,
and young men refrain from courting.

In a land without a ruler
pandits receive no gifts,
ascetics stop their wandering,
and the learned cease
to debate in honeyed groves.
Travelers fear to venture out,
archers no longer twang their bows,
horses stop their prancing before shining chariots,
elephants no longer lumber along highways,
ringing their bells.

Where there is no king
there is no wealth,
no ghee-laden offerings,
no alms for the poor,
no festivals of merry singers and dancers,
no armies victorious over foes.

Like a river without water,
like a chariot without a horse,
like a mountain without peaks,
the land without a ruler
cries in the night.

For the king is truth.
He is righteousness.
The protector of good,
he is the father of the orphan,
the mother of all.

When Sumantra bade farewell to Rāma on the banks of the River Gangā, he thought his heart would break. He stood watching until Rāma, Sītā, and Lakshmaṇa crossed the river and disappeared into the woods on the opposite shore. And then he was alone.

Sumantra wandered by the shore for several days, talking with Guha and waiting for news from Guha's spies, who followed Rāma's progress. When he heard that Rāma had reached Bharadvāja's āshram and traveled on, he knew there was no hope of ever rejoining his master's son. So

Sumantra hitched the horses to King Dasharatha's chariot and started the lonely journey home.

It was just as he feared. From afar, Ayodhyā no longer beckoned like a bejeweled queen. Bleak and desolate, the gates shuttered, the city looked more like a widow who had just lost her husband. When he drove into the silent city, people heard his chariot and ran into the streets, their weary faces lit with a glimmer of hope. But when they saw the empty chariot, they cried out, "Where is he?" When Sumantra told them that their beloved Rāma had crossed the wide Gangā, people burst into tears, their last hopes shattered.

Hearing the women of Ayodhyā weeping behind their window screens was trying enough, but for Sumantra the worst was yet to come. Nothing could prepare him for the fallen state of the king, who lay like a withered leaf on his couch. When Kausalyā whispered Sumantra's arrival to the king, the aged monarch slowly turned his face to face him. His old friend could see that the king was cherishing the hope that Rāma was with him.

When Sumantra gently told the king that he had returned without Rāma, Dasharatha found strength enough to ask, "Then tell me, O faithful friend, your news of Rāma. How does the royal prince, accustomed to sleeping on silken beds, endure nights on the hard ground? How does the delicate Sītā walk so far, without a chariot to relieve her fatigue? What did Rāma, Lakshmaṇa and Sītā say when you parted?"

Sumantra, who always spoke the truth, did not hold anything back, though his voice choked with emotion. "Rāma asked that I salute you again and again, and that I touch your feet, as he would do if he were here. He offers his greetings and love to all the royal mothers. He greets his mother Kausalyā with reverence and says that all is well. He entreats her to be vigilant in pursuing her Dharma—to light the sacred fire at the proper hours, to always serve his father as she would her God, to treat Kaikeyī as she would treat Sumitrā, without pride or rancor, and to serve Bharata as she would the king himself, for rulers must be honored for their power.

"He also left a message for Bharata," Sumantra continued. "Rāma said, 'O Bharata, please my father by ruling the kingdom, and always respect his wishes.'" At that point Sumantra could barely continue, as he recounted that Rāma's tears fell like rain when he entreated Bharata to treat all his mothers equally, and to take special care of Rāma's aged mother Kausalyā, now bereft of her son.

"Seeing Rāma's tears, the faithful Lakshmaṇa could not contain his feelings," said Sumantra. "Lakshmaṇa said, 'Rāma is my brother, my father, my king, and my master. I fear that my father cannot expect to continue ruling, having exiled the virtuous Rāma, who is adored by all.' But the blameless Sītā said nothing. Her breast heaving with sobs, her face pinched with grief and bathed in tears, she helplessly watched me take my leave.

"The royal horses at first refused to return home without Rāma, and tears rolled from their large eyes. And as I journeyed back to Ayodhyā," said the brokenhearted Sumantra, "I saw a land in which buds wither, water boils in rivers and lakes, and wild beasts have lost the will to hunt their prey. Flowers wilt, birds shrink from view, and men and women are exhausted by tears. For no creature cares to live without Rāma."

At these blunt words of Sumantra's, Dasharatha again lamented his fatal mistake. "How could I have acted so foolishly, swayed by Kaikeyī's poisoned words, without consulting my friends, ministers and citizens? O Sumantra, if I have ever done good to you, take me to Rāma now. Let me rest my head near his, for I cannot live without seeing him and his brother Lakshmaṇa and the devoted Sītā once more. Please, take pity on an old man, and bring me to them."

Sobbing, the king said to Kausalyā, "There is no way for me to cross over this ocean of grief. How great my sin must have been, for my children to be torn from me."

Hearing the king's heart-rent words, Kausalyā could not contain herself. Her body shook and she fell to her knees, begging Sumantra again and again to bring them to Rāma.

That good servant wished he had bitten his tongue. Now he tried to reassure the queen. "Sītā has taken to forest life like a creeper to a tree. She delights in the blossoming flowers and the songbirds, and is learning their names from Rāma. She wears her lovely ornaments and silken sārīs, and trips along in the forest as if it were her own pleasure garden. Because her pure heart is overflowing with love for Rāma, her natural serenity and beauty, like the petals of a lotus flower, are undiminished by the wind or sun. Those three, fulfilling their father's vow, delight in the forest life."

"Oh my son, my son!" The more Sumantra tried to soothe her, the louder Kausalyā cried. Then suddenly she stopped crying, and for the first time since Rāma's exile, Kausalyā turned to King Dasharatha and chastised him for causing this unthinkable misfortune.

"When I see Rāma's face before me, with his lotus eyes and crown of thick curls, my heart breaks into a thousand pieces. And who is to say that Bharata will even relinquish the throne when the fourteen years of exile are over? And why would Rāma accept the leftovers of his younger brother? Such an insult cannot be borne by that tiger among men, who with his invincible strength and golden-tipped arrows can devour the ocean itself. But he is the knower of Dharma, so he has respected your vow. He has been undone by you like a fish swallowed by its own parent. And I, too, have been destroyed. For a woman depends first on her husband, second on her son, and third on her relations. All of these are no more. By destroying our son, you have destroyed me. Worse, you have destroyed this city, this kingdom, this state, yourself, and your ministers. Only your one son and one wife are happy."

Pierced by these scorching arrows from the normally serene and dutiful Kausalyā, King Dasharatha could scarcely breathe. In his misery, his mind swirling with emotion, he fell unconscious. After a long time, he came to his senses.

"O my faithful queen," cried out King Dasharatha, trembling with remorse. "Take pity on me." Folding his hands together like a mendicant, he begged her, "You are ever loving and kind to all, even your enemies. I beg you, my dear queen, who is anchored in Dharma, forgive your unworthy husband's misdeeds, as you have been taught. Do not treat me unkindly, even though you are drowning in grief."

Seeing her proud husband begging for forgiveness, the good and humble Queen Kausalyā burst into tears again. "It is I who must be forgiven," she said. She tenderly placed his hands, folded like a lotus bud, on her head. "I fall at your feet for what I have done, to cause a great and just man to beg for his wife's forgiveness like a common thief. I have always clung to Dharma, and I know that you, too, are a man of utmost integrity. It is my sorrow that has caused me to say words I did not mean to say. Surely, grief chokes courage, blinds knowledge, and clouds the senses. There is no greater enemy than grief."

King Dasharatha removed his hands from her head and tenderly clasped her delicate hands in his own, and so the two righteous and heartbroken parents of Rāma were reconciled. His wife's soft words soothed him like a healing balm, and finally the tormented king fell into a deep and restful sleep.

THE NIGHT STILL covered the earth in a veil of darkness when King Dasharatha woke up. His mind brooded over the events of the last weeks, churning over them again and again, hoping to discover how this calamity could have befallen his family. Then, like a flash of sunlight on a cloudy day, he recalled a misdeed he had unwittingly committed many years before, as a youth. Waking Kausalyā, he told her this strange and tragic story.

"Long ago, before we married, in that long-forgotten time when I was a young king, I was known as a skilled archer, because I could hear the sounds of an animal and direct my arrow to it without even seeing the target. Like a man who longs to eat poison fruit because it looks pretty, I did not know the consequences of shooting by sound alone. But whether you know the consequences or not, you reap the fruit of your action.

"It was the season of rain, and the waters cooled the scorched earth like a mother's caress. Birds splashed happily, elephants drank long and deep, and withered leaves shed their dust and sparkled with vitality. In this happy time I went hunting alone in the lush woods near the River Sarayu. I hunted at night, hoping to kill an elephant.

"My bow and arrow in hand, I crept quietly through the forest and stopped by a tranquil pool. Staying absolutely still, I waited. Soon I was rewarded by the sound of an elephant stomping to a pond and drinking from its waters. I sent the arrow flying to meet its mark.

"A man cried out in agony, 'Why would someone want to kill me, a hermit devoted to austerities? I was only filling my pot with water, to carry to my aged parents. What have I done to be pierced in the middle, my vital parts torn in two?'

"I was paralyzed with fear and shaking with grief. Surely I would wake up from this nightmare, I thought, for even at that young age I always tried to follow Dharma. And now I had mistakenly struck down a Brahmin, the most heinous sin of all.

"Hoping to help him, I crashed through the palms and reached his side. There I found a youthful ascetic, lying on the ground and clutching his side, his water pot rolling at his feet. Even in his agony he shone with an inner light made brilliant through long meditations.

"Recognizing me, he reproached me. 'What harm did I do you, O mighty king, that you would want to strike me?' he said in anguish. 'Your one arrow has killed three, for my aged mother and father are blind, and I am their sole caretaker. What made you shoot a man who was carrying water to his ailing parents? You must go quickly to my father's āshram and tell him, lest he destroy you with his anger. But first, remove the arrow and put me out of pain.'

"I knew that by my removing the arrow, the youth might die. Seeing my fear and regret he said, 'Do not worry that you will be killing a Brahmin. I am the son of a merchant and laborer.' And so I did as he asked, and he passed to the next world.

"For a long while, I was paralyzed with remorse. Finally, I gathered myself together and, taking the water pot, made my way to the āshram nearby. There I found an old man and woman, radiating light but unable to move without their son to carry them on his back, like a forest that must wait for the rain.

"At first they thought I was their son. 'Dear son, why have you taken so long to bring water to your mother?' asked the sage. 'Have we done something to offend you?'

"Trembling all over, placing my palms together in respect, I finally found the courage to tell them about the dreadful accident.

"At first the sage said nothing. A wave of unspeakable grief passed over his face, and tears fell. Then he said quietly, 'It is fortunate that you yourself have told me of this inconceivable act, for otherwise your head would have shattered into a thousand pieces. The entire line of Ikshvākus could have been destroyed today.' Then he asked me to lead them to the place where their son lay.

"While performing the last rites for their slain son, the weeping couple cried out again and again, 'Take us with you, for we cannot exist without you to feed and care for us. You will reach the highest heaven, for your faithful service to us on earth and for the power of truth you have attained.'

"Throughout all this, I stood with my hands folded, too stunned to move. Finally, the sage turned to me, his face radiating such light that it nearly blinded me. 'As a warrior, it is a grievous sin to kill a holy man, but because you did it in ignorance, you will not suffer the most severe consequence. Yet the misery you have created will find you, as surely as your own arrow found its mark. As I die of grief now at the death of my son, so you too will die of grief from losing your son.' Having cursed me, the old man and his wife left this world to join their son."

Having finished his story, King Dasharatha said, "Like an illness caused by eating poisonous food, I now face the inevitable consequences of that regrettable mistake. The words of that grieving father stretch across the long corridor of time to reach me, and now I will surely die, grieving for my son."

Reaching out to touch Kausalyā, he said, weeping with fear, "Lay your hand on mine, O auspicious one. I can no longer see you, for men who are near death cannot see. My senses will retract, one by one, until finally my mind will fail, like a lamp whose oil has dried up, and then my heart will stop. If only I could feel the touch of Rāma once more, my Rāma who knows Dharma and who is undefeatable. The sadness dwelling in the deep pools of my heart is swelling to consume me, just as the river consumes its banks in a flood."

Then the king cried out, "O Rāma, fortunate are those who will live to see you again. O Kausalyā and Sumitrā! O Rāma! O Sītā! O Lakshmaṇa!"

Overwhelmed with sorrow, his last thoughts on Rāma, attended by Kausalyā and Sumitrā, the noble King Dasharatha gave up his life.

THE BODY WAS discovered the next morning by the maidservant, who saw Kausalyā and Sumitrā lying unconscious at the dead king's feet and ran from the room crying. Wailing began in the women's quarters, and all the servants of King Dasharatha crowded into the room, sobbing as if the world had ended.

Cradling the king's head in her lap, Queen Kausalyā said to Kaikeyī, "See where your selfish designs have led? This king could not live without Rāma. By banishing that worthy son, you have killed our husband." The other women, too, cried out in despair, "Who will protect us now?" Among themselves, they whispered, "Who will save us from the evil deeds of Kaikeyī, a woman without human feeling?"

Soon the ministers and holy men came and removed the body. They immersed it in oil to preserve it, for not one of the four sons of Dasharatha was present to perform the funeral rites. Headed by Vasishtha, they held an emergency meeting.

"Bharata must be summoned to conduct the rites of the dead," said one of the Brahmins to Vasishtha.

"And he must take the reins of the kingdom," a minister said. "For without a king, this land will surely dissolve into anarchy." So it was that Vasishtha ordered the messengers to summon Bharata home to a kingdom without a ruler, a kingdom shrouded in mourning like the dark night.

पुत्रव्यसनजं दुःखं यदेतन्मम साम्प्रतम् ।
एवं त्वं पुत्रशोकेन राजन्कालं करिष्यसि ॥

As I die of grief now at the death of my son,
so you too will die of grief from losing your son.

—Ayodhyā Kāṇḍa 64.54

Chapter 14

Bharata's Grief

Far from the fertile fields of Kosala, in the charming kingdom of Kekaya, the land of his mother's birth, Bharata slept fitfully. Little did he know that messengers were drawing near the city to summon him home.

The next morning, his brightness dimmed, Bharata did not smile or greet his friends. He sat brooding in a corner of the elegant room where he and his cousins usually gathered. Shatrughna stood beside him, as always. Reflecting his brother's mood, he too felt withdrawn from the usual banter. Seeing Bharata's strange state of mind, his cousins tried to cheer him up with songs, jokes, and dancing. They even performed a humorous skit.

Finally, one of his closest friends asked, "Dear Bharata, when your friends try their best to make you happy, why do you keep staring with a long face?"

Bharata struggled with his emotions and could not speak. Finally, his voice quivering, he said, "In a dream, I saw my father in dire straits. The strong-limbed Dasharatha, smeared with mud, his hair unkempt and his clothing disheveled, fell from a mountaintop into a pool polluted by cow dung. Standing in that pool, he drank oil from cupped hands and laughed like a madman. Then he dived headfirst again and again into a vat of oil. Finally—and this is the worst part—wearing a red garland and red sandalwood paste, he climbed into a chariot drawn by asses, driven by a red-faced demoness who laughed hideously, heading south."

Bharata looked around at his dear friends. "I fear that one of us will soon die, either Rāma, Lakshmaṇa, Shatrughna, my father or me. This is why I do not respond to your kindly efforts to cheer me. I cannot shake the fear I felt upon seeing my father in such a wretched condition."

The group of friends fell silent now, for everyone knew that such a dream did not bode well. Just then messengers from Ayodhyā were announced. As they entered the room, Bharata and his friends leapt to their feet to welcome them.

The faithful Bharata could hardly wait until the formal greetings ended. "Tell me," he said, "how is my father? Are my mothers well? How are Rāma and Lakshmaṇa? And do the people prosper?"

Having been instructed by Vasishtha to avoid telling Bharata the sad news, they answered in general terms. "They are all well, only you have been summoned home on urgent business. You must leave today." Then they handed Bharata gifts of costly garments and jewelry for his relatives, as well as two bags of gold pieces. "The larger is for your grandfather, and the other for your uncle, to thank them for hosting you so graciously."

Bharata gratefully accepted the gifts, generously rewarding the trustworthy messengers with gold.

Filled with foreboding, Bharata bade farewell to his maternal grandfather, King Ashvapati. "You have my blessings on your journey," said the monarch. "Offer my greetings to your mother, your father, the holy men who surround your family and your two radiant brothers, Rāma and Lakshmaṇa. You are a noble son to my daughter and are always welcome here." Then, to honor Bharata and his family, he sent with him two thousand gold pieces, horses, elephants, mules, well-bred dogs, luxurious carpets, deerskins, and other items of wealth.

Bharata barely took time to express his thanks for their kindness, so anxious was he to mount his chariot for home. Flanked by their grandfather's army and most trusted officials, Bharata and Shatrughna left the city where they had been treated like gods.

The journey took them over mountains, across rivers, and through uninhabited forests. At one point they rode on elephants through dense woods. Later the pure and high-souled Bharata, with Shatrughna, hitched swift steeds to his chariot and left the army behind. By changing the teams they were able to keep traveling through the night and reached Ayodhyā at dawn on the seventh day.

Home at last, Bharata saw inauspicious signs when he entered the city. "Where are the Brahmins who chant their hymns at daybreak?" he cried to Shatrughna. "Where are the merchants selling flowers? Why do the gardens look empty, with no young children playing about? Where is the smell of sweet incense, entwined with the cool breeze? Birds have lost their voices, the front porches are unswept, and the temples stand empty, their fires untended. No smells of sumptuous food fill the air, no one eats, no one worships, no one celebrates. Tears streak the faces of the people, and their clothing is unwashed and torn. I fear the worst, as this city bears all the signs of the passing of the king."

His eyes welling with tears, the weary Bharata made his way to his father's palace. When he found the chambers silent and his father absent, he hurried to his mother's palace, hoping to find him there.

Kaikeyī, resting on her couch, rose to greet her son. Clasping him to her breast, she covered him with caresses. Sitting down on her divan, she drew him to her side. "Tell me, how long was your journey? You must be so tired. Tell me, how are your grandfather and your uncle? Did you enjoy staying there? Tell me everything."

Bharata answered her questions dutifully, but when he could no longer contain himself, he burst out, "Where is my father? Why isn't he here to greet me? I have been summoned home so abruptly. Please, dear Mother, tell me what is wrong!"

When his devious-minded mother told him, in unconcerned tones, that his father had gone the way of all earthly mortals, the mighty warrior Bharata fell to the ground like a *shāla* tree felled by an ax.

"I am destroyed!" cried Bharata. "How can I live without my beloved father to wipe away the dust from my face? Fortunate are Rāma and Lakshmaṇa, for at least they could perform his last rites."

Bharata writhed on the floor in anguish, crying out, "I must see Rāma immediately, for now he is my father, my brother, my friend, and my master. I am his devoted servant. Only by serving Rāma can I feel happy, now that my father is gone."

Kaikeyī tried to raise him. "It is not seemly for royalty to wallow in grief," she said coldly. "Rise up, for in bravery, in the recitation of the Vedas, and in the performance of righteous acts, you are more radiant than the sun."

Bharata knelt by her couch, sobbing with his head in his hands. "Tell me, what were his last words, he who was the model of perfection and protector of all?"

Kaikeyī said impatiently, "He cried out, 'How fortunate the ones who will see Rāma returning. O Rāma! O Sītā! O Lakshmaṇa!'"

Bharata felt a chill pass through his body and he shuddered. He was afraid to ask the next question. Unable to meet his mother's eyes, he finally whispered, "Where is Rāma?"

"He has been banished to the Daṇḍaka Forest with Sītā and Lakshmaṇa, clad in bark cloth."

Bharata's eyes darted around wildly. Surely he must be going mad. "How could the pure-minded Rāma have done something so wrong?"

Then Kaikeyī, thinking her moment of glory had finally arrived, told Bharata all she had done—starting with the night in the chamber of anger, the king's promise, the exile. "I did this all for you, Bharata," she concluded with a proud smile. "So abandon your sorrow, perform the funeral rites, and be installed as lord of the world."

Bharata turned away from his mother, whose smile now seemed hideous. For a long time he could not even speak, so great was the turmoil in his heart.

"You, whom Rāma cherished as tenderly as his own mother; you, whom Kausalyā treated as a sister—how could you harm them?" he said finally, his voice shaking with emotion. "Now I see that it was you who killed my father. Now I see that he died of grief. You have consumed our family. How could you even conceive of such evil deeds?"

Then the noble-hearted Bharata, gathering his strength about him like armor, stood up to leave. "Know this. I will never fulfill your ambitions. I will never rule in Rāma's place. In spite of you, I will bring back from the forest my faultless brother, who is dearly loved by the people. I want nothing to do with your schemes."

Stunned by this turn of events, Kaikeyī sank to the floor.

She was sobbing now, but the usually gentle Bharata, unable to contain his rage, his chest heaving like a bellows and his eyes blazing with fire, continued to denounce her actions. "By killing my father and banishing the one who was loved and respected by all, you have brought dishonor to me and to the whole line of Ikshvākus. How can I face my other mothers, who have been separated from their husband and their sons by you? For everyone knows that to a mother, none is so dear as a child."

Distraught, the pure and loyal Bharata left Kaikeyī and made his way to Kausalyā's palace. He stopped short when he saw the mother of Rāma looking so pale and thin, her face lined by rivers of tears.

"The throne that you envied is now yours," said Kausalyā, her voice shaking. "The ruthless Kaikeyī has taken it from my son, who must now live as a poor wanderer in the forest, while you will enjoy the kingdom, with its vast wealth and storehouses of grain."

The blameless Bharata could not bear to hear these bitter accusations from Kausalyā and he fell to the floor. Finally recovering enough to speak, he said, "O faultless one, I am innocent. I beg you, do not blame me for schemes of which I knew nothing. You know that my heart is bursting with affection for Rāma."

Kausalyā said nothing. Then Bharata uttered a scorching oath: "May those who sent Rāma to the forest spend the rest of their lives as slaves. May they forget the teachings of the scriptures. May they suffer the fate of one who treats his teachers with irreverence or harms a cow. May they endure the destiny of the seller of poison. May they be excluded from the society of the virtuous."

"O my beloved son," cried the tenderhearted Kausalyā, who was now weeping, "through God's grace, your heart is still noble, and your soul is among the blessed. Stop now, for I cannot bear to hear you utter these sad curses." She raised Bharata to his feet and clasped him tightly in a maternal embrace.

Bharata spent the rest of the day in a daze, trying to fathom all that had happened in his absence. He spent the night tossing and turning, heaving great sighs, the peace of sleep eluding him.

The next morning, Vasishtha, who had ruled the kingdom in the absence of a king, spoke calming words to Bharata. "It is time to perform your father's funeral rites. It is time to end your grief."

Bharata, ever conscious of his duty, began preparations. But as he stood by the king's body and attendants lifted it from the bath of oil, he again gave way to his emotions. "What were you thinking, O dear Father, when you sent Rāma away?" he lamented. "Why have you gone away, leaving me alone with a city drained of light, mourning for you?"

"Gather yourself, O Bharata," Vasishtha gently advised him. "For the sake of your father, these rites must be performed with a steady mind." Once again Bharata checked his emotions and helped the priests perform their tasks.

Carrying the king's body on a palanquin, his servants slowly walked to the banks of the River Sarayu on the edge of the city, where the funeral pyre awaited. Men from Ayodhyā scattered gold and silver coins on the path ahead while the women watched from afar. More people followed on foot, on horses, and on camels. The pandits chanted sacred mantras. Bharata lit the pyre, and the air became dense with smoke.

Twelve days later, Bharata bathed in the river to purify himself, as part of the *shrāddha* ceremonies, sacred rites for ancestors and departed parents. To ensure the happiness of his father in heaven, Bharata gave the Brahmins goats, cows, and piles of gems, cloth, and rich foods.

On the thirteenth day, when Bharata was completing yet another rite, he broke down again, sobbing. "Without my father and brother Rāma to guide me, I will enter the flames. I will retire to a hermitage."

Shatrughna, seeing his brother's anguish, remembered all his father's acts of kindness and felt his own sadness stabbing at his heart. And Shatrughna, too, fell down sobbing next to Bharata.

"Why do you delay in your duties?" the self-composed Vasishtha admonished Bharata, to bring him to his senses. "All beings must experience hunger and thirst, pleasure and pain, life and death. These cannot be avoided."

"All things have a beginning and end," added Sumantra as he helped Shatrughna and Bharata to their feet.

Finding peace in Sumantra's kind words, the two lionhearted brothers, their eyes red from tears, completed the ceremony. Despite their grief, Bharata and Shatrughna stood resplendent, like two glorious flags of Indra, unfaded by sun and wind.

एष त्विदानीमेवाहमप्रियार्थं तवानघम् ।
निवर्तयिष्यामि वनाद्भ्रातरं स्वजनप्रियम् ॥

In spite of you, I will bring back from the forest
my faultless brother, who is dearly loved by the people.

—Ayodhyā Kāṇḍa 73.26

Chapter 15

Bharata Seeks Out Rāma in the Forest

Crowded with ministers, representatives, and holy men, not a seat remained in the palace hall. It was the fourteenth day after the death of their monarch, and they had assembled to decide who would fill the empty throne.

The eldest member rose to speak. "Only because of strong unity has this fatherless kingdom been spared from anarchy. With Rāma in exile, it falls on the next eldest son to rule. O Bharata, take up the crown!"

There was a long silence. Finally, Bharata stood up, radiant in his silken robes and gold ornaments. After reverently circling the crown and other materials that had been assembled earlier for Rāma's coronation, he faced the assembly.

"Surely it is the eldest who should rule," said Bharata, his voice ringing in the great hall of the palace, with its walls made of gold. "This is the tradition of kings and the tradition of our family. You should know me better. I will not take the crown that my mother sought for me. I will spend the years of exile in the forest instead of my brother, and with my armies I will deliver Rāma to his rightful place on the throne."

Flowers rained down from the heavens. Tears fell from the noble ones' eyes. All the people rejoiced, their sorrow vanquished by Bharata's heroic words.

"May the giver of plenty, Lakshmī, shower you with rewards for such an unselfish act," cried one minister. "Who but the high-minded Bharata would give up a kingdom for the sake of his brother?"

Immediately the assembly decided that a highway should be built so Bharata could lead his army to the forest. Having spent the last weeks immobilized by depression, the people of Ayodhyā threw themselves into the task. Masons, carpenters, bridge builders, and dam builders happily went about their work. They spent weeks leveling, cutting, digging, and smoothing the way.

When it was finished, the road arched through the countryside up to the banks of the River Gangā, with its cool waters and leaping fish. Flanked by landscaping as beautiful as the gardens of heaven, the royal way glistened with white pebbles. Sprinkled with water mixed with fragrant sandalwood paste, its smooth sidewalks looped through flower beds and groves of blossoming trees, lined by banners swaying in the wind. Songbirds rejoiced in its completion.

Elegant roadside resting camps for Bharata and his followers were built along the path. Surrounded by moats, each royal camp was graced by serene gardens and luxurious resting areas.

The highway and its camps were completed on a day when the moon joined with auspicious stars. The people poured into the streets, ringing conch bells in jubilation. Musicians sang and the sages chanted.

After the ceremony, while resting high up in the palace, Bharata and Shatrughna heard the bards joyously praising Bharata with glad songs, just as they lauded King Dasharatha in happier times. The pure-hearted Bharata burned with shame and grief.

Summoning his ministers, Bharata quickly gave the order for silence. "I am not the king!" he told them. Sinking onto a couch, his head in his hands, he moaned, "O Shatrughna, what a disservice has been done to the people by my mother!"

Just then, a messenger arrived. He announced, "Honored Prince, the revered Vasishtha requests your presence in the court." Bharata and Shatrughna exchanged worried glances and hurried there.

As Bharata entered the palace hall, with its luxurious seats covered in gold-threaded cloth, he wondered why it was crowded with all the most important leaders of the kingdom, including a representative from each realm. Without Bharata's knowledge, Vasishtha, having perceived the support for him among the people, had summoned all the royal advisors and holy men.

The wise Vasishtha, who knew the Dharma of kings, rose to speak in kind tones. "O Bharata, your brother Rāma, so devoted to truth, will never agree to rule against his father's wishes, any more than the sun will give up its light. You have inherited this kingdom through no action of your own. So now take up the throne, rule happily, and receive gifts from all the kingdoms under your rule."

Bharata could not speak. He was anxious to follow the words of his preceptor, as he had been taught. Yet his thoughts dwelled on Rāma, who had been treated so unjustly on his behalf. His mind whirled. When he spoke, his lips trembled and his voice shook with emotion. "How could a son of Dasharatha become a throne-snatcher? I would surely go to hell if I accepted the repulsive arrangement my mother contrived for me."

His voice stopped shaking and he now spoke with conviction. "I will go to the forest. I will try diligently to persuade Rāma, who is enlightened among men, to return to his rightful place on the throne of Ayodhyā. If I cannot, then I will live with him in the forest with Lakshmaṇa." All who heard his words shed tears of joy, knowing that the righteous Bharata was determined to bring back their beloved Rāma.

Bharata saw the people nodding their heads and smiling in agreement. "The road is now ready. Let us start at first light!"

The people cheered and cheered in an ovation that went on for many minutes.

Vasishtha, seeing the will of the people, gave Bharata his blessings. Immediately, Bharata instructed Sumantra to ready the army. "Prepare my chariot as well," he said.

Everyone in Ayodhyā rushed home to prepare for the journey. The next morning, as the first rays of the rising sun streaked the horizon, Bharata and Shatrughna set out in their chariot. Ahead rode the ministers and Brahmins in grand horse-drawn chariots sparkling with gold. Behind marched the army, mounted on elephants, chariots, and horses. Kausalyā, Sumitrā, and Kaikeyī followed in their royal chariots, and then the village elders, who were honored for their wisdom. Wealthy citizens, merchants, artisans, and physicians—all the people of Ayodhyā, wearing spotless new clothing, their bodies adorned with jewels and smeared with dyes in auspicious hues—rode horses, camels, and elephants.

Filled with gladness to be ending the painful separation from their adored Rāma, the entire procession crept along the new royal highway, which followed the path Rāma had taken.

After a few days, they reached the bank of the Gangā, and Bharata directed the army to spread into camps to spend the night. Then he said to Shatrughna, "I will perform oblations in the river on behalf of our departed father." He dipped in the purifying waters of the Gangā and prayed that he would be able to persuade Rāma to return to Ayodhyā.

As Bharata finished his evening meditation and prayers and joined his ministers, he was unaware that hundreds of eyes watched him. Guha, the forest king, and his warriors were hidden behind a rise of land above the river. They surveyed the sprawling army that swallowed the banks of the river.

"What can Bharata have in mind?" wondered Guha, who was ever faithful to Rāma. "Does he wish to destroy us and Rāma with that ocean of an army?"

Thinking awhile, he formed a sensible plan. "Send all our boats to the spot along the Gangā where the army is camped," he ordered. "Let each boat be armed with youthful marksmen to guard against anyone crossing the river. Fill the boats with food, fish, roots, and fruits. We will offer this food to Bharata if he proves his faithfulness to Rāma."

Then Guha and his ministers walked on foot through the forest to meet Bharata, followed by people carrying welcoming gifts of food and drink.

Guha greeted Bharata as warmly as he had greeted Rāma. "Your army is welcome to stop here tonight for nourishing food and entertainment. All that is ours is yours."

Bharata, who recognized Guha from their time as fellow students at Vasishtha's āshram, graciously thanked the forest king. "Dear friend of my brother, how can I cross this wide river, and how can I find Bharadvāja's hermitage through the tangle of thorns and foliage that awaits us on the other side?"

The faithful Guha, even though he could see that Bharata's army was formidable, said simply, "My fishermen and I can take you. But first, please tell me your intentions. I pray you do not harbor hostile feelings for the innocent Rāma, for this massive army makes me wonder."

Blameless as the sky, Bharata felt no anger, but answered earnestly, "Please, do not suspect me of wrongdoing. Rāma is my father, my brother, my master. I wish only to persuade him to return with me. That is the truth, dear Guha."

Relieved beyond words, Guha at last relaxed and smiled widely.

"Then you are blessed, to give up a kingdom for the love of your brother. Surely, your fame will never end in all the three worlds."

That night, as Bharata tried to sleep in the place where his brother had camped, he felt the heavy weight of despair returning. Undeserving of such pain, the righteous Bharata nonetheless felt sadness burning his heart like a flame in the hollow of a tree. And like an avalanche, it obliterated his hopes and smothered his happiness.

The next morning, Guha saw Bharata's dejected mood and tried to reassure him with stories of Rāma's stay by the Gangā. He pointed to a distant banyan tree. "That is where your brother Lakshmaṇa refused to sleep, so faithful was he in guarding your brother." Guha told how the two young warriors matted their locks before boarding the boat with Sītā.

When he heard that his brothers now traveled as mendicants with matted locks, Bharata sank to the ground as if struck by an arrow. Shatrughna tried to comfort him, but overcome with sorrow, he also fell down.

Mother Kausalyā, seeing her sons' distress, tenderly bent over Bharata, uttering gentle and motherly words. "Bharata, are you well? The hope of the Ikshvākus now rests with you, for with Rāma and King Dasharatha gone, you are our only salvation. Have you heard some bad news of Rāma? Pray tell us."

Realizing that he should not upset Mother Kausalyā, Bharata struggled to his feet. "Please, Guha, show me the hallowed spot where Rāma spent the night," he entreated Rāma's friend, even as he wept. "Tell me what he ate."

Guha gladly recalled the details, and then Bharata, followed by his mothers and ministers, walked to the ingudī tree whose branches had sheltered Rāma while he slept. Staring at the leaves, Bharata said softly, "Because of me the noble-born Rāma spent the night on the hard forest floor, his stomach empty, bereft of blankets to keep him warm. Here the tender Sītā joined him; here you can see the threads her garments left in the grass. My mind is dazed at this nightmare."

Then he made a solemn vow. "From this day on, I will lie on the ground, eat roots and fruits, and wear matted locks and robes of tree-bark cloth. I will live happily in the forest with Shatrughna, to fulfill Rāma's pledge. Rāma will return to rule Ayodhyā with Lakshmaṇa." Heartened by this plan, he stopped weeping.

The next day, Bharata and his army crossed the River Gangā in Guha's gaily decorated fishing boats, their colorful sails billowing in the wind. The elephants splashed in the water.

On the other side, Bharata and Shatrughna left the army behind and traveled on foot to Bharadvāja's hermitage, accompanied by Vasishtha and his ministers. When they saw the quiet abode in the distance, the two princes shed their weapons and approached with reverence.

Inside the āshram, the venerable sage greeted them with refreshing fruit juices to drink and water to bathe their feet. He inquired after the family, kingdom, treasury, and army, tactfully not mentioning King Dasharatha. In turn, Bharata and Vasishtha asked about the sage's health, his yagya fires, his trees and birds and beasts.

After they had welcomed each other with kind words, Bharadvāja asked, "What brings you here, dear Bharata, when you should be ruling the kingdom? I hope you do not wish to do injury to your brother, who has been exiled."

The pure-hearted Bharata could not bear such unkind words. "My life is a failure, if a blessed sage such as you thinks such ill thoughts about me," he said, his eyes flooding with tears. "I have not agreed to what my mother arranged in my absence. I have come here to ask Rāma to rule. I pray, grant me your blessings for this worthy task. Please, tell me where Rāma is now."

Pleased with his answer, the great sage said, "You are truly a son of the Ikshvākus, for you speak with self-control, obeying your elders, keeping to the ways of the good. I knew your mind before you spoke, but by so answering my question, you have enhanced your glory. You will find Rāma, Sītā, and Lakshmaṇa on Chitrakūta Mountain. But grant me one wish: stay here with your army today."

Bharadvāja instructed Bharata to bring his entire army to the quiet āshram. Then he used his considerable yogic powers to lavish Bharata's army with food, drink, and entertainment as could only be found in heaven. Servants served mounds of delicious, steaming food on golden platters. They poured sweet drinks from crystal urns. Celestial Gandharvas and dancers delighted the senses. Cool breezes wiped away all fatigue, and the heavens showered fragrant flower blossoms like rain. Far into the night the soldiers danced and celebrated, yet when they awoke at dawn they felt refreshed and invigorated.

In the morning Bharata and his mothers waited patiently by

Bharadvāja's hut to bid him goodbye. The hospitable sage completed his morning meditation and stepped outside. He asked kindly, "And did your army pass the night comfortably?"

Bharata expressed his thanks again and again for the uncommon welcome they had received from the generous sage, far more lavish than any ruler on earth could have provided. Then the three mothers respectfully circled the celebrated Ṛishi. Kaikeyī, her eyes cast downward, scorned by all the world, fell to the sage's feet in a silent plea, and then withdrew to one side.

Seeing Kaikeyī's distress, the compassionate sage said to Bharata, "I would like to know more about your mothers."

Bharata began introducing them with love and respect. "Mother Kausalyā, the king's first wife and mother of the illustrious Rāma, who is wan from fasting and grief, is known the world over for her piety. Mother Sumitrā, who is so weak from fasting that she holds her arm in her hand, wilting like a flower, is the good mother of the valiant Lakshmaṇa and Shatrughna."

But when it came to introducing his own mother, his voice cracked and he wept in despair. "It is because of my cruel mother Kaikeyī that my brother has been banished and King Dasharatha has gone to his death, and my days are numbered by ignominy and heartbreak. It is because of her selfish and vain ways that you find us in this deplorable condition."

Then the wise Bharadvāja said gently, "You must not think this way about your mother, O Bharata, for this exile of Rāma will bring happiness to all. All good will come to sages, gods, and men as a result of Rāma's banishment."

Heartened by these words, Bharata set out for Chitrakūta Mountain.

न दोषेणावगन्तव्या कैकेयी भरत त्वया ।
रामप्रव्रजनं ह्येतत्सुखोदर्कं भविष्यति ॥

You must not think this way about your mother, O Bharata,
for this exile of Rāma will bring happiness to all.

—Ayodhyā Kāṇḍa 92.30

Chapter 16

Bharata Debates Rāma

Do you honor Vasishtha, our family's preceptor,
as you would our father?
Do you pay homage to the gods, your ancestors,
the ministers, Brahmins, and physicians?

Are your ministers good-hearted and noble,
masters of their senses?
Are they incorruptible,
honest, and wise?
Do you listen to their advice?
For that is the source of
victory for a king.

Do you nightly reflect on ways
to ensure success for your kingdom?
Do you treat your military leader,
master of mantra-propelled missiles,
with due respect?
Is the leader of your army
brave and adventurous,
honest, devoted, and skillful?
Do you honor courageous

officers with gifts?
Do you pay your army on time?

Is your messenger learned,
alert, highly intelligent,
and precise in speaking?
Do you keep the ministers under
your rule informed
as to your goals and desires?
Are you aware of plans
your ministers make among themselves?
Do you prefer one wise advisor
to a passel of fools?
For one prudent counselor
can lead a king to success.

Do you choose enterprises that cost little
yet bring great return?
Do you act on your plans immediately without procrastinating?
Do you manage your servants
according to their merits,
giving those who are superior
work that is superior,
and those who are inferior
tasks that are inferior?

Do you study the Veda?
Do you follow the path
of our father, our grandfather,
and all who are honorable?
Are the leading citizens of your kingdom
devoted to you with their whole hearts?
Do you share your meals with friends?

These were the questions
Rāma asked of Bharata
when they met
on Chitrakūta Mountain.

For the king who governs his subjects
with fairness, who is just to all,
conquers the world
and finds his place in heaven.

Rāma and Sītā sat on the grassy banks of the pure River Mandākinī, basking in the warm sun after bathing in the cool waters. The lilt of birdsong mingled with a gentle breeze, and shady trees cooled the earth.

Rāma offered Sītā choice pieces of *jambu* fruit. "Try this rose-apple," he said. "And this one is even more tender."

Suddenly, in the quiet forest they heard a sound like the trampling of elephants. Herds of deer fled the river banks. Rāma asked Lakshmaṇa, who was always near, to climb a tall arjuna tree to see what was happening.

"I see an army shrouded by billowing dust clouds," Lakshmaṇa called down from the top of the tree. "It is advancing on us quickly. Take Sītā to a cave, and string your bow and arrow."

"Look again," said Rāma. "Do you see a standard?"

"I see nothing but the chariot of Bharata," said Lakshmaṇa in tones that could scorch the earth, "driving his horses like a madman. The throne was not enough for him. Now he comes to kill us."

Lakshmaṇa scrambled down the tree and grabbed his bow. "Let's take our place on the mountain or, if you prefer, make our stand here. How I long to face Bharata, the cause of all our woes. Today I will let loose the arrows of my wrath, so long stored."

"What good would it do to attack the virtuous Bharata, who comes to me with an open heart?" asked Rāma patiently. "What good would the throne do me if it were tainted by my brother's blood? I say this with all truth: I desire only the fruits of righteous living.

"Surely Bharata returned to Ayodhyā," Rāma continued, "and finding that I was in exile with matted locks, is coming in all love to offer me the throne. He could never harm us. What has he ever done to you, to cause you to fear him today? Know this: an insult to him is an insult to me. How could a son think to strike down his father or his brother, as dear to him as his own life? If it is the kingdom you want, then I will tell Bharata, and he will willingly give it all to you."

Hearing the honorable Rāma's words, Lakshmaṇa's anger drained away like water down a slope. To cover his shame, he said, "I think it is our father who comes today."

"Yes," said Rāma, smiling now. "He has probably come to take us home or to fetch Sītā. Here I see his ancient elephant, swaying like an oak in the wind. But where is his standard? Let us go to the hermitage and wait for them."

Later that day, Bharata left the army behind and continued on foot, fanning out with Sumantra, Guha, and his hunters to search the forest for Rāma. As he drew near Rāma's hermitage, he said, "See how Lakshmaṇa has marked the trees, to make it easier to find his way in the dark." Bharata's heart lightened now that he would soon reunite with his beloved Rāma.

Finally Bharata reached Rāma's hut. A thick arbor stood nearby, covered with vines, pine boughs, and palm leaves and decorated with the golden quivers and sunbeam swords of Rāma and Lakshmaṇa. Neat stacks of wood and mountains of flowers filled the yard. Through the open doorway he could see that the dirt floor of the hut was spread with auspicious kusha grass. By the light of the sacred fire flickering across his brother's noble features, Bharata could just barely discern Rāma sitting before an altar inside.

Bharata was overcome with emotion. "Because of me, the highly-esteemed son of Dasharatha, born to be waited on in luxury, now sits on the ground wearing scratchy robes of bark. Dust covers his body—he who was once anointed with rare sandalwood paste and wore silken robes. I should be struck down, shunned for this cruel injustice and hated by all." Entering the hut, his face bathed in perspiration and tears, he fell at Rāma's feet, able to articulate only one word, *Ārya* (noble one).

Rāma wept as he embraced Bharata, Shatrughna, Sumantra, and Guha. Then Rāma drew Bharata to him again and fondly kissed the crown of his head. "I hardly recognize you of the mighty arms, for your face is so pale and your limbs are so thin."

Then he began to question Bharata on the state of the kingdom. "How is my father? I trust that you are looking after him. I fear he is not well, or else why would you come here? And how are our mothers? Are the people prosperous and contented?" One by one, he thoughtfully inquired about all the affairs of the kingdom and gave Bharata advice.

"O beloved brother, what use is political science to me, when I have fallen from my Dharma?" cried Bharata. "Come to Ayodhyā with me now. I beg you, take the mantle of the throne. For as soon as you left Ayodhyā, our father joined the gods in heaven. Thinking only of you, his heart stricken with sorrow, he clung to the thought of you at his death."

Pierced by this sudden revelation, Rāma fainted. Sītā and his three weeping brothers knelt beside him, sprinkling water on his face to revive him.

"What good am I now that my father has died of grief over me?" cried out Rāma in agony. "O Bharata, you and Shatrughna are the fortunate ones, for at least you were able to fulfill your duty to your father and perform his last rites. How could I return to Ayodhyā now, without him to guide me and lift me up with graceful words?"

Then Rāma placed a cake, made from the fruit of the ingudī tree, in a coconut shell bowl. He turned to Sītā, whose soft eyes brimmed with tears. "O Sītā, will you and Lakshmaṇa follow me to the River Mandākinī to perform water libations and offer food to the earth in my father's name?"

Standing in the river, Rāma cupped water in his hands and performed the traditional offering. Then he placed the ingudī cake on the grassy bank, saying, "This humble cake, which we eat, is to honor you, O Father. For it is said that you should offer to the gods what you partake in yourself."

Then the three sadly returned to their hermitage, where Bharata and Shatrughna waited. Having performed his duties to his father, Rāma could at last give in to his heartbreak. He fell into Bharata's arms, crying out again and again for his dead father. The other brothers and Sītā joined in grieving, and a wail as loud as the trumpeting of elephants filled the forest.

The army of Ayodhyā, camped nearby, heard the sound of the four brothers lamenting for their father. They knew immediately what it meant.

"Bharata has found Rāma, and now Rāma has heard the news of his father's death!" As if with one mind, they mounted their horses, elephants, and chariots. Others followed on foot, trampling the tender grasses and vines in their haste to reach their cherished Rāma. The noise reverberated through the forest like thunder, frightening the wild elephants, boars, and deer, which fled in every direction. Flocks of birds wheeled across the skies, while below the army blanketed the earth.

At the first sight of their revered prince, sitting in his hut, the people's eyes filled with tears. Sobbing, they surrounded Rāma, eager to draw near. He embraced his friends and greeted others as a father his children, graciously welcoming them all. Overcome with emotion, they wailed and moaned, and the tumult echoed through mountain caves like the beating of drums.

Meanwhile, the three queens and the holy Vasishtha, who were following Bharata at their own pace, slowly made their way to the hermitage. They stopped by the banks of the Mandākinī.

"See here," said the softhearted Kausalyā. "Sumitrā, this is the place where your son bends to draw water for my son. Even though he acts as a servant now, there is no dishonor in serving his brother, who abounds in every virtue. Once Rāma and Lakshmaṇa return to Ayodhyā, may your royal-born son forever be freed from performing servile tasks!"

They walked a little farther and came to a cake lying on the grass. "This must be the food offered by Rāma in his father's name," said Kausalyā, her eyes filling with tears. "My heart breaks into a thousand pieces, for I know that it is this coarse cake on which our dear sons now subsist."

Finally they came to the hermitage, and seeing Rāma sitting in his coarse bark-cloth garments like an immortal driven from paradise, his mothers again wept. As Rāma bowed to touch his mother's feet in honor, Kausalyā brushed the dust from his back with her hands.

After greeting Lakshmaṇa with equal tenderness, Queen Kausalyā embraced Sītā as she would her own daughter. "Oh Sītā, how have you, treasured wife of Rāma and lovely daughter of King Janaka, come to live in such a wretched and lonely place? My heart is swollen with grief, to see your brightness diminished like gold covered in dust."

Rāma and Lakshmaṇa touched the feet of their guru, Vasishtha, and invited all to be seated. Bharata, ever conscious of his duty to honor his brother, seated himself at a lower level than Rāma. Amidst his friends and family, Rāma sat like an ancient Ṛishi, resplendent in purity. The four brothers, shining like four fires surrounded by priests, conversed with their friends and family long into the night.

The next morning, Rāma, Bharata, Lakshmaṇa, and all their family and friends sat resting on the sun-dappled banks of the Mandākinī. In that peaceful place, Bharata suddenly stood up, crossed the grass to where Rāma sat and prostrated himself, touching his brother's feet.

Then, after taking his seat before his brother, like the petals of a lotus opening one by one, Bharata haltingly made his heart known to Rāma, his voice weak from the strain of the past weeks. "I do not desire the kingdom my mother won for me. I give it to you, as it was given to me. Only you can repair the rent in the fabric of the kingdom; only you can rebuild the bridge washed away by flood. Only then will our father Dasharatha's death be vindicated, for surely he died of grief when you were banished. I cannot fill your shoes, any more than a mule can keep pace with a racehorse. Without you, the kingdom is like a mango tree that flowers but does not bear fruit, and in my misery I am like a garden that has withered from lack of water.

"All the people of Ayodhyā have come this long distance to beg you to reign over the land as the noonday sun reigns over the sky, so my father can at last rest, happy and fulfilled in the heavens," he concluded.

"Wonderful!" cried the people of Ayodhyā. "These words are tipped with honey!"

Rāma smiled compassionately at his brother. "Assuredly, it is not wise to spend too much time in regret over our father's untimely passing or my loss of the kingdom, for man cannot escape change. It is our fate on earth. Wealth that is accumulated gets dispersed, that which is built up tumbles down, meetings end in parting, and life ends in death. Even if a man goes on a journey to avoid death at home, it will find him.

"Just as pieces of wood join together in the ocean and eventually drift apart, so do sons, fathers, mothers, brothers, wives, and wealth join us for a while and then, in time, leave us. No one on earth can keep those he loves forever. There is no reason to pity the dead or loss of kingdom, for eventually all will follow the same road. Why shed tears over the inevitable?

"Life is like a river flowing to the ocean; it never returns. That is why the wise spend their days pursuing knowledge and performing right action, and from this they derive true happiness. Our father spent his days in good works, supporting his dependents, ruling with compassion and justice, and performing many yagyas. For this he is enjoying a divine reward in the afterlife. It is not for a wise and learned man like you to mourn one who, having cast off his worn-out body, enjoys the grace of heaven. The wise should not give in to endless lamentation and tears. Therefore, end your grieving and return to Ayodhyā.

"What you can do is take up the throne as our father requested. I will fulfill my promise to him by living here in the forest. I must respect his wishes and the wishes of my mother Kaikeyī, and so must you. You too have been raised by Dasharatha, so these actions come naturally to you. Be true to your own nature and follow the example of our father, who lived a life of perfection."

All was silent for a moment and the people heard only the sound of the river rushing and birds calling.

Then Bharata exclaimed, "There is no one in this world equal to you! Neither misfortune nor joy affects you. You know the cause and effect of all; you are divine, you are as wise as a great sage. Constant in pleasure and pain, nothing can harm you, not even the most fearful calamity.

"Whereas I am inferior to you in knowledge, intelligence, and birth,"

Bharata went on. "How could I rule in your place? What good is it for you to abandon your throne and forsake your Dharma as protector of the people, for the sake of this ill-fated design of my mother's? Have compassion on us all. Save us—our mother Kaikeyī, our father, our friends, our relatives, and me—from carrying out this unlawful act. Be crowned today in the forest and reign in triumph in Ayodhyā," Bharata begged Rāma with his words, his eyes, and his heart.

The people cried out, "Yes, well said!" at the words of Bharata, the devoted brother. Yet they could also plainly see that Rāma would never forsake his father's vow. It was satisfying for them to witness his steadfast devotion to Dharma, and at the same time painful, for they grieved that Rāma would not return with them.

Rāma again spoke smilingly to his brother. "Such an eloquent speech is worthy of your devoted heart. But you must remember, dear brother, that when our father married your mother Kaikeyī, he offered an unparalleled dowry. He promised to give her the kingdom. And then in the war between the Devas and asuras, he offered her two boons in love and gratitude. She had every right to claim these boons, and bound by his vow, he promised to fulfill them. So I must spend my exile in the forest, and you must rule from the throne.

"You will be sheltered from the sun's rays beneath the royal umbrella, O Bharata, and I too will be sheltered in comfort beneath a canopy of forest trees. Shatrughna with his brilliant mind will be your advisor and friend, and Lakshmaṇa will be my faithful companion through every challenge. In this way, we four brothers will uphold the reputation of our illustrious father as a knower of truth."

Bharata was consoled by Rāma's words and fell silent.

Ever thinking of the needs of the kingdom, Vasishtha spoke next. He too tried to persuade Rāma to give up his life in the forest. He recited the long lineage of Rāma's royal family since the time of Manu, the father of the first king of the glorious solar dynasty. "You see that it is always the eldest son who takes the throne," he pointed out. "You are the eldest son of King Dasharatha; while you live, a younger son may not be anointed. This is the tradition of your line, so take up the throne and rule the earth. While the father gives life, the guru gives wisdom, and therefore the guru is considered superior. By obeying me and your virtuous mother Kausalyā, you will not stray from the path of virtue."

Rāma, always respectful of his revered guru, said, "A child can never repay his mother and father for all that they do to raise him. His parents shower him with gifts, food, clothing, and infinite amounts of tender guidance and loving advice. In the face of this debt, how can I refuse to obey my father?"

Hearing this, Bharata cried out, "I will lie at your feet, facing you, until you agree to relinquish your vow!" Glaring impatiently at Sumantra, who was absorbed in gazing at Rāma and did not get up to help him, Bharata himself spread kusha grass on the ground and lay down at Rāma's feet.

Rāma felt that his heart would break. "Rise up, I cannot bear to see you like this. What have I done that my dear brother should prostrate before me like a beggar?"

Bharata glanced around at the crowds, imploring them, "Why do you remain silent? Will you not say something to persuade Rāma?"

The people gazed at Bharata lovingly, but no one spoke. Then one of the elders spoke up, "Having heard Rāma's words, we do not believe he will ever relinquish his vow."

Finally Bharata stood to ask his brother's forgiveness. He said to all assembled, "I never desired to be king. I will take Rāma's place in exile, and then the vows of our father will be fulfilled."

"I will never break my father's word and bring shame to him or to myself," Rāma answered. "Let Bharata be crowned king today!"

It is said that as they watched this glorious debate between the two luminous brothers, the people's hair stood on end.

Also watching were the celestial Ṛishis, the Devas, and the Gandharvas. Floating in the air, invisible, they felt mounting concern. What if Rāma, out of compassion for his people, was persuaded to return to Ayodhyā? For the good of the world, they knew that Rāma must remain in the forest in order to destroy the demon Rāvaṇa and fulfill the purpose of his birth.

छायां ते दिनकरभाः प्रबाधमानं
वर्षत्रं भरत करोतु मूर्ध्नि शीताम् ।
एतेषामहमपि काननद्रुमाणां छायां
तामतिशयिनीं शनैः श्रयिष्ये ॥

You will be shaded from the sun's rays beneath the royal umbrella, O Bharata, and I too will be sheltered in comfort beneath a wide canopy of forest trees.

—Ayodhyā Kāṇḍa 107.18

CHAPTER 17

Rāma Leaves Chitrakūta

THE AIR FILLED with celestial chimes and a soft breeze as the shining ones made themselves visible, floating just above the ground. Their robes and bodies emanated a bright effulgence not seen on earth. All the people gazed in wonder at the sight of these auspicious visitors, their faces radiant with divine light.

The celestial Ṛishis, Devas, and Gandharvas addressed Bharata, "O hero of wisdom, virtue and knowledge, you must accept Rāma's resolve to fulfill his father's wishes. This is necessary for his happiness and yours. Indeed, it is precisely because Rāma has been steadfast in his vow that your father has ascended to heaven." Then the divine Ṛishis disappeared, and only the sounds of the forest remained.

Rāma, his heart filled with joy at these words, smiled with delight. Bharata stood humbly before him. In a faltering voice, he begged Rāma one last time, falling at his feet. "I am not fit to rule this kingdom. Everyone looks to you for guidance. Will you not return to Ayodhyā and save us from ruin?"

Rāma drew his brother to him now, embracing him tenderly. "You have been trained since birth to rule, dear brother, and are blessed with native intelligence and virtue. Know this: even though the moon may withdraw its splendor, the Himālayas may lose their snow, and the ocean may exceed its boundaries, I will never abandon my father's vow. And you must obey your mother Kaikeyī, even if you do not agree with her actions."

Bharata bowed his head silently for a long moment. Finally, he said,

"O Rāma, hero among men, then give me your sandals. They will bring peace and harmony to our kingdom."

Rāma slipped his feet out of the wooden sandals he wore in the forest.

Bowing low before Rāma's shoes, Bharata said, "For the next fourteen years, I will dwell outside the city in bark-cloth robes and matted locks. I will eat only the roots and fruits of the forest and will lie on the ground at night. As your servant, I will offer the kingdom to your sandals. And if in fourteen years you do not return, I will offer myself to the flames!"

"So be it," said Rāma. "I will return." Then he clasped Bharata to his breast tenderly once again. After embracing Shatrughna with equal feeling, he said to his brothers, "Do not be angry with your mother Kaikeyī. Cherish her always, on Sītā's behalf and mine." His eyes spilling over with tears, he bade goodbye to his preceptor, mothers, ministers, and beloved friends from Ayodhyā.

Receiving with reverence the pair of bright wooden sandals, the celebrated Bharata, who knew Dharma, reverently circled Rāma and placed the sandals on his head. As he walked slowly into the forest, carrying the sandals on his head like a crown, the people of Ayodhyā followed him. Rāma retired to his hut, quietly weeping as his brother and mothers disappeared from view.

BHARATA AND THE entire procession made their way back to Ayodhyā. Seeing the city in the same desolate state of mourning, he immediately called a meeting with Vasishtha and his other advisors.

"I seek your permission to rule the kingdom from Nandigrāma, a village to the east of Ayodhyā," said Bharata. "From there I will endure Rāma's exile. From there I will await his return, for he alone is lord of Ayodhyā."

"Your devotion to your brother is beyond all praise," said Vasishtha, giving his blessings with the other ministers.

In Nandigrāma Bharata and Shatrughna built a hut. Addressing the crowd that had followed him there, he said, "Bring the royal canopy and install the throne. The sandals will rest here, as a symbol of Rāma's authority. I will bow to his exalted feet in all affairs of the kingdom, and in this way the kingdom will be ruled by him. In fourteen years, I will restore the throne to him and wash away the stain of dishonor brought on me by my mother."

Placing Rāma's sandals reverently on the throne, Bharata humbly took up residence in the hut as a servant of Rāma, wearing forest clothes and eating forest foods like his brother. Surrounded by his ministers, as well as Vasishtha and other holy men, he offered all affairs of the kingdom first to Rāma's sandals. In that way, the kingdom truly was ruled in the spirit of Rāma. Bharata announced, "I administer, but Rāma rules."

After Bharata and his army left Chitrakūta, Rāma and Sītā tried to settle into their peaceful lives again. Only now the garlanded woods had been trampled by elephants and men. Worse, Rāma saw the sages whispering about him behind their hands.

He decided to pay a special visit to Vālmīki in his āshram. "Have I done anything to displease you?" Rāma asked Vālmīki. "Has Sītā been remiss in performing her duties to you?"

Vālmīki shook his head. "The pure-minded lady Sītā, always so happy, could never veer from the path of Dharma. What you perceive is the sages' concern about the rākshasas who dwell in this forest. One of them, Khara, is the evil brother of Rāvaṇa, the king of the rākshasas. He is angry that you are here and has started attacking the sages and spoiling their yagyas. Thus I and the other ascetics are moving to a pleasant woods nearby."

Rāma returned to his hut, troubled that he was causing the sages to leave their peaceful abode on Chitrakūta Mountain. He also felt restless. "Now that Bharata and Shatrughna and my mothers have visited me in these woods, it is impossible for me to forget their sorrow," he said to Sītā.

Thus Rāma decided to leave the lovely Chitrakūta. The very next day the three wanderers set out, carrying their weapons, Sītā's clothing, and a basket and shovel for digging roots.

At the end of the day they came upon the peaceful āshram of Atri. Treated to the customary hospitality offered the weary traveler, the three soon felt revived. As they sat talking with the venerable sage, his wife entered the room. Her hair was white and her limbs bent with age, but her face radiated happiness and peace.

Atri greeted his wife with affection and introduced her to his guests. "This is the renowned Anasūyā, who is surely known to you for her high-minded deeds. By the power of her meditations, she ended a ten-year drought, causing the skies to open and the rains to fall. She inspired the River Jāhnavī to flow once more, thus replenishing precious herbs and restoring the withered roots of trees."

Then Atri said to Rāma, "It would be a blessing to the pure-hearted Sītā to wait on that lady of brilliant light."

Sītā humbly stood before the enlightened Anasūyā. She folded her hands in reverence and said, "I am Jānakī, the daughter of King Janaka, named Sītā by my parents."

Delighted to see the lovely Jānakī before her, who was known the world over for her devotion to Rāma, the aged one praised her. "Great are the rewards for a wife such as you, who abandons family, home and comforts to follow her husband. Even without his riches, you serve him as God. Such a wife, who loves her husband no matter the circumstances, gains the highest heaven. For a woman, there is no greater friend than the husband."

Her heart light with happiness, Sītā thanked the esteemed Anasūyā. "These precious words remind me of the advice my mother gave me beside my wedding fire. And they are reminiscent of the parting words of my dear mother-in-law, who also loves Dharma. I have always sought to follow these precepts, instilled in me at a young age. But for me it has been easy to love my husband with all my heart. For he has faithfully loved me, has never swerved from Dharma, and has sought always to make me happy. Such a husband is dear, and following him to the forest was like following water down a slope to the sea."

Sītā smiled and said further, "Of a woman, no austerities are expected except to love her husband with all her heart. That is how Sāvitrī reached the higher realm. And you too have attained glory through service to your husband. The goddess Rohiṇī, ever devoted to her spouse, the moon, never wanders far. Many other devoted women, by serving their husbands, have been exalted by the gods for their good deeds."

Charmed by these words, the radiant Anasūyā drew Sītā to her and kissed the top of her head. "It would give me joy to grant you any wish. Name what you desire and it will be done."

"You have already fulfilled my heart," said Sītā.

These humble words pleased Anasūyā even more. "Here, then. I wish you to wear this heavenly garland of jasmine, these shining jewels, this golden sārī, and these rare oils and cosmetics. You are worthy of these celestial gifts, which will never fade nor grow dim from dust. They will always look as fresh as today. Anoint your body with this oil, and you will glow with the luster of Lakshmī and delight your husband as she delights Vishṇu."

Sītā gratefully accepted these gifts of Anasūyā, and stood quietly, her hands folded.

"I have heard that your husband won you in a svayaṁvara," said Anasūyā. "Please, I would like to hear your story, told from your heart."

Happily Sītā told how she had been born of the earth and adopted by her mother and father, King Janaka; how her father despaired of ever finding her a worthy spouse; how he had offered her hand in marriage to anyone who could string the great bow of Shiva; how none could move it even an inch until Rāma lifted it as easily as a stick, snapping it in two when he strung it.

"How wondrous are these events," said Anasūyā. "How charming and how sweetly told. But now the night has laid its cloak over the forest. See how the sacred fires waft streams of gray smoke. See how the stars sprinkle the skies and the birds cease their entertaining, overtaken by sleep. Go now to rest with Rāma. You have delighted me with your joyful words. But before you go, let me see you wear these ornaments. Allow me that pleasure."

Then the beautiful Sītā, like the daughter of the gods, adorned herself with the celestial ornaments, given with affection by the saintly Anasūyā.

Later, when Rāma saw Sītā looking so radiant, his heart overflowed with happiness that she had been so honored by Anasūyā. They spent the night resting peacefully in that happy abode.

The next morning the three travelers said their farewells. Advising them on the best path to take into the dense Daṇḍaka Forest, the sages warned, "Stay clear of the rākshasas. For if anyone who loves Dharma walks in the forest alone, he becomes their prey. You must stop these demons, O Rāma."

Bowing to the saints with their hands folded, Rāma, Lakshmaṇa, and Sītā received their blessings and disappeared into the forest as the sun disappears behind clouds.

स पादुके ते भरतः स्वलंकृते महोज्ज्वले सम्परिगृह्य धर्मवित् ।
प्रदक्षिणं चैव चकार राघवं चकार चैवोत्तमनागमूर्धनि ॥

Receiving with reverence the pair of bright wooden sandals,
the celebrated Bharata, who knew Dharma,
reverently circled Rāma and placed the sandals on his head.

—Ayodhyā Kāṇḍa 112.29

End of the Ayodhyā Kāṇḍa

THREE

Āraṇya Kāṇḍa

The Forest

Chapter 18

The Sages Beg Rāma for Protection

When Rāma and Lakshmaṇa,
with Sītā of dazzling beauty,
entered the dark Daṇḍaka Forest,
they came upon a circle of huts
spread with sacred kusha grass,
inhabited by holy sages
radiating light from within.

Flowers carpeted the forest floor.
Celestial nymphs gamboled in
lotus pools that cooled the air.
Flocks of birds and families of deer
settled peacefully there.
Vedic hymns of old echoed through the trees,
and a rare light of heaven
suffused the grounds.

"We beg protection from you,"
said the sages.
"Shelter us in the practice of virtue
as a mother shelters a child."
This is how the holy sages

who had subdued the senses
and mastered the Self
honored the hero Rāma
and his lionhearted brother Lakshmaṇa.

Not long after entering the dark Daṇḍaka Forest, Rāma, Sītā, and Lakshmaṇa came to a place where all the trees, shrubs, and vines stuck out at strange angles, cracked and broken. They noticed that no birds sang here, and the hum of crickets foretold something ominous.

Suddenly, a mountain rose in front of them. It was a hideous titan, his eyes sunk in an oversized head, with a bulging stomach and enormous mouth, jaws open and snapping. On his giant spear hung three lions, four tigers, two leopards, four deer, and an elephant—all food for his dinner.

He rushed at them like a mighty storm and snatched Sītā, who trembled like a palm leaf in the wind. "I will kill you and make this lovely lady my wife!" roared the giant.

Rāma's bright complexion drained of blood. "This is the worst tragedy of all," he said to Lakshmaṇa. "To see my gentle wife touched by him is worse than my father's death and my exile."

Lakshmaṇa too felt his eyes sting with tears, but said, "With me as your servant, why do you lament? I will direct all my bitterness for your exile to this beast and send his head rolling on the earth."

As Lakshmaṇa reached for his bow, the giant roared, "Who are you and why are you here?"

"We are warriors of the Ikshvāku race," answered the two brothers. "And who are you?"

"I am the rākshasa Varādha. Run along now. Do not bother trying to kill me, for a boon from Brahmā makes it impossible for anyone to vanquish me with weapons."

To answer his arrogant words, the brothers let loose a volley of arrows. Agitated, the giant set down Sītā and charged at Rāma and Lakshmaṇa with his spear, which Rāma broke with his swift arrows. Roaring with laughter, the giant again rushed at them. Rāma and Lakshmaṇa threw down their weapons, which the giant's boon had rendered useless, and fought him with their bare hands. Suddenly, the monster grabbed Rāma in his right hand and Lakshmaṇa in his left, placed one on each shoulder, and stomped down the forest path.

"Let him take us a ways, after all it's in the direction we want to go," said Rāma calmly.

But then they heard Sītā crying out, "Take me instead of those two Ikshvāku warriors, for I will perish in this forest all alone!" They had no choice but to destroy the hideous monster immediately. Rāma twisted the right arm and Lakshmaṇa the left. His arms hanging limp, the giant slumped to the ground, like a mountain in a landslide.

"Dig a pit, Lakshmaṇa," said Rāma. "Since his boon prevents us from killing him with weapons, we will bury him."

Hearing Lakshmaṇa's name, the giant said humbly, "O hero, whose blows equal Indra's, until this moment I did not recognize you. Now that I am dying, I see that you are Rāma, that lion among men. I was cursed to live in this monstrous body by Kubera, the god of wealth, but inside I am, in reality, a Gandharva. I was told that only Rāma could end this curse by ending my life. I die willingly at your hand. I honor the one who frees me."

Before Rāma and Lakshmaṇa buried him in a pit big enough for several elephants, he told them where to find Sharabhanga, a sage as radiant as seven suns. Then he breathed his last breath and ascended to heaven, liberated from his horrible fate by Rāma.

The danger over, Rāma rushed to Sītā and embraced her, murmuring consoling words. "Let us go to Sharabhanga's āshram right now," he said to Lakshmaṇa. "This forest is too dangerous."

When they drew near to Sharabhanga's hermitage, they saw an amazing sight. There before them was a celestial being, his feet floating above the ground and his robes sparkling, free of dust. Radiating light like the sun, he boarded his golden chariot, driven by celestial bay horses. Two divine women held a canopy of luscious garlands over his head and fanned him with yaks' tails mounted on rods of gold. The chariot also floated above the ground, surrounded by Ṛishis, gods, and other celestials, who sang divine chants to him as he took leave of the sage Sharabhanga.

"O Lakshmaṇa," said Rāma, "surely this is Indra, the king of the gods, who attends every yagya performed on earth. Do you see hundreds of youthful warriors surrounding him? Each one looks to be twenty-five years old, the perpetual age of the Devas. Wait here, and I will find out for certain who this hero is."

But Indra saw Rāma approaching and said to Sharabhanga, "I must leave before Rāma reaches me. I will greet him later, when he returns victorious, having achieved his purpose on earth, having accomplished a deed no other could." Then Indra respectfully took leave of the great sage and rose to heaven.

Later, when Rāma, Lakshmaṇa, and Sītā had been welcomed by Sharabhanga and were seated at his holy feet, Rāma asked the highly regarded sage about Indra's visit.

"O Rāma, Indra came to take me to Brahma Loka, that highest of heavens, the abode of the gods. I have earned a place in that realm of unsurpassed beauty through my *tapas*, my long meditations, and through the performance of yagyas. But I did not want to go just yet, because I wanted to see you first."

Rāma placed his palms together and bowed to the humble sage in respect. "O revered Ṛishi, can you tell me of a safe place to dwell here?" he asked. "A place where Sītā will be safe."

Sharabhanga replied, "Follow the River Mandākinī to the āshram of Sutīkshṇa, who can suggest where to find a peaceful forest home. But first, stay with me until I cast off this body."

Then Sītā, Rāma, and Lakshmaṇa watched, amazed, as the sage built a fire and entered it. He emerged with a youthful and shining body and ascended to Brahma Loka, having achieved all of his desires on earth.

After the glorious departure of Sharabhanga, the other sages in the āshram greeted the three illustrious travelers. Among the sages there were those who were born of the nails and hair of Brahmā, those who lived on moonbeams, those who lived on uncooked husked grains, those who lived on water, those who slept on the bare ground, and those who never slept at all. Their bodies shone with a rare light born of their deep austerities.

These holy men surrounded Rāma and Lakshmaṇa, standing humbly with their hands folded in respect. They seemed shy to speak. Finally, the eldest stepped forward. "We honor you, who are the upholders of Dharma," said the luminous Ṛishi. "Know that we say the next words in desperation, so please forgive us. These woods are filled with vicious rākshasas who harass and kill any holy man. We tremble in fear. Will you save us from the night-rovers, O Rāma? There is no greater savior on earth than you."

Rāma folded his hands respectfully and said, "Most exalted ones, you did not need to phrase this as a question; it is for the sage to command the warrior. It is my good fortune to have come here, where I can protect those who know the Self. My brother and I will kill these evil rākshasas in the Daṇdaka Forest. In this way, our time spent in the forest will become a blessing."

The saints were so relieved by this assurance from Rāma that they themselves decided to lead him through the dense and silent Daṇḍaka Forest to Sutīkshṇa's āshram.

Rāma first saw the hermitage at a distance on a high mountain, where it seemed to float like a cloud. A little later, walking through a thick grove of trees heavy with fruit, Rāma and the sages came to a clearing. There they saw the sage Sutīkshṇa sitting in the center of his āshram, performing his duties by the sacred fire. Rāma respectfully approached the saint, who was smeared with ashes and sat with his eyes closed, absorbed in meditation.

"O revered sage, I am Rāma, who has come to visit you," said Rāma.

Sutīkshṇa opened his eyes and smiled broadly. He rose and embraced Rāma, who was surprised to hear him say, "I have been waiting for you ever since I heard that you had left your kingdom. Indra, chief of the gods, came to tell me I have achieved Brahma Loka, but I put him off, because I wanted to see you first. All that I have gained through austerity, all the enjoyment of the three worlds, I now offer to you, your wife and your brother."

The radiant Ṛishi then invited Rāma to stay in his hermitage. "This pleasant place is frequented by sages, for it is easy to gather roots and fruits in all seasons. The only problem is the multitude of enchanting deer, which sometimes trample the garden."

Before Rāma could answer, Lakshmaṇa impulsively held up his bow and arrow and said, "If I stayed here, I could not refrain from hunting those herds of deer, and that would make you unhappy, O gentle sage. For this reason I do not wish to stay here long."

Rāma did not object, and so it was decided that they should only spend the night. After their evening devotions, the sage himself served them hulled grain. The next morning, rising as usual at dawn, Rāma and Sītā bathed in the pure waters of the River Mandākinī, fragrant with the scent of lotus flowers.

Bidding goodbye to Sutīkshṇa, Rāma bowed before him. "Thank you for showing us every honor, but we must travel early before the sun becomes too hot. We wish to visit all the holy men of the Daṇdaka Forest, and we ask your blessings for our journey."

The generous sage embraced the two brothers affectionately. "Go safely, Rāma, with Lakshmaṇa and Sītā, who follow you like your own shadow. Enjoy the silent beauties of the Daṇḍaka Forest, with its hidden sylvan retreats, clear lakes filled with swans, and blossoming groves that echo the cry of the peacock. Go, and when you have seen all, come back to this āshram."

After the three travelers circled the sage in reverence, Sītā handed the brothers their celestial arrows, thundering bows, and swords glittering with gold. The two brothers and the princess of unsurpassable beauty then set out briskly on their pilgrimage.

As they walked, Sītā sweetly said to Rāma, "You who are most noble, even you could suffer from a small defect that could grow slowly into something greater. Yet it is always possible to avoid the three failings of man, each rooted in desire. The first failing is to tell a lie, the second is to associate with another's wife, and the third is to commit a violent act without just provocation.

"You have never told a lie and you never will; you are known for speaking the truth. As for the second failing, your heart has always been true to me and you have never been possessed by the passion that destroys Dharma. You are devoted to me and faithful to your vows.

"It is for the third failing, that of committing a violent act without just provocation, that I am concerned. You have promised the sages to kill the rākshasas. When I see you walking through the forest, armed with your bow and arrow, my mind is in tumult and I wonder how I can help you in this world and the next. Entering the Daṇḍaka Forest with arms does not find favor with me, and I will tell you why.

"The simple act of carrying a bow and arrows increases the probability of using them. There is a story of a devout and gentle ascetic who was so pure that Indra was afraid of his powers. Indra disguised himself as a warrior, and while visiting the holy man, asked him to keep watch over his sword. The conscientious sage took Indra's sword with him everywhere he went—to gather roots and fruits, to collect water. By carrying that sword, the hermit began to crave violence, and eventually lost his self-control and fell from the path of virtue. As contact with fire alters a piece of wood, so contact with arms alters the minds of men.

"I speak of this only because of my unbounded love and affection for you. I do not intend to instruct you," continued Sītā in her quiet and pleasing voice. "But I beg you to give up the thought of striking the rākshasas in the Daṇḍaka Forest without provocation, for the world detests such an act. Even a warrior should resort to arms only to defend souls in peril.

"Oceans separate the world of the warrior from the world of the ascetic; they are opposed to each other. Here in this quiet forest, the abode of ascetics, it is best to be an ascetic. When you are back in Ayodhyā, you can be a warrior and follow the *kshatriya* code again.

"From Dharma flows wealth, from Dharma flows happiness. Adhering to Dharma, one obtains everything. The heart of this world is Dharma. With a pure heart, devote yourself to Dharma in these holy woods, my beloved."

Then Sītā modestly added, "You already know everything there is to be known about Dharma. How could anyone instruct you, O Rāma? But please think over what I have said and then do what you feel is best."

Rāma, who loved his wife dearly, was filled with delight at Sītā's words. "You have spoken these words in affection, my darling Sītā, and they are noble words, worthy of your birth. How can I answer you? As you said yourself, it is the Dharma of a warrior to carry a bow to save those in peril, and the sages of the Daṇḍaka Forest are in peril. They begged me to protect them from the night-roving, man-eating rākshasas, who like to attack them at the fire offerings and when the moon is full.

"My heart broke to see those venerable sages kneeling before me, when I should be kneeling to them, for it is they who are the true refuge of the world. Loath to use their hard-won powers to curse the rākshasas, the sages asked me to destroy the evil demons with my bow and arrows. Responding to their plea for help, I made a promise, and thus I must honor it as long as I have breath in my body. It is my duty to defend them in any case—but now that I have given my word, I would yield up my life, and even yours or Lakshmaṇa's, my beloved, before I would dishonor my vow.

"So even though I cannot give up my arms, having made this vow to protect the saints of the Daṇḍaka Forest, it makes me happy to hear your words, my lovely one, for we offer advice only to those we truly love. Your words befit your high-souled nature. It is by following the path of Dharma that you have become dearer to me than life itself."

And so the two brothers and the princess wandered through the dense twilight of the Daṇḍaka Forest. They roamed over hills, flowering groves, and lotus-covered pools, their only companions the families of bears, herds of elephants, horned buffaloes wallowing in riverbeds, and flocks of birds darkening the sky.

Whenever they came to a hermitage, they were welcomed by the sages there. Sometimes they stayed for a few months, sometimes a year. In this way, imbued with the peaceful rhythms of forest life, the three blissfully passed ten years of their exile honoring the Ṛishis.

At the end of ten years, having visited many āshrams of the Daṇḍaka Forest, Rāma and his cherished wife Sītā, followed by the faithful Lakshmaṇa, returned once more to the āshram of Sutīkshṇa. There they dwelled happily for some time in the company of the wise.

धर्मादर्थः प्रभवति धर्मात्प्रभवते सुखम् ।
धर्मेण लभते सर्वं धर्मसारमिदं जगत् ॥

From Dharma flows wealth, from Dharma flows happiness.
Adhering to Dharma, one obtains everything.
The heart of this world is Dharma.

—Āraṇya Kāṇḍa 9.30

Chapter 19

Ṛishi Agastya Gives Rāma Celestial Weapons

"The season I love best is here,"
Lakshmaṇa said to his brother Rāma
as he drew water from the river.
"Frost covers the earth,
making it sparkle like a jewel.
The ground is cold to sleep upon,
and fire dispels the chill.

The country folk enjoy their harvest
of ripened grains with milk and butter.

"Kings dream of conquest
and embark on ambitious quests.
The sun passes its equinox
and veers to the land of Yama,
leaving the northern sphere
as forlorn as a woman
without her tilaka mark.
The mountain peaks earn their name
'Himālaya'—robed in snow.

"The midday sun kisses the skin softly
and is an agreeable friend.
Shade and water
are no longer one's companions.
Dove-gray mists blot the sun,
and crisp winds play in calm forests.

"No one sleeps in the open
from the cold Pushya month on,
for the moon is shrouded in clouds,
and the west wind sprinkled
with snowflakes.

"Golden barley and wheat stalks rustle,
swaying gracefully as the date flower,
and the plaintive call of the heron
sounds through the woods at dawn.

"In the pale morning sun
elephants snap back their trunks
from the cold water,
and geese clutch the river banks,
afraid to dive in.
Grassy glades sleep under frost blankets,

and the sweet taste of snowmelt lingers in the mouth.
This is why I praise winter,"
said Lakshmaṇa,
devoted brother of Rāma.

One day, while Rāma, Sītā, and Lakshmaṇa sat in silence at the feet of Sutīkshṇa, Rāma said, "I wish to pay my respects to the high-souled sage Agastya. Where would I find him in this vast and mysterious forest?"

"I was just thinking myself," said Sutīkshṇa, "that you should visit that esteemed Ṛishi of old. Why not start out today?" Then he told them how to find the āshram of Agastya's brother, where they could spend the first night of their journey.

Rāma, Sītā, and Lakshmaṇa walked quickly past clear mountain lakes and streams, elated to be meeting the great Agastya at last. As they walked, Rāma told Sītā and Lakshmaṇa a story of the renowned saint. "Ṛishi Agastya made it safe to live in the South," he said. "With the power of his radiance, he destroyed the two asura brothers named Ilvala and Vātāpi, who made a sport of killing thousands of Brahmins here. Neither rākshasa nor asura dare threaten this area now."

After spending the night in the āshram of Agastya's brother, the three set out again. As they walked in the direction he had indicated, Rāma said to Lakshmaṇa, "The hermitage of Agastya must be nearby. See how various types of flowering trees are heavy with fruits and nuts, their fragrance sweetening the air. See how it is shady and cool here, and herds of tame deer walk without fear. Do you hear the sweet call of songbirds, and feel your fatigue lifting in this peaceful place? See the smoke of ghee-fed fires, like the crest of black clouds. The walks are lined with auspicious *darbha* grass, brilliant as blue sapphire."

Enchanted by the beauty of this place, Rāma said, "The South is celebrated in all three worlds because the renowned sage Agastya lives here. At his request, the great Vindhya Mountains, which tried to block the sun and moon, stopped growing. Here the Gandharvas, perfected beings known as *siddhas* gather, attracted by his purity. In his radiant light, neither liar nor evildoer can live. From here enlightened sages, having earned the fruit of their tapas, ascend to heaven in celestial chariots and become immortal in other worlds. I will ask this celebrated sage where we should live, and he will guide us."

They reached the āshram at the end of the day. After Lakshmaṇa requested an audience, the radiant Agastya himself greeted them, shedding light all around like the sun. "I have been waiting for your visit," he said to Rāma. "You are the king of all the world, and the upholder of Dharma. You deserve all honor." Agastya and disciples offered the guests a seat, washed the dust from their feet, and circled their heads with light from a ghee lamp. Then they brought water and large trays of fruits to eat.

After the three travelers were refreshed, the sage Agastya gave Rāma auspicious gifts. He asked one of his disciples to bring a magnificent bow, studded with jewels and flashing with gold. Agastya handed the bow to Rāma. "This is the celestial bow, made by the divine artist Vishvakarman, that Vishṇu wielded to vanquish the asuras in battle, bringing untold power and glory to the gods. Here is a golden arrow, brilliant like the sun, given to me by Lord Brahmā. None can ever escape it. These two quivers, for you and Lakshmaṇa, can never be emptied of arrows. They were bestowed upon me by Lord Shiva. Here is a sword with a golden hilt and scabbard. Take the bow, arrow, quivers, and sword, endowed with the powers of the celestials, and use them to conquer your foes, as Indra conquers all with the thunderbolt."

Rāma thanked the sage with his hands folded and his head bowed in respect.

Then Ṛishi Agastya said, "O mightiest of warriors, I am happy that you have come to visit me. Through my intuition and my affection for you, I know all that has happened to you and Dasharatha. Blessed is King Dasharatha to have his honor upheld by a son such as you. It pleases me also to see Lakshmaṇa, who tirelessly serves you, and Sītā, who is so devoted to you. The journey has fatigued you, and it has also been a strain on Sītā, who has been delicately brought up in all comfort, yet left her royal home because of her love for you. By following you, she has faced tremendous hardships. Be careful, Rāma, to be certain that she is happy here. Unlike other women, who love their husbands only when they meet with prosperity, she is free from all sin and is a model to all others."

Rāma smiled at the magnanimous sage, whose radiance blazed like an open fire. "You have blessed us many times over by your honors and wise counsel. I would be grateful if you could tell us of a place, secluded by trees and near pure water, where we could set up our hermitage."

"There is a place nearby called Panchavatī, where flowers never stop blooming beside the crystal waters of the River Godāvarī," said the magnanimous Agastya. "It is a pleasant and secluded spot, near five ancient fig trees, and dates and mangoes abound. Having completed most of the years of your exile, you can live there until you return to rule your kingdom. I think Sītā will be very happy in Panchavatī."

Rāma, Lakshmaṇa, and Sītā respectfully took leave of Ṛishi Agastya, thanking him again and again, and set out for Panchavatī that day.

As they strolled through the forest, Rāma and Lakshmaṇa saw a giant vulture sitting on a branch of a tall evergreen tree. He was so enormous that at first they thought he must be a rākshasa.

Yet Rāma addressed him respectfully. "I am Rāma. May I know who you are, revered elder?"

"I am a friend of your father," answered the great bird.

Rāma, delighted to meet his father's friend, greeted him warmly. He asked the bird's name and inquired about his family.

"I am Jatāyu, king of the vultures, son of Aruṇa," answered the bird with dignity. Then he told them the story of the ancient ones, and how, in the milky dawn of creation, they gave birth to birds and all other creatures—cows, horses, lions, elephants, bears, and monkeys. Jatāyu himself was born at the beginning of time.

"I will live near you," the venerable bird said to Rāma, "and watch over Sītā while you and Lakshmaṇa are away hunting."

Rāma, touched by Jatāyu's kind offer, bowed to the ancient bird and embraced his feet. He thanked him for protecting Sītā. Taking leave of his father's friend, Rāma led the way to Panchavatī. The woods appeared just as Agastya had described them.

"We have arrived at the place of five fig trees," said Rāma, gesturing to the ancient trees, their branches spread wide to offer shade. "Lakshmaṇa, you are the expert in building forest homes. Choose a place that will make Sītā happy, with a pool or spring nearby, a beautiful landscape to gaze upon, and plenty of branches and kusha grass to build a hut with."

Folding his hands in reverence, Lakshmaṇa said, "Even if you live to be a hundred, I will always be your servant. Therefore, you choose the spot that pleases you, and I will build the hermitage there."

His heart flooded with love for his younger brother Lakshmaṇa, Rāma selected the site. Then, clasping his brother's hands in his, he said, "Here is a glorious place that is level, teeming with trees in flower and a pool wreathed in lotuses. The River Godāvarī flows nearby, with swans and geese flocking around. The cry of peacocks echoes through the hills, and herds of deer frequent the woods. Mango, jackfruit, and āmalaka trees offer abundant fruits, and hundreds of flowering trees and vines shower the banks of the river with blossoms. There is a holy and pure feeling in the air. We will live here happily with Jatāyu as our friend. Here you should build a pleasant hermitage."

Lakshmaṇa built the hut, and they entered it after performing the yagya for a happy dwelling. They lived there for several seasons.

One winter's day, as he drew water from the river for Rāma and Sītā, Lakshmaṇa said, "Winter makes me think of our brother Bharata, who must be suffering from the cold in this season. I cannot bear to think that at this very moment, in the darkness before dawn, he who was raised in luxury is bathing in the cold River Sarayu.

"Ever devoted to you, he has spurned the kingdom to spend his days fasting and his nights sleeping on the freezing ground. He speaks sweetly and lives his whole life for you. By serving you, the faithful Bharata has won his place in heaven. It has been said that men take after their mothers, but he has proven the opposite, for he is completely unlike his cruel-hearted mother."

"We must never speak ill of our mother," said Rāma. "But please, continue in your praises of Bharata. Although I am resolved to live fourteen years in the forest, my love for Bharata makes me wish it were over. I long to hear his loving words, which soothe my soul like the nectar of the gods. O Lakshmaṇa, when will we four brothers be together again?"

Rāma and Lakshmaṇa bathed in the cold River Godāvarī and performed *Sūrya namaskāra*, saluting the rising sun. After his morning prayers and meditation, Rāma shone like Shiva, accompanied by the bull Nandi and Pārvatī, the daughter of the Himālaya. In the company of Sītā and Lakshmaṇa, Rāma lived in Panchavatī like a god in heaven.

अयं देशः समः श्रीमान्पुष्पितैर्तरुभिर्वृतः ।
इहाश्रमपदं रम्यं यथावत्कर्तुमर्हसि ॥

Here is a glorious place that is level, surrounded by trees in flower.
Here you should build a pleasant hermitage.

—Āraṇya Kāṇda 15.10

CHAPTER 20

Rāma Defeats Shūrpaṇakhā, Khara, and Fourteen Thousand Demons

There is a youthful prince,
son of King Dasharatha—
his powerful arms
reach to his knees.
His broad muscular chest
angles to his waist
like a tight fist to the wrist.
They call him Rāma.

Never defeated in battle,
he equals Indra in prowess.
He battled an army of demons
alone, and won.
He multiplied himself
fourteen thousand times,
so each demon faced the
purifying fire called Rāma,
and attained liberation.
His eyes red,
his voice swelling like a kettledrum,
he destroyed all foes
with his golden-winged arrows.

Virtuous and brave,
he swallows oceans
in his wrath against wrongdoing.
He turns rivers in their courses,
shatters the ground,
shivers the planets and stars.
He lifts the earth
and spins it on his finger,
rolls seas over continents,
raises mountains
from the watery deep.
He conquers all evil
and directs the wind itself,
creating a new universe.

Rāma spent his days quietly in his humble āshram at Panchavatī. Often the sages of the area would gather around him under the arbor in front of his hut. With Sītā by his side, Rāma shone like the moon in spring. Rāma entertained the sages with legends of great men and women of long ago.

One day, as Rāma sat under the arbor, a *rākshasī* happened by. Stunned by Rāma's radiant good looks, she stood staring at his broad, massive shoulders, and thin waist; his thick, shining locks; his dark, smooth, blue-tinted complexion; his delicately formed features; his confident air of authority; his winning and compassionate smile; his eyes like lotus petals; and his demeanor royal and majestic as an elephant.

She was the opposite of him in every way. His voice was clear and melodious, her raspy voice croaked harshly; his eyes were open and trusting, hers squinted in malice; he radiated youth, she looked old and withered; he spoke truth, she spoke lies; he pursued the path of Dharma, she pursued the path of evil. In every way that she repulsed others, he filled them with charm. Yet this hideous rākshasī was struck with a burning passion for Rāma.

"Who are you?" she asked, her voice hoarse. "And why do you wear your hair matted like a hermit when you carry a bow and arrow and live with your wife?"

"I am Rāma, son of Dasharatha," said Rāma in his calm and simple way. "I have come to this place to fulfill a vow to my father. This is my brother and my wife. And now would you tell us who you are and why you are here? By your charms, you appear to be a rākshasī."

Her heart pounding with runaway infatuation, she said, "I am Shūrpaṇakhā, a rākshasī who can change into any form I desire. I terrorize these woods as I wander about. My eldest brother is the all-powerful Rāvaṇa, who rules the world. My other brothers are the sleeping giant Kumbhakarṇa, the famous warriors Khara and Dūshaṇa, and the virtuous Vibhīshaṇa, who is not like the rest of us at all."

Then she smiled lovingly at Rāma and said, "I have taken a liking to you. Why do you live with such a distasteful wife, who is so pale and thin, when you could live with one of equal beauty, like me? I am much more powerful, being able to manifest any thought at will. I will devour your ugly wife today, as well as your brother. Then you and I, who are suited for each other in every way, can roam these woods as our pleasure garden."

Rāma suppressed a laugh, not wishing to hurt the rākshasī's feelings. He gently teased her, saying, "I am attached to my wife, and you are not the sort to live with a co-wife. Take my brother instead. He is handsome and youthful, and he needs a spouse. Enjoy him without a rival, as Mount Meru enjoys the sunlight."

Having no sense of humor, the rākshasī did not realize she was being teased. She stopped gazing raptly at Rāma and immediately focused on Lakshmaṇa, who stood beside Rāma as handsome as the god of love. "I am a beautiful and worthy wife for you. Come with me and we will wander the Daṇḍaka Forest together."

Lakshmaṇa smiled and said, "How could you be happy to be the wife of a slave? I serve my brother day and night, and as my wife, you would also be forced to labor."

Frustrated, the demoness pointed at the fawn-eyed Sītā. "It is because of this ugly and deformed woman that you reject me. No matter, I will devour her and then I will live happily with you, without a rival." Her red hair flying like the tail of a meteor, her teeth sharp as knives, her eyes blazing like red suns, she let out a piercing shriek and rushed at the innocent Sītā.

Rāma swiftly stood up to block her from harming his wife. He said to Lakshmaṇa, "I should never have teased the violent and wicked. Although we cannot kill a woman, no matter how evil, stop her with your sword."

When the demon flew at Sītā from another direction, Lakshmaṇa swiftly chopped off her nose and ears. Shrieking in pain, holding her nose and ears to stop the stream of blood, the repulsive monster fled from the forest, her howls filling the air long after she left.

Shūrpaṇakhā fled to the palace of her brother Khara and found him sitting on his throne, bolstered by his army of demons. Screaming in terror, she hurled herself at his feet like an ocean storm hurling waves on the shore. The rākshasa Khara shouted, "Who has disfigured you so hideously, you who are all-powerful and can go anywhere in any form? They should know that they have placed the noose of death around their necks, for I will make their blood flow today!"

"Two brothers, who look more like gods than men, did this to me on account of a young, beautiful woman covered in jewels," shrieked Shūrpaṇakhā. "It is because of her that I have been dishonored like an adulteress. Now I only wish to drink the blood of that woman and those two youths, who live in the Daṇḍaka Forest like hermits!"

Khara, his face red with fury, ordered fourteen of his fiercest, most dreadful demons to seek out the brothers and kill them.

Rāma and Sītā were seated under the leafy arbor when the fourteen rākshasas raged into the forest, goaded by the cruel Shūrpaṇakhā like a cloud driven by wind. Seeing the unsightly band before them, Rāma said quietly to Lakshmaṇa, "Stay with Sītā, and I will kill these evil demons who have come to destroy us."

Rāma twanged his great bow, inlaid with gold and jewels. His legs planted firmly, his face reflecting calm resolve, he said, "We are the sons of Dasharatha, Rāma and Lakshmaṇa, who have come here to fulfill my father's vow. We pass our days in quiet meditation, harming no one. Why do you wish to attack us, wicked creatures that you are? It is by the request of the holy sages that I reside here. Stop, turn back, if you wish to live."

Angered by Rāma's unshakable courage and sweet speech, they answered, "It is you who will die, standing all alone." The gruesome monsters with anger-red eyes bore down on Rāma, brandishing spears, maces, and arrows. Their cavernous mouths screamed in fury.

Rāma quickly let loose fourteen arrows tipped in gold and snapped their fourteen spears like straw. Then he calmly strung fourteen new arrows and let them fly. Each one hit its mark, piercing the fourteen rākshasas through the heart.

Seeing the blood of Khara's fourteen ace warriors spilt all around, Shūrpaṇakhā once again ran screaming to her brother and threw herself at his feet, rolling on the palace floor and sobbing.

"Why are you still in hysterics?" asked Khara. "I've sent my fourteen best warriors and surely they must have killed those three hermits by now. Sit up, there is no need for tears."

"I run to you in desperation," Shūrpaṇakhā managed to say between sobs. "Only you can save me. Those fourteen warriors are dead, killed by Rāma alone. Now I am drowning in an ocean of tears, hunted by crocodiles of fear. You must leave your palace and kill Rāma and Lakshmaṇa before they destroy all demons. If you do not have the strength or courage to kill these two men, how can we live here?"

Khara slammed his hand on the arm of his throne. "Say no more! Your traitorous speech makes me burn with rage. Rāma is no threat to me. I will send him to Yama today. Stop your crying, for soon you will quench your thirst for his blood."

He ordered his brother Dūshaṇa, the commander of his army: "Mobilize fourteen thousand of the fiercest and most bloodthirsty titans. Bring me my chariot, for I will lead them in battle."

Outside his palace, the demon king Khara climbed into his chariot, inlaid with gold. Chiming with bells, its panels decorated with paintings of fish, flowers, trees, and other good luck symbols, it was drawn by spirited horses.

"Charge!" he roared to the multitude of fierce rākshasas, who were armed with every deadly weapon imaginable. Their tumultuous shouts echoed in four directions, like a colossal thunderstorm.

As Khara, Dūshaṇa, and their hordes rumbled through the Daṇḍaka Forest in search of Rāma, bad omens appeared. A black shadow eclipsed the sun, making the rim appear red as blood and the day appear as night. The swift horses pulling Khara's chariot stumbled on their way, jackals howled at the army as it swept by, hyenas and vultures shrieked ghastly cries. Lotuses withered, fruits and flowers disappeared, winds blew violently, and dust clouds covered the forest. As the earth trembled and shook, the army faltered.

"Only the weak are influenced by such trifles," said Khara with an arrogant laugh. "These mean nothing to one as powerful as me. I can shoot down the stars with my shafts. I have never known defeat in battle.

I can vanquish Indra, the king of the Devas, so what do I have to fear from two ordinary men?"

Khara's loud boasting renewed his army's courage. They roared louder than ever, and hurtled on, destroying everything in their path.

Sitting outside their hermitage, Rāma and Lakshmaṇa saw the same omens. "These brown clouds, raining blood, portend the death of the rākshasas," said Rāma. "See the smoke rising from my arrows, as if they are eager for the fight. My right arm twitches; victory will be ours."

As the pounding of drums echoed through the forest, Rāma said, "Take Sītā to a mountain cave, one difficult to reach and screened by trees. Do not leave her under any circumstances. I know that you could defeat these demons, but I wish to slay these night prowlers single-handedly."

Lakshmaṇa bowed to Rāma and immediately set out for the cave with Sītā. His heart cheered by Lakshmaṇa's willingness to follow his every command, Rāma donned his coat of armor, shimmering like a flame.

Hearing the thunderous din of the rākshasas crashing through the forests, the Devas, Gandharvas, and celestial Ṛishis assembled in the skies to watch the battle. "Just as Vishṇu vanquished the asuras, may Rāma triumph over the titans," they cried. "Yet how will Rāma vanquish these fourteen thousand monsters by himself?" They floated in their celestial chariots high above the battlefield, talking among themselves.

The army of demons plunged into the clearing beside Rāma's quiet āshram. Shouting "Kill the enemy!" they loosed bloodcurdling screams that shook the forest trees.

Rāma calmly stood and surveyed the field with the eyes of an experienced bowman. Taking one celestial arrow from his quiver, he strung his bow, its twang resounding like thunder through the trees, causing his enemies to quake.

"Destroy him!" shouted Khara, and drove his chariot straight at Rāma, his army clustered around him like the planets around the sun.

Khara's bow spat a thousand arrows at Rāma, and lumbering ahead like elephants the giant demons let loose clubs, swords, spears, and axes on him, coming at him from all sides like a typhoon surrounding a boat at sea.

Without flinching, Rāma bent his bow like a sickle and shot a thousand arrows, each piercing a demon in the heart. The rākshasas, their legions slaughtered, scrambled over heaps of bodies to escape from the battlefield. Then the rākshasa commander Dūshaṇa, invincible in battle, rallied the army, and they charged Rāma straight on, wielding boulders and trunks of tall arjuna trees.

Watching from the heavens, the Devas sometimes thought Rāma was winning, other times the demons. Then, just as demons engulfed him like the ocean, Rāma shouted so loud that his voice rang around the forest like a gong. Stringing a celestial Gandharva weapon on the bow, he fired a thousand arrows in all eight directions. For a while, Rāma's arrows flew so fast and thick that the Devas saw only a black cloud covering the sun, and no one could see when he strung his bow and when he shot the arrows. Rāma stood at the silent center, unmoved by fear, his eyes closed like a bull in a rainstorm. Titans, horses, and elephants lay in heaps around the battlefield, slain by the arrows of Rāma.

Seeing his army decimated, Dūshaṇa wheeled his chariot to charge Rāma. Rāma's arrows shattered Dūshaṇa's horse, the charioteer, and his bow, and struck Dūshaṇa in the chest. Staggering with injuries, Dūshaṇa hurled his mace, large as a mountain peak and studded with sharp nails, which had conquered the Devas and smashed heaven's gates. Rāma pierced it with his arrows, and it shattered in eight directions. A few more swings of Rāma's sword, and Dūshaṇa was dead.

"Well done!" cried the Devas who watched from above. "Well done!"

Now Khara, enraged to see Rāma strike down his brother as lightning fells a great tree, ordered three generals and the remaining army to kill Rāma. Rāma's arrows pierced them all, so that only Khara remained.

Standing alone, Khara finally understood that Rāma had single-handedly vanquished his powerful brother and the entire demon army, and for the first time in his life, he felt fear. Nevertheless, he mounted his chariot, let loose a hundred poisonous arrows, and darted about the battlefield, revealing his formidable skill in battle.

The arrows flew so thickly from both sides that soon the battlefield was covered in darkness. At first Khara thought that Rāma was overcome with fatigue, because he stayed rooted to one spot. But Rāma continued to loose his arrows, as unconcerned with danger as a mighty lion in the company of a deer.

Then Khara made a bold move. He drove his chariot straight into

Rāma and broke Rāma's bow. Letting loose seven shafts like Indra's thunderbolt, he shattered Rāma's armor and wounded him. Khara whooped in victory.

Rāma raised a second bow, the one that Ṛishi Agastya had given him, named Vaishṇava. Like a clear, smokeless flame, Rāma advanced on Khara, shooting arrows that cracked the demon's bow, killed his horses and charioteer, and smashed his shield. Watching from above, the Devas shook their heads in wonder at such prowess in battle.

Now Khara faced Rāma on foot, wielding his mighty mace. Seeing him about to attack, Rāma's voice rang out in the forest. "You who love the darkness, see how your evil deeds, the killing of innocent sages in this Daṇḍaka Forest, have led to your death. The tyrant who causes pain to others can never gain happiness. It is to save those innocent saints that I have come to this forest. Now you will reap the inevitable harvest sown by your actions; now I will cut off your head like the fruit of a palm tree." At this, Rāma raised his bow and dispatched a single arrow, cracking the mighty mace of Khara into smithereens.

His ugly mouth foaming with anger, Khara hurled abuses at Rāma. Glancing about wildly for a weapon, he uprooted a giant axlewood tree. "With this you are dead!" he cried as he charged at Rāma.

Rāma easily broke the tree with his arrows, and then, his patience having run out, pierced Khara's body with countless arrows. Still, Khara hurtled on like an arrow that, once unleashed, cannot be stopped. Taking up the shaft of Brahmā and uttering the sacred mantras to empower it, Rāma let fly the fatal arrow that pierced the demon's heart. The terrible demon Khara crashed to the earth, dead.

The celestial crowds above cried out, "Jai Rāma!" and showered flower garlands on Rāma below. They rejoiced with the beating of drums, the ringing of bells, and the blowing of conch shells. "Wonderful is this great deed of Rāma, the knower of the Self. Wonderful is his might. In strength he resembles Lord Vishṇu himself." Chattering happily to one another, they recounted again and again how Rāma, possessed of the Self, single-handedly destroyed fourteen thousand demons in the course of an hour.

Soon the famed Ṛishis of the Daṇḍaka Forest, led by Agastya, assembled to give thanks to Rāma. "It was for this heroic deed that you were brought to this lonely place," rejoiced Agastya. "Now holy men can live in peace in the Daṇḍaka Forest, without fear of attack."

After Rāma returned to the hermitage, Lakshmaṇa and Sītā emerged from their mountain hiding place and joined him there. Seeing her adored husband victorious over the enemy, Sītā embraced him happily. Delighted by Rāma's victory, suffused with bliss to find her beloved Rāma unharmed, Sītā washed his face and feet, served him food and drink, and soothed away the fatigue of battle with songs of praise.

अहो बत महत्कर्म रामस्य विदितात्मनः ।
अहो वीर्यमहो दार्ढ्यं विष्णोरिव हि दृश्यते ॥

Wonderful is this great deed of Rāma, the knower of the Self.
Wonderful is his might. In strength he resembles Lord Vishṇu himself.

—Āraṇya Kāṇda 30.32

Chapter 21

Rāvaṇa Plots to Kill Rāma

Blazing like the sun
he sits on his throne,
Rāvaṇa, the lord of the three worlds.
Twenty arms fan out like a peacock's plumes,
striped with emeralds and gold.
Ten heads gape open-mouthed,
like caves armed with stalactite teeth.

Neither gods nor Gandharvas
nor Ṛishis can vanquish him,
nor Death himself.
He bears the scars of
Vishṇu's discus,
yet his limbs still punch the air
like mountain peaks.

He snatched the magical car
Pushpaka from the god of wealth,
he wrecked the pleasure gardens
of the Devas,
and stole their Soma elixir.
He alone can churn the seas.

Through austerity he won
Brahmā's boons,
freeing himself from death
by Devas, Gandharvas, or demons.
All but the humble creatures—
monkeys and bears,
and man.

In his arrogance,
he forgot to ask for
immunity against those he deemed
too weak to stop him
from stealing the wives of others
and terrorizing the holy.

In his arrogance,
he forgot to save himself
from the bottomless ocean
that is Shrī Rāma.

Rāvaṇa, the king of the rākshasas, sat on a throne inlaid with a most lavish and rare assortment of gems. Through the windows of the great hall where he held court, he could see the golden rooftops of his domain, the fabled city of Lankā. It had been built by the divine architect, Vishvakarman, and there was no other place like it on earth. The citizens of Lankā lived in ornate palaces, the walls lined with gold and the doors studded with precious gems. The city sparkled in brilliant hues of cat's-eye, emerald, ruby, diamond, and sapphire. Demons dressed in luxurious robes and feasted on delicacies unknown to man. Singers and dancers entertained them in bejeweled halls, and everyone lived in opulence and ease.

Yes, Rāvaṇa's day had started pleasantly, like any other—his bards sang his praises at the first light of dawn, recounting all the Devas, Gandharvas, and Ṛishis he had conquered. This always put him in a good mood, because it reminded him that he had never been defeated. There was no one, not even Indra in heaven, who did not fear him. He was the undisputed ruler of all three worlds.

On this day, however, a messenger dared to bring him the disturbing news of Dūshaṇa and Khara's destruction. "Who would dare attack my brothers?" Rāvaṇa roared at the unlucky messenger, Akampana. "I will destroy him, just as I have conquered Indra, Varuṇa, and Death himself!"

Akampana, who had barely escaped Rāma's arrows on the battlefield, visibly quaked under the harsh storm of Rāvaṇa's wrath. "A prince by the name of Rāma, the youthful son of Dasharatha, faced the rākshasa army alone in the Daṇḍaka Forest at Janasthāna and destroyed them," he managed to say in a voice strangled with fear.

"He must have been helped by the Devas!" screamed Rāvaṇa. He hoisted his mammoth body from his throne and stomped up and down the hall in a rage.

"His golden-winged arrows twisted into five-headed serpents, killing five with one," said the messenger. "But the Devas did not help him."

"I will go there myself and kill him!" bellowed Rāvaṇa. His voice echoed off the golden walls and rattled the jeweled chandeliers.

"This man can destroy the worlds and create a new universe," said the messenger. "There is no one who can defeat him."

Seeing Rāvaṇa about to explode in anger, the hapless messenger quickly added, "But I know of a way. Rāma is inordinately attached to his wife, who accompanied him to the forest. Adorned with jewels, she is the most beautiful woman in the world. She is far more lovely than the nymphs or Devas. Kidnap her, and Rāma will die of grief."

Rāvaṇa liked the idea, and for the first time he smiled. He immediately climbed aboard his aerial chariot, drawn by mules. Gleaming with gold, it swiftly bore Rāvaṇa high above cities and villages, tranquil lakes, and dense forests. Soon he landed in a clearing in the woods, where the rākshasa Mārīcha sat outside a hut performing austerities, wearing the guise of a hermit.

Mārīcha served Rāvaṇa a sumptuous feast. Then he said, "I feel apprehensive. What brings you to this quiet retreat?"

Rāvaṇa laid out his plan to steal Sītā. Mārīcha held up his hands in protest. He did not want to tangle with Rāma.

"Surely the fool who suggested this plan was your enemy, craving your destruction," he said. "It is not possible to defeat Rāma. Like an elephant, he has the lineage of heroes as his trunk, valor as his blood, and muscle-knotted arms as tusks. Do not hurtle yourself into the bottomless ocean that is Rāma. His bow is the crocodile, his arms are nimble as quicksand, his shafts are like rising waves that submerge the battlefield in endless waters. Return to your kingdom in peace and let Rāma dwell in the forest."

Rāvaṇa returned to his kingdom. It would have ended there, except for Shūrpaṇakhā. That hideous demon, who had watched her brothers die in battle, waited impatiently at Rāvaṇa's palace, eager to seek revenge on Rāma.

"How can you sit there, consumed in your quest for pleasure, while doom is descending on you like a dark cloud?" wailed Shūrpaṇakhā when Rāvaṇa arrived. "The king who does not protect his lands lives without glory, like mountains flooded by the sea. Rāma has single-handedly slain the multitude of demons of the Daṇḍaka Forest. No one helps the degenerate monarch who fails in his duty. He is swept from his kingdom like straw. The king who is vigilant, on the other hand, is revered by all."

Rāvaṇa, chastised severely by his sister, was quiet for a moment. Then he said, "Tell me all you know about Rāma."

Shūrpaṇakhā, her voice shaking with rage, again told Rāvaṇa the story of her disfigurement by Rāma and Lakshmaṇa. Then she cunningly added, "Rāma's tender wife, Sītā, is by far the loveliest lady in existence. Whoever wins her as a consort will live in all happiness. It was when I tried to capture her for you that Lakshmaṇa so cruelly attacked me. When you see her, you will be pierced by the arrows of the god of love, so do not delay. Rāma must be repaid for the deaths of Khara and Dūshaṇa."

His hair standing on end, Rāvaṇa weighed her words. Then he set out again in his chariot for Mārīcha's āshram, flying through the clouds.

Mārīcha was not happy to see him.

"I am terribly distressed, and you can help me," began Rāvaṇa, who was a persuasive orator. "I am distraught with the news from my sister,

Shūrpaṇakhā. She tells me that this insignificant mortal, Rāma, has been thrown out of his kingdom. Ruthless and without principle, he attacked my army without provocation and killed my brothers, Khara and Dūshaṇa. Passionate and a slave to his senses, he even dared to harm Shūrpaṇakhā, a defenseless female. Having abandoned his duty as king, he lives in a hermitage, seeking to harm others without just cause, flaunting his strength. To punish him for his misdeeds, I am resolved to take his beautiful wife, Sītā, by force."

Employing his considerable charm, Rāvaṇa said to Mārīcha, "You are unequaled in skill and courage. Moreover, you are a master magician. I want you to transform yourself into a golden deer, one that will win the heart of Sītā. When she sees you bounding by, she will surely say to Rāma, 'Capture it for me.' While Rāma and Lakshmaṇa are chasing you in the forest, I will carry Sītā away in my chariot. Then Rāma will die of grief and will no longer rule the Daṇḍaka Forest."

Mārīcha turned as pale as a swan's feather. He licked his dry lips, his eyes fixed in terror on Rāvaṇa.

Folding his palms together, he begged Rāvaṇa to come to his senses. "It is easy to flatter a powerful king; it is more difficult to speak truthfully. You are deluded and your spies are incompetent. Rāma's wrath will be the death of all rākshasas. Sītā's smile will become the instrument of that destruction. Rāma has never been disowned by his father, nor is he angry, selfish, or harmful to others. He is the embodiment of Dharma, he is virtuous, and he is brave."

Mārīcha saw the demon king was not convinced. He tried one more argument. "You will never conquer Rāma. He will no more be parted from his beloved Sītā, whom he values more than his own life, than the sunbeam from the sun. Unless you wish to see your opulent Lankā laid waste, its temples and gardens destroyed, and the limbs of your subjects pierced by arrows, stay clear of Rāma. Take counsel with your ministers, headed by the virtuous Vibhīshaṇa, before embarking on this cruel and foolhardy plan. I speak for your own good, O king of the night prowlers."

Then Mārīcha explained why he himself feared Rāma. For Mārīcha was the same demon that the young Rāma had shot years ago when defending the āshram of Vishvāmitra. The impact of Rāma's powerful weapon did not kill him, but struck him with such force that he was flung a hundred yojanas into the sea. "Rāma was just a boy when he shot me and, being generous, spared my life. Later, still filled with contempt for him, I confronted him again in the Daṇḍaka Forest and only barely escaped because I ran away. Now just the sound *rā* makes me so frightened, I jump when I hear it! That is why I took to the hermit's life. Having seen his strength, I know that you, Your Majesty, cannot defeat him. Plus there is no greater sin than consorting with another's wife. You have thousands of concubines; look to them and save your honor, your fortune, your kingdom, and your life."

Just as a patient who is about to die refuses the remedy, Rāvaṇa blindly refused to listen to Mārīcha's forthright words. Instead he lashed out at the unfortunate Mārīcha. "You miserable wretch! You will see me conquer this stupid and inconsequential human. I did not ask you for advice; I only asked you to help me. A gloomy response does not please a king; no sovereign likes having his dignity affronted by his advisors. A king embodies the five Devas: Agni (ardor), Indra (valor), Soma (gentleness), Yama (retribution), and Varuṇa (forgiveness). At all times you should honor these qualities in me; yet you have offered me only arrogance and have treated me, your guest, as a reprobate. My mind is fixed. You will help me capture Sītā. If you refuse, I will put an end to your miserable life now."

Mārīcha did not quake, nor did he shrink in fear. He was not afraid of Rāvaṇa's blustering. "The king is the source of all righteousness and virtue in his subjects. A cruel leader cannot protect his subjects any more than a jackal can protect a herd of deer. Ministers who counsel violence will certainly reap violence along with their king, as a chariot driving swiftly on rough roads is destroyed along with its dull-witted charioteer. Who is this foolish person who advises you on this course? It will surely lead to your destruction. The rākshasa race, under your leadership, is doomed to extinction.

"But since you are determined to offer up your life to Rāma, I will go with you. I would rather die by the arrow of Rāma, and thus attain liberation, than be killed by you. May you be prosperous, O mighty king."

Rāvaṇa felt rage rush through his body, from his ten heads to his ten toes. Mārīcha deserved to be punished for his arrogance—yet Rāvaṇa restrained himself. He knew he needed Mārīcha's skills in sorcery if his plan was to succeed.

Thus Rāvaṇa subdued his anger and smiled at last. "Now you are talking like the Mārīcha I know. Lead me to Sītā."

Sweeping across the sky in Rāvaṇa's aerial chariot, far above the land, they traveled to the Daṇḍaka Forest.

ये तीक्ष्णमन्त्राः सचिवा भुज्यन्ते सह तेन वै ।
विषमेषु रथाः शीघ्रं मन्दसारथयो यथा ॥

Ministers who counsel violence will certainly reap violence
along with their king, as a chariot driving swiftly on rough roads
is destroyed along with its dull-witted charioteer.

—Āraṇya Kāṇḍa 41.12

Chapter 22

The Golden Deer

I am devoted to Rāma,
unshakable as Mount Meru,
invincible as the ocean.
I embrace Rāma,
who shelters me
as the limbs of the banyan tree
provide shade to the earth.
I am Rāma's shadow,
clinging to the
lionhearted and brave.
I am loyal to Rāma,
whose face shines like
the full moon,
the soul of the universe.

And who are you,
who dare to desire me,
a lioness beyond your reach?

Trying to win me
is as futile as trying to shoot the
sun from the sky,
tear the moon from its orbit,
or swim the seas
with a boulder on your back.

For an infinite ocean separates you from Rāma,
as wide as the gulf between
jackal and lion.
You and Rāma are as different as
crow and peacock,
straw and silk,
lead and gold.

You could no more
steal my heart from Rāma
than a wasp
could swallow
a diamond.

Sītā wandered through the flowering groves outside their hermitage. The sun shone on her golden skin, lighting it with even greater brilliance than usual. Blessed with an inner happiness that never faded, her voice rose in melody while she plucked blossoms of crimson, magenta, and butter yellow.

Suddenly she stopped in her tracks, her song broken off in the middle. Before her pranced the most enchanting animal she had ever seen. It was a golden deer, its horns shining with silver and crusted with emeralds, pearls, and rubies. Its mouth glittered bright as the red lotus, its eyes the color of turquoise, its dainty feet sparkled like blue sapphire. As it leapt in the sunlight, its iridescent coat rippled in a rainbow of colors. Sometimes this rare creature bent to nibble the undergrowth, sometimes it gently pawed the earth. Shimmering with light, its radiance illumined the entire forest, like the moon frosting the trees with silver.

"Rāma, come here quickly!" called Sītā. "Bring Lakshmaṇa!"

The two brothers came running. Sītā pointed and exclaimed, "Will you catch this enchanting deer for me? It will make a magnificent pet for our āshram. We can charm our mothers and Bharata with its wonders when we return to the palace."

Lakshmaṇa frowned. "This beast is a fantasy, not found in nature. Surely this is the work of the sorcerer Mārīcha, who wishes us harm."

But Rāma, too, was enchanted by the gilded deer with its gem-studded horns. Wishing to please Sītā, he said, "Who could not be mesmerized by this extraordinary creature? We should add its wealth to the coffers of the king. If it is a demon in disguise, then I will end its life and bring home its skin for Sītā to sit upon, for this wicked Mārīcha has preyed on the Ṛishis of Daṇdaka Forest long enough."

Then he ordered Lakshmaṇa, "Stay here and guard Sītā with your life. Protecting her is our most important duty. Maintain utmost vigilance while I shoot this deer."

Rāma fastened his sword around his waist and carried his bow. Seeing him approaching, the deer bounded away. Rāma followed him into the forest, but the deer leapt ahead of him and, just as Rāma was about to shoot, disappeared. Then it suddenly appeared again, like the moon showing its face from behind the clouds. Thus the deer led Rāma deeper into the woods in a treacherous game of hide-and-seek. Finally, growing impatient at being led so far from the āshram, Rāma made up his mind to end the chase. Drawing his Brahmā arrow, he sent the fiery shaft straight into Mārīcha's heart.

Pierced by the arrow, losing blood, the demon reverted to his normal monstrous shape. Honoring his promise to Rāvaṇa, Mārīcha completed the final stroke of deceit. He called out loudly in Rāma's voice, "Alas Sītā, alas Lakshmaṇa!" And then he died, liberated by Rāma's arrow.

Rāma shuddered when he heard the dying rākshasa call out in his own voice. "What will Sītā think, when she hears me calling? What will Lakshmaṇa do?" His heart filled with dread, he quickly hurried home.

Rāma's fears were well founded, for Sītā was highly alarmed. Her mind flooded with frightening thoughts and her heart pounded. "Quickly, go help Rāma!" she cried to Lakshmaṇa. "That long, plaintive call was surely a cry for help!"

But Lakshmaṇa remembered Rāma's instructions and stood silently, unmoved.

Wild with anxiety, Sītā burst into tears. "Lakshmaṇa, you are nothing but an enemy to your brother," she sobbed in fear and confusion. "Otherwise, how could you stand here while he calls you? You obviously have no love for him. Why wouldn't you protect him, when that is why you came to the forest in the first place? O brother of Rāma, what can I do to make you move?"

Lakshmaṇa calmly reassured her. "There is no need to worry about Rāma, dear Sītā, for there is no one in this world or the next who can harm your husband. You have no reason to speak to me so harshly, for I cannot possibly leave you alone in the forest. I gave my word to Rāma, and I will stay here until he returns. Surely that voice was just a rākshasa trying to trick us. Do not worry, Rāma will soon return."

Hearing Lakshmaṇa's comforting words, Sītā grew even more agitated. Her eyes stinging with tears and flashing with anger, she railed at him, her one thought to help Rāma. "Surely you have come to this forest as an enemy in disguise, perhaps sent by Bharata, perhaps to have your way with me. But your plan will never work, for how could I ever love anyone but the compassionate Rāma? I will give up my life first, for I cannot live a day without him."

Now Lakshmaṇa shuddered. "You are like a goddess to me, and it is not for me to answer. But truly, I cannot endure such unjust and bitter words from you. They pierce my heart like flaming arrows. So be it—I will follow Rāma, against his command. I fear for your safety, for the omens are evil. May the trees protect you! May the creatures of the forest protect you! May we find you safe on our return!"

The faithful and good-hearted Lakshmaṇa bowed to Sītā's feet. Out of her mind with distress, she refused to look at him or answer him. Tears streaming down her face, she wailed, "If Rāma does not return, I will take poison, I will drown in the Godāvarī, I will throw myself in the fire—but I will never touch a man other than Rāma."

Again stung by Sītā's words, Lakshmaṇa ran into the woods to find his brother, glancing back at Sītā until she disappeared from his view.

This was the moment Rāvaṇa had been waiting for. Disguised as a wandering holy man carrying a staff, his saffron robes covered with dust, his gray hair matted in a knot on top of his head, he walked briskly along the forest path. As he passed, the wind stopped playing in the trees, the River Godāvarī slowed in its course and the birds stilled their chatter.

When he entered the clearing, Rāvaṇa stopped suddenly as he glimpsed Sītā for the first time. Sitting desolate in front of her hut on a pillow of leaves, she wept uncontrollably. Even in distress, her golden complexion, her narrow waist, her lotus-red lips, and her radiant inner light pierced Rāvaṇa with desire.

Feigning old age, Rāvaṇa hobbled to the hut with his stick and addressed Sītā in words oozing with deceit. "Who are you, lovely lady, with the coal-black eyes, the playful looks, and the raven hair? Surely you are the Devī Lakshmī, come down to earth."

He could barely refrain from leering. "With your yellow silken robes and garland of flowers, you look as ravishing as a divine nymph. Why are you all alone in this forsaken forest that teems with rākshasas? One as divinely beautiful as you belongs in a tall mansion, attended by a multitude of servants, or in a pleasure garden, agreeable to the senses."

Sītā looked up then, her eyes flooded with tears. She saw a holy man standing before her, and, accustomed to welcoming the guests of the forest, the pure-hearted Sītā stood up, offered him a seat under the arbor, and brought him water. She glanced around frequently, anxiously awaiting Rāma and Lakshmaṇa. This holy man spoke strangely and she was all alone, yet if she did not answer his questions respectfully, he might curse her. So to be hospitable she told him all about Rāma and Lakshmaṇa, the story of Rāma's banishment, and their stay in the forest.

"You may rest here awhile," she concluded in her soft voice. "In a moment, my husband will return with food. And now please tell me where you are from and what is your name."

Not wanting to waste another moment, Rāvaṇa revealed his identity. "I am Rāvaṇa, the demon king," he said in a loud, arrogant tone. "I rule over the richest kingdom in the world, the fabled Lankā of unimaginable wealth and beauty. I have many other wives, but none please me as much as you. Come with me to Lankā and be my first queen. I will reward you with five thousand servants and a life of luxury, far from this wretched forest."

Sītā's eyes blazed with indignation. "I am devoted to Rāma. I could never be your queen, nor any other's. If you think you can steal Rāma's beloved wife, you may as well poke out your eyes with a stick. Compared to his lionlike greatness, you are a mere spider." Having said these brave words, Sītā trembled all over.

Seeing her quivering with fear, Rāvaṇa only wanted her more. "I do not think you heard me, fair lady," he said with a frown. "I am Rāvaṇa, the half brother of Kubera, the god of wealth. I have conquered the Devas and Indra himself. Even the wind ceases and the rivers stop flowing when I pass by. I am the most powerful king in the world. My city,

Lankā, is a pleasure ground fit for the gods. With its lofty palaces, its gates set with gems, you will forget your life as a human. When you can have me, why would you want Rāma, so helpless that he allowed his father to banish him? He is weaker than my thumb. If you do not come with me, you will regret it."

Sītā could barely contain her disdain. "If you are the brother of the god of wealth, how did you come to live such a low life? Your evil ways will bring the destruction of your kingdom and your entire race. It may be possible to steal the wife of Indra, but if you lay even a finger on Rāma's cherished wife, you will never escape his arrows."

At this, Rāvaṇa could not hide his anger. He smacked his fist to the palm of his other hand. Twisting about, he grew until he reached his true size and assumed his usual ten-headed form. Towering above her, he grabbed Sītā with one hand and lifted her body with another. Blinded by passion, he dragged her to his golden aerial chariot, which hovered nearby.

The spirits of the woods fled in a panic, seeing this unforgivable act. Sītā writhed in Rāvaṇa's arms, struggling to break free. She pleaded, "Rāma, save me! Lakshmaṇa, stop this demon!"

As Rāvaṇa directed his car over the treetops, Sītā lamented, "O Rāma, you who have sacrificed fortune, kingdom, and home for the sake of Dharma, can you not stop the worst violation of all? You defend the weak from the wicked; will you not protect your chaste wife from evil?"

Speeding through the sky, with Rāma farther away every moment, Sītā begged the forest, "O noble trees, tell Rāma that Rāvaṇa has stolen Sītā! O creatures of the forest, large and small, tell Rāma that Rāvaṇa has taken Sītā. O River Godāvarī, noisy with swans and cranes, quickly tell Rāma that Rāvaṇa has carried Sītā away!"

Hearing her agonized pleas, the birds stopped singing and the trees wept.

हंससारससंघुष्टां वन्दे गोदावरीं नदीम् ।
क्षिप्रं रामाय शंस त्वं सीतां हरति रावण: ॥

O River Godāvarī, noisy with swans and cranes,
quickly tell Rāma that Rāvaṇa has carried Sītā away!

—Āraṇya Kāṇḍa 49.31

Chapter 23

Sītā and the Blade of Grass

As Sītā flew through the skies in Rāvaṇa's chariot, there was another who heard her cries. Waking from his nap, the ancient bird Jatāyu, his giant wings hunched like two mountains, saw Sītā passing above.

"O noble bird," cried Sītā from the chariot, "you will not be able to stop this demon Rāvaṇa, who carries me off by force—but please, tell Rāma of this wicked deed."

Jatāyu called out to Rāvaṇa, "I am Jatāyu, king of the vultures, knower of the Veda and knower of Dharma. You also are a king, so others follow your example. It is your duty to uphold the scriptures, to protect the wives of other kings. Stop this evil plan and release her."

Rāvaṇa's arrogant laugh echoed through the forest like the braying of the mules that drew his chariot.

"O Rāvaṇa," said Jatāyu, "I am old and have ruled with wisdom and justice. You are young and armed with sword, arrows, and an aerial chariot. Yet you cannot carry off Rāma's wife while I look on any more than one can change the eternal meaning of the Veda through convenient arguments. While I still live, I will defend Rāma's honor, even if it brings my death."

Thus challenged, Rāvaṇa rained arrows upon the courageous bird. Jatāyu flew up and landed on Rāvaṇa, and with his thick talons tore into the rākshasa king's back and arms, inflicting deep wounds. Seeing Sītā standing in the chariot, her face wet with tears, Jatāyu was filled with strength. He snapped Rāvaṇa's bow in his claws, shattered his blazing shield, and swept aside his arrows with his giant wings. He broke off the head of Rāvaṇa's charioteer with his beak, killed Rāvaṇa's mules, and smashed the chariot into pieces with one swipe of his wings. Rāvaṇa, clutching Sītā in his arms, darted into the sky before the chariot hit the ground.

Seeing the ten-headed Rāvaṇa humbled, the beings of the forest, who had gathered to see the heroic fight, cried out, "Long live Jatāyu! Jai Jatāyu!"

As Rāvaṇa tried to escape, carrying Sītā, Jatāyu blocked his path. "Where can you go to escape the noose of death? Rāma and Lakshmaṇa will find you. Your death is assured."

Then the valiant Jatāyu lit on Rāvaṇa and again sank his talons deep, yanking out the demon's hair with his beak and tearing off his ten arms. But like water in a fountain, ten new arms sprang up in their place.

Filled with rage, Rāvaṇa set Sītā on the ground and used his hands and feet to beat off the bird, who attacked him repeatedly in a furious struggle. Finally Rāvaṇa drew his sword and sliced off the bird's two enormous wings. Jatāyu fell to the ground, bleeding, his strength spent.

Sītā ran to the bird and cradled his enormous head in her lap, weeping for him as she would for her own kin. When the valiant bird had breathed his last breath, she cried out, "Because of me, this brave and noble bird now lies dead."

Looking up, she saw Rāvaṇa coming for her. She sprang to her feet and wrapped her arms tightly around a tree trunk. "O Rāma! Do you not see the bad omens of birds and creatures fleeing? Rāma, Lakshmaṇa, save me!" she cried piteously.

Rāvaṇa yanked Sītā by the hair and, pressing her to his side, flew above the treetops. Seeing that prince of darkness drag the blameless Sītā by the hair, the wind stopped blowing, the sun dimmed, and darkness covered the earth. The Devas cried out in distress, but at the same time they rejoiced, "The destruction of Rāvaṇa is now complete."

As Sītā streaked through the air in Rāvaṇa's clutches, her golden skin shone like lightning against a storm cloud. Her yellow sārī streamed behind her like a flag, and her fire-bright bracelets fell like meteors to the earth below. The princess continued to wail, "Rāma! Lakshmaṇa!" as she was borne through the skies.

All the creatures in the universe trembled. "There is no justice, no truth, no kindness in this world now that Sītā has been stolen by Rāvaṇa," the mountaintops whispered to one another. With their crests reaching to the sky like giant arms, they seemed to be lamenting for her as she passed. Seeing the gentle Sītā's anguish, the forest deities shuddered.

Sobbing, Sītā continued to twist and turn in Rāvaṇa's arms to free herself from his deadly grip. "Aren't you ashamed of this cowardly act?" she railed at him. "Afraid to face Rāma, you used trickery to lure him away, then seized me when I was alone. Jatāyu showed far more bravery than you, and now he lies slain. What kind of king are you, that you steal another's wife when she is defenseless? It will do you no good, for I will never take a husband other than Rāma. Let me go, before Rāma finds you and destroys you. He has slain fourteen thousand demons without help. What will stop him from slaying you?"

Suddenly Sītā saw five immense monkeys sitting on the top of a mountain. Thinking quickly, she managed to free her arms and gather her jewels into her silken shawl. After knotting them into a bundle, she dropped them amidst the monkeys as she flew over. "May you whisper my fate to Rāma," she prayed.

In his haste to carry Sītā to Lankā, the wicked rākshasa king did not notice what had happened. On and on he flew, not realizing that he carried the means of his destruction in his arms.

Rāvaṇa dragged Sītā over the hermitages and lakes of the vast Daṇdaka Forest, until finally they reached the ocean, the journey's end for all rivers. Seeing the sobbing princess in Rāvaṇa's arms, the ocean churned in furious waves and the fish dived to the bottom. To comfort the sea, the siddhas and *chāraṇas* (celestial singers) called down from heaven, "The destruction of Rāvaṇa is at hand!"

They flew over the ocean until they came to the rooftops of Lankā poking through the clouds. Rāvaṇa carried the struggling Sītā into his palace and set her down in his private chambers.

"Let no one talk to Sītā without my permission," Rāvaṇa ordered his servants, who were hideous female demons. "Give her rubies, diamonds, silken robes, ornaments—anything she desires. If you speak harshly to her, it will cost you your life."

Foolishly feeling safe from Rāma's reprisal, the deluded king reveled in the ecstasy of capturing Sītā. "Now Sītā will be my wife," he thought. Feeling pangs of passion for her, he hastened to her side.

Guarded by the demon servants, Sītā sat weeping, her face shrouded in sorrow. Deluded by his own power and lust, Rāvaṇa said, "See this beautiful city, inhabited by ten thousand night prowlers. Darling one, become my first, most cherished queen and rule over this city and my thousand other queens. Make me your servant. This city, surrounded by ocean waters, can never be conquered. You cannot expect Rāma—deprived of his kingdom, traveling barefoot—to rescue you now. Besides, I am a much more worthy consort for you. Forget about Rāma, let me lavish you with silks and jewels, and live by my side in delight."

Sītā covered her moonlike face with the end of her sārī and sobbed.

"Do not worry that our union will be against Dharma, for we shall have a Vedic wedding," the arrogant rākshasa king continued. "I will press your tender feet with my hands. Grant me my prayer and free me from the thorny torments of love, for I have never before bowed my head to a woman." With this humble plea, the proud rākshasa king thought, "Now she is mine."

Sītā could bear these insults no longer. She held up a single blade of grass between herself and Rāvaṇa. Her eyes flashed with anger like sparks from a fire as she spoke to the blade of grass rather than directly to Rāvaṇa. "There is a man who is known as the lover of Dharma. He is my husband and my God. If you had not been so cowardly, and had laid hands on me in his presence, you would already be dead. Your boon may protect you from gods and asuras, but you will never escape the fury of Rāma.

"A virtuous wife, faithful to her vows, can never be tempted by a sinner such as you, O last of the rākshasas. Why would a swan, swimming happily with her mate, be attracted to a dull, dark cormorant on the river bank? You can bind or destroy this body, but I will never be dishonored by you."

Anger stirred Rāvaṇa's blood. "Consider carefully, lovely princess. If you do not submit to me before twelve months have passed, my cooks will cut you to pieces and serve you to me for breakfast."

Then Rāvaṇa privately instructed the demon women who surrounded Sītā. "Break her will, as hunters break the will of a female elephant. Flatter her, then terrify her in turns."

With Rāvaṇa's orders, those gigantic and terrifying women, who shook the earth when they walked, seized Sītā and dragged her to the

Ashoka Grove inside the palace wall. A gazelle ensnared by lions, thinking only of Rāma, Sītā fell to the ground in a faint.

मुमोच यदि रामाय शंसेयुरिति भामिनी ।
वस्त्रमुत्सृज्य तन्मध्ये निक्षिप्तं सहभूषणम् ॥

Sītā gathered her jewels into her silken shawl
and dropped them amidst the monkeys.
"May you whisper my fate to Rāma," she prayed.

—Āraṇya Kāṇḍa 54.3

Chapter 24

Rāma's Lament

In this enchanted valley
Sītā sat beside me.
Smiling, she spoke gentle words.
Perhaps she still wanders the sides of the river
or gathers flowers.
Yet I know she would only walk
these winding banks
with me by her side.
Never caring to stroll in solitude,
she of the lotus eyes,
wreathed with blossoms
and trailed by songbirds,
was too timid to enter
the forest alone.

O radiant sun, you are the witness
of all good things on earth
and all evil.

Has Sītā wandered away
or has she been stolen?
O relentless wind, you pry into every hidden crack
in this world.
Has Sītā, my tender flower,
lost her way,
been carried off
—or is she no more?

As Rāma rushed through the forest toward the hermitage, leaping over logs, ducking his head to avoid low branches, oblivious of shrubs grazing his legs and tearing at his skin, he trembled at the sound of jackals howling and the cries of birds and beasts fleeing the forest in fear. Alarmed by these omens, Rāma thought, "Surely Mārīcha aimed to lead me away so he could harm Sītā."

Trembling with apprehension, he spotted Lakshmaṇa striding toward him, pale and discouraged.

"My dear brother," said Rāma as he took Lakshmaṇa by the hand, "why have you left Sītā unprotected? You were wrong to leave her. I see so many evil omens. That deer turned out to be the demon Mārīcha, who called out in my voice to lure you here. My left eye throbs and my heart is heavy. I fear the worst for Sītā."

Lakshmaṇa could find no words to answer him, but only looked down.

The two brothers raced back to the hermitage to find Sītā. As they ran, Rāma, his emotions overwhelming him, cried out to Lakshmaṇa, "Where is Sītā, my life's strength, who is like a daughter to the gods? O Lakshmaṇa, without her I cannot live, even for a moment. If something has happened to her, I will die. Then what will happen to my poor mother, who, without a son to protect her, will fall under Kaikeyī's sway? If I return to the āshram and do not find Sītā, who always smiled before she spoke, I will give up my life. I am drowning in an ocean of sorrow. I tremble before my fate."

When the two brothers reached the āshram, it was empty. The grass mats were scattered on the ground in disarray. The deserted hut was like a lake in autumn, shorn of its lotus flowers. Bereft of Sītā, the trees drooped as if weeping and the color of their blossoms faded away. Deer no longer leapt, birds no longer sang. Rāma ran to all of Sītā's favorite places crying, "Sītā! My Sītā!"

As he stumbled over a banyan tree root, he shook all over. "O Lakshmaṇa, why did you desert Sītā, when I left her in your care?" he asked, his voice weak and choked to a whisper.

Seeing Rāma so stricken, Lakshmaṇa nearly broke into tears. "Please believe me, it was not I who wanted to leave her," he said. He told Rāma how Sītā had wept and pleaded with him. "I was forced to leave because of her cruel words, my lips trembling, my eyes flaming with anger."

"O dear brother," replied Rāma in anguish, "it was wrong to abandon her. You know well that I could defend myself without your help. Yet reacting to her indignant words, spoken out of extreme anxiety, you gave in to anger and disobeyed my command. This was truly a breach of Dharma."

Rāma ran to the trees, calling them by name. "O jambu tree," he pleaded, "have you seen my dear love, whose hair your rose-apple blossoms loved to adorn? Tell me, where has she gone?"

"O ashoka tree," he cried, "you are the dispeller of grief. Prove worthy of your name and reveal where my beloved is hiding."

Then he ran after the beasts, calling, "O gentle deer, where is she of the doe-like glances, who fed the fawns out of her hands?"

"O brave tiger," he cried, "where is my gentle spouse, who is radiant as the moon? Tell me, O fearless one!"

Overcome with anxiety, he thought he glimpsed her yellow sārī flitting behind a pomegranate tree and called, "Why do you hide from me, my lotus-eyed one? I see you, lady of lovely smiles. Stay, if you have any love for me."

When it proved to be a shadow he was chasing, he sobbed, "My Sītā has been devoured by a demon. She with her golden complexion, her white teeth and rose-red lips, her queenly nose, her delicate ears, her skin like jasmine, her slender neck smooth as sandalwood—she has perished, like one who has no husband to protect her."

Rāma ran from mountaintop to riverside, from cave to meadow. Overcome with despair, he staggered like one who had lost his wits. Searching frantically throughout the woods for his love, he finally returned to the hermitage and collapsed in exhaustion.

"O Sītā, if you are hiding from me in jest, come out now. You have enjoyed my anguish long enough. O my darling one, the gazelles want to play with you. See how their eyes are filled with tears, they miss you so. O Sītā, more graceful than the bough of the plantain tree, end my pain. O goddess of my heart, enough of this laughing at me. It is not fitting to play so much at a hermitage, although I know laughter comes naturally to you. Come home."

When Lakshmaṇa also returned alone from his search, his face blanched with fear, Rāma cried out, "I cannot live without Sītā! I will join my father, who will reproach me for not keeping his vow. I could never go back to Ayodhyā without her. And what would I say to King Janaka, when I left with her and returned alone? No, Lakshmaṇa, you go without me and embrace Bharata tenderly. Tell him that I command him to rule the earth. Comfort our mothers and tell them of Sītā's death and mine."

Lakshmaṇa shuddered to see Rāma so distraught. He tried to console his brother. "You are a man of wisdom. Do not waste your energy in grieving. Let us search this forest together. Sītā has undoubtedly wandered after a colorful bird, or perhaps she has hidden in a cave to tease us. It is by searching the forest that you will be reunited with Sītā."

But Rāma would not hear of it. "We have searched the forest, and no trace of my gentle Sītā can be found." He sank to the ground, barely conscious, sobbing and crying out, "O Sītā, do not leave me!" He fell deeper and deeper into an abyss.

Lakshmaṇa stood before Rāma with his hands folded together in respect, begging, pleading, trying everything in his power to rouse the heartbroken Rāma.

"Surely there is no one in this world more miserable than me!" cried out Rāma. "I must have done something sinful in a previous lifetime. First the loss of the kingdom, then the exile from all who love me, then the parting from my father and mother. I had forgotten all this sadness, living happily here with Sītā. But now that she is gone, these memories sear me like a log falling from the fire. My tenderhearted wife has been carried off by a demon. How can I endure these sleepless nights?"

Lakshmaṇa now spoke sternly. "O brave hero, give up your grieving. You need your strength to search for Sītā. Great warriors do not lose themselves in emotion, even when faced with insurmountable hardships."

Rallying for a moment, Rāma said, "Lakshmaṇa, search the River Godāvarī. Perhaps she has gone there to gather lotus flowers."

When Lakshmaṇa again returned without Sītā, Rāma jumped up and ran to the Godāvarī like a wild man, crying to that holy river, "Where is Sītā?"

Silence greeted his anguished cries.

"Where is Sītā?" he beseeched a herd of deer. The deer rose as one and faced the south, craning their necks upward. Then they ran to and fro in front of Rāma and Lakshmaṇa.

Lakshmaṇa understood. "Rāma, the deer are trying to tell you something. They are pointing to the south. Perhaps if we go that way we will find Sītā."

"So be it," said Rāma. He strode briskly on the path to the south. Suddenly he cried out, "O Lakshmaṇa, look! Here are the flowers I gathered for my darling Sītā just this morning. She braided them in her hair. It looks as if the sun, the wind, and the earth saved them for me, here on the path."

Then he cried out to the mountain, "O lord of the hills, have you seen the graceful princess Sītā?"

Once more, there was silence.

"Show me where Sītā has gone, or I will break your peaks!" shouted Rāma, his voice echoing off the mountainside like the roar of a lion in his den. "I will burn you to ashes. No more will the trees find a home in your arms. I will dry up your rivers if Sītā is not found."

Again confronted only with silence, Rāma would have destroyed the mountain. But just then, he saw a giant footprint in the earth and, beside it, the delicate footprint of Sītā. Searching the forest floor, the brothers found the shattered remains of a chariot, a pearl-inlaid bow, and hundreds of arrows.

"Alas, a great struggle took place here, on account of Sītā," said Rāma. "These golden arrows and broken bow must belong to a great rākshasa, who surely carried off Sītā and devoured her."

His body shook with anger. "Who is there in this world that dares to mock me? Someone mistakes my softhearted disposition for cowardice, my compassion for weakness. Today I will suppress those gentle qualities and show the world my full power. Today I will stop the planets in their orbits, cover the moon, blacken the sun, and dry up the ocean."

Rāma's wrath burned like the fire at the dissolution of time. His eyes glowing red, his body shooting forth sparks of gold, he raised his bow and fitted it with an arrow as deadly as a snake. "If the lords of the universe do not deliver my beloved Sītā, they will see what I can do. My arrows will darken the sky and flood the earth. If the flawless Sītā of charming smiles is not returned to me unharmed, I will destroy every Deva, rākshasa, earthly creature, and man. I will destroy the three worlds!"

Lakshmaṇa faced Rāma, his hands again clasped together in respect and his lips white as parchment. "Dear brother, never before have you let rage overpower you. You have always been self-controlled and intent on doing good to all creatures. Just as beauty is natural to the moon, splendor to the sun, patience to the earth, and quickness to the wind, all of these qualities, as well as fame, are natural to you.

"What good would it do to destroy the three worlds when only one demon committed the crime? You are the refuge of all beings. The mountains and oceans, the Devas in heaven, the celestial beings, and the good men on earth could never wish to harm you. It is your duty now to find Sītā and to punish her abductor. With me by your side, we will search every cave, hill, lake, and mountain. We will seek guidance from the gods, the Gandharvas, and the men who live in each place. If through gentleness, humility, and sensible efforts you do not retrieve Sītā, then only will you be justified in shooting your arrows like Indra's thunderbolts."

Hearing these words, Rāma felt another wave of gloom wash over him. Immobilized by his loss, he wailed like an orphaned child.

Now the faithful Lakshmaṇa, ever the nurturing and supportive friend to Rāma, clasped Rāma's feet lovingly. In an effort to comfort his brother, Lakshmaṇa entreated him, "Remember that you are the fruit of our father's yagyas, just as *amṛitam*, the nectar of immortality, is the fruit of the yagya of the Devas. If you cannot bear misfortune, how can an ordinary man?

"Who in this world can escape challenges that burn like fire? Vasishtha, our enlightened guru, lost a hundred sons in one day. Our revered Mother Earth, whom all worship, trembles at times. The eyes of the universe, the sun and moon, are occasionally eclipsed. Even Indra and the gods are subject to consequences of good and evil. Therefore, do not grieve.

"Even if Sītā has met the worst of fates, it is not worthy of you to lament like an ignorant man. Men of wisdom bear pleasure and pain with equanimity, O Rāma.

"I am only repeating what you have taught me in the past—for how can I presume to teach you anything? Even the gods could not fathom your intelligence. I am merely trying to rouse your wisdom, which is dulled by grief. What good would it do to seek revenge on the Devas and men? Now is the time to decide the best course of action, to seek out your foe and put an end to him."

Rāma was not accustomed to receiving advice from his younger brother, yet he saw the wisdom in Lakshmaṇa's words. His anger drained away, and he lowered his massive bow. "Where shall we search for Sītā? What shall we do, Lakshmaṇa?" He struggled to set aside his devastated feelings.

"First we must scour this area together, leaving no corner unvisited," suggested Lakshmaṇa. As they beat aside the underbrush with their swords, again checking every foot of the forest floor for clues, they saw a giant bird lying wounded on the ground.

"This great bird is surely the rākshasa who devoured Sītā," said Rāma, raising his bow. "I will end its miserable life." He rushed on the bird as if he would destroy the whole earth.

His voice barely audible, the dying bird whispered, "O Rāma, true to my promise to protect Sītā, the lady you seek like the rarest of herbs, I fought Rāvaṇa, the king of the rākshasas. But when I grew exhausted he cut off my wings with his sword. I am dying, so there is no need to kill me."

Rāma, recognizing Jatāyu, flung aside his bow and dropped to his knees. With Lakshmaṇa at his side, he caressed the bird as he would his own father, sobbing for his friend and distressed at hearing such fearful tidings of Sītā. "My misfortunes could consume fire itself," cried Rāma. "Now my father's dear friend is dying, his blood staining the earth."

Taking the bleeding bird tenderly in his arms, he gently asked, "If it is possible for you to speak, will you tell me where my Sītā has gone, she who is dearer to me than my life? I beg you, tell me all."

The loyal bird faltered, his life's breath ebbing away. "Rāvaṇa used his sorcery to stifle the wind and hide the sun. He flew away with her, facing the south. But he stole her in the hour of *vinda*, when all that is lost is soon recovered. So do not despair, you will defeat him and recover Sītā." And then the noble bird gave up his life in Rāma's arms.

"Speak, noble bird, please tell me more," cried Rāma, his face streaming with tears.

Shaken with grief, Rāma clasped the bird's feet. "This selfless bird lived many years happily in this forest, and now he has died in my service, using his last breath to save Sītā. This proves that high-souled beings live among all the wild creatures. His death weighs heavily on my heart."

Then he instructed Lakshmaṇa to gather firewood. "This bird deserves the same funeral rites as our own father."

Lighting the funeral pyre after gently placing the massive bird on it,

Rāma said, "O mighty Jatāyu, who died for my sake and Sītā's, go beyond the worlds of fearless warriors, beyond the worlds of those who perform yagyas, beyond the worlds of those who give away their fortunes—go to the realms of perpetual bliss."

Then Rāma chanted in a low voice the sacred hymns and performed all the auspicious ceremonies to gain the blessings of nature for their father's friend. The grieving brothers walked to the river bank and waded into the Godāvarī. After bathing in its pure waters, they cupped their hands and solemnly offered water oblations for the great bird, just as they had done for their own father.

Remembering the words of Jatāyu, who assured them that they would recover Sītā, the two left Panchavatī and strode like Vishṇu and Indra toward the southwest, the dense forest closing behind them like a door.

यां विना नोत्सहे वीर मुहूर्तमपि जीवितुम् ।
क्व सा प्राणसहाया मे सीता सुरसुतोपमा ॥

Where is Sītā, my life's strength, who is like a daughter to the gods?
O Lakshmaṇa, without her I cannot live, even for a moment.

—*Āraṇya Kāṇda 58.4*

Chapter 25

The Two Princes Search for Sugrīva

Sandy beaches circle Lake Pampā
like a necklace
and swans, herons, and ospreys call sweetly
across her tranquil waters
where lotus flowers collect like clouds.

Rainbow blossoms gently
float from trees

and light plays melodies on
her sapphire waves.

Sparkling fish
slip through underwater gardens.
Giant monkeys roar like bulls,
inhaling the crystal waters like nectar.
Elephants rush to her shores,
crimson trunks raised high,
intoxicated by champa flower fragrances.
Bears, panthers, wolves,
and azure-colored deer
live in peace on her banks.

Across her placid face rise
the peaks of Mount Ṛishyamūka,
shaped by Brahmā's thoughts.
The fortunate ones who pass the night
dreaming of treasure on its cliffs
find wealth awaiting them at dawn, it is said,
while the sinful who climb its high paths
are devoured by demons.

High on Mount Ṛishyamūka,
in a hidden cave,
its entrance guarded by a cool lake,
live Sugrīva and his four loyal ministers,
waiting to help Rāma find his beloved.

As they continued their search the two princes left the Godāvarī River basin and headed into impenetrable jungles to the south. Vines and creepers covered the forest floor, making it difficult to traverse.

"I see many evil omens," said Lakshmaṇa. "My left arm trembles, and fear shrouds my mind. But the cry of the dreaded *vanjulaka* bird tells me we will be victorious."

Just then a deafening noise blasted through the forest, assaulting their ears. As they drew closer, they saw a strange creature towering above the trees. Shaped like a round barrel with no head or neck, he sported a single eye blinking from the belly. Tufts of hair prickly as pine needles covered a mountainous shape. Long, powerful arms swung through the forest like pendulums, sweeping lions, bears, and deer into a ravenous mouth ringed with icicle-like fangs.

Rāma and Lakshmaṇa stood watching from what they thought was a safe distance. Without warning, the rākshasa suddenly stopped, swung his long arms in their direction, and snatched the princes in his massive claws. As the demon dragged them toward his cavernous mouth, Lakshmaṇa remembered his premonition and feared they were doomed. He cried out, "Dear brother, offer me to this monster and save yourself! I am convinced you will be reunited with Sītā and regain the throne of Ayodhyā. When you rule the earth once more, think of me often, your humble servant."

Rāma did not succumb to emotion. "Scatter your fear to the winds, dear brother. Such a valiant warrior as you need never despair."

"It is my good fortune that has brought you here to feed my ravenous hunger," roared the rākshasa in a voice that clapped like thunder. "You may as well be dead."

Hearing this murderous threat, Lakshmaṇa drew his sword and said, "Let's cut off this despicable rākshasa's arms before he eats us."

The monster opened his mammoth mouth to swallow the two brothers. With perfect timing, Lakshmaṇa swiftly sliced off his left arm and Rāma his right. Both arms severed, the rākshasa's trunklike body swayed and crashed to the earth. His howl of pain rang through the earth, the sky, and the four quarters.

"Who are you and what is your purpose?" asked the monster as he gasped for his last breath.

"This is Rāma, and I am his brother Lakshmaṇa." Lakshmaṇa patiently explained how they had come to the forest and how they now searched for the chaste Sītā, who had been dragged off by Rāvaṇa.

"And who are you?" Lakshmaṇa asked politely.

"I am Kabandha. God praise you, Rāma and Lakshmaṇa, for at last you have come!" His horrible mouth smiled with happiness.

As his life seeped away, Kabandha told them a curious story. "O Rāma, as the shining Gandharva Danu, I once was known for my splendor in all the three worlds. As beautiful as the moon, I foolishly took on this hideous body to torment saints for sport. Once I terrorized a powerful Ṛishi named Sthūlashirā while he gathered wild fruits. He cursed me, saying, 'May you forever stay in this body.' I pleaded with him to take back his curse. Finally he said, 'When Rāma and Lakshmaṇa cut off your arms in battle, you will regain your original beauty.'

"After that I performed tapas and earned the boon of immortality from Lord Brahmā himself. Unfortunately, this made me so arrogant that I attacked Indra one day, thinking that I could conquer him. Hurling his thunderbolt, he smashed my head down into the trunk of my body, and created this repulsive eye and mouth in my middle so I could see and eat. I implored him to kill me outright, but he said, 'I must honor the boon Brahmā gave to you. But, as Sthūlashirā said, you will be freed the day Rāma and Lakshmaṇa cut off your arms in a fight.'

"O compassionate Rāma, at last you have come to liberate me. Burn me in the funeral pyre, and when I have regained my true body and intelligence, I will be able to help you find the rākshasa who stole your wife."

"Let it be so," said Rāma. Without delay, the powerful princes lifted the dying hulk and set him down near a shallow pit in the forest, in which they piled tree trunks that had been felled by elephants and cured dry by age. They rolled the giant body on top and lit the fire.

From the pure flame rose the resplendent form of the Gandharva Kabandha, clad in spotless white garments, flower garlands, and golden ornaments. Radiating light all around, he was enthroned in a floating chariot drawn by silver-white swans. From there he called to Rāma, his melodious voice chiming like soft bells.

"Now I will tell you how to recover Sītā. Of the various means to end misfortune, it is best for you to seek a friend who shares your difficulties. I see no other path to success than this. For without army or wealth, you are alone and helpless.

"Listen carefully," continued Kabandha. "High on Mount Ṛishyamūka, beside Lake Pampā, lives a monkey king who, like you, has been exiled unjustly. His name is Sugrīva, and he is endowed with strength, courage, and intelligence. This monkey will become your friend and help you find Sītā. Go to him and swear your loyalty to each other with the fire as your witness. Do not worry that he is a mere monkey, for Sugrīva is powerful and can grow tall as a tree or shrink small as an ant. He knows all the habits and haunts of the rākshasas, and his monkey army will search every cave and crevice for your beloved Sītā, even if the monkeys have to scour the home of Rāvaṇa himself. Sugrīva will prove a worthy friend to you."

The now radiant Kabandha pointed to a forest path. "Take this trail west through groves of blossoming trees, which provide fruit in all seasons. Sustain yourselves on their fruits as you journey toward Lake Pampā. On the shores of that lotus-filled lake, you will meet an ancient woman named Shabarī, who has served the holy Matanga and other exalted sages of Lake Pampā. She is waiting in Matanga's hermitage to serve you." Then he faded into the heavens.

"May peace go with you," the two princes called after him.

"You will recover Sītā," Kabandha called back, as he dissolved into the sky. "Befriend Sugrīva, O Rāma."

The two brothers immediately headed down the path the Gandharva had pointed out, through thick undergrowth and thorny bushes. As they passed through groves of rose-apple, mango, and champa trees, they stopped occasionally to eat the plump mango fruits, ripened in the sun. Winding their way through the mountains, they spent the night on a high plateau.

The next day they reached the sandy shores of Lake Pampā and spotted a quiet hermitage in the woods nearby. Outside, as if waiting for them, sat a woman with snow-white hair. She rose to greet them, smiling with a rare radiance.

"I have been expecting you," she said. She trembled with tender devotion as she bowed to the feet of Rāma and Lakshmaṇa again and again. Raising her up, Rāma said, "It is I who should be bowing to you, revered Shabarī."

Shabarī brought them water to wash their feet and rinse their mouths, as was the custom. She offered the weary travelers a seat that she had prepared for them that morning, covered with blossoms. She served them ripe berries she had just picked.

"Since the time you first set foot on Chitrakūta Mountain, my teachers told me to expect you," Shabarī explained. "Even though they ascended to the celestial realms, they asked me to stay behind. 'Welcome Rāma and Lakshmaṇa as your guests,' they said. 'When you behold Rāma, you will attain the highest heaven.' So each day for thirteen years I have spread this seat of rose-apple blossoms from the jambu tree, and each day I have gathered wild fruits from the shores of Lake Pampā for you to eat."

After Rāma graciously thanked the sage for her remarkable hospitality, he inquired after her welfare in kindly tones. "Have you attained eternal bliss and inner tranquility? Has devotion to your guru yielded fruit? Have you quelled all anger and the need for food?"

Shabarī smiled her brilliant smile, glowing with the light of purity. Despite her extreme age and countless wrinkles, she looked strong and healthy. Standing with her hands folded, her eyes shining with divine love, she said, "Now that I have bowed to you, I have achieved the purpose of my birth. Now that I have touched your holy feet, I have honored the teaching of my guru. Now that my eyes have feasted on your radiant being, I shall reach the heavenly realms. With your favor I will now attain all worlds."

Rāma smiled, his heart swelling in appreciation for this blissful and devoted saint. Then he said, "The Gandharva Danu has told us about the renowned gurus of Lake Pampā, whom you have served. Can you show us where they spent their days?"

She led them down a secluded path, beneath blossoming trees. "We are walking in the Matanga Wood, the abode of my guru, the great sage Matanga. Each day he and other praiseworthy ascetics purified their minds in the silent depths of meditation and sanctified their every action by chanting the hymns of the Vedas. They made this wood holy. Due to its silence and purity, even the wild elephants stopped tramping through it, and the deer and the tiger live in harmony."

They entered a clearing. "Behold the altar, facing east, where the ascetics conducted yagyas to raise the fortunes of the world. Behold the sparkling streams of water flowing from the seven seas, drawn here by the power of the wise ones' thoughts. Behold the blue-tinted lotus garlands, gathered by them for worship, still unfaded and fresh. This is a place of eternal renewal, a place to erase all cares."

The two brothers waded into the sacred flowing waters, splashing their limbs as they performed their evening ablutions. They cupped their hands and offered homage to their ancestors.

When they returned to her hermitage, the devoted sage Shabarī faced the two brothers with her hands folded together in respect. "Now that I have shown you all that you desired to see, please grant me leave. I wish to shed this body and join my pure-souled teachers, whom I am accustomed to serving."

"Wonderful! Wonderful!" cried Rāma, his heart touched by all that he had seen and heard. "You have surely honored me today, radiant Shabarī. Take your leave and go swiftly to the abode of happiness."

With that blessing, the gentle Shabarī, wearing the humble tree-bark robes and matted locks of an ascetic, stepped into the fire she kept ever burning at the hermitage. In a flash she rose from the pure flame into the air, her limbs adorned with celestial robes and garlands, emitting a divine fragrance sweeter than sandalwood. Lighting the skies, she ascended to the highest heaven, joining her guru and other high-souled Ṛishis who had already passed to their heavenly abode. The sound of conches, celestial music, and bells filled the air.

The two brothers stood in silence for a long while. Finally Rāma said, "O Lakshmaṇa, surely this sacred place has washed away our sad karma. Now my heart rests in peace. Soon we will enjoy good fortune."

Rāma set out walking from the hermitage. "Let us follow the shores of this enchanting Lake Pampā. I am anxious to reach Mount Ṛishyamūka, floating above the lake in the distance. There lives Sugrīva, who will help us find Sītā."

"That mountain beckons me too," said Lakshmaṇa. And so the two princes, their bodies shining like the sun, strode resolutely beside the lotus waters of Lake Pampā, its shores shaded by blossoming trees.

स ते प्रतिग्रहीतव्यः सौमित्रिसहितोऽतिथिः ।
तं च दृष्ट्वा वराँल्लोकानक्षयांस्त्वं गमिष्यसि ॥

Welcome Rāma and Lakshmaṇa as your guests.
When you behold Rāma, you will attain the highest heaven.

—*Āraṇya Kāṇḍa 74.16*

End of the Āraṇya Kāṇḍa

FOUR

Kishkindhā Kāṇda

Kingdom of the Monkeys

Chapter 26

Rāma Meets the Servant of His Heart

In this spring without Sītā,
I wander the sandy banks of Lake Pampā,
shaded by flowery boughs.
My feet tread softly
as blossoms
of dawn's pastel hues
wash these shores
in frothy tides.

The gentle wind
frolics in tune with humming bees,
swaying the treetops
until their branches touch
like courting birds.
The breath of spring
brushes against flower petals
and scatters the scent of sandalwood.
O Lakshmaṇa,
in this season of tender breezes,
how can I bear the loss of my doe-eyed one?

Sītā would thrill
at the cry of the dātyūhaka bird

trilling from the waterfall.
How can I live without my beloved
of gentle speech and loving glances?

See the strutting peacock adorned with turquoise,
fanning a thousand eyes in the wind,
intoxicating the pea-hen with desire?
Sītā followed in my footsteps
as the peacock's mate follows him.
Now he cries in sympathy for me.

All that brought me joy
in her presence
now pains me like the sting of ice.
Without her, the crystal waters of Lake Pampā,
teeming with blue water lilies and swans,
pierce my bones like the winter wind.

In every lotus I see her eyes.
In every breeze I feel her breath.
In every birdsong I hear her voice.
If I could see her now,
resting on that hillside erupting in blossoms
amidst flocks of birds,
I would want for nothing.

To live apart from Sītā
in the season of spring
is beyond bearing.

As Rāma and Lakshmaṇa walked along the shores of Lake Pampā under the blossoming trees, a gentle breeze showered petals that caught in their hair and fell in drifts on the ground. As he inhaled the earthy, honey-scented breath of spring, Rāma could think only of Sītā.

"You know that this season was Sītā's favorite," said Rāma in an unsteady voice. "Everywhere I look, I see reminders of her slender waist, her thick eyelashes, her melodious voice, her smiling glances. The dance of mating birds and the caress of soft breezes only intensify my feeling of loss. I cannot bear this pain. I fear that she, too, cannot endure this separation. For she has always been true to me, just as I have loved only her. O Lakshmaṇa, it is time for you to go home to Bharata and leave me here. For I cannot live without Sītā."

Rāma slumped on a fallen log, holding his head in his hands, his gleaming weapons trailing on the forest floor.

Ever the faithful brother, Lakshmaṇa said, "Stay steady on your path, Rāma. Do not give in to sadness, for the only way to recover what you have lost is through your own resourcefulness. Nothing is more powerful in this world than a strong will and the energy to exert yourself. The only way to reunite yourself with Sītā is to find Rāvaṇa. Even if he should hide himself in the womb of Diti, the mother of the demon race, you must find him there and slay him. Put aside your emotions for now. Remember who you are, O Rāma. The light of your intelligence and courage can never be dimmed."

Braced by his brother's words, Rāma rose above his grief. Though he still felt the pain of being separated from Sītā, his mind was steady once again. Established in equanimity, he searched for Sītā under the blossoming trees of Lake Pampā.

As the two powerfully built brothers made their way toward Mount Ṛishyamūka, others were watching. Monkeys playing in the woods saw the princes walking purposefully through the forest, their shining weapons slung over their shoulders, and fled to the nearby Matanga Wood, where they felt safe.

These monkeys were not ordinary primates, for they had come into being in an unusual way. At the time when the Devas had begged Lord Vishṇu to take birth as the warrior-king Rāma, the farseeing Lord Brahmā instructed the Devas, "O immortal ones, may you give birth to *vānara* (celestial monkeys) and bears to assist in the destruction of Rāvaṇa, for in Rāvaṇa's boon he neglected to ask for protection from men or animals. I have already created Jāmbavān, the chief of the bears, who emerged from my mouth when I yawned."

The Devas then gave birth to numerous vānara of uncommon abilities. These celestial monkeys could fly through the air and grab onto clouds with their tails. Immensely strong, they could uproot trees and conquer lions. These monkey tribes, versed in the art of warfare, served either Bāli, son of Indra, or his brother Sugrīva, son of Sūrya, the Sun. A multitude of monkeys waited to fulfill the purpose of their birth.

High on Mount Ṛishyamūka, Sugrīva, the king of the monkeys, watched the brothers far below and felt his stomach knot up. Restless with worry, he paced the cave that served as his hiding place, anxiously checking the progress of the two godlike warriors, who came closer every minute.

"I am afraid that these two were sent by my brother, Bāli, to kill us," he told his monkey ministers. "Disguised as wandering mendicants, they are armed and ready."

"Yes, surely Bāli has sent them!" cried Sugrīva's ministers. As fear overtook them, they bolted from the cave and flew from peak to peak, racing over the mountain to escape the two men. As they trounced on trees, the tops broke off under their weight, frightening the deer and tigers, which stampeded in confusion.

Finally, worn out, the frazzled ministers returned to the spot where they had started and stood quietly beside Sugrīva, awaiting his command. Seeing his opportunity, the wisest and most eloquent minister, Hanumān, known as the Son of the Wind, quietly said to Sugrīva, "It is fear of your brother Bāli that makes us flit from place to place. Yet he is not here. You are giving in to the flighty indecisiveness of common monkeys. A leader must remain calm. Use your formidable intelligence and experience to determine the intentions of these men. Only then can you prevent danger."

His minister's wise words calmed Sugrīva. He said, "These two are surely spies of Bāli. So let us spy on the spies. Hanumān, disguise yourself as a human being, and go to meet them. Praise them, and with your courteous address, win their confidence. Ask them why they have come here, armed with bows. If they wish me harm, their speech and manner will betray them."

"So be it," said the noble Hanumān, his hands folded in respect.

In one bound, the great vānara Hanumān leapt from the peak of Mount Ṛishyamūka to its base, where Rāma and Lakshmaṇa were walking.

Through his powers of transformation, Hanumān made himself appear as a wandering ascetic. As he walked on the path toward the two brothers, he studied them to ascertain their character. When he finally spoke, it was from his heart.

"You who radiate light like gods, how have you come to this forest?" He bowed his head and pressed his palms together in respect, addressing them in Sanskrit, the language of the Vedas. "Though you wear the matted locks of an ascetic, you surely are men of courage. How have you come to the shores of Lake Pampā, clad in tree-bark robes but carrying bows bright as rainbows and swords gilded with gold? With your lion's strength and broad chests you dazzle the eye. Your eyes are as large as lotus flowers and your arms powerful as trunks of elephants. You light up the distant mountain with your brilliance, power, and beauty. The two of you, looking so much alike, could be the sun and moon come to earth."

When the two brothers did not respond to his gentle and pleasing words, he asked in courteous tones, "Why do you refrain from answering, even though I utter your praises? Sugrīva, the king of the monkeys, who has been banished to this forest by his brother Bāli, wishes to make friends with you. I am Hanumān, Son of the Wind and minister of Sugriva. I can go anywhere and take any form at will. At the request of my king, I appear before you as a monk rather than a monkey."

Rāma's face lit up with joy at the mention of Sugrīva's name. He turned to Lakshmaṇa and advised him privately, "Sugrīva has sent his minister to meet me. Talk to Hanumān in engaging tones, for he understands the subtleties of speech. He is extremely learned, for only by knowing *Ṛik*, *Sāma*, and *Yajur Veda* could he speak such perfect Sanskrit without hesitation. He surely has heard all the rules of grammar repeated many times, for he has not made a single mistake.

"His forehead, eyebrows, and eyes reflect the pleasing quality of his speech. He speaks in agreeable middle tones, neither too fast nor too slow, neither too wordy nor too obscure. Each word is enunciated clearly, never slurred or drawn out, each syllable given its proper accent. Resonating from his chest, throat, and head, his wholesome and harmonious speech charms my heart. A king with such a minister will surely meet with success, for such eloquence speeds all undertakings."

Thus guided by Rāma, Lakshmaṇa stepped forward and answered Hanumān cordially. "We know of your king, Sugrīva, and we have come to this forest to seek his assistance. Please tell us how we can meet him."

Hanumān smiled with delight. Always eager to serve his king, he immediately thought, "Here is one who can help Sugrīva regain his kingdom." And so he asked, "How is it that you have come to this forest?"

Lakshmaṇa explained their circumstances in his own eloquent way. "I have answered your questions with sincerity," he concluded. Then his eyes flooded with tears. "My brother Rāma, who once ruled the earth, now seeks the favor of the monkey king. Rāma, who has given away enormous wealth, now looks to King Sugrīva for sustenance. Rāma, the compassionate refuge of all beings, now seeks refuge with the chief of the monkeys. May Sugrīva offer his friendship to Rāma, who is overwhelmed with grief."

"It is the good fortune of King Sugrīva that men who have mastered the Self, controlled the senses and conquered anger have sought him out," replied Hanumān in his courteous and dignified manner. "King Sugrīva, too, has met with difficult times, having lost his kingdom and his wife to his brother Bāli. Sugrīva, son of the Sun, will help you search for Sītā. I will take you to meet him now."

Cheered by this harmonious response, Lakshmaṇa turned to Rāma, who was still standing behind him. "Hanumān, who is extremely intelligent, says Sugrīva will help us. Our task is as good as done. We can trust him, for his face is bright and we have gained his esteem."

With that, Hanumān dropped his disguise and bowed to Rāma. Then he swelled his body to an enormous size. Taking Rāma and Lakshmaṇa on his back, he flew in one leap to the top of the mountain where Sugrīva waited.

नानृग्वेदविनीतस्य नायजुर्वेदधारिणः ।
नासामवेदविदुषः शक्यमेवं विभाषितुम् ॥

He is extremely learned, for only by knowing
Ṛik, Sāma, and Yajur Veda could he speak such perfect Sanskrit.

—Kishkindhā Kāṇḍa 3.28

Chapter 27

Rāma and Sugrīva Become Friends

Carrying Rāma and Lakshmaṇa on his back, Hanumān flew to the top of Mount Ṛishyamūka and landed at the edge of a shimmering pool. From this spot high on the mountain, Rāma and Lakshmaṇa looked down on the sandy shores of Lake Pampā, the dense Matanga Wood and the rainbow hues of the flowering trees where they had walked far below.

After stepping to the ground they followed Hanumān as he circled the pool, arriving at a spot where a giant boulder guarded the entrance to a cave. Hanumān deftly rolled the boulder aside and beckoned them inside. Sugrīva and his four ministers had made a home out of the cave, with straw mats and a fire pit. After making his guests comfortable with water to wash their feet and food and drinks to refresh them, Hanumān disappeared into the shadows of the cave to report to Sugrīva.

When Hanumān told Sugrīva that Rāma, the embodiment of Dharma, had come to the forest seeking his aid, the monkey king smiled with relief. His fears dispelled, Sugrīva came forward to warmly greet Rāma and Lakshmaṇa.

"I salute you for upholding Dharma," said Sugrīva to Rāma. "The Son of the Wind has told me of your valor, your all-embracing love and compassion, and your other supreme qualities. I feel honored that you wish to befriend me, a mere monkey. If you desire to be my friend, take my hand, and we will enter into a fruitful alliance."

Rāma warmly clasped Sugrīva's hand to secure the friendship. Then he embraced Sugrīva heartily, delighted by his sweet words.

Hanumān quickly kindled a sacred fire. With flowers he made offerings to the fire and, with his mind serene, beckoned Rāma and Sugrīva to join him, one on each side. Having made their offerings, Rāma and Sugrīva circumambulated the sacred fire, their shadows dancing on the cavern walls. Rāma and Sugrīva gazed at each other fondly, each delighted with their new friendship.

"You are a friend for all time," said Sugrīva. "We will share our joys and sorrows alike." He offered a branch from a flowering shāla tree, which Hanumān had brought, as a seat for Rāma. Then he joined Rāma, sitting next to him on the branch. Hanumān placed the bough of a fragrant sandalwood tree on the floor of the cave and offered the seat to the humble Lakshmaṇa.

"Each day I wander these forests, O Rāma," said Sugrīva. "Exiled by my brother Bāli, who has stolen my wife, I live in fear of him. Save me from Bāli and dispel this crippling fear."

"To help and serve another is the sign of friendship, just as harming another is the sign of enmity," said Rāma, who knew Dharma and embraced it wholeheartedly. "I will defeat your brother Bāli, who has abducted your wife. This very day you will see my sun-bright arrows strike Bāli and lay him flat."

Sugrīva's depression lifted and he felt joy for the first time in many months. He knew in his heart that his purpose was as good as achieved. As faithful friends have done throughout time, he reciprocated the favor, pledging to rescue Sītā in return.

As Rāma and Sugrīva sealed their pact, the left eyes of Bāli and Rāvaṇa quivered, portending their deaths.

Sugrīva's next words made his visitors' hair stand on end. "I cannot be certain, but I think I saw your wife flying across the skies, struggling to escape Rāvaṇa's arms. My four ministers and I were seated on this mountaintop when she passed overhead, crying piteously, 'Rāma, O Rāma!' Seeing us, she threw down her shawl and jewels. I have them here, if you wish to identify them."

Rāma's dark skin turned pale. "Please, bring them to me, my friend."

When he saw Sītā's shawl and jewels, Rāma gathered them in his arms and slumped to the ground, tears blurring his eyes. Pressing them to his heart again and again, he cried out, "My darling one!"

Recovering himself, he said, "O Lakshmaṇa, without a doubt these are Sītā's jewels, which she scattered on the ground to warn us of her abduction."

"I cannot identify the armlets or earrings," said the virtuous Lakshmaṇa, wiping tears from his eyes, "but the anklets I remember well, for I bowed to her feet each morning."

Then Rāma, his face bathed in tears, questioned Sugrīva. "Show me the place where you saw Sītā. Who is this monster who bore her away, and where does he live? What is his strength? Tell me all you know, and I will send him to his death this day."

Moved to tears himself, the good Sugrīva joined his palms together and said, "I do not know where that beast can be found, but I do know that I will find Sītā and bring her back to you. Until then, I beg you to set aside your heartache and show your courage. An illustrious hero such as you cannot be moved by adversity, separation from loved ones, loss of wealth, or fear of death. Those who succumb to sorrow can never succeed; their strength slips away, as a boat overturned in high waters slips beneath the waves. Please believe me—I speak to you as a friend, with my hands folded in respect. I do not presume to teach you anything; I speak only for your good. For the sake of our friendship, do not let grief overtake you."

Touched, Rāma wiped away his tears and embraced Sugrīva. "You have spoken as a good friend, one who is concerned for my welfare. Thanks to your well-chosen words, I am my true self again. To find an ally like you, who has suffered similar misfortunes, is rare indeed, especially in troubled times."

Thus sitting side by side on the shāla bough, the man and the monkey spoke intimately of their hopes and their fears, for which they shared a common bond.

"The Devas have blessed me in every way to send me such an ally, imbued with every remarkable quality," said Sugrīva. "Gold and silver, clothes and jewels are to be shared with one's friends. A friend is a safe harbor, whether he is rich or poor, happy or sad, flawless or full of faults. Those who value friendship will sacrifice wealth, happiness, and life itself for the sake of a friend."

The radiant Rāma, pleased with Sugrīva's devotion, said, "Now tell me how your brother Bāli came to be your enemy."

Sugrīva sighed deeply and said, "Only because you have given me your hand in friendship, with the fire as my witness, will I tell you the wrong that eats away at my heart."

"Speak freely," said Rāma. "Tell me all. The thought of your humiliation both angers me and engulfs my heart with sadness. Tell me every detail, so I can carefully consider how to ensure your happiness."

"This is my story, Rāma," said Sugrīva. "Bāli, my older brother, was dearly loved by my father and, in those days, by me too. When my father died and Bāli became king, I obeyed my elder brother in all things, just as the trustworthy Lakshmaṇa obeys you.

"My brother had a famous fight over a woman with the asura Māyāvī. In the dead of night, Māyāvī came to the gates of our monkey kingdom, Kishkindhā, and with a roar that shook the stones of the palace walls, challenged Bāli to fight. Awakened from sleep, Bāli rushed outside to fight him, even though his wives and I pleaded with him to stop.

"Determined to help my brother, I followed him outside the gates of our kingdom. The asura fled into a wide, yawning cave. 'Stand watch for me here,' commanded Bāli. 'Guard the entrance while I kill this demon.'

"I begged Bāli to let me help him, but he charged into the cave alone, his mind furious on Māyāvī. I stayed outside that cave for an entire year, anxiously waiting for my brother to return. Sick with worry, I was determined to follow his orders. Then one day I heard a terrific roar from the asura and saw blood trickling out of the cave. Not hearing my brother's voice, I concluded that he had been killed. Wishing to save the people from certain destruction by Māyāvī, I blocked the entrance with a huge boulder.

"Stricken with grief, I returned home. Even though I did not wish to tell them, my friends learned of Bāli's death and insisted on crowning me king. I ruled the kingdom with justice. But then Bāli returned home—he had killed Māyāvī and with his incomparable strength pushed the boulder away from the mouth of the cave.

"I tried to explain that I had truly thought he was dead. I laid my crown at his feet, offering him the kingdom and my services. But he would not bless me, and instead chased me out of the kingdom, shouting, 'The cruel Sugrīva tried to kill me in order to usurp the kingdom.' I did not want to commit violence against my own brother, so I ran from him with only the clothes on my back.

"Since then Bāli has abducted my wife, the radiant Rūmā, and chased me over the earth. Through no fault of mine, I have been persecuted by him. Only on this mountain, where he is forbidden to set foot, am I safe from his torments. Many times he has sent other monkeys to kill me. When you arrived on this mountain, it was from fear of him that I did not greet you. It is only because Hanumān and my other friends have stayed with me that I survive at all.

"You are my only hope to end this misery. Only you are capable of helping me recover my wife by killing Bāli. My life and my happiness depend on you; you are my friend, my heart's haven, my hope."

Rāma smiled reassuringly. "The wicked Bāli, who has stolen your wife, will die today. I will ferry you across the ocean of your grief, which I feel as my own."

Sugrīva's heart swelled with joy. He thanked Rāma again and again. Then he said, "I am convinced of your power and your courage, yet Bāli is extremely powerful. For exercise, Bāli leaps to the oceans in the east, west, and south before breakfast each day. He breaks off mountain peaks like icicles, tossing them in the air and catching them like a juggler. He snaps giant trees like twigs. He has never been defeated in battle, even by the Devas themselves. The son of Indra, he is invincible and ruthless. That is why I fled here. I do not see how you could defeat him in battle." Sugrīva's head was in his hands now, for the monkey's emotions swung quickly from joy to despair.

Lakshmaṇa smiled. "What must Rāma do to convince you of his strength?"

Sugrīva thought for a moment. "If Rāma could kick the carcass of the immense buffalo asura who was killed by my brother one hundred yojanas, and if he could slice off the tops of seven shāla trees with one arrow, then I would know he has strength enough to conquer Bāli."

He added humbly, "O dear Rāma, you are my brave and revered friend. I am well acquainted with Bāli's power, and I do not yet know the extent of your skill in battle. I myself am known to be cowardly, while your speech, confidence, and strength blaze forth like fire."

Now it was Rāma's turn to smile. "If you do not yet trust my prowess, then let me instill confidence, for trust is essential for success in battle." With those words, the monkey king Sugrīva led Rāma and Lakshmaṇa to the place where the massive buffalo carcass lay. Raising one foot, Rāma kicked it a hundred yojanas.

Sugrīva considered this deed thoughtfully. "It is true that the carcass is now just dried bones, and Bāli kicked it all the way here while it was still heavy with flesh and he was exhausted by combat. I am sure that you will pierce those seven shāla trees with your arrow, and then I will be satisfied. For you are chief among men, just as the sun rules the planets."

Hearing those courteous and candid words of Sugrīva's, Rāma let loose a golden arrow. With the sound of a thunderbolt it sailed straight through the trunks of seven towering trees that stood in a row. Their limbs tumbled to the earth, crushing the woodland plants below. Then the arrow returned to Rāma's quiver like a messenger pigeon.

Overjoyed, the good monkey king prostrated himself at Rāma's feet, heaping praises on him and holding Rāma's feet to his head. "I am the most fortunate creature on earth, to have as my friend one who has the strength of the vast sea. You will surely destroy Bāli."

"Let us go at once to Kishkindhā and challenge Bāli, who is your brother in name only," said Rāma.

Passing through the woods, they soon arrived at the golden gates of Kishkindhā, the enchanting monkey kingdom built inside a vast mountain cave, hidden by a grove of trees. Sugrīva stepped forward and let loose a stupendous war cry, roaring so loudly that Bāli heard it deep inside his palace and rushed outside in a rage, ready to fight.

नाहं जानामि केयूरे नाहं जानामि कुण्डले ।
नूपुरे त्वभिजानामि नित्यं पादाभिवन्दनात् ॥

I cannot identify the armlets or earrings,
but the anklets I remember well,
for I bowed to her feet each morning.

—Kishkindhā Kāṇḍa 6.22–23

Chapter 28

Rāma Slays Bāli

When she saw the body of valiant
Bāli lying on the ground, his
virtuous wife Tārā lamented,
"You who hurled mountain peaks
like thunderbolts,
whose valor matched Indra's,
who tossed the titan buffalo
across the skies
like a discarded cloak—
you, hero among monkeys,
lie still before me,
dead to my cries.

"Why do you embrace the earth?
Rise and rest on your silken couch
befitting a great king.
Or do you love lying on the
cold ground,
since now you scorn me?
Never again will you frolic with me
under fragrant bowers.

You have found a new and more golden
Kishkindhā in heaven.

"I who have never known pain
must spend my life as a widow.
And our tender son Angada
craves your embrace in vain.
You who were born a hero,
who struck down your enemies
with bare hands,
must return to the elements alone.
If only you had listened to my pleas
and made peace with the magnanimous Rāma."

Like the sun rising above the mountaintop, Bāli appeared before Sugrīva. Burning with anger, he did not speak a word, but rushed at his brother, striking the first blow. A ferocious struggle began between the two brothers, like a clash between Mercury and Mars in the heavens.

As they struck each other with diamond-hard fists, Rāma stayed hidden in a grove of trees. He strung his bow and took aim. But he could not tell one brother from the other, as they resembled each other like the two divine *Ashvins*. Afraid to shoot his friend by mistake, Rāma let his bow fall slack at his side.

Sugrīva fought valiantly for a time, but finally, weary and discouraged that Rāma had not helped him, he ran away from his powerful brother. Covered with wounds, he hid himself on Mount Ṛishyamūkha. There Rāma and Hanumān found him later that day.

Sugrīva hung his head in despair and humiliation. "Why didn't you keep your promise? I never would have subjected myself to such a battering if you had frankly told me that you did not wish to kill him."

Rāma knelt at his friend's side. "Sugrīva, you are my dear friend. Please do not be angry, for when you hear my reason you will understand. When you were wrestling with your brother, the two of you looked exactly alike. There was no way for me to tell you apart. I was afraid to dispatch my arrow for fear it would hit you by mistake. To kill one's ally is a grave sin. Lakshmaṇa and Sītā and I are completely dependent on your good will; you are our only hope. So let us go back and challenge Bāli again. Only this time wear something around your neck so I can tell you apart."

At Rāma's bidding, Lakshmaṇa gathered a blossoming vine and twined it around Sugrīva's neck like a garland. Revitalized, Sugrīva shone golden and radiant.

On their way back to Kishkindhā, they passed herds of elephants and deer. They saw flocks of birds swimming in an emerald lake thick with water lilies. Rāma found himself gazing at the densely clustered trees ringing the lake. "What is that forest, gathered like a mass of clouds and circled by plantain groves?" he asked.

"Deep inside that woods you will find a peaceful and enchanted āshram that removes all weariness," Sugrīva said. "It is said that seven monks who maintained severe ascetic practices once lived there, submerged up to their necks in the lake. They ate once every seven days, and even then their only food was the mountain breeze. After seven hundred years they ascended to heaven, their bodies intact.

"Due to the power of their purity, no one can penetrate their āshram, even the Devas. Those who enter by mistake never return. A divine fragrance wafts from there, celestial music echoes from there; and the smoke of the monks' sacred fires, which burn eternally, forms a golden cloud above the trees like the wings of a dove. O Rāma and Lakshmaṇa, with hands joined together in reverence, offer your salutations, for those who offer blessings to these pure-souled Ṛishis banish all sorrow."

After bowing to the sacred place, Rāma and Lakshmaṇa continued on their way, following the monkey king Sugrīva down the wild mountain paths.

When they reached Kishkindhā, crawling with monkeys and guarded by watchtowers, they once again hid behind the trees.

"Set aside your anxiety," said Rāma. "I will fulfill my promise to you. Bāli will fall today." Sugrīva, filled with courage now that his victory was in sight, again shattered the earth with a roar. Shining like the sun, he stepped forward to confront Bāli.

Deep inside the inner apartments of the palace, Bāli was relaxing with his wives, celebrating his victory over Sugrīva. When he heard Sugrīva's shout, lashing the walls of the kingdom like waves in a tempest, he could not contain his rage.

He stomped out of the palace, shaking the earth with each step. Radiant as the stars, his devoted wife Tārā followed him outside and gently caught him by the arm. Tenderly circling her arms around his neck, the daughter of the divine Bṛihaspati said in a voice trembling with fear, "I beg you to check your anger, which rages like wild waters flooding the river banks. Put off this fight with Sugrīva, at least until you know who his allies are. It does not make sense that he should roar with such confidence after being so severely beaten by you.

"The spies of our son, Prince Angada, tell me that the two powerful princes of Ayodhyā, Rāma and Lakshmaṇa, have allied themselves with your brother. Rāma welcomes all who seek his aid; every good quality finds its home in him. Rather than fighting him, make your peace. Seek his blessings with flowers, gifts, and pleasing words. Now is the time to win back your brother's affection, for the thick-necked Sugrīva is incomparable in strength and wisdom. Invite him to live near you. If you care at all for me and wish to return my infinite affection for you, then put off this fight and make peace with the Prince of Ayodhyā."

Bāli paid no heed to these wise words. "My lovely lady, I would rather be dead than be called a coward. When the foolhardy Sugrīva challenges me to fight, I must meet his challenge. Do not fear, Rāma is Dharma incarnate and will do no wrong to me. As for Sugrīva, I will not kill him, but I will crush his pride with my blows. You have shown your sweet affection and followed me far enough, O lady of smiles. Now it is time for you to turn back, my beloved one."

The virtuous Tārā, who knew right from wrong, embraced Bāli and circled him, keeping him to her right shoulder as she recited the sacred hymns of a warrior's wife to bring him good luck in battle. Then she quietly returned to her palace, filled with foreboding.

Bāli strode outside the city gates toward Sugrīva, his eyes flashing red sparks. He gathered his loincloth closely about him and, doubling his powerful fists, rushed at his brother like a bull. A fierce fight ensued, like a thunderstorm with claps of thunder and sparks of lightning. But Bāli was the stronger, and when Sugrīva felt his strength ebbing, he looked over to Rāma, who stood ready with his bow. Rāma's arrow hissed through the air, streaming flames red as the ashoka tree blossom. It struck Bāli, who fell like a tree in a tempest.

The sky darkened and the wind stopped. Mortally wounded by Rāma's arrow, the courageous Bāli still wore the gold necklace bestowed by his father Indra, which imbued him with vitality, radiance, and power. He shone like the sun in its last blaze of glory as it sinks below the horizon.

Rāma and Lakshmaṇa quietly drew near the great warrior to pay their respects.

"O Rāma, why did you sneak up on me from behind while I fought another?" Bāli called out bitterly. "I have heard that you uphold Dharma and are full of generosity and valor; your praises are sung throughout the world. Yet you have behaved like a common scoundrel who wears the mask of virtue. What have I ever done to harm you, that you should trick me with such a wicked deed? I am a mere monkey, living on roots and fruits; it is your job to protect me, not to shoot me from base desire. Who will be the earth's refuge, now that you have become treacherous and evil-hearted? If only I had listened to Tārā! If you had come to me for help, I would have trounced Rāvaṇa and restored Sītā to you in a moment. Sugrīva will never reach heaven, having stolen the throne by illegitimate means. How can you justify your conduct?"

Rāma replied with conviction, "Why do you rail against me like a child, when you do not know what is right and what is wrong? You have not consulted your elders, yet you attack me, who wishes you only good. This land belongs to my brother Bharata, who not only rules Ayodhyā but is emperor of neighboring kingdoms such as this one. I uphold his commands, punishing wrongdoers and rewarding the virtuous.

"Even for the virtuous, the laws of Dharma are subtle and difficult to grasp, O mighty one. Only the soul, residing in the heart of all beings, knows what is right and what is wrong. It is the duty of the younger brother to serve his older brother, as a son his father. It is the duty of the elder brother to treat the younger brother as his own son.

"You have committed a grievous wrong by stealing your brother's wife, Rūmā, and taking her as your own while he still lives. Such a sin is punishable by death. How can you who break the law expect to escape punishment? Sugrīva is my friend and in my heart I consider him as equal to Lakshmaṇa. I have pledged my word to help him regain his wife and kingdom.

"As it says in the Manu Smṛiti, men who have done wrong are washed free of sin by fulfilling the punishment given by the king—or by his pardon. But the king who pardons the wrongdoer, or overlooks the crime, must himself assume the guilt and do penance. I did not act in anger, nor hastily. I acted in accord with the traditions of my ancestors. One should never reproach a king, nor address him with disrespect. Yet you have insulted me."

These words pierced Bāli's heart deeper than Rāma's arrow. Seeing his errors, he felt ashamed. Though weak, he managed to join his palms together in the timeless gesture of respect. "Out of ignorance, my mind bewildered, I have clearly done wrong in insulting you. In the serenity of your mind, which can never be ruffled, you see the nature of action and its results. Please forgive me, for you are concerned with the welfare of all."

Then, his life ebbing away, he said, "O Rāma, I am worried that my only son, Angada, will die of grief without me. The son of Tārā, he is virtuous, though young and immature. Please watch over him like a father. Show your benevolence to Sugrīva and watch over him as he governs the nation; treat him and Angada as you would Lakshmaṇa. Make certain that Sugrīva treats Tārā with respect and does not hold her responsible. I should have listened to Tārā's words, but my body was destined to die by your arrow, thus liberating me from all cares, O Rāma."

Rāma knelt by Bāli's side and soothed him with comforting words. "You have removed the taint of wrongdoing by paying the penalty. Your soul is cleansed. Do not grieve or be afraid. Angada will be cared for by Sugrīva and by me, just as he was by you. I will make sure he is anointed crown prince, to rule next after Sugrīva."

Bāli, comforted by Rāma's forgiving words, fell into a swoon and did not wake up.

सूक्ष्मः परमदुर्ज्ञेयः सतां धर्मः प्लवंगम ।
हृदिस्थः सर्वभूतानामात्मा वेद शुभाशुभम् ॥

Even for the virtuous, the laws of Dharma are subtle and difficult to grasp.
Only the soul, residing in the heart of all beings,
knows what is right and what is wrong.

—Kishkindhā Kāṇḍa 18.15

Chapter 29

Rāma Grows Impatient on Prasravaṇa Mountain

The sky inhaled the essence of the seas
and stored the elixir in its womb for nine months.
Now it yields up the waters of life,
marking the start of the rainy season.

Water rushes down mountain cliffs
like strings of pearls,
the skies strike in drums of thunder,
and rains fall on the parched land.
Lightning flashes through black clouds
like Sītā writhing in Rāvaṇa's arms.

Steam rises as raindrops
quench the thirst of the hot earth,
bathing the golden hibiscus with cooling nectar,
wrapping the mountainside in green sashes,
sending peacocks into riotous rain dances,
and swans to their mates.

The rains quicken my senses
and heighten my longing for Sītā.
The ripened rose apple oozes red juice.
Bees drink the intoxicating nectar of arjuna blossoms
and elephants trumpet in tune
with the cries of birds.
Clouds thread through the mountains like Sītā's garland
and cover the earth with a curtain of Sītā's tears.

Rāma stood at the mouth of the long, narrow cave where he and Lakshmaṇa were waiting out the rainy season on Prasravaṇa Mountain, near Kishkindhā. After instructing Hanumān to arrange the coronation of Sugrīva, Rāma did not enter the city of Kishkindhā for the coronation, in keeping with his vow to never enter a village or town for the fourteen years of exile. Instead he retired to this quiet cave to reside for the four months of rain, agreeing with Sugrīva to begin the search for Sītā in autumn.

Pacing back and forth, he stopped occasionally to watch the rains pouring down, drumming at the mouth of the cave. The incessant drops were a constant reminder of Sītā's tears.

"O Lakshmaṇa," he said, "I can hear the sounds of music and laughter wafting their way from Kishkindhā. Surely Sugrīva is happy, now that he is reunited with his wife and his kingdom. But I, still bereft of my wife, know not a moment of happiness. Like my tears, the rains pound on and on without end. Each night I lie down to sleep, but I find no rest. To vanquish Rāvaṇa seems impossible." Tears filled his eyes and dropped onto the floor of the cave like rain.

"You can turn the earth from end to end," said Lakshmaṇa. "Surely nothing is impossible for you. Do not let your heart be overcome with grief, for you know that will only bring ruin. Tear out the sorrow from your heart—that is how to tear out the roots of your enemy. Surely Sugrīva will fulfill his promise and summon his army once the rains end. Nurture your intention to destroy Rāvaṇa."

Then he abruptly turned aside so Rāma would not see him wiping away his own tears.

As the weeks passed, the clouds slowly cleared. Finally the sun shone for the first time in months, drying the swollen rivers and soaked earth. Autumn had finally come.

In the monkey kingdom of Kishkindhā, Sugrīva had, indeed, forgotten his vow to Rāma. So long deprived of affection and comfort, he neglected the affairs of the state to revel in pleasure with his wives.

Hanumān, the son of the wind, who was versed in Dharma and knew what acts should be performed at what times, sought out Sugrīva to remind him of his promise to Rāma. He chose words that inspired right action, that considered his ruler's best interests and yet were diplomatic—words that reflected humility yet conveyed confidence that his advice would not be ignored.

"Those who treat with equal respect crown, wealth, friends, and life-breath rule the earth," Hanumān advised Sugrīva, who was lying drowsily on his couch after a night of merrymaking. "Moreover, he meets with disaster who does not set aside everything and help his friend with zeal. It is to Rāma that you owe your good fortune, yet that wise and powerful prince will not remind you that it is time to keep your vow, for that is your responsibility.

"You are powerful and courageous; you help even those who have done nothing for you, so why not help Rāma, who has restored your kingdom? Assemble your army of ten thousand monkeys. Search under the ocean and through the skies for Sītā. Try with all your heart to do what Rāma asked, for he has achieved all that you desired."

Hearing these well-measured words, King Sugrīva came to his senses and called Nīla, the commander in chief of his army, to his side.

"Take Angada, the crown prince, and travel to all the corners of the kingdom," he commanded. "Approach each general in person and tell them to bring their armies to Kishkindhā before fifteen nights are over, on pain of death."

With those words the monkey king retired to his palace.

After the rains stopped, Lakshmaṇa went out each day to hunt for roots and fruits on the mountainside. The lovely Prasravaṇa Mountain was covered with fruit-bearing trees and dense tangles of creepers and undergrowth. One day when he returned, he found Rāma sitting outside the cave, lost in despondent thoughts.

"How can my Sītā live without me?" lamented Rāma. "Sugrīva has forgotten me. He treats me with contempt while I am distraught with grief. Now that the rainy season has ended, he does not wish to honor our pact. Instead he spends his days drinking. It is a marvel to me that he would not keep his vow, when he knows my strength and yours. The valiant stick to their promises. There is none lower than he who refuses to come to the aid of the friend who helped him. Go to Kishkindhā and give that foolish king this message: 'Do not follow the path of Bāli.'"

Seeing his brother overwhelmed with anguish, Lakshmaṇa swelled with anger. "Today I will kill that monkey who has broken his word to you." He jumped up, grabbed his bow, and was halfway out of the cave before Rāma stopped him with soothing words.

"You would not wish to kill a friend, Lakshmaṇa. A warrior should control his anger. Honor the ties of friendship we forged with Sugrīva. Renounce harshness, yet calmly remind him that the time we set for action has already passed."

Thus checking his anger, Lakshmaṇa started down the mountain to Kishkindhā. In his haste, he did not follow the path, but charged down the cliffs, uprooting trees and crunching rocks underfoot. When he reached Kishkindhā and saw all the monkeys guarding the kingdom, his wrath against Sugrīva flared. His eyes flaming red, his lips quivering, his brow furrowed in anger, he frightened the monkeys, who began breaking off trees and hoisting boulders to defend themselves. They clustered outside the gates, baring their teeth. This only made Lakshmaṇa angrier.

Several monkey ministers ran to the palace to warn Sugrīva. Intoxicated, pursuing pleasures with his wives, he did not even hear them.

Finally Bāli's son, Angada, bounded outside the fortress walls to meet Lakshmaṇa.

"Tell your uncle that Lakshmaṇa, the brother of Rāma, awaits him at the gate," commanded Lakshmaṇa.

The young Angada, frightened by Lakshmaṇa's harsh tone, rushed to his uncle and shouted, "Lakshmaṇa has come!" He respectfully bowed to his uncle's feet and to his mother, Tārā, and Rūmā. Sugrīva, sunk in a drunken stupor, did not wake up. Outside, the monkey guards began crying out in tumultuous shouts to welcome Lakshmaṇa, hoping to soften his wrath. The shouting finally penetrated the sleep of Sugrīva, who sat up in a daze.

The ministers, seeing him finally awake, spoke in urgent tones. "Lakshmaṇa stands outside the gate, bow in hand, firing angry glances at the guards. Appease his fury by resting your head on his feet. Fulfill your vow to Rāma and be true to your word."

Sugrīva at last came to himself. He addressed his counselors. "I have not spoken harsh words nor acted wrongly. Why are Rāma and Lakshmaṇa angry with me? It makes me nervous that I have not yet been able to return Rāma's favor to me."

The wise Hanumān stepped forward. "It is clear to me that Rāma is offended because you are letting the autumn pass without honoring your promise. Lost in pleasure, you have been negligent and forgetful. Lakshmaṇa is here to remind you. The only thing to do is to beg Rāma's pardon and submit to his will. It is my duty as a counselor to tell you the truth, and that is why I have spoken thus after thinking deeply."

Angada bounded to the gate and invited Lakshmaṇa inside. The monkey guards parted to make a path, folding their hands respectfully. Suppressing their monkey nature to hop about, they kept their tails tucked under them and barely dared to move as Lakshmaṇa stomped by.

Still breathing fire, Lakshmaṇa followed Angada into the vast cave that was the kingdom of Kishkindhā. It teemed with monkeys, all descendants of the Devas and Gandharvas. Rare jewels of unusual luster decorated the buildings, which were seven stories high. The gardens were filled with fragrant flowers and celestial blossoms that never faded. Lakshmaṇa followed Angada toward the palace of King Sugrīva, rising in high white domes lined with gold. After entering the palace they passed through seven courtyards, finally reaching the innermost chambers, where the chords of the vīṇā sweetened the air. A cluster of female monkeys, adorned in silk and jewels, chatted nearby as they strung garlands of flowers. The shy Lakshmaṇa felt his skin prickle with embarrassment. To hide his discomfort, he twanged his giant bow, making the palace and everyone in it tremble. In the next room Sugrīva turned pale on his throne.

"Tārā," he begged, "will you speak with Lakshmaṇa first? Even though he is angry with me, he will not be harsh with a woman. After you have soothed him with pleasing words, then I will meet him."

The virtuous Tārā, who by custom had become the wife of Sugrīva, her dead husband's younger brother, ambled out to meet Lakshmaṇa. Her hair loosened, her normally modest attire in disarray under the influence of wine, she swayed slightly. Seeing her coming, the bellicose Lakshmaṇa immediately lowered his bow, stared at her feet, and became as docile as a holy man.

"Why are you angry, O greatest of men?" asked Tārā. "Who has failed to please you?"

Lakshmaṇa answered directly, but as courteously as a student in school. "The four months of waiting have long passed, but your husband, lost in sensual pleasures, does not even realize he forgot his oath. Surely you must know that drunkenness brings loss of wealth and virtue, and even sours the ability to enjoy. What's more, it is against the laws of Dharma to fail to return a favor. To lose a friend destroys Dharma. You know the path of Dharma, O daughter of Bṛihaspati. What do you think should be done?"

The wise and lovely Tārā pleaded with Lakshmaṇa, "You who are endowed with all heroic qualities, have patience with those who are lacking them. How could one as pure as you fall prey to anger? I know why you and your brother are frustrated, and I know well what you have done for Sugrīva. But I also am familiar with the power of passion. Even the most exalted Ṛishis have fallen prey to it, so can you not forgive this monkey, who is by nature fickle-minded? Besides, even though he has been boggled by love, Sugrīva has arranged for thousands of monkeys to assemble on this very day."

Having soothed the warrior's anger, Tārā invited him into the inner chamber to meet Sugrīva. When Lakshmaṇa saw Sugrīva sitting on the golden throne, adorned with golden robes and garlands, his beautiful wives surrounding him as the stars surround the moon, his nostrils flared and his eyes turned blood-red with anger once again.

Sugrīva jumped up when he saw Lakshmaṇa enter. In spite of his daze, he stood strong before Lakshmaṇa, like *kalpa-vṛiksha*, the divine wish-fulfilling tree.

"The king who is ungrateful to the friends who have helped him is as guilty as a murderer!" shouted Lakshmaṇa.

Once again, Tārā soothed Lakshmaṇa. "The king of the monkeys is not cruel, nor ungrateful for what Rāma has done. He has only been enjoying his good fortune after years of adversity. Like the sage Vishvāmitra when he was tempted by the nymph Ghṛitāchī, Sugrīva has become lost in physical pleasures and has forgotten that the time has passed for repaying the favor to Rāma."

Seeing Lakshmaṇa's anger melt before Tārā's sensible words, Sugrīva shed his sloth like wet clothes. He tore off his gaudy-colored garlands and snapped out of his drunken haze.

"I owe my life, my kingdom, and my fortune to Rāma," said Sugrīva, pressing his palms together and bowing low. "Rāma will recover Sītā by his own prowess; I am merely his assistant. If I have betrayed his friendship, please forgive me."

Hearing these forthright words, the valiant Lakshmaṇa's anger dissolved. He said in affectionate tones, "O humble king, with the aid of your valor and sincerity, my brother will slay Rāvaṇa in battle. Equal to Rāma in strength, you are brave and virtuous, and you know the way of right action. What other king could recognize his own faults and speak so humbly? No one but my own brother Rāma, and you."

His hands folded in respect, Lakshmaṇa added, "Please forgive me for my harsh words. I spoke hastily because my brother is so acutely distressed. Let us go now to help him."

"Yes, we should act without delay," agreed Sugrīva, now completely recovered from his revelries. To Hanumān, the monkey king said, "I have already sent the swiftest messengers in all the four directions to call the monkey armies here today. Now I call upon the fleetest emissaries to fly to the mountains, to the caves of hills, to the slopes of Mount Meru, to fragrant forests and sheltered glades, to the mansions of the sun, to every quarter of the earth. Summon all the monkeys in their hundreds and thousands to come here today!"

Having done all he could for the moment to help Rāma, Sugrīva turned to his attendants: "Bring the royal palanquin." Soon the glorious conveyance arrived, carried on the shoulders of strong, muscular monkeys and festooned with marigold garlands. Dazzling the eyes with its bejeweled, gilded carvings of birds and trees, it was designed by the divine architect Vishvakarman.

Lakshmaṇa and Sugrīva mounted the royal litter, resting on silken pillows beneath the red and gold canopy. Monkey servants trailed them, waving fans of white yak tails to keep them cool. Conches trumpeted and bards sang the king's praises. Hundreds of monkey warriors swarmed around them as they made their way to Rāma's cave on Mount Prasravaṇa.

Seeing the monkey king arriving with his armies, Rāma drew his breath inward with relief. When Sugrīva stepped down from the palanquin and prostrated himself at Rāma's feet, Rāma raised Sugrīva from the ground, embraced him affectionately, and offered him a seat.

"A true king divides his time between pleasure, the acquisition of wealth, and his responsibilities to others," said Rāma. "To neglect his Dharma is like falling asleep on top of a tree and waking up after he's already fallen. Happy is the monarch who honors his friends, destroys his foes, and pursues equally his duty, wealth, and pleasures."

"Until you restored my kingdom to me, I had lost everything," said Sugrīva humbly. "Now through your grace and your brother's I have regained all. Only a fool would not honor the one who bestowed such favors.

"O Rāma, monkeys and bears are traveling here as we speak. The sons of Devas and Gandharvas, they are mighty and fierce. They know every tree and every crevice in this country, and they can change their shape into any size or form. They will soon arrive with their armies in the thousands. They will join you in searching for Rāvaṇa, they will fight by your side, and they will restore Sītā to you."

At these words, Rāma's heart filled with happiness, and he radiated light like the blue lotus.

Embracing Sugrīva, he said, "Having a friend as noble as you makes me understand how the moon lights the night, how the sun dispels darkness at dawn, how the rains quench the earth's thirst. Now that you support me, I will rescue Sītā and vanquish Rāvaṇa."

Just then the sky turned dark, dust filled the air, and the earth, mountains, and forests shook.

संत्यज्य सर्वकर्माणि मित्रार्थे यो न वर्तते ।
सम्भ्रमाद्विकृतोत्साहः सोऽनर्थेनावरुध्यते ॥

He meets with disaster who does not set aside
everything and help his friend with zeal.

—Kishkindhā Kāṇḍa 29.13

Chapter 30

The Monkeys Search for Sītā

Roaring like thunder,
monkeys of rainbow colors—
pink as the rising sun,
white as the moon,
blazing red as the ginger flower stamen,
golden as the lion's mane,
and black as ash—
blanket the earth,
forests and mountain peaks.

Hanumān and Sushena,
Nīla, Nala, Angada,
illustrious monkey chiefs all,
command armies of thousands.
Shouting, leaping, saluting,
they gather 'round Sugrīva
like storm clouds converging in the sky.

Rāma and Sugrīva looked up to see thousands of monkeys bounding toward them from all directions. Bursting with energy, they gleefully hopped on stones, boulders, and hillsides, leaping over the earth. The leaders of the armies gathered at Sugrīva's feet, offering him gifts and bowing to him as befitted a king.

Sugrīva stood amidst his valiant monkey generals like a mountain in the sea. With his hands folded in devotion to Rāma, he said, "Assembled here are the leaders of my armies, each commanding thousands of ferocious monkeys, strong as titans. They await your orders."

Rāma embraced his friend and said affectionately, "My loyal and courageous friend, you have my best interests at heart. You give the command."

Sugrīva called out his instructions to his valiant generals, first recognizing each for his special abilities. "O Vinata, you are able to turn back time with your hordes of monkeys as bright as the sun and the moon. Take your thousands of monkeys and search for Rāma's highly regarded wife in the mountains, valleys, and rivers to the east. Scour the lowest crevices and the highest mountain peaks, the deepest caves, and crowded cities. Seek also the fortress of Rāvaṇa. Return before a month has passed with your findings. If you wish to live, do not exceed the time, even by a day."

"Angada," commanded Sugrīva, his voice ringing, "you are born to a noble family and are imbued with strength and vitality. Now is the time to reveal your heroism as you explore the regions to the south. Besides all the monkeys in your army, take Hanumān, son of the wind. Take Nīla, son of Agni, the god of fire, and Nala, son of Vishvakarman, the divine architect of the Devas. Take Jāmbavān, king of the bears, and his army. Whoever returns saying, 'I have found Sītā,' will spend the rest of his days in splendor, honored and cherished by me like a brother."

With bowed head and palms placed together in respect, Sugrīva humbly approached the eminent monkey chief Sushena, his wife Tārā's father, and touched his feet. He then turned to the monkey army and announced, "Sushena will lead the army to the west. Listen carefully to all that he commands. Renowned for his bravery and skill in battle, he is also my spiritual teacher."

To the north Sugrīva sent Shatabali. "Search everywhere for Rāma's wife, and do everything that you can to help him," he told the monkeys under Shatabali's command. "Do not go beyond the mountain Soma, for in that region the never-ending night awaits. Return before the month is over."

To each group Sugrīva gave detailed directions, naming every mountain peak, river, valley, and town the armies would encounter. To Hanumān, though, he confided the wishes of his heart, for he fully expected this trusted and enlightened hero to be the one to find Sītā. "Nothing on this earth, in the sky, or in the regions below can stop your progress, most trusted one," said Sugrīva. "You are as quick and energetic as your father, the wind. In your wisdom, strength and courage I place my trust."

Hearing Sugrīva's words to Hanumān, Rāma thought, "Hanumān, the one who has shown his superior valor through his deeds and is considered the most valuable servant by his king, will surely succeed in his duty." With this realization Rāma felt a release of his heavy burden, and happiness filled his heart and mind.

Slowly Rāma extended his hand to Hanumān, offering in his open palm a ring inscribed with his own name. "By this token, most loyal of monkeys, the daughter of King Janaka will know without fear that you are a messenger from me."

Hanumān lifted the ring and touched it to his forehead. He bowed in reverence at Rāma's feet. Resolute in his intention, confident of reaching his goal, Hanumān prepared to depart. Angada's monkey army circled him like a garland.

"Search the four quarters and achieve your purpose!" cried Sugrīva. With that final command, the four monkey armies swarmed north and south, east and west, covering the earth like locusts. Howling and cheering, those brave and skillful warriors set out to vanquish Rāvaṇa.

"We will return Sītā to her lord and destroy the wicked Rāvaṇa!" they shouted. "We will travel to the ends of the earth, even to hell," some cried. "We can leap from the mountains to the sea," said others. "Nothing can stop us."

As the ground trembled beneath their feet, Sugrīva, Rāma, and Lakshmaṇa watched the monkeys depart. When Angada led Hanumān and the vast monkey and bear army to the south, Rāma raised his hand in a final salute. "O Son of the Wind, I depend on your valor," he called after them. "Bring my beloved home to me!"

For the next four weeks, the monkey armies scoured the countryside, seeking the princess of Videha in the north, south, east, and west. They climbed mountains and tramped through forests. At night they slept on the ground, nourished with ripened fruits plucked from the trees. No valley or thicket, peak or plain was left untouched by Sugrīva's massive monkey armies, who combed their assigned regions again and again.

The first army to return was led by the valiant commander Vinata, who came from the east without having seen Sītā anywhere. Next, Shatabali returned from the north with his monkey hosts. He too had nothing to tell Rāma.

Finally, before the month had passed, Sushena arrived from the west, disappointed and empty-handed. After greeting Sugrīva, who sat next to Rāma on the ridge of the mountain, the revered general Sushena said, "It is for the noble-born Hanumān to find Sītā now. Surely he has reached the place where she is hidden."

AT THAT MOMENT, far to the south, Hanumān, Angada, and his followers were lost in a cave, unaware that the month had passed. Here is how it happened. When they left Sugrīva and Rāma, the army searched every crevice of the Vindhya Mountains looking for Sītā. Later they came to a region where no fruits grew, no water flowed, and no birds or animals lived. According to legend, the sage Kaṇdu had cursed the land in anguish when his ten-year-old son was killed.

As they searched this desolate place, a giant rākshasa appeared and charged the monkey army. Thinking it was Rāvaṇa, Angada struck him in the jaw and felled the raging monster like a mighty tree. Later, after searching two caves nearby without finding Sītā, the weary and famished army came to a halt near a stand of spiny bamboo.

Wishing to fulfill his duty to Rāma, Angada tried to rally the monkeys' sagging morale. "Until Sītā has been found, we must comb the area once more. When Lord Rāma entrusts his future to us, it is not right to stop for food, drink, or sleep. Let us not think of ourselves—let us keep searching until we find his cherished wife."

The wisest monkeys, including Hanumān, cheered Angada for his noble leadership. The monkey army, recharged with energy, once again bounded over the thick forests and precipitous valleys of the Vindhya Mountains, searching for Sītā.

Alas, she was not to be found. Yet the weary and thirsty monkeys, their tails dragging and their spirits at a low ebb, continued to hunt for her in the deep caves, high cliffs, and impenetrable forests of the mountain range.

Then they came upon an astonishing sight. A flock of waterfowl, dripping with water, flew from an opening in the mountainside. Concluding that there must be water nearby, the monkeys drew closer. Peering deep into a mammoth cave, they glimpsed a lush and enchanting land. Their senses were delighted by the sight of waterfalls falling from high cliffs, trees laden with fruits and blossoms, and animals ambling on the grassy banks of a river.

"We have wandered far without finding Sītā," said Hanumān. "Let us replenish ourselves with food and water from this cave."

With Hanumān's assent, the monkeys entered the Ṛikshabila Cave. But instead of coming to the lush and verdant valley they had seen from the cave's entrance, they found themselves walking deeper and deeper into a dark and ominous cavern. They heard the roar of lions and bears, and their hair stood on end and they pressed close together for comfort as they wandered for days without light from the sun or stars.

Hungry, thirsty, and almost drained of hope, they finally saw a light far in the distance. As they surged forward, the light became brighter and brighter, until they were enveloped in a shower of light. Fragrance filled the air, and they beheld trees bursting with blossoms of gold, their twigs ruby red, their trunks studded with emeralds. Glittering fish flashed through a tranquil lake crowded with blue lotuses. The path was lined with palaces of gold and silver, their windows draped in pearls, their walls embedded with diamonds and glittering precious gems. Vats of honey, vessels of food, sumptuous piles of silken fabrics, and golden chariots beckoned from all sides.

The light shone on the hollow cheeks of the thirsty monkeys, shrunken with fatigue and hunger, as they wandered through this enchanting land.

In the distance they saw a woman dressed in the garb of an ascetic. After bowing in reverence to her, Hanumān asked courteously, "Who are you? Who owns this magnificent cave with all its splendor and jewels?"

"I am Svayamprabhā," said the pure and holy woman. "I live here with the nymph Hemā, who is skilled in the arts of singing and dancing. Brahmā created this cave for Hemā to live in, and I am her guardian."

Then the sage said, "Please, satisfy your hunger pangs on the enchanted fruits you see all around you. Once you have regained your energy, tell me how you came to this impenetrable place, if your story is fit for me to hear."

After they feasted on the fruits and drank from the jeweled waters, Hanumān told Svayamprabhā about the abduction of Sītā and their search for her. Always courteous, he said, "You have saved us from dying of hunger and thirst. What can we do for you in return?"

The omniscient Svayamprabhā smiled and said, "It was my duty to serve you. You owe me nothing, for you have pleased me."

"Please, holy one," asked Hanumān, "will you help us find our way out of this cave, for only then can we continue to serve Lord Rāma."

"It is difficult for any being to emerge from this cave alive, but with the grace of the spiritual power I have earned through long meditations I can help you," answered the ascetic. "Now you must close your eyes. No one will leave alive if they keep their eyes open."

With dark, slender fingers, thousands of monkeys covered their eyes and a moment later found themselves standing on the opposite side of a mountain than the place where they had entered the cave.

"Behind you soar the auspicious Vindhya Mountains, blanketed with herbs and trees, and before you stretches the endless ocean," said Svayamprabhā, who had accompanied them. "May you enjoy good fortune in your search," she blessed them as she faded out of sight.

But the monkeys had a serious problem. Judging from the blossoming trees, it was already spring. While they were lost in the enchanted cave, they had unknowingly stayed far beyond the time when Sugrīva had ordered them to return.

Angada, his massive shoulders bulging, spoke to the hordes of monkeys as they sat on a wide ledge, watching the waves crashing against the shore far below. "It is not safe for us to return to Sugrīva, for he will surely keep his word and put an end to those who did not follow his orders. He will not spare me, for sure, for the enmity between my uncle and my father is well known. There is no recourse for us but to die fasting here in the wilderness."

The monkeys cried out in terror. "Sugrīva is harsh and Rāma wants only to find his spouse. One who does not follow a king's orders cannot wait upon the king. Unless we find Sītā, we must die."

Then the general Tāra, shining like the moon, tried to soothe them. "Why do we need to die? We can enter this bountiful cave and live out our lives here, feasting on fruits and drinking pure water falling from the heavens. No one, not even Rāma, could find us here."

"Yes," cried the monkeys, "we must save ourselves from an untimely death."

Hanumān stood slightly apart. Seeing that the monkey army was being swayed by fear, he stepped forward to reestablish their minds on their Dharma. Knowing that Angada, the son of Bāli, was wise and brave, Hanumān addressed him first.

"O Angada, you are more valorous than your father and are certainly capable of ruling. But these fickle-minded monkeys will change their minds and want to return home if they are separated from their wives and children for very long. And if you shrink from fulfilling your Dharma, you will never draw Nala, Nīla, Jāmbavān, and myself to your side, not with gifts, not with threats.

"The strong will always overcome the weak, so it is foolhardy for the weak to make the strong their enemy. This cave will provide no safety from the fiery arrows of Lakshmaṇa. These monkeys, far from home, bereft of their loved ones, terrified by Lakshmaṇa's arrows, will desert you.

"If we present ourselves humbly to the magnanimous Sugrīva, he will surely forgive us. He is devoted to your mother, Tārā, and lives to please her. You are her only son; thus Sugrīva will restore you as heir to the kingdom."

Angada shook his head, his eyes burning with tears. "That ruler among monkeys is ruthless. Why else would he seal the cave while my father was inside and take his brother's wife for his own? He will surely imprison me if I return home. The rest of you can return to Kishkindhā, but I will stay here and fast to death. Console my mother, who is pure-hearted and loves me dearly."

With this distressing speech, Angada and the other monkeys groaned and wept at their fate, their cries echoing through the caverns and cliffs of the mountains.

अनेन त्वां हरिश्रेष्ठ चिह्नेन जनकात्मजा ।
मत्सकाशादनुप्राप्तमनुद्विग्नानुपश्यति ॥

By this token, most loyal of monkeys, the daughter of Janaka
will know without fear that you are a messenger from me.

—Kishkindhā Kāṇḍa 44.13

Chapter 31

The Monkey Army Reaches the Ocean

I am the Son of the Wind,
who shatters mountains,
befriends fire,
and spins the earth
on my finger like a ball.
I can circle Mount Meru
a thousand times without stopping.
I can churn the ocean 'til it overflows,
leap to the sun and back
before it sinks in the west.

I can touch the stars and planets,
drink up the infinite ocean,
or flood its shores.
I can shatter mountain peaks
and uproot trees when I fly.
As I flash through the air like lightning,
I can scatter the clouds
and slip through space.

In my heart I have already rescued Sītā,
burned Lankā
and returned victorious.

While Angada and the monkey army wailed and mourned their fate, a vulture watched from a cave high above them. Seeing the monkeys preparing to die, the giant vulture said to himself, "It must be because of good acts in the past that finally this food comes to me."

Angada heard the vulture and said to Hanumān, "All creatures wish to serve and please Rāma; he brings out their natural affection. Just as Jatāyu, the king of the vultures, laid down his life trying to save Sītā, so we monkeys, exhausted from our search, now lay down our lives."

"Who are you, that you speak of Jatāyu?" cried the bird. "I am Sampāti, older brother to Jatāyu. Please carry me down from this peak so I can join you. I cannot fly, for my wings are scorched."

Angada did not wish to help Sampāti move closer, for he feared the great bird would eat them. But the other monkeys said, "He will only help us fulfill our desire to die." They carried the aged bird from the high cliff to their camp on the side of the mountain.

Once Sampāti was seated beside them, Angada told the giant bird the story of Rāma's exile, Sītā's abduction, Jatāyu's valiant fight, and their own miserable plight. "We will surely be put to death by Sugrīva, so we have vowed to end our lives here," he concluded, and the monkeys moaned and wailed once more.

Sampāti listened with tears in his eyes. "You say that my brother was felled by Rāvaṇa's sword, yet I have no way of avenging his death. My wings were singed one day long ago when my brother and I, in our youthful arrogance, wished to fly to the sun. We flew closer and closer, our eyes burning. Grand cities far below looked like tiny chariot wheels and mountains like small stones. My brother started to falter, so I spread my wings over him to shield him. My wings were scorched and I fell here, never to fly again, not knowing what fate befell my brother until now."

"Do you know anything of Sītā?" asked Angada.

"I saw a beautiful woman flying across the skies in a chariot, struggling in the arms of the demon Rāvaṇa. Her golden garments flashed against his dark arms like a lightning bolt among thunderclouds. She cried out again and again, 'O Rāma! O Lakshmaṇa!' Rāvaṇa carried her one hundred yojanas across the sea to the island-kingdom of Lankā, where he lives in unimaginable luxury. Even now, by the power of my extraordinary sight, my eyes can travel across the expanse of the ocean to see her. Sītā is kept under a tree in a garden. You must find a way to cross the crashing waves and rescue her."

The monkeys were transported with joy to finally learn where Sītā was hidden. They somersaulted and leapt down the mountainside, tagging each other and swinging from trees.

"Now I wish to perform the water rites for my dead brother," said Sampāti, his quiet dignity contrasting with the youthful energy of the monkeys. "If you would carry me to the sea that lies at the foot of this mountain, I would be most grateful."

Profoundly moved to have received such valuable information from the ancient bird, Angada dispatched six powerful monkeys to carry Sampāti down the mountain to the ocean below.

After bathing at the shore of the sea and performing his duty to his brother, Sampāti was carried back up the steep mountain path, where he sat amidst a sea of monkeys, who were eager to learn more of Sītā.

"I will tell you how I first learned of Sītā's abduction," said Sampāti. "When I fell, my wings scorched by the sun, I did not regain consciousness for six days. Finally I opened my eyes, but I didn't know where I was. But when the deep caves and high ridges of this mountain came into focus, I realized I had landed on the Vindhya Mountains, home of the ascetic Nishākara, whom my brother Jatāyu and I had visited many times. I dwelled on these mountains for eight thousand years, hoping to see the holy man once again. Finally, I could wait no longer and crawled down the mountain. Near the bottom I found his peaceful hermitage, where the monkeys, tigers, and bears flocked like a river.

"'What has happened to your wings?' asked the compassionate sage when he saw me. 'What dreaded disease has befallen you?' When I told him how I had scorched my wings in the sun due to arrogance and pride, I started to weep. I wished only to end my miserable life by hurling myself down a cliff.

"Nishākara sat quietly for a while, and then he said, 'Your wings will grow again, and you will regain your energy and power. This will happen after you tell the messengers of Rāma where to find his beloved wife, Sītā. It would be possible for me to grow your wings now, but if you wait here long enough, you can perform a great service to Rāma and Lakshmaṇa, as well as to Indra and all the Devas.'

"The sage Nishākara told me the entire future of Rāma's exile, Sītā's abduction and imprisonment on Lankā," Sampāti said to the monkeys. "So many times, in the hundred years since then, I wanted to die, but I remembered his words and waited to tell you this story."

As the bald vulture spoke, a wondrous thing began to happen. Tawny-colored down sprouted on his wings. The monkeys watched, wide-eyed, as the fuzz became feathers and the feathers became golden wings. Slowly, Sampāti spread his immense wings, majestic and youthful once more.

"My new wings are a sign that you will be successful!" cried Sampāti. "Do not delay—cross the wide sea to find Sītā." He could not contain his joy and flew to the top of the mountain.

The monkeys, having witnessed this marvelous sight, were surcharged with energy. They joyously bounded down the mountain, through the valley, and to the shore, eager to rescue Sītā. Yet when they reached the ocean, stretching like a mirror to the cloudless horizon on three sides, they suddenly grew quiet and subdued. Once again, their flighty hearts filled with despair. How would they ever cross it?

"We must not give in to fear," said the valiant Angada. "Doubt and fear will only weaken us."

They spent the night on the sand by the sea. In the morning, Angada wisely called his ministers and elders together. With all the monkey army listening, he addressed them.

"Which one among you can cross the wide ocean to reach Sītā? Which one can leap a hundred yojanas and accomplish the purpose of our king? Who can bring glory to his family and this army, having saved Rāma from despair?"

The monkeys stared at the ground, tucking their tails under them. No one stirred. Not one among them could attempt such a feat.

Angada tried again. "Tell me, praiseworthy leaders of this army, how far each of you can leap."

"I can leap ten yojanas," said Gaja.

"And I twenty," said Gavāksha.

"I can leap thirty," said Sharabha.

"Forty," said Rishabha.

And the mighty Gandhamādana, "Fifty."

Mainda said, "For me, sixty," and the shining Dvivida said, "More than seventy." Susheṇa topped them all, shouting, "Eighty yojanas!"

Then Jāmbavān, the wise leader of the bears, spoke. "When I was young I could leap wondrously far, having circled Vishṇu when he took three steps across the entire world. Now I am old and unsure of my strength, but to help Rāma and Sugrīva we must all give our utmost, so I will leap ninety yojanas."

"I can leap a hundred yojanas," said Angada, "but of the return, I cannot be certain."

"It is not for you to leap ahead," the sagacious Jāmbavān said. "It is for you to command this army. Like a wife by her husband, a commander should be sheltered by his warriors. It is your role to guard the root of the expedition; let others pluck the fruits. You are the essence of this army, the underlying principle, superior in wisdom and valor."

"But if I do not leap the distance," said Angada, "and none of the others can do it, we may as well take up our fast again. For we dare not return without success. Revered Jāmbavān, I leave it to you, as our elder, to point out our path of action."

"There is no obstruction to our success," said Jāmbavān firmly. "I will now call on the one who can carry out the mission without any obstacle."

The entire monkey army held their breath. Quietly and with great dignity, the king of the bears called upon Hanumān. All eyes turned to that foremost of monkeys, who was sitting quietly by himself, his eyes closed, meditating beneath a coconut palm.

"Why are you sitting apart, O Hanumān?" asked Jāmbavān. "You are the equal of Rāma and Lakshmaṇa in strength, versed in the scriptures, wisest and most valorous of all monkeys. You have the strength of Garuda, the king of the birds. Just as his wide wings can carry him across the seven seas, you are strong enough to leap hundreds of yojanas in a single bound. You possess the wisdom, intelligence and courage of the Devas. Prepare yourself to leap across the ocean."

Jāmbavān was the oldest creature present. Like Sampāti, he had been alive at the beginning of time, when the Devas and asuras churned the ocean and the nectar of immortality streamed forth. He knew that Hanumān possessed immeasurable strength, even though Hanumān himself did not remember.

So Jāmbavān began to tell the story of Hanumān's birth, to help him reawaken his dormant powers. "As you know, you are the son of Vāyu, the god of the wind. Your mother, Anjanā, was the most noble and beautiful of all the apsarās. Because of a curse, she was born as a monkey who could assume any form, and later married the monkey Kesarī. One day she assumed the form of a young, radiantly beautiful woman and took a walk on a mountain peak. Your father saw her and was completely enamored. He embraced her, but she called out, 'Who would approach a virtuous wife and destroy her marriage?'

"'Do not be afraid,' your father said. 'You will give birth to a son unsurpassable in strength and wisdom.'

"And so she raised you in a mountain cave. One day when you were playing outside, you saw the sun and thought it was a ball. You leapt over three thousand yojanas to the sun without getting burnt. Indra saw you, and threatened by your strength, struck you down with his thunderbolt. You plummeted to the earth and still survived, although you broke your jaw. And Hanumān, that is how you got your name, 'the one of the fractured jaw.'

"Angry with Indra, your father stopped the wind from blowing across the three worlds. Finally, to appease your father, Brahmā bestowed the boon of invincibility upon you. Indra, amazed at how you were barely affected by his thunderbolt, offered yet another boon: you would never die until you chose to. Thus mollified, the wind started to blow across the land again."

Jāmbavān's next words were full of joy. "You are as swift and powerful as your father, the wind. You are the lord among monkeys. We look to you to save us. No one else can accomplish this task. Look to your inner strength, your own infinite power. Rise up and leap over the ocean, O Hanumān!"

As the monkey army watched in astonishment, Hanumān began to swell, as the ocean swells when the moon is full, and soon he rose far above them, as tall as the mountain itself. The Devas arrived from the four quarters to watch this miraculous event, and the monkey army cheered and shouted in jubilation. As Hanumān grew in size, he waved his tail slowly like a flag, showing his incredible strength.

Towering far above the monkey crowds, his hair standing on end, Hanumān stretched his mouth wide, blazing like a smokeless flame. "*Bhara, bhara!*" he cried. "Back, back to the Self!"

"O hero, you have dispelled all fear," cried Jāmbavān. "We stand on one foot until you return. Our lives depend on you!"

Roaring with joy, Hanumān leapt to the top of a nearby peak, Mount Mahendra. And as he leapt with terrific force, elephants fled, waterfalls spouted, and cliffs dropped away. The flower-carpeted mountain uttered a cry as Hanumān prepared to leap again, this time all the way to Lankā. Having settled his mind, the spirited Hanumān, hero among monkeys, slayer of enemies, gifted with great swiftness and possessed of immense strength, fixed his awareness on speed and took himself to Lankā in thought.

स वेगवान्वेगसमाहितात्मा हरिप्रवीरः परवीरहन्ता ।
मनः समाधाय महानुभावो जगाम लङ्कां मनसा मनस्वी ॥

Having settled his mind, the spirited Hanumān,
hero among monkeys, slayer of enemies,
gifted with great swiftness and possessed of immense strength,
fixed his awareness on speed and took himself to Lankā in thought.

—Kishkindhā Kāṇda 67.49

End of the Kishkindhā Kāṇda

FIVE

Sundara Kāṇda

The Beautiful City

Chapter 32

Hanumān's Great Leap

He followed the path of the wind,
Hanumān, the pure of heart,
his monkey limbs covered in blossoms
fallen from trees uprooted with his first leap.
He scattered the waves
and devoured the sky,
soaring through the clouds
so quickly the air clapped like thunder.
He parted the heavens,
rushing like the wind,
his eyes burning like two fires,
the ocean below rising
in mighty waves to greet him.
His shadow spread forty yojanas on all sides
like the wings of the king of birds.
To help this servant of Rāma,
the sun cooled its rays,
and the wind softened its blows.
The sea offered its hidden mountains as footstools,
and Gandharvas sang joyful songs
to speed him on his way.

Hanumān leapt with such force that blossoming trees were uprooted and spun after him through space, following him like subjects follow their king. As they plunged into the sea, they scattered their blossoms over the multitude of astonished monkeys and bears, who watched from the shore.

"I fly to Lankā with the speed of the wind!" exclaimed the ecstatic Hanumān before he flew out of sight. "I will return with tidings of Sītā or with the rākshasa king himself in chains."

The Devas, Gandharvas, and Ṛishis, watching from above, rang bells and blew conches, delighted with Hanumān's strength. The lord of the sea, Sāgara, vowed to help Hanumān. He spoke to his highest mountain, hidden beneath the waves, which guarded the gate to the underworld. "Golden-wreathed Maināka, who protects the earth from the demons below, rise up and greet the messenger of Rāma, who flies above you and needs a place to rest. In days of old the sons of Rāma's ancestor King Sagara, protector of the Ikshvākus, hollowed out the ocean and created a place for me to rest. So I must return the favor to this servant of Rāma."

As Hanumān soared across the sky, he saw Mount Maināka suddenly burst from the waters, blocking his path. Its charming peaks of gold reached to the sky, its cliffs covered with trees and celestials playing lutes. Determined to let no obstacle stop him, he flew straight into it, smashing its peak.

Instead of being angry, Mount Maināka rejoiced in Hanumān's strength. Taking the form of a human being, he sat on his own summit and lovingly called out to Hanumān, "O jewel among monkeys, take a moment to rest on your heroic journey. The king of the ocean, who received help from Rāma's ancestor Sagara and his sons, wishes to serve you by offering my mountain peak as your seat. Rest here, feast on my fruits and drink from my waterfalls."

When Hanumān didn't appear to be stopping, Maināka added, "There is another reason for me to honor you. Many years ago, when all the mountains had wings and flew across the skies, the celestials and ascetics who lived on the mountainside trembled in fear of falling off. So Indra struck off the wings of the mountains with his thunderbolt. Your father, the wind god Vāyu, saved me by hiding me under the sea, where I could keep my wings intact. I honor you, O Son of the Wind, and welcome you with great joy!"

Hanumān smiled and touched the mountain affectionately with his hand as he passed overhead. "I thank you for the warm welcome from you and Sāgara, the ocean king," he said with respect. "But I must keep going. The day is passing, and I have vowed not to rest until I reach Lankā."

"Well done!" cried the Devas and other celestials. Indra praised Mount Maināka for offering help to Hanumān and granted the boon that the ancient mountain would never lose its wings. Then Mount Maināka sank to its place under the sea.

Now the Devas, having glimpsed Hanumān's true strength and determination, decided to test him. They called forth Surasā, mother of the serpents, who rose from the depths of the ocean to greet them. "Take the form of a female demon, as tall as a mountain, with jaws that stretch to the sky," they ordered her. "Try to stop Hanumān."

Honored to serve the wishes of the Devas, Surasā swelled into a hideous rākshasī, her jaws yawning. When she saw Hanumān flying toward her, she howled, "O mightiest of monkeys, you are destined to feed me. Fly into my mouth so I can eat you." With those words she opened her mouth so wide that she blotted out the sun.

Hanumān smiled politely and said, "I cannot feed you now because I have vowed to help Rāma recover his wife, Sītā. Once Sītā is safely restored to Rāma of the great deeds, then I will return to enter your mouth."

"No one can pass by me alive," screeched the rākshasī, her frightful body hovering above the sea, blocking his path. "Due to Brahmā's boon, you must first enter my mouth before you search for Sītā."

Seeing that gigantic monster in his way, Hanumān swelled with wrath. "Open your mouth wide enough to swallow me," he dared. Hanumān grew until he was forty yojanas wide, but Surasā's jaw merely opened wider. Hanumān grew by fifty yojanas, and her jaws spread still wider to swallow him. Every time she increased the size of her mouth, Hanumān swelled his body so he was even bigger. Finally, when Surasā was busy stretching her ghastly mouth still wider, Hanumān abruptly shrank to the size of a thumbnail. As quick as a blink of the eye, he flew into her mouth and out again.

"I salute you, O lady of the sea," said Hanumān respectfully. "I have honored your boon by entering your mouth. Now I must continue my search for Sītā."

Seeing Hanumān fly out of her mouth, Surasā shrank to her usual form and bowed her head in respect. "I honor you, chief of monkeys. You have done well. Now go and fulfill your divine purpose."

"Wonderful!" cried the Devas, Gandharvas, and Ṛishis. Celestial beings thronged the sky in chariots driven by lions, elephants, and tigers. Satisfied with Hanumān's prowess and delighted with his feats, they showered him with rose petals.

On Hanumān flew, piercing the clouds. He floated through the air as gracefully as a bird, traversing the canopy of the sky along with the sun and moon.

Suddenly Hanumān felt something tugging him backward. "What has stopped me like a cloud blown back by headwinds?" he wondered. Glancing behind, he saw another terrifying female rākshasī rising from the ocean, grasping his shadow in her claws. Hanumān immediately recognized the frightful demon Siṁhikā, who was known to capture her prey by first seizing its shadow.

Now again Hanumān swelled to the size of a thundercloud. Siṁhikā stretched her mouth wider than the sky to devour him. Howling like the wind in winter, she pounced on him. But just as with Surasā, Hanumān was too quick for Siṁhikā. He disappeared into the cavern of her mouth like the full moon being devoured by Rāhu. As quick as thought, he snapped her heart with his teeth and flew out again. Howling in pain, she dropped his shadow. Then he swelled even larger, waxing in strength like the moon, while the giant rākshasī fell into the ocean.

"Well done, O hero!" shouted the crowds of Devas, Gandharvas, and Ṛishis, still watching from the heavens. "Now you will accomplish your purpose with no hindrance. This is the way to succeed—with wisdom, courage, and skill—and with your mind focused on your purpose."

Long before nightfall Hanumān reached the far shore, alighting on one of the three peaks of Trikūta Mountain, which was crowded with trees. He shrank his body to its normal size, not wishing to attract the attention of the demons that lived there. Having crossed the vast ocean without stopping, Hanumān felt no fatigue. "I can fly hundreds of yojanas, so one hundred is not such a great feat," he thought.

There he stood, not even out of breath, and gazed across the valley to the tallest peak of Trikūta Mountain, crowned with the legendary city of Lankā. Even from a distance, he could see the city's glistening white buildings reaching high into the clouds, as if they were floating in the air. Flower gardens, parks, and ponds, flocked with birds, graced the shining city. Tall marble buildings with countless towers lined wide boulevards, and arches covered with flowering vines spanned the highways. Created by Vishvakarman, the architect of the Devas, it rivaled Amarāvatī, the city of the gods.

Bounding with vigor, Hanumān leapt down from the peak where he stood and hopped nimbly over the woods and wide fields until he faced the lotus-filled moat of Lankā. Facing the high golden walls, inlaid with cat's-eye gems, Hanumān saw that they were heavily guarded by demons armed with giant bows and arrows. He sat still and pondered how to enter the guarded city, inaccessible even to Devas and asuras.

यस्य त्वेतानि चत्वारि वानरेन्द्र यथा तव ।
धृतिर्दृष्टिर्मतिर्दाक्ष्यं स कर्मसु न सीदति ॥

O best of monkeys, this is the way to succeed—with wisdom, courage, and skill—and with your mind focused on your purpose.

—Sundara Kāṇḍa 1.201

Chapter 33

The Jewel of Lankā

Behold Lankā,
high on Mount Trikūta.
Born of Vishvakarman,
her pavement studded with pearls, crystals, and gems,
the notes of pealing bells and musical instruments
ride on her breezes.
Banners stream from her golden wall,
and her towers touch the heavens.

Her streets are lined with mansions
upheld by golden pillars,
with crystal stairways
and emerald floors,

windows of diamond,
screens of gold,
and balconies of silver.
Beautiful women walk freely,
their precious ornaments tinkling.
Peacocks cry
and swans glide in pools of lotus flowers.
Thinking of Sītā, Hanumān
sees only a prison
that must come down.

As Hanumān gazed across the moat at the impenetrable fortress that was Lankā, he felt a twinge of doubt. "Besides myself, only Angada, Nīla, and Sugrīva are capable of leaping the ocean," he thought. "And how will Rāma, even if he can cross the wide sea, penetrate these formidable ramparts?"

Then he shook his head, to banish doubts and focus on the task at hand. "First I must find Sītā." He decided to begin his search at night, at an auspicious moment. The wise Hanumān thought through his strategy in detail, for he knew that even the best plans can go awry if the messenger is not careful.

"I will disguise myself as a rākshasa," he thought. But he soon realized that the real rākshasas would find him out. Finally, he decided to go as himself, but smaller, so he could enter the mansions undetected.

As nightfall crept over the city, the milky moon rose like a swan in the sky, and Hanumān thanked that celestial orb for lighting his way. He sprang across the moat and stood outside the northern gateway of Lankā, which rivaled in splendor the entrance to Kubera's residence high on Mount Kailāsa. He saw what looked like a foothill beside the gate, which turned out to be a hulking rākshasī, irritable from having her sleep interrupted.

"Who are you and why do you come here?" the giant ogre roared as she stood up and blocked his way. "No one enters the city of Rāvaṇa!"

"I will answer if you first tell me who you are," said Hanumān amiably.

"I am Lankā, the deity of the city," said the giant. "I guard the gate. Anyone who tries to enter will be crushed by my blows."

The courageous Hanumān said, "I wish to see this fair city, to explore its gardens and its mansions of many stories."

"Are you deaf?" shouted Lankā. "No one enters the city of the rākshasas unless they wish to face me."

"If you let me in, I promise to return here, auspicious lady," said Hanumān politely.

Lankā could bear it no longer. Swinging her massive arm, she cuffed Hanumān with the palm of her hand. Hanumān roared and, pouncing on her back, struck her with his left fist. He softened the blow because she was a woman, but even so the giant fell to the ground, moaning and crying for mercy.

"O monkey of the mighty fist, spare me!" she cried. "You have conquered me with your courage and strength. Listen now, for Brahmā predicted long ago that when a valorous monkey overcame me by force, the rule of the evil King Rāvaṇa would end and Lankā would be destroyed. Enter this doomed city and roam it freely, for Rāvaṇa has brought his own destruction by abducting the chaste Sītā."

The brave Hanumān scaled the wall and peered at the fortress city below, lit by lanterns as if it were daylight. To avoid being detected, he shrank to the size of a cat. Landing on his left foot, auspicious for vanquishing enemies, he moved silently through the golden streets.

From lighted mansions poured the sounds of women laughing and the chiming of their golden bangles. Looking for Sītā, Hanumān leapt from rooftop to rooftop, climbing walls to peer in the windows. He saw garlanded rākshasīs resting in the arms of their husbands. He saw courtesans with their slanted eyes and flashing jewels. Passing other dwellings he heard the low, rhythmic recitation of Vedic texts floating through the windows. Gatherings of rākshasas sang the praises of Rāvaṇa, while others engaged in heated debates, pounding the tables with their ferocious fists. In other homes rākshasas spoke intelligently and with courtesy.

He passed wandering mendicants, their faces smeared with paste, golden robes shining in the night. Some rākshasas were repulsive to see, others beautiful and radiant.

In a wide courtyard Hanumān saw scores of rākshasas armed with spears, swords, and clubs. Beyond these guards, he came to the royal citadel, set high on its own hill, girded by a lotus-filled moat and tall golden walls. A low rumble of elephants, horses, and chariots milling about filled the air, mixing with the pleasant sounds of music and laughter. Hanumān gazed at the radiant moon, splendid with cooling light, dispelling the sins of the world, swelling the oceans. Slipping under high arches, still the size of a cat, Hanumān entered the famed palace of Rāvaṇa unimpeded.

Precious jewels covered the palace ceiling, its walls clad in fragrant sandalwood. Highborn women reclined on cushions or strolled about, dressed in silks of brilliant colors. Dancers shook their tambourines and singers sang pleasing melodies. The charming music of drums and flutes sweetened the air.

"So this is the jewel of Lankā," thought Hanumān. He had never seen such a splendid palace; it was said to surpass even the abode of Indra. Hanumān wandered through vast art galleries, pavilions, and entertainment halls graced by gem-studded pillars. Inner courtyards abounded with lush gardens populated by waterfowl and deer. One garden replicated Mount Mandara, soaring to the sky, home to peacocks and exotic birds, complete with trees and flowers.

Jeweled chariots and golden palanquins filled a cavernous warehouse in the palace. There Hanumān saw Rāvaṇa's heavenly chariot Pushpaka, which could fly above the rooftops as swiftly as the wind, propelled by the thought of its driver. Stolen from Rāvaṇa's half brother Kubera, it was made by the divine architect Vishvakarman of burnished red sandalwood and decorated with life-size statues of horses studded with precious metals and gems. Birds made of emerald, silver, and coral adorned its sides.

The astonishing chariot rose like a mountain peak covered with flowers. The interior was lavishly outfitted with a gleaming pearl-studded floor, blue sapphire galleries, shining pavilions, winding golden staircases, and pillars embedded with rubies. A statue of Shrī Lakshmī graced a lotus pool, flanked by white marble elephants holding lotus leaves in their tapering trunks.

Not finding Sītā in that resplendent chariot, Hanumān began to search the private suites in which Rāvaṇa himself resided.

These chambers were even more opulent. Illuminated by golden ghee lamps, the walls were draped with intricately woven tapestries. Thick carpets adorned the floors and the sweet smells of incense and ambrosial wines filled the air. Like a mother, Rāvaṇa's palace soothed all the five senses, making Hanumān wonder, "Can this be the dwelling of Rāvaṇa? Is this paradise, the city of the Devas, or have I entered the state of supreme bliss?"

The lovely wives of Rāvaṇa lay dozing, entwined in each other's arms like flowers in a garland. Having fallen into slumber in the midst of their revelries, some still grasped vīṇās or tambourines. The smell of sweet wine perfumed their lips, and their loosened jewelry lay scattered like stars across the sky. These consorts, the daughters of celestials, kings, and Ṛishis, had been won by Rāvaṇa in battle or had surrendered to him in love. Unlike Sītā, whose heart belonged to Rāma, not one had been taken against her will, and not one had been the wife of another. Endowed with grace, beauty, and nobility, they were devoted to Rāvaṇa.

"Sītā must be superior to all of these women," thought Hanumān, "because the lord of Lankā has risked everything to capture her."

Now Hanumān saw, in the midst of the sleeping women, the luxurious royal bed of Rāvaṇa, emblazoned with gold and encrusted with pearls and diamonds, with a gleaming white canopy festooned with garlands of ashoka blossoms.

Hanumān shrank back, for lying before him was the king of the rākshasas himself. With his ten heads lying across the bed like the fan of a peacock, his earrings sparkled, and his golden robes dazzled the eyes. Big as a mountain, dazzling as the sun reflecting on the open sea, Rāvaṇa lay sleeping on the bed, his wine-stenched breath masking the sweet perfume from the agarwood walls. As he snored, he alternated between the rumble of an unhappy elephant and the hiss of an angry serpent.

Hanumān gazed at the twenty mighty arms tumbling from the bed like a waterfall, laced with rings and jeweled bracelets, and smeared with sandalwood paste and red saffron by his loving wives. Unvanquished by the sharp tusks of Indra's white elephant Airāvata or Indra's thunderbolt, these were the arms that struck fear into the hearts of Devas, Gandharvas, and men.

Then Hanumān saw another royal bed slightly apart from Rāvaṇa's. On it lay a lovely woman clad in silken robes and precious jewelry, whose inner radiance lit the room. Thinking it was Sītā, he leapt about in joy, fanning his tail and frolicking up and down golden pillars in monkey fashion.

Then he came to a standstill, for Hanumān knew suddenly and surely that Sītā would never sleep in Rāvaṇa's chambers. "Sītā would not be able to eat, sleep, or dress in lavish garments. Her mind and heart fixed on Rāma, she would submit to no other consort." He realized that the radiant woman sleeping near Rāvaṇa was none other than his favorite queen, Mandodarī.

Hanumān crept away from the royal bedchamber and made his way out of the palace, through the banquet hall, where golden couches shone like flames. Delicate sauces and the meat of rare animals filled exquisitely decorated plates. Vessels inlaid with ivory and pearls held rare wines made from the blossoms of trees. Sumptuous desserts and fruits lay scattered among sleeping women.

As he silently passed by, the honorable Hanumān regretted gazing on the women while they were sleeping. "Yet I must look for Sītā," he reflected. "It is also true that my mind remains untroubled, unstirred. It is with a pure heart that I search for Sītā among these women."

Ruminating on these thoughts, Hanumān left the palace. By now he had searched the greater part of Lankā without finding Sītā.

"She may have slipped from Rāvaṇa's arms and fallen into the ocean as he flew across the wide sea," he thought in despair. "Or perhaps Rāvaṇa has killed her because she would not submit to him."

Doubts crowded his mind. "What will I say to Sugrīva and Rāma, when I return without finding Sītā? Perhaps it is better to fast to death than to return empty-handed."

Fortunately, it wasn't long before his usual equanimity began to restore itself. "Perseverance is the source of success and happiness," he remembered. Then he made a vow: "I will search the gardens and palaces that I have not yet searched, and then I will search again in those areas I have already seen."

Having resolved to continue, he peered into the balconies, galleries, and gardens of the mansions of Lankā. He glanced at women of every shape, beautiful and revolting, who lived in Lankā. He opened and closed doors, crawled through windows, climbed towers, and combed every inch of the kingdom.

He had explored every corner of the wondrous city and still could not find Sītā. The valiant Hanumān sank into a chasm of dark thoughts, certain he had crossed the ocean in vain.

अनिर्वेदः श्रियो मूलमनिर्वेदः परं सुखम् ।
भूयस्तत्र विचेष्यामि न यत्र विचयः कृतः ॥

Perseverance is the source of success and happiness.
I will search the places that I have not yet searched.

—Sundara Kāṇḍa 12.10

Chapter 34

Hanumān Finds Sītā

O Sītā!
Under the ashoka tree
she sits on the bare ground
refusing food, water, or rest.
Pale and thin,
her radiance shadowed,
her tears soak the earth.
The sun veils its face in shame,
hidden by clouds.
Sītā grieves like a night without the moon,
a flame snuffed out,
a garden without rain.
Yet Rāma fills her heart,
Rāma is her salvation,
and Rāma is all that she sees.

Having scoured the city of Lankā twice in one night without finding Sītā, Hanumān could not contain his despair. Sitting on a wall overlooking the palace, his tail drooped and he held his head in his hands.

"Sītā must surely be dead," he thought. "But how can I tell Rāma? It would be wrong to withhold information, yet how can I offend him by telling him my fears? If I return without news of Sītā, then Rāma and

Lakshmaṇa will die of despair, and Bharata, too, will give up his life. Without their sons, the worthy mothers of those warriors will not go on living. And Sugrīva, Rāma's perfect friend, will die of grief."

Drowning in despair, Hanumān couldn't stop his mind from spinning dreadful thoughts. "And what will happen to Rūmā without her lord, and Tārā? They will surely die, too. Without his parents, the youthful Angada will wander through the forest sunk in misery. Deprived of his loved ones, he too will die. Then what will happen to the monkey kingdom, with no leaders to defend them? They will hurl themselves into canyons or impale themselves on their weapons. By returning with this devastating news, I will destroy two illustrious kingdoms."

Hanumān determined never to return to Kishkindhā. "That way those two noble brothers can at least live with the hope of finding Sītā," he thought. "I will become an ascetic in the forest, or I will enter the flames. My heroic deeds of the past have faded like a garland, now that I have failed in my quest."

But once again the wise Hanumān could not be lost long in these dark thoughts. He shook his head, drew a sharp breath, and rallied his courage. "I will not return empty-handed, because that would mean death to Rāma and all the others," he resolved. "I will not take my life, because that brings innumerable evil consequences. If I continue to search for Sītā, then there is still hope that she will be found. At the very least, I will kill the demon Rāvaṇa to avenge Sītā's death!"

While thinking these courageous thoughts, he suddenly noticed for the first time a grove of ashoka trees set away from the palace and illuminated in the moonlight.

"This must be Rāvaṇa's famous Ashoka Grove, the pleasure garden of his wives," he thought. "After calming my mind, I will enter that auspicious Ashoka Grove to continue my search for Sītā. May Brahmā, Agni, Varuṇa, Vāyu, Indra, Sūrya, Chandra, and all the celestial beings grant me success. Let me find the chaste Sītā and deliver happy news to Rāma."

Having already found Sītā in his mind, Hanumān bounded from the wall. In one leap he landed in the Ashoka Grove, his courage and vigor renewed.

There cuckoos, peacocks, and exotic birds flocked, and deer slept under the ashoka trees. As Hanumān leapt from tree to tree, he showered bright orange flower petals on them like rain.

As he swung through the grove, snapping creepers and vines in his haste, Hanumān marveled at lovely lotus pools surrounded by fragrant flowers of all kinds. Crystal streams meandered through clusters of flaming red ashoka trees, and in the distance, flowering jasmine bushes sparkled in the moonlight like women's bracelets.

"This sumptuous garden of Rāvaṇa's is even more delightful than the legendary Nandana Grove of Indra or the Chaitraratha Grove of Kubera," thought Hanumān. "I will wait high in a tree beside this clear stream, for surely Sītā will visit here, thinking of her days in the forest with her lord."

Seating himself on a branch, he saw that he was near a gleaming marble temple with walls of gold, steps of coral, and pillars covered in starry gems. Beside the temple, a woman sat on the bare ground guarded by female demons. Even from a distance, Hanumān could see that she was of uncommon beauty. Though tears washed her face, her inner radiance lighted the night. Her eyes roved to and fro like a doe in distress as she sighed again and again.

"This lovely-eyed lady, so pure, must surely be Sītā!" thought Hanumān.

Her face was like the full moon, her lips like ripened *bimba* fruit, her eyes like lotus petals, and her eyebrows arched like butterfly wings. With graceful limbs and neck, her skin glowed, despite the darkness that covered her.

"In looks and nobility, she is surely Rāma's mate," thought Hanumān. "It is clear that she thinks only of him; that thought alone keeps her alive. I can see now why Rāma has turned the world upside down to find her."

Hanumān also saw that she wore a bracelet on her arm that matched the ornaments flung down from the sky on that fateful day when Rāvaṇa carried her across the skies. Her yellow garment matched the bright silken scarf she had dropped to the monkeys below. As Hanumān watched, tears streamed down her face and she closed her eyes as if to stop them, covering her face with her sārī. Yet despite the tears, her face looked resolute. "Her mind is fixed on Rama," thought Hanumān.

Seeing the chaste and tender spouse of Rāma in such distressing circumstances, her face thin and pale from lack of food and water, Hanumān felt his own tears slipping down his face. "Surely destiny is all-powerful; otherwise, how could the rival of Lakshmī, protected by the powerful Rāma, be sitting here in the midst of these vicious rākshasa women?"

Oblivious to the gruesome rākshasas surrounding her, Sītā sat unadorned, her chief ornament her devotion to Rāma. Some of the rākshasa guards had only one eye, some only one ear, some sported a nose sticking out of their forehead. Like a water lily snapped from its stem, like Rohiṇī being harassed by evil planets, Sītā was trapped in the midst of these monsters.

Having found Sītā at last, Hanumān bowed to Rāma in his mind, offering words of praise, grateful that he was able to accomplish his great purpose.

As Hanumān sat high in the tree observing Sītā, the night slipped away. The golden chariot of dawn drew near, and Hanumān heard the chanting of the Vedas far in the distance. Then, just as the sun shed its first rays of light on the enchanting Ashoka Grove where Sītā sat, patient as the earth, the jingle of bells and women's jewelry filled the air.

Far in the distance Hanumān saw Rāvaṇa walking slowly toward Sītā, his passion drawing him like a bee to honey. Close behind him trailed a hundred of his devoted wives, their eyes droopy from sleep and wine. Some carried golden vessels of water, others followed with golden cushions, and still others with fans. Several women bore ghee lamps to light the way, one carried a gem-decorated cup filled with wine, and another held up a parasol over her lord, spread wide like the wings of a swan.

Wearing a silken cloak, his twenty arms adorned with countless jeweled ornaments, his eyes flaming red with desire, Rāvaṇa entered the garden gate. For just a moment, the power and brilliance of the demon king's body made even the valiant Hanumān shrink behind the boughs of the tree.

As Rāvaṇa strode toward her, surrounded by his proud wives like the planet Jupiter surrounded by its moons, Sītā saw him coming and began to shake like a palm in the wind. She drew her garments around her and again fixed her mind on Rāma. The haughty, impeccably attired Rāvaṇa towered above the helpless Sītā, hoping to win her favors.

"Why do you try to hide from me in fear, O radiant lady?" asked Rāvaṇa in his softest voice. "You know that I love you. Your beauty is renowned throughout the world. You have no rival. I could take you by force, but I am enchanted by you, so I will not lay hands on you."

Sītā said nothing, sobbing quietly.

"Stop lying in the dust, refusing water and food, and become the ruler of my palace, filled with gems, silks, servants, singing, dancing, feasting, and music," Rāvaṇa wheedled. "Your youth is passing like a river to the sea. All this magnificent kingdom—indeed, all that is mine—I lay at your dusty feet and offer to your father Janaka."

Sītā still did not respond.

"Rāma cannot even find you," said Rāvaṇa, his voice louder now.

"Nor can he, weak and deprived of his kingdom, conquer me. No one can. So, lady of graceful beauty, cease this asceticism and enjoy all the pleasures of the world with me."

Hearing these insults to her husband, the virtuous Sītā, her heart faithful to Rāma, stood up. Once again she held up a single blade of grass between herself and Rāvaṇa. Her voice quivering with emotion, she said, "Take back your heart and give it to your lawful wives. I will never be unfaithful to my husband. Just as the sun's rays cannot be separated from the sun, so I cannot be separated from Rāma. No riches in the world exist that can make me wish to rest in the arms of another man."

Then she added, "The ruler who is not master of himself brings ruin to his kingdom. This Lankā, overflowing with treasure, is doomed. If you continue in these evil actions, the whole universe will rejoice at your death. If, on the other hand, you return me to Rāma and seek to reconcile with him, he will offer his mercy to one who seeks safety in him. Otherwise, nothing can save you. You may have escaped the thunderbolt of Indra, you may have escaped Death itself, but you will never escape the terrifying bow of Rāma." With these powerful words, Sītā turned her back to Rāvaṇa.

Rāvaṇa was beside himself with fury. He had never been refused by a woman, as all were enamored by his power and glory. He spat his words instead of speaking them. "I have heard that women respond to gentleness, but you become more resistant the more I shower you with kindness. It is a sign of my unfathomable love that I do not kill you for your impertinence. But even I cannot stand much more of this. If you do not succumb to me in two months, I will have my chefs cook you for my breakfast and I will drink your blood."

The wives of Rāvaṇa, themselves daughters of Devas and Gandharvas, were filled with pity for Sītā, and without Rāvaṇa noticing, some of them silently made sympathetic gestures to Sītā.

Seeing their support, Sītā gained courage. She turned to face Rāvaṇa once again. "It appears that your advisors desire your destruction, otherwise they would prevent you from persisting in this suicidal path. Who would dare to insult the consort of Rāma? It is easy for you to say wicked things about him when he does not stand before you. O vile demon, you will not escape the fury of Rāma."

Her voice growing stronger as she spoke, Sītā continued, "By the power of my virtue and tapas, I could turn you to ashes this instant if Rāma wished it. All who are wise and righteous in the world wonder why your eyes didn't burn when you first gazed at me with evil intent. Why didn't your tongue fall out when you addressed these despicable words to me? There is only one answer—the Devas allowed you to capture me only to orchestrate your own destruction."

Rāvaṇa's eyes rolled in rage and shot angry sparks. "I will destroy you today, you perverse wretch!" He raised his hand to strike her.

Then Mandodarī, the beloved first wife of Rāvaṇa, rushed to his side. With gentle and charming words she quieted the raging king of the demons. "What need have you for Sītā? Come, enjoy yourself with me."

Subdued for the moment, Rāvaṇa spoke privately to the ogres who surrounded Sītā, "Find a way to bring her to me, whether it be through threats or bribes, fearful or sugary words."

Whirling around, Rāvaṇa stomped back to the palace, shaking the earth. He did not look back, leaving Sītā at the mercy of the vicious rākshasa women.

एवं सीतां तथा दृष्ट्वा हृष्टः पवनसम्भवः ।
जगाम मनसा रामं प्रशशंस च तं प्रभुम् ॥

Having seen Sītā at last, the joyful Hanumān bowed down to Rāma in his mind, offering words of praise.

—Sundara Kāṇḍa 15.54

Chapter 35

Sītā in the Ashoka Grove

Closing in around her, brandishing their weapons, the rākshasīs shrieked at Sītā in anger. "You do not properly respect Rāvaṇa, who is the grandson of the holy Pulastya, the son of the Creator himself," screeched Ekajatā, a demoness with red-flaming eyes. "Give up your foolish pride and marry this descendant of Brahmā, lady of long eyelashes."

One with the face of a cat snarled, "Unite yourself with the scourge of foes, who has conquered the thirty-three celestials, defeated the Devas, and rules the earth."

"Lady of sweet smiles, forget about Rāma, who has lost his kingdom, and submit to the one who is king of kings, who can offer you all the luxury and pleasures of Lankā," a rākshasī with only one eye tried to coax her.

Sītā shrank from their weapons and her eyes filled with tears. "What you suggest is morally wrong. If you wish to eat me, you may do so, but I will never be untrue to Rāma. My husband is my spiritual guide, whether he is reigning on the throne in Ayodhyā or wandering penniless through the forest. I will follow him always, as the faithful Arundhatī follows her husband Vasishtha, the nakshatra Rohiṇī follows the moon, and Lakshmī follows Vishṇu."

Sītā's innocent words only made the rākshasa women more angry. "You think you are too good for Rāvaṇa," they screamed. They crowded around her, shouting and grimacing, and their horrible faces became even more terrifying. Sītā edged away and huddled under the tree where Hanumān was hidden. Weakened by hunger and thirst, lost in grief, she covered her moonlike face with her sārī.

The demons followed her there and surrounded the tree where she sat, like wolves encircling a fawn. "Foolish woman," the ugliest ogre of all shouted, "this entire kingdom could be yours, along with the favors of the king. Thousands of women will wait on you, and even Mandodarī, the favorite queen, will move aside. Take this boon, or I will tear out your heart and eat it this minute."

Another ugly rākshasī yelled, "Looking at this young thing, with eyes like a deer, I suddenly feel hungry for her liver, her spleen, her heart, limbs, and head."

"Let's tell Rāvaṇa we have killed her, and then he will let us eat her," cried another.

"Let's eat her and dance!" they screamed in unison, over and over.

Sītā, overwhelmed with fear, burst into tears. "A human cannot be the wife of a rākshasa," she said between sobs. "I could never be untrue to Rāma. You can tear my body to pieces, but I will never do what you ask."

She trembled violently, tears streaming down her body. "O Rāma!" she wailed. "O Lakshmaṇa!" She cried out again and again for Mother Kausalyā, for Sumitrā, for all those who loved her.

In her misery, she began to think terrible thoughts. "I must have committed unforgivable sins in the past, to be separated from Rāma and tormented by these demon women. Why doesn't my lord rescue me, when he was able to kill fourteen thousand rākshasas in the Daṇḍaka Forest? Why haven't his fiery arrows crossed the sea and destroyed Lankā? Either he does not know where I am, or he has merged with the eternal absolute and no longer has need of a consort. Or has he been killed through Rāvaṇa's trickery? Without him, having fallen into the clutches of the evil Rāvaṇa, I have nothing to live for. I will give up my life."

Hearing her despairing words, the angry demon women only increased their jeering until Trijatā, the oldest among them, who had just awakened from sleep, stepped between the demons and Sītā.

"Stop, you wretched beasts!" she said. "You can devour me, but do not touch Sītā. For in the morning twilight I dreamed that Lankā lay destroyed and burning, and this woman's husband was our destroyer."

The fierce rākshasa women stopped their taunting for a moment and gathered around Trijatā, begging to hear about the dream. "I dreamed that Sītā was dressed in immaculate white, standing on a snow-white mountain by the sea. Rāma and his brother Lakshmaṇa, mounted on a towering four-tusked elephant, adorned with garlands and radiant with light, rode to greet her. She joined Rāma on his magnificent elephant and then rose up to touch the sun and the moon with her hands. Later I dreamed that Sītā, with Rāma and Lakshmaṇa, departed for the north in a sun-bright, flower-laden chariot.

"Then I saw Rāvaṇa. Smeared with blood, he wandered across the scorched earth like a madman, babbling and laughing deliriously. He entered a lake that had no water, only red mud. There he joined his brother Kumbhakarṇa and his sons, whose heads were shaven and smeared with oil. A terrifying woman clad in red and black slid a noose around Rāvaṇa's neck and dragged him to the south, the region of death. Lankā was burning and falling into the sea, her arches shattered. Drunken demons flooded her streets.

"Only Rāvaṇa's brother Vibhīshaṇa floated above this unthinkable chaos, his garments spotlessly white, shaded under a white canopy. So stop your tormenting. Beg this woman for mercy, for only through her kindness can you be saved."

When the demon women became silent with fear, the compassionate Sītā said, "I will be your protector."

"Look at her—she quivers with good omens," said Trijatā. And indeed, Sītā noticed that her left eye and her left arm tingled, a sign of good luck for women, and that the birds nesting above her were singing happily as if the hour were auspicious. That graceful and youthful lady suddenly felt revived like a desert plant after a long-awaited rain, and her heart filled with joy. Shedding her fatigue and hopelessness, once again Sītā radiated the beauty and vitality of the adored daughter of King Janaka and the cherished wife of the hero Rāma.

All this time Hanumān had stayed hidden in the branches of the leafy tree above where Sītā was sitting. Since the rākshasas continued to guard Sītā closely, he wondered how he could ever talk to her.

"I have breached the fortress walls of Lankā, and I have found Sītā hidden in this secret garden," reflected Hanumān. "Yet my mission will fail if I do not speak to her before I leave, for she is desperately in need of encouragement. Her spirits have lifted for the moment, but it's possible that she could even take her life if she hears no word from Rāma. And what would I say to Rāma, if I returned with news of Sītā but no message from her?"

He studied the rākshasa women surrounding Sītā. "If I speak Sanskrit to her like a Brahmin, Sītā will be frightened, thinking I am Rāvaṇa. She will cry out, and then the demon women will come running. Being so excitable, they will rouse whole armies, and then I will have to fight them all. Yet if I do not talk to her, she will surely die of hopelessness."

His mind seesawing with contradictory thoughts, Hanumān stayed hidden, wondering how to give Sītā his message from Rāma. Finally, the wise monkey came up with a plan.

High up in the tree, he waited patiently until the women, calmed by Trijatā, fell asleep in another area of the garden a short distance away. When Sītā was finally alone, he began to sing a song of Rāma's character and deeds, his voice sweet and melodious like a nightingale's. He sang of Rāma's auspicious birth, his winning of Sītā, his exile, his triumph over fourteen thousand rākshasas, his fury and grief when Sītā was stolen by Rāvaṇa, his quest for his wife, and his alliance with Sugrīva. Then he sang, "I am one of Sugrīva's ministers, and I have crossed this wide ocean to find the doe-eyed Sītā, overjoyed to behold her at last."

Sītā, whose heart was filled with love for Rāma, was astonished to hear her innermost thoughts echoed in the voice coming from above her. She brushed aside her unbraided hair, which had fallen all about her face, and peered up into the tree. Smiling, her whole being filled with happiness to hear the name of Rāma, she finally saw the small monkey Hanumān, his body shining in the leaves and his face the color of coral.

Seeing the monkey's scars from having crashed to the earth and broken his jaw, she cried out in a faint voice, "O Rāma! O Lakshmaṇa!" When the monkey gazed at her with compassion and reverence, she thought it must be a dream.

"A dream of a monkey is surely inauspicious," she thought. "Perhaps something is wrong with Rāma." Moaning, she fell into a faint.

When she revived, she realized that it could not be a dream, because she had not slept since being separated from Rāma. "All I think about is Rāma. My whole being flows to him," she thought. "Is this an illusion of my mind, which is ever absorbed in Rāma? Yet I wish with all my heart that it not be so."

Finally, she folded her hands in prayer and said in her gentle voice, "I pray to Brahmā, to Indra, to Vishṇu, that this creature who speaks so well of Rāma be real and not a dream."

Hearing her prayer, Hanumān hopped down from the tree, and standing far enough away so Sītā would not feel threatened, he bowed to her in all humility.

"Pray tell me your name, O graceful lady," said Hanumān in humble tones. "From your radiance and your purity, I think you must be the daughter of a sage or of divine birth. From your royal bearing, I think you must be the daughter of a king. From your tears, your ascetic's clothing, and your matchless beauty, I think you must be Sītā, the wife of Rāma."

Again Sītā smiled. "I am the wife of Rāma, whose wisdom rivals the Devas. My name is Sītā."

"O faithful Sītā, I have come to you at Rāma's request," said Hanumān with great joy. "He is safe and waits anxiously to hear news of your well-being. And Lakshmaṇa, the powerful brother of Rāma, also bows to you."

Sītā wept tears of delight. "The wise say that happiness comes to everyone, even if they must wait a hundred years," she said.

यदि वाचं प्रदास्यामि द्विजातिरिव संस्कृताम् ।
रावणं मन्यमाना मां सीता भीता भविष्यति ॥

If I speak Sanskrit to her like a Brahmin,
Sītā will be frightened, thinking I am Rāvaṇa.

—Sundara Kāṇḍa 30.18

CHAPTER 36

Hanumān Consoles Sītā

Under the ashoka tree
Hanumān sang Rāma's praises:

"In radiance he is like the sun,
in patience like the earth,
in wisdom like the preceptor of the gods.
He shelters all beings
and defends Dharma and tradition.
Imbued with humility,
he is versed in the Vedas and Vedāngas.

"He is known for his broad shoulders,
long arms, wide forehead,
and muscular and taut chest.
His thighs, fists, and wrists are hard,
yet his lustrous skin is soft.

"His eyes are like lotus petals,
his face shining like the moon.
His complexion dark,
his voice low like the dundubhi drum,
he walks with the royal pace of an elephant.

Moving with grace, he is renowned by all.
His eyesight is clear,
his intellect sharp.
He delights in the true,
he delights in the just,
and he is compassionate to all."

Thus Hanumān convinced Sītā
that he served her beloved with his heart.

As Hanumān talked quietly to Sītā in the Ashoka Grove, he stepped closer. Immediately Sītā felt frightened. What if this monkey were Rāvaṇa in disguise? Her hopes dashed, fearing that Rāvaṇa had devised a new trick to get close to her, she sank to the ground once again.

"If you are Rāvaṇa," she cried to Hanumān, "who once before tricked me by disguising yourself as a sage, it is not right to approach me now, when I am weak with hunger and fear." She shuddered at the thought of that dreadful day.

Yet as the humble Hanumān bowed before her, she took hope. "Surely you cannot be Rāvaṇa, for my heart fills with joy in your presence. Tell me more about Rāma, gentle monkey, for your words make me happy. Unless, of course, this is a vision brought on by my long fasting. But no, I am in control of my senses." Her mind wavered, not knowing whether to trust Hanumān or not.

As Sītā fell silent, Hanumān saw her thoughts and sought to console her. He again began to sing praises of Rāma in his melodious voice. "Rāma shines with the light of the moon and the sun together. Ever speaking the truth, ever sweet-natured, pleasing to look upon, brilliant in mind and heart, Rāma is the protector of all. The destroyer of evil on earth, he will soon destroy Rāvaṇa. To find you, he has joined forces with the king of the monkeys, Sugrīva, who also sends his greetings through me.

"I am Hanumān, the Son of the Wind. I have leapt across the wide ocean in a single bound for your sake. Do not doubt me. Trust your heart and have confidence in me."

Hearing these nourishing words from Hanumān, Sītā raised her head. She desperately wanted to believe him, but asked more questions for proof. "How did you meet Rāma? Tell me again of his unrivaled qualities—hearing you praise him dispels my grief as the sun dispels the clouds. How is Rāma, and how is Lakshmaṇa? Tell me everything."

Hanumān again began extolling Rāma, never tiring to speak of his nobility, charm, and beauty. Hanumān described Rāma's auspicious marks. "His thumb is marked with four lines, showing his mastery of the Vedas; four lines mark his forehead, the sign of a long life; his arms and thighs are strong; his cheeks, lips, and jaws are full; his nose long; his nails, eyelids, and palms pink; his arms, fingers, and legs slender."

Hanumān told Sītā that he was one of the monkeys who had been sitting on the hillside when she dropped her jewels. He told how he met Rāma and Lakshmaṇa, how Rāma killed Bāli, how Rāma sent the monkeys to the four quarters to find her.

At last Sītā said, "You are certainly a real monkey, and a true friend to Rāma—how could I think otherwise? As the dry earth is gladdened by the rain, so am I gladdened to see you." Sītā's long lashes shuddered with tears of joy, for finally she knew that she could trust the faithful Hanumān.

Seeing that her heart was settled, Hanumān pulled out a ring, which looked large in his small monkey hand. He held it out on his palm for Sītā to see. "Take this ring, given to me by Rāma, to erase your doubts. See, that illustrious hero's name is engraved on it. Now is the time to take heart. Rāma will soon end your sorrow."

Sītā took the ring that had been worn by her lord and, gazing on it, nearly swooned with joy. Her eyes shone with the light of the stars, as if Rāma himself were in her presence. As she looked at Hanumān, whom she now knew to be her most trusted friend, she could not contain her happiness.

"You are no ordinary monkey, but are stronger than the strong, for you crossed the ocean as if it were only a puddle. You are valorous, for you are not afraid of Rāvaṇa. You are worthy, for Rāma has trusted you to find me. Answer me this, then. Why doesn't Rāma burn up the earth with his arrows of fire? Has my absence caused him to forget about me? Or is he torn with anxiety on my account? In my heart I know that the love he bears for me is greater than that for his mother, his father, and even his brother. I live only to be reunited with him."

After expressing these conflicting emotions, Sītā again was silent. Hanumān humbly joined his hands together in respect and replied, "Rāma does not know where you are. That is the only reason he has not yet rescued you. There is nothing that will stop him from saving you now. Like you, he no longer sleeps, and he thinks of nothing but you. Lost in thoughts of you, when he sees a flower or fruit or any tender object, he cries, 'O Sītā!' He has poured his entire being into his search for you."

Sītā's heart spilled over with joy to be reassured of Rāma's devotion, yet she was pained to hear of his suffering. "Your words are like nectar tinged with poison," she said. "Surely no person, no matter how fortunate or powerful, can escape his destiny. How else could Rāma, Lakshmaṇa, and I be trapped in this abyss of grief? Rāvaṇa has been warned by his virtuous brother Vibhīshaṇa to return me to Rāma, but instead he continues to seek his death as an arrow seeks its mark. This was told to me by Vibhīshaṇa's eldest daughter, Kalā. Avindhya, Rāvaṇa's trusted minister, also has foretold the destruction of Lankā at Rāma's bow. I anxiously await the day when Rāma destroys this dark ocean of ferocious rākshasas. I feel hopeful, for my heart is pure, and Rāma, the knower of the Self, has infinite strength, courage, power, and compassion. But it must be soon, for the wretched Rāvaṇa has given me only two more months to live." At this, Sītā began to weep again.

"My lady, you must not suffer another minute," cried Hanumān. "This very day, I will carry you on my back across the sea. You will be in Rāma's arms tonight!"

Sītā was surprised that this tiny creature, though obviously no ordinary monkey, thought he could carry her on his back. Filled with wonder at his valor, and wishing not to offend him, she hesitantly asked, "Dear Hanumān, how could you carry me, when I am much bigger than you?"

Hanumān felt crushed. "Sītā has no idea of my power. I must show her," he thought. Swelling like a seed in the rain, Hanumān grew until he was enormous, his teeth flashing like diamonds, his body radiant as the sun.

"I can smash this city into the sea, uproot its trees, and destroy Rāvaṇa himself. Delay not another moment, pure-hearted lady. Let me take you to Rāma and end his suffering today." Then he shrank back to a small size, so as not to draw the attention of the sleeping demons that guarded Sītā.

Sītā smiled radiantly. "O brave Hanumān, now I know your true stature and strength. I know now that you are capable of carrying me away. But first I must consider if it is in my own and Rāma's best interests. What if I became dizzy, clinging to your back as you flew the skies faster than the wind, and fell into the watery deep? And surely if you took me away, Rāvaṇa would send his armies to fight you. Unarmed, how would you prevent those demons from tearing me to pieces? Or they might hide me away in some secret place where Rāma could never find me. Rāma and Lakshmaṇa's lives depend on me. If something happened to me, they would give up their last breaths.

"But even more, I do not wish to touch another save Rāma. When Rāvaṇa dragged me through the skies, it was against my will. It will bring Rāma honor and glory to rescue me. Dear Hanumān, you will help most, and make me happy once again, by bringing Rāma to me."

"Who could think with such nobility and purity of heart!" exclaimed Hanumān. "You have honored all women with your modesty. Please forgive me, it was only my affection and devotion to Rāma that made me propose such a foolhardy plan. Now I will return to Rāma and tell him all that has happened. Will you give me a token to make him certain that I have seen you?"

Sītā sobbed as she unwrapped a pearl that was knotted in a corner of her sārī. "I once wore this on my forehead, but I have hidden it away. It has given me strength to endure all these misfortunes."

Hanumān took the lustrous pearl in his hand. He suddenly felt as though he had entered the calm eye of the hurricane, and his last fears were dissipated. "What do you wish me to tell Rāma when I see him?" he asked.

"Tell Rāma I can last only a month. Ask him if he remembers that day in spring when we sported by the river in Chitrakūta, when I was covered with garlands that he made for me. Ask if he remembers how he replaced the tilaka mark on my forehead when mine faded.

"Ask if he remembers that a crow started to bother me, and I became frightened and tried to chase it away. Vexed at my impotence, crying in fear, I found solace in his arms. He laughed and wiped away my tears, and I fell asleep in his embrace. He too slept peacefully, but when I awakened, the crow caught my sārī in his beak, tore off a piece, and flew away. Rāma saw that the crow had harassed me and, his eyes rolling with fury, grabbed a single blade of kusha grass and invoked the dreaded weapon of Brahmā. He flung it at the crow. That crow, who was actually Indra's son in disguise, flew through all the three worlds, even to his father's heavenly abode, trying to escape the Brahmā weapon. Finally, exhausted, he landed at Rāma's feet, begging forgiveness.

"Ever compassionate, Rāma said, 'I will forgive you, but the Brahmā weapon, once invoked, cannot be called back.' And so Rāma closed the crow's right eye, to use up the power of the weapon in the least harmful way.

"Ask Rāma if he remembers how the insult from a mere crow caused him to hurl the weapon of Brahmā for my sake. Ask him how, then, can he and Lakshmaṇa allow me to languish here, the captive of bloodthirsty demons? How can he allow Rāvaṇa to remain unpunished? I know that his power extends beyond the ends of the earth. No one can defeat him in battle. It must be that I have committed an unspeakable sin for Rāma and Lakshmaṇa to forget me like this.

"Repeat these words to Rāma again and again: if Rāma does not rescue me by the end of one month, I will give up my life."

Now Hanumān, his kindly heart overwhelmed with Sītā's sadness, tried everything in his power to console her. "Believe me, O gentle heart, Rāma is beside himself with grief. Hearing news of you, his strength will be increased a thousandfold. Soon he will destroy this kingdom for you. Have patience, for you will soon be restored to happiness." Then Hanumān circled Sītā in respect and bowed down at her feet.

Seeing Hanumān swelling again to his giant size, preparing to leave her, Sītā said, "Bow low to the long-armed Rāma, the scourge of foes, and wish him good fortune. Give my good wishes to the courageous Lakshmaṇa, who looks upon me as a mother and Rāma as a father. Also give my good wishes to Sugrīva and his court. Think carefully how you can help them and end all my suffering. May success stay with you."

Holding up the palm of her right hand to bless him, the dark-eyed Sītā honored the devoted monkey, Hanumān.

गृहीत्वा प्रेक्षमाणा सा भर्तुः करविभूषितम् ।
भर्तारमिव सम्प्राप्तं जानकी मुदिताभवत् ॥

Sītā took the ring worn by her lord and, gazing on it,
was filled with joy, as if she had obtained her husband.

—Sundara Kāṇḍa 36.4

CHAPTER 37

Hanumān Destroys Rāvaṇa's Generals

AFTER HANUMĀN TOOK leave of Sītā, he paused for a moment to plan his next move. "He who accomplishes the most with least effort is truly a useful servant," he thought. "If I can now ascertain the strength of Lankā's armies, I will have served Rāma well."

Considering the four means of gaining success over an enemy—negotiations, gifts, sowing dissension, and valor—Hanumān realized that the first three would have no value here. "Negotiations would not work, for the rākshasas are too untrustworthy. Gifts would have no effect on these wealthy rākshasas. It would be impossible to sow dissension among those who are so proud of their strength. That leaves only valor. If the rākshasas see me vanquishing their invincible warriors, it will strike fear into their hearts and weaken them."

Hanumān wondered how he could incite Rāvaṇa's army. "I will destroy this Ashoka Grove, the pleasure park of Rāvaṇa's wives, which looks like a garden of the gods," he decided. "Then Rāvaṇa will send out his army, and by fighting them, I will measure their strength."

Having decided on a plan, the immensely strong Hanumān raged about the garden, uprooting trees, overturning pavilions, and breaking off the tops of the hills as if they were children's toys. Eager to fight Rāvaṇa's forces, Hanumān boldly stood at the gate of that ruined pleasure garden, blazing with light.

The rākshasa women who guarded Sītā woke up to the cries of deer, tigers, and birds as they fled from the garden. Terrified, they watched Hanumān as he grew in size until he became as large as Mount Meru. "Who is this animal who tore up the garden while our eyes were closed?" they interrogated Sītā. "Weren't you talking to him while we slept?"

"Since you are rākshasīs and can change your shape at will, you know more than I do of such creatures," said Sītā, shaking her head. "I think he must be a demon, come to terrify me."

Sītā's guards escaped the garden and ran to Rāvaṇa's palace. Finding him in the magnificent throne room meeting with his ministers, the frightened women collapsed at his feet. "O merciful king, a terrifying monkey, whose head touches the clouds, has uprooted all the trees and overturned the pavilions in the garden where Sītā stays. He has been seen conversing with that lady and may even be a messenger from Rāma. The entire Ashoka Grove is destroyed, save the one tree where she sits, shaded by its blossoms."

Rāvaṇa's eyes dripped tears of anger like a ghee lamp dripping hot oil. "Send eighty thousand demons to destroy this monster!" he roared.

Armed with maces and clubs, this formidable army of rākshasas marched to the gate of the Ashoka Grove, where the valorous Hanumān stood waiting. Waving his massive tail, Hanumān created a din with his ferocious war cries. Birds fell from the sky, confused by the noise and buffeted by winds from the fanning of Hanumān's tail.

"Jai Rāma!" he shouted. "Victory to Lakshmaṇa! I am the Son of the Wind, messenger of Rāma. Even if I face a thousand Rāvaṇas, I can crush them all beneath my feet. I have come here to find Sītā and destroy Lankā."

Screaming in fury, the titans rushed at him in a ferocious snarl of teeth, clubs, and weapons. Hanumān grabbed an iron bar from the gate and roared as he wielded it, leaving heaps of dead rākshasas. The few remaining fled to Rāvaṇa. Flinging themselves at Rāvaṇa's feet, they cried, "He has destroyed all!"

Rāvaṇa's ten heads swiveled on his ten necks. "Send the invincible Jambumālī, son of Prahasta!" he screamed.

Meanwhile, Hanumān, feeling friskier than ever, bounded up the hill to the temple. One thought filled his mind: "I have destroyed Rāvaṇa's pleasure garden. Now I will burn his temple."

Radiant like the sun, he attacked the magnificent temple and toppled its pillars inlaid with gold, ivory, and jewels. Roaring from that peak, he terrified the citizens of Lankā, who could see the giant monkey wreaking havoc on the hill above Rāvaṇa's palace.

"Victory to Rāma!" he shouted. "Victory to Lakshmaṇa! Victory to King Sugrīva!"

One hundred guardians of the temple, armed with sharpened teeth, spears, axes, and arrows, attacked Hanumān. Hoisting one of the temple's bejeweled pillars, which flashed in the sun, that invincible warrior whirled it around his body, creating a vortex of light. After mowing down the demon guards, he spun the pillar so rapidly that it burst into flames, setting the temple on fire.

Hanumān stood triumphant on the hill, his colossal form silhouetted against the sky. The hundred demons vanquished, the temple in flames, he bellowed to the citizens of Lankā gathered below, "There are more like me coming to destroy Lankā. Hundreds of thousands of monkeys with sharp nails and teeth have joined forces with Rāma. Some have the strength of one elephant, some of an entire herd—some the strength of Indra, and others have strength unimaginable. Neither you nor Rāvaṇa will survive, for your foolish king has invoked the wrath of Lord Rāma."

Then Hanumān heard the thunder of a war chariot bearing down on him from above. It was the floating chariot of Jambumālī, the skilled warrior with ferocious teeth. Charging Hanumān, Jambumālī let loose a volley of iron-tipped arrows, piercing Hanumān's face and drawing blood.

Hanumān roared with anger. He tore up a shāla tree by the roots and raised it above his head. Jambumālī shot ten more arrows at Hanumān's arms. His arms covered with blood, Hanumān bashed the body of Jambumālī with the tree trunk, and the ferocious rākshasa fell to the earth, wounded, and retreated to the palace.

Next Rāvaṇa sent the seven sons of his ministers. These young warriors, courageous and fierce, rode in golden chariots that rumbled through the sky like thunder. When these invincible youths reached the gate where Hanumān stood, they shot a thick volley of arrows that showered him like a rainstorm.

Hanumān lithely dodged the arrows, turning this way and that. Letting loose an earsplitting war whoop, striking terror in the hearts of his foes, he leapt on the rākshasas, striking them with his palms, feet, and nails. One by one they fell to the ground, some knocked down by the force of his bellowing alone. Their bodies lay in a heap on the earth, along with broken chariots and slain elephants and horses. Blood flowed from the temple hill down through the streets of Lankā, and the families of the ministers cried out in anguish. Filled with energy, eager to fight the next demon, Hanumān once more took his stance at the gate.

When Rāvaṇa heard of the destruction of his minister's sons, his red eyes bulged in his ten heads and shot sparks. Quickly he summoned his top five generals, who were each the leaders of vast armies, masterful in strategic planning and valor.

As they stood before him, their armor and weapons gleaming, Rāvaṇa said, "Brave generals, I do not think this is an ordinary monkey, but a celestial being. Perhaps Indra has sent him to vanquish us. So proceed carefully, even though you are victorious among Devas, demons, and men. Take him prisoner."

The five generals led their armies with confidence, never having been defeated in battle. But when they saw Hanumān standing on the hill below their flying chariots, with his massive arms, unbounded strength, and keen intelligence, they felt tremors of fear course through their hearts for the first time.

It was not long before Hanumān again brandished his shāla tree and knocked three of them from the skies, along with their horses, chariots, and armies of demons. Then he broke off the peak of a nearby mountain, complete with its trees and animals, obliterating the other two generals beneath it. The streets of Lankā were now littered with the bodies of the demon generals and their armies. Having crushed the brave generals along with their chariots and armies, the hero Hanumān rested for a moment at the side of the gate, destructive as time itself at the end of creation.

As Rāvaṇa heard the news and cast his eyes about the hall, his gaze rested on his youngest son, Aksha. Seeing his father's nod, Aksha sprang forth eagerly, thrilled to prove himself in battle.

Dressed in fine gold bracelets and jeweled earrings, shining with youth and beauty, he drove his chariot to the gate where Hanumān waited. Aksha surveyed the scene with awe, taking the measure of Hanumān's boundless strength and valor. Then he rallied his courage and attacked Hanumān in a rage. A terrific struggle took place, causing the sun to cease from shining, the wind to stop blowing, and the mountains to shake.

Aksha let loose a spray of arrows that pierced Hanumān in the forehead. Blood ran into his eyes and blinded him, yet Hanumān was not frightened. On the contrary, facing a worthy foe exhilarated him, and he felt his energy surge.

Hanumān roared in exultation. Aksha, in the eagerness and overconfidence of youth, rushed at him like an elephant rushing to a pit concealed in the grass. Driving his chariot high above Hanumān, Aksha rained down arrows, covering the valiant monkey like a cloud.

Seeing Aksha's valor, Hanumān thought, "This youth has skill and courage far beyond his years. I do not wish to kill him, yet if I let him go, he will kill me. It is unwise to leave a fire burning without putting it out."

His mind made up, Hanumān flew through the air, and with the palms of his powerful hands, struck the eight noble horses that pulled Aksha's chariot, knocking them from the sky and overturning the chariot. Aksha deftly slipped out of the plummeting chariot and emerged mid-air with his bow and sword, eager to keep fighting.

Hanumān ended the battle quickly. Grabbing hold of the valiant Aksha's legs, that fearless monkey spun him around like a top and threw him to the earth below. Having trodden on the heads of his foes, the mighty Hanumān took his stance by the gate like Death itself.

Rāvaṇa's blood coursed with anger when he heard of Aksha's death. Controlling his anger and grief, his mind focused, he turned to his eldest and most beloved son, who was called Indrajit because he had once captured Indra, the king of the Devas.

"You are the most skilled warrior in the world," Rāvaṇa said to his son. "I have faith in you, even though these other great warriors have been vanquished. You have proven that you can defeat both Devas and asuras. You are Indrajit, who bound the invincible Indra and dragged him to a cave. Yet you must use your shrewd intellect against this monkey, for he is fast like Vāyu, the wind, and immune to weapons like Agni, the god of fire. It appears he cannot be killed."

Indrajit, shining with valor, circled his father in respect and gathered his inner strength for battle. His heart free of fear, exuding strength, Indrajit drove his shining chariot, pulled by four snow-white lions. As this ferocious warrior and his army drew close to the gate where Hanumān waited, the sky grew dark and jackals howled.

When Indrajit reached the spot where Hanumān stood, he alighted from his chariot and motioned for his army to stand back. He wanted to fight Hanumān alone. Then the two warriors, perceiving an equal match, joyfully entered the fight. Indrajit let fly his gold-tipped arrows, flashing through the sky like lightning. Hanumān, twisting and spinning, ducking and leaping, dodged them all. Yet Hanumān could not deliver his usual fatal blows to Indrajit, for he could not catch that brilliant warrior unawares.

After a time, Indrajit stopped to think deeply. He realized that Hanumān could not be killed. So he decided to capture him. His mind focused within, he released the weapon of Brahmā, which he had won as a boon.

Hanumān felt himself being bound by the invisible fetters of that celestial weapon, but he did not fight back. Nor did he feel pain. Rather, his heart was filled with devotion to Brahmā, the Creator. He knew that no harm could come to him from Brahmā. He also knew it was useless to resist.

"Besides," he thought, "it will be to my advantage to be captured. For then I can meet Rāvaṇa and measure his strength."

And so Hanumān lay motionless as he was bound with ropes by Indrajit's army. Although the rākshasas who were binding him did not realize it, the Brahmā weapon had ceased to work the moment Hanumān had surrendered to Brahmā. Hanumān only pretended to be helpless. Roaring like a lion, he allowed the demons to drag him through the streets of Lankā, bound like a maddened elephant.

"Kill him!" shouted the demons who now poured into the city streets, rejoicing that the pillager of their city had been captured. They mocked and taunted him as he was dragged to Rāvaṇa's palace to face the demon king.

ततः कपिस्तान्ध्वजिनीपतीन्रणे
निहत्य वीरान्सबलान्सवाहनान् ।
तथैव वीरः परिगृह्य तोरणं
कृतक्षणः काल इव प्रजाक्षये ॥

Having crushed the brave generals along with their chariots and armies,
the hero Hanumān rested for a moment at the side of the gate,
destructive as time itself at the end of creation.

—*Sundara Kāṇḍa 46.41*

Chapter 38

Hanumān Burns Lankā

Rāvaṇa smiled as Hanumān, arms roped to his sides, was roughly shoved in front of the powerful king of the rākshasas and his court. Rāvaṇa nodded to his four learned and distinguished ministers, who surrounded him like the four seas.

"Who are you, and why do you come here?" demanded Prahasta, the eldest minister, who was also the commander in chief of Rāvaṇa's army.

"I am a messenger from King Sugrīva of the kingdom of Kishkindhā," said Hanumān quietly.

As he stood there before Rāvaṇa, Hanumān stared intently at the king of the demons, trying to learn as much as he could about Rāma's adversary. Hanumān was dazzled by the golden ornaments on Rāvaṇa's body, which was polished smooth and smeared with red sandalwood paste. Precious gems, created by the concentrated power of the titan's mind, made him shine like a universe of stars. Graceful and lavishly ornamented women stood nearby, gently wielding fans and waiting to serve him.

"How surprising to see such power, such beauty, such magnificence and dignity," reflected Hanumān. "If only he used his power for good, he could befriend the Devas or Indra himself. Instead he uses his unlimited prowess for destruction, and thus he himself will be destroyed."

At Rāvaṇa's bidding, Prahasta said, "I see that you are not a mere monkey. Are you Bāli? Or are you Indra himself? No, I think you must be Yama, or perhaps Vishṇu, come here to settle an ancient score. Do not be afraid to tell us why you have wreaked havoc on Lankā. If you tell us the truth, you will go free. If you lie, we will take your life."

"I am not Bāli, nor am I Indra, nor Death itself. I am a monkey, and I wished to see Rāvaṇa, which is why I tore up your Ashoka Grove. When you sent those waves of demon warriors to me, I fought them in self-defense. I have received a boon from Lord Brahmā which does not allow me to be killed by any weapon. I only submitted to gain this audience with Rāvaṇa, to deliver this message from Lord Rāma, whose virtue and power are infinite."

Prahasta signaled for Hanumān to continue.

Addressing Rāvaṇa directly now, Hanumān's clear voice echoed through the hall. "Listen to my words, O king of the titans, for they are your only hope. I am Hanumān, the son of the wind. I have come here to find Sītā and have discovered her in the Ashoka Grove. To retrieve her, Lord Rāma has joined forces with Sugrīva, after felling the mighty Bāli with one blow. Soon hundreds of thousands of monkeys and bears will descend on Lankā to destroy it. I myself have crossed a hundred yojanas in a single bound.

"O king of the night prowlers, you are known for the power of your austerities. The son of the sage Vishravā and the grandson of Ṛishi Pulastya, you are familiar with the wisdom of the Vedas. One as wise as you should not transgress the laws of righteousness. It is not right to steal another's wife. So far you have reaped only the blessings of your austerities. Now you will harvest the consequences of your evil deeds. This heinous act is not worthy of you. Return Sītā to Rāma, and save yourself, your family, and your kingdom from destruction."

Hanumān went on. "It is true that you are invincible against Devas, demons, celestial beings, and Gandharvas. But Sugrīva is a monkey and Lord Rāma is a man. I myself could destroy you and your city, only Rāma has not commanded me to do that. It is known by all that no one can resist the arrows of Lord Rāma. He can destroy the worlds and re-create them at will. By offending him, you give up your life. His valor has no equal."

Rāvaṇa could contain his wrath no longer. Driven by pride, lust, and his own destiny, he bellowed, "For this impudent speech you will be put to death!"

Then the wise and gentle Vibhīshaṇa, brother of Rāvaṇa, rose to speak. "For just a moment, brother, cool your anger and listen to me with a settled mind. You know the moral code regarding messengers. It is against ordinary justice to put a messenger to death. A wise king must overcome anger and do what is right. Think carefully, invincible hero, and mete out just punishment to your foes."

"It is no sin to kill an evil wretch such as this!" roared Rāvaṇa.

Vibhīshaṇa again answered Rāvaṇa's crude words with quiet reasoning. "It is never right to kill a messenger. You can punish him in other ways to humiliate him and his sovereign, but a man of honor and strength such as yourself does not need to resort to killing. You are the king of the rākshasas, the ruler of the whole earth. Why would such a great warrior fall to such low actions? You must master your anger and deliver the punishment to the rulers who sent this envoy, for this messenger has merely uttered these words in service to them."

Seeing that Rāvaṇa was unmoved by his words, Vibhīshaṇa appealed to his brother's vanity. "Besides, if you put him to death, Rāma and Lakshmaṇa will not know where to find you. Why deprive the Devas and celestials of the glorious sight of the magnificent king Rāvaṇa fighting Rāma in battle?"

His pride at stake, Rāvaṇa finally saw the truth in his brother's words. "In a monkey, the tail is his most valued possession," he said. "Set fire to this monkey's tail and lead him through the streets of Lankā so all may see his humbling."

As the wicked rākshasas wrapped his tail in cotton rags and set it afire, Hanumān grew larger and larger and his tail grew longer and longer. As it flamed, the demons roared and held him in place.

"I could destroy all these demons and end this game," thought Hanumān. "But for the sake of Rāma, I will endure this heat so I can survey the city once more. Despite this pain, my mind is free."

Thus Hanumān allowed himself to be dragged through the city streets at the end of a rope, his tail burning. He carefully noted the position of the ramparts, moats, walls, streets, mansions, and palaces of Lankā. "Spy, spy, spy!" the crowds jeered at that illustrious champion.

From her seat in the Ashoka Grove, Sītā could hear the clamor of the crowds. "They have captured that monkey who was conversing with you," her demon guards told her. "Now they are dragging him through the city with his tail on fire."

Sītā, having endured unimaginable hardship herself, could not bear to think of Hanumān suffering on her account. Her large eyes, gentle as a fawn's, filled with tears. She prayed to Agni, the god of fire, "If I have proven to be a faithful wife, if Rāma is still devoted to me, then may Hanumān feel no burning, but only cooling winds."

Immediately, Hanumān began to feel an icy breeze wafting across his tail. "Why don't I feel the burning of the flame?" he wondered. "It must be Sītā's purity and Rāma's power that shield me."

Heartened by Sītā's help, Hanumān suddenly thought, "Why should I remain a captive of these disgusting creatures?" When he had been dragged as far as the city gate, he shrank to a miniature size and slipped out of his bonds as easily as a snake shedding its skin. Once free, he swelled again to an enormous size. Before his guards could catch him, he bounded to the top of the wall, his tail still burning like a flare, and surveyed the city.

"Having destroyed the Ashoka Grove and part of their army, now I will burn their fortress. With the god of fire helping me, I will destroy this entire city!"

Leaping across the rooftops from house to house, with his burning tail Hanumān set fire to the mansions of Prahasta, Jambumālī, and countless others. Then he leapt across the palace moat and landed on the dwelling of Rāvaṇa. Across the roofs of the magnificent palace he danced, touching off fires on the palace roof wherever he landed, his tail lighting up the sky.

Winds fanned the fires and soon every building in Lankā ignited. Demons fled the buildings screaming in terror, or fell flaming from balconies like fireworks. As the structures melted, molten precious metals flowed through the streets like lava, mixed with diamonds, pearls, and rubies. Thousands of demons shouted and milled about trying to escape the fire, and others were trapped in their collapsing homes. Horses, elephants, and deer stampeded in terror. With smoke curling upward like the petals of a blue lotus, the flames licked the skies.

"This is not a mere monkey," cried one of Rāvaṇa's ministers who, with the rest of Rāvaṇa's court, had run from the palace to the garden below. "Only Death himself could wreak such havoc!"

"Or perhaps he is Brahmā, the Creator, trying to destroy the rākshasas," suggested another minister.

Having torched the city, Hanumān plunged his burning tail into the sea, which hissed and steamed as it cooled. Then he rested outside the wall of the city, his mind fixed on Rāma. The Devas, Gandharvas, and Ṛishis, watching from above, felt their hearts swell with joy to see the evil city burning.

As Hanumān sat quietly, a disturbing thought came to him. With all of Lankā burning, where was Sītā? Mortified, Hanumān could only lament. "Due to my anger, Lankā lies in ashes. Anger is the greatest folly—it prevents one from thinking clearly. Due to anger I have cut away the root of my mission. If Sītā is dead, Rāma too will die, and Lakshmaṇa, Bharata, and Sugrīva will be unable to live without Rāma. I will plunge into the depths of the sea. I cannot bear to live."

Nearly lost in despair, Hanumān suddenly saw auspicious omens and remembered that Sītā was the one who cooled the flames burning his tail. "If she can cool the god of fire with her purity, surely she herself will be immune from its flames. For the sake of Rāma and Sītā the ocean itself yielded up Mount Maināka to help me rest along the way. No fire could consume Sītā, given her stainless virtue and unyielding devotion."

Then the faithful Hanumān heard voices above him. They were the divine heavenly bards, who had come to earth to see Lankā in flames. "Look, the mighty Hanumān has burned the city to the ground, yet the exalted Sītā still lives."

When he heard these nectar-like words dropping from the skies, Hanumān's heart blossomed in happiness. With the auspicious omens and his own intuition now confirmed by the words of the celestial Ṛishis, Hanumān felt assured that Sītā was safe.

Even so, he decided to visit her once more before leaving Lankā and flew to the garden where he had last seen her. His heart pounding, he entered the ruined garden and searched for her amidst the uprooted trees. Finally, he glimpsed Sītā sitting quietly under the ashoka tree where he had left her—the only tree left standing in all of Lankā.

The hero Hanumān bowed humbly to Sītā, his eyes flowing with tears of devotion. "It is only by God's grace that I find you here, unharmed," he said, his hushed voice trembling with emotion.

Sītā gazed on him affectionately, as she would a favorite son. Then she cried, "Oh, if only you could stay one more evening! I could hide you here, so you could rest before your long journey. With you here, I forget all my troubles. Once you are gone, I will surely suffer even greater misfortune and will be devoured by grief. I cannot stop wondering how Rāma and the monkey armies will pass over the ocean. I now know that you are capable of conquering Rāvaṇa and returning me home all by yourself—yet it is for Rāma to do such a deed. Help him in every way you can, faithful Hanumān."

"Take heart, O lovely lady, for soon Rāma will destroy Rāvaṇa and his army and return to Ayodhyā, bringing you with him. Hundreds of thousands of monkeys have pledged to help him in this task. They will see that he crosses the vast expanse of the sea."

After circling Sītā with all respect and honor, Hanumān of immeasurable strength bounded up the nearby Arishta Mountain, with tall trees reaching like a giant's arms to the sky. Waters tumbling down the mountain mimicked the chanting of the Vedas, making it a favorite pleasure garden for Ṛishis and celestials. Its peaks yawned at the heavens and its jagged cliffs and rich caves of gold ore added even greater beauty.

When he reached the summit, Hanumān closed his eyes and settled inside himself, gathering his inner resources for his long leap home. As the Son of the Wind rose into the air, from the force of his leap that lofty mountain was stomped to the ground, its peaks toppled, its trees uprooted. Lions roared from their caves.

सरणं राक्षसं हत्वा नचिराद्रघुनन्दनः ।
त्वामादाय वरारोहे स्वा पुरीं प्रति यास्यति ॥

Take heart, O lovely lady, for soon Rāma will destroy Rāvaṇa
and his army and return to Ayodhyā, bringing you with him.

—Sundara Kāṇḍa 56.18

Chapter 39

Hanumān Returns to Rāma

Scattering the clouds, Hanumān sailed across the skies in a single bound. Having found Sītā, vanquished the rākshasa armies, and burned Lankā, he returned home a glorious hero. Landing on the northern shore, he gazed up at Mount Mahendra and bellowed like a lion, his long tail rattling the earth as he climbed to the cliff where the monkeys waited.

"Surely Hanumān has good news, or he would not be roaring so," cried Jāmbavān. Pure ecstasy bubbled up among the monkeys, and they swung from tree to tree, leaping and jumping as they rushed to meet him. Laughing and cheering with joy, the monkeys surrounded him like water around an island.

Bursting with happiness, Hanumān bowed to his superiors, first to the ancient Jāmbavān, leader of the bears, and then to the youthful Prince Angada. "I have found her!" he cried, and was answered by a tumult of shouting, cheering, and dancing that shook the mountain. Finally Hanumān sat beside Prince Angada. Some offered branches for him to rest on and fruits to sustain him after his arduous journey.

Taking the young warrior's hand, he related all that he had seen, all that he had heard, and all that he had done in Lankā. Listening with rapt smiles, the monkey host was silent long after Hanumān stopped speaking, absorbing the glorious feats he had described. Finally Angada spoke. "There is none to equal your courage, your valor, your prowess, O Son of the Wind. You have given us back our lives. Such endurance! Such bravery! Such skill! Now, by the grace of the gods, Rāma will smile once more."

After Hanumān had refreshed himself with food and drink, other monkeys dragged boulders over and arranged them in a circle around him. Sitting on the boulders, they asked, "How did you find Sītā?" and "What did she say?" Again he told the whole story of his visit to Lankā, keeping his head slightly bowed in respect for Sītā. More monkeys arrived and crowded around his feet, listening to his glorious exploits with delight.

When he had come to the end of his tale, Hanumān left the celebration and met with Jāmbavān, Angada, and the other monkey leaders. "It made me supremely happy to see Sītā's unwavering devotion to Rāma," he told them. "By the power of her virtue, she herself could destroy Rāvaṇa. I leave it to you to decide what we should do next."

"Let us cross this sea to Lankā, destroy it and Rāvaṇa, and return Sītā to Rāma," suggested the youthful Angada.

Jāmbavān, who knew the wisdom of the Vedas, gently advised, "It is true that we are powerful enough to destroy Rāvaṇa and rescue Sītā. Yet we must consider carefully the task Sugrīva and Rāma asked us to accomplish. They asked us only to find Sītā, not to bring her back. Rāma, if you remember, has vowed to slay Rāvaṇa and rescue Sītā. Why should we prove his words false? What good would it do to displease him? Let us return to Rāma and tell him the success of our mission. Your thoughts are valorous, Angada, but we will find supreme victory only by following Rāma's commands."

"Yes," cried the other leaders. "Our good fortune lies in serving Rāma." Hanumān and Angada agreed.

With the victorious Hanumān at their head, massed together like a dense cloud, leaping and frisking about, the monkeys set out on their journey back to Kishkindhā.

MANY DAYS LATER, as they drew near Kishkindhā, they came upon an enchanted garden owned by Sugrīva and guarded by his maternal uncle, Dadhimukha. Known for its golden honey, it was called *Madhuvana*, meaning "the honey-sweetened woods." Bees swarmed around orchards of fruit-bearing trees, and abundant streams of honey poured out of beehives, tawny-colored like the monkeys' fur.

"Drink the honey and enjoy yourselves," said Hanumān. "I will protect you from anyone who tries to stop you."

Angada, who knew that the garden belonged to Sugrīva, his uncle and king, said, "We will do whatever Hanumān wishes, for he has succeeded in finding the divine Sītā and is beloved by the Devas."

"Splendid!" cried the monkeys. "Marvelous!" They swarmed into the orchard and scrambled up the trees to drink the honey. Soon they started to riot, inebriated with honey and high spirits. Monkeys jumped and tumbled, wrestled and shouted as they swung merrily from the trees. When the guards of the garden came running to stop them from ripping it up, the mischievous monkeys smacked them with their powerful hands and feet and chased them away. Even Dadhimukha, the garden's chief guard, was treated roughly.

Barely escaping from those rascal monkeys, Dadhimukha leapt from tree to tree all the way to Kishkindhā to complain to Sugrīva. He threw himself at his sovereign's feet, breathless, his clothes in disarray.

"Tell me, is all well in Madhuvana?" asked Sugrīva. "Tell me everything."

"The royal forest, brimming with honey and fruit, which you kept off-limits from all the monkeys in order to protect it from harm, has been overrun by them. Your guards tried to stop them, but they brazenly kept up their feasting and merriment. In their wanton revelry, they have uprooted the trees and plundered the fruits and honey."

Lakshmaṇa, who was sitting beside Sugrīva, wanted to know who had done such a deed.

Buoyed with excitement, Sugrīva exclaimed, "It must be Angada's monkeys who have gorged themselves on honey and fruits from the royal garden. This is extraordinary news, for they would never behave with such abandon if they did not bring us good tidings. This can only mean that Hanumān has found success in his search for Sītā. Tell Rāma his suffering is over."

Instead of censuring those monkeys, Sugrīva said to Dadhimukha, "We can forgive the reckless behavior of the victorious. Send a delegation to Madhuvana and bring the lionhearted Hanumān home with all speed." Elated that their long wait was nearly over, the monkey king's tail curled and uncurled, and he lifted off the ground in bursts of happiness.

"So be it," said Dadhimukha. He bowed respectfully to Sugrīva and Lakshmaṇa and flew back to Madhuvana, where the monkeys were resting after their revelries, sober once again.

Dadhimukha sought out Angada. Bowing to the youthful leader, he said, "Forgive me, O prince, for setting my guards on your troops. I did not realize it was you, the heir apparent. I was only trying to save the royal garden from destruction. I have informed your uncle, Sugrīva, of all that happened. He is not upset; on the contrary, he wishes you to return home immediately."

"You have brought us good tidings," said Angada. For now he knew that Sugrīva would pardon them for exceeding the one-month time limit.

Immediately Angada turned to the monkey troops and said with all humility, "Sugrīva has welcomed us, and by now Rāma, too, knows of our victory. We should delay no longer. But it does not seem fitting for me to give you orders, now that you have returned with your hands firmly grasping victory. Tell me what to do and I will do it."

The troops shouted words of praise and joy. "Only one who is truly great can utter such humble words. We are ready, but will go only with your blessings."

"Then let us return home without delay!" shouted Angada. The horde of monkeys shot into the sky like pebbles being flung from a boy's hand.

Shouting "*Kila! Kila!*" the exuberant monkeys flew like a cloud before the wind to Mount Prasravaṇa, where Sugrīva, Rāma, and Lakshmaṇa waited in almost unbearable anticipation. As they heard the riotous clamor of the monkeys descending on them, their hearts throbbed with joy, and Sugrīva's tail curled and uncurled.

"With Angada and Jāmbavān as generals and Hanumān as inspiration, their victory is in hand," cried Sugrīva.

Suddenly Hanumān landed in front of Rāma, Lakshmaṇa, and Sugrīva. As the monkey army alighted giddy with happiness from the sky, Hanumān bowed low to Rāma first.

"I have seen Sītā, who is uninjured and whose heart is fixed upon you," he said with great joy.

"How is my Sītā?" implored Rāma. "Where is she to be found? Tell me everything."

Keeping his head bowed to show respect to Sītā, the divine Hanumān faced south, toward Lankā, and began his story. He told how Sītā, bereft without Rāma, was like a lotus plucked from the water. How, ever devoted to Rāma, she steadfastly suffered the torments of Rāvaṇa and the demon women.

Kneeling before Rāma, Hanumān pressed Sītā's pearl into Rāma's outstretched hands. "She who is your very soul entrusted this to me," said the brave Hanumān. "Sītā said, 'Give this to Rāma, so that he may remember how he placed the red mark on my brow, how he chased to the ends of the earth the crow that tore my sārī. Tell him I cannot live one month more without him.'"

Rāma clasped the pearl to his heart and nearly fainted.

"O Lakshmaṇa," he cried. "This pearl is the one my darling Sītā wore on her brow on our wedding day. Plucked from the depths of the sea, worshipped by the Devas, this pearl was given to her by her father, Janaka. To see this pearl is to see Sītā, as real as life. Yet to hold this pearl without holding her is more pain than I can bear. I cannot live another moment without my sweet-smiling Sītā."

When he had somewhat recovered, Rāma implored Hanumān, "Tell me more. How is my tenderhearted consort able to withstand these hardships?" Again and again he questioned Hanumān, who recounted the words of Sītā, how she remained ever true to Rāma but feared she could only last one more month, until Rāma at last grew silent.

हनूमांश्च महाबहुः प्रणम्य शिरसा ततः ।
नियतामक्षतां देवीं राघवाय न्यवेदयत् ॥

Then the mighty Hanumān bowed low to Rāma and said,
"I have seen Sītā, who is uninjured and whose heart is fixed upon you."

—Sundara Kāṇda 64.42

End of the Sundara Kāṇda

SIX

Yuddha Kāṇḍa

The War

Chapter 40

Rāma Marches to the Sea

They say that time heals all wounds,
yet my heart weighs heavier with each passing day.
It is not only that Sītā has been swept far from me,
it is her youth fading
that sears my heart.

O gentle wind, I call on you to go to her,
and having caressed her,
return to caress me.
As I lie awake at night, I hear one thing—
her last words as she was carried off:
"O Rāma, save me!"
Only news that she is alive keeps me
from throwing myself into the sea.

O Sītā of the slender waist,
when will my arms circle your lovely form again?
When will you hold me in sweet embrace,
and when will I drink the nectar of your lips?
How can you, the daughter of Janaka,
lie down to sleep amidst the titans?
Already delicate in stature, you are wasting away.

When will I shoot my arrow deep into Rāvaṇa's heart
and release you from the demons
like the moon scattering the darkness?
Gentle Sītā, when will I feel
your tears of joy on my neck,
O daughter of the immortals?

While the monkey army camped in the surrounding hills, Hanumān and the other leaders sat in a circle around Rāma like the crescent moon around a star.

Rāma thanked Hanumān again and again. "No one but Garuda, Vāyu, and you could cross the infinite ocean," he said. "You have not only accomplished the purpose of your mission by finding Sītā, but you have destroyed much of Lankā. They say the finest messenger completes a difficult task with dedication, exactly as the king asks—and then does something more." Thus Rāma praised Hanumān.

"The only thing that disturbs me," said Rāma as he smiled at the brave Hanumān, "is that I have no gift to give you. All that I have is my embrace. Let that stand for my Self, which I offer to the high-souled Hanumān." With these words, Rāma joyfully clasped the valiant Hanumān to his breast.

Later, after rejoicing with the monkey army, Rāma said to Hanumān, "Now that I know Sītā is alive, I should be thrilling with joy. Yet one thought still plagues me. How will we cross the sea to reach her?" Having voiced his doubt, Rāma suddenly looked down, his face drained of color.

Sugrīva hastened to comfort his friend. "What is this gloomy mood?" he asked gently. "It is not fitting for a hero to waste his energy on dark thoughts. You must set aside your doubts, just as an ascetic sets aside the thoughts that do not help him attain his goal. Giving in to grief only makes you weak."

Sugrīva gestured to the waiting army with a grand sweeping motion. "Look around you, observe this ocean of valiant monkeys. They are so devoted to you that they will risk their lives for Sītā. With this army you can build a bridge, cross the sea and destroy Rāvaṇa. No one who faces you in battle can survive. Let us not sit here talking another moment. I see all good omens for your success. Turn your heartbreak into resolve and vanquish your foes."

Encouraged by his friend Sugrīva's wise words, Rāma felt heartened. With renewed vigor he turned to Hanumān and said, "I will find a way to cross the wide ocean. If I have to, I will dry up the sea! Now tell me, dear Hanumān, what are the fortifications in Lankā? How large is their army? What are their weak points?"

The intelligent Hanumān spoke clearly and eloquently about the drawbridges, walls, moats, palaces, guards, armies, roads, houses, and weapons of Lankā, which he had carefully observed.

"I will destroy that city myself," said Rāma. "Let us leave now for the ocean shore, for the moon is in an auspicious *nakshatra* and the sun is overhead. If we start now, we will have good luck. All the omens are good. Sītā will wish to live long, once she knows we are on the march."

Then Rāma, trained by his father in warfare, determined which leaders would go to the fore, which behind, which to the east, and which to the west. "Let any exhausted or weakened troops remain here," he said. "Let Jāmbavān and his army of bears march where there is cool, fresh water and abundant fruit to eat. Let the monkeys leap high into the air and scout for rākshasas, who may be hiding in the hollows and valleys, wishing to poison our food and water."

When Sugrīva gave the orders, the army burst from the forest like water from a dam. The ecstatic monkeys swelled in size and shouted loud enough for all to hear, "We will destroy Rāvaṇa and rescue Sītā!" Bounding and leaping, cartwheeling and catapulting, the exuberant monkeys lifted one another playfully on their backs and leapt into the sky. They roared with delight as they passed by flowering blossoms, crowning one another with wreaths and uprooting whole trees to use as walking sticks.

Behind this bubbling, roiling sea of tawny-colored monkeys the high-souled Rāma rode serenely on Hanumān's back, and the mighty Lakshmaṇa straddled the shoulders of Angada.

Avoiding cities and towns, the army feasted on fruits and drank from mountain streams along the way. Finally, the eager monkeys reached the peaks of Mount Mahendra. Gazing down from that great height, Rāma glimpsed the sea for the first time. Quickly the army pressed on and soon arrived at the sandy shore.

The monkeys grew silent as they contemplated the bottomless sea, crowded with fish, turtles, and whales, its expanse stretching so far in all directions that it merged with the sky at the horizon. Home to all streams and rivers, tumultuous and churning, its waves thundered on the shore like war drums beating.

"Let us camp here and decide how to cross this vast ocean," said Rāma. And so the army of thousands of monkeys camped along the shore.

Later, as Lakshmaṇa made his way to the water's edge for his evening prayers, he found Rāma there, sitting with his head in his hands, his face wet with tears. "When will Sītā be free and this bottomless grief be ended?" cried Rāma in anguish. Lakshmaṇa, ever the faithful servant, gently reassured him in soft tones and led his all-powerful brother into the waves for his ablutions.

AT THE SAME time the monkey army was marching to the sea, Rāvaṇa was sitting in his jeweled throne room, with its gold-leafed walls, gem-studded chairs, and sumptuous silken cushions. The rākshasa leader looked careworn and pale. Belatedly, now that war seemed inevitable, he had decided to consult his ministers, who sat before him.

"Our fair city of Lankā, which was impregnable even to the Devas, has been laid waste by Hanumān, a mere monkey," he said. "I've called you here to discuss how we should deal with Rāma, who will undoubtedly cross the sea with his monkey army, being powerful enough to dry it up.

"I am asking you, my ministers, to advise me in a plan of action. I intend to follow your counsel, for I always seek the advice of friends and family members who are concerned with my success. Together we will weigh the pros and cons of the situation carefully and then act in the way we think best.

"As you know, ministers fall into three categories. Superior ministers make their decisions by the light of the Vedas, never sway from the truth, and spontaneously agree with each other from the start. Ordinary ministers consult each other even though they have different views, and eventually agree on a course of action. Weak ministers never come to an agreement.

"Advise me, then, on the question of Rāma arriving at Lankā's gates with his horde of monkeys."

"I myself will destroy that monkey army," cried one of the foolish advisors. Another ventured, "You have never been defeated by Devas, celestials, or rākshasas. How can a mere monkey army do you harm?"

"We were taken by surprise by Hanumān," cried another. "Just order us to attack them now, and we will wipe them out before nightfall."

Shouting and brandishing their clubs, javelins, and spears, in their fury the rākshasa leaders jumped to their feet and ran to the door as if to attack Rāma at that moment. They were stopped by the exalted, high-souled Vibhīshaṇa, brother of Rāvaṇa. He stood in their way, calmly raising his hand and motioning them back to their seats. Then he took the floor.

"According to the science of warfare, we should resort to force only if the first three tactics of conciliation—negotiations, giving gifts, and sowing dissension—have failed. Even then, the wise know that an attack will succeed only in certain circumstances: if the enemy is evil, is caught off-guard, is already fighting with another foe, or is doomed by fate," he said in a firm, clear voice. "Why should we attack Rāma, who is waiting for battle, alert and fully prepared? In addition, he has Dharma on his side, for he has been wronged by you. The only way to avoid being destroyed by Rāma's superior forces is to give his wife back to him. I speak the truth, and I advise you only out of brotherly affection. Take pity on your people, let them live long, and follow the path of righteousness."

Rāvaṇa, who had grown thin and weak from his obsession with Sītā, quickly ended the meeting and retired to his private palace. But the truthful and wise Vibhīshaṇa followed him even there. He knew that it was dangerous to press his view on Rāvaṇa, but the situation had become so extreme that he felt he had no choice. He was treading a path that he knew was the way of Dharma. That thought emboldened him.

As he entered the lavish palace of Rāvaṇa and made his way to the king's private apartments, passing throngs of beautiful women and gaily decorated elephants, he heard the bards wishing their ruler victory in battle. Vibhīshaṇa approached his brother with reverence, winning him over with kind and deferential words, and took his seat humbly where Rāvaṇa indicated with his eyes.

When the moment was right, Vibhīshaṇa said quietly, "There is something that your ministers are afraid to tell you, yet everyone in this city knows it but you. Ever since you brought Sītā here by force, there have been ill omens. Sacred fires smoke and fizzle; crows gather in the hundreds; elephants and horses, refusing their food, grow thin and lackluster; and jackals howl. The way to reverse this ominous trend is to return Sītā to Rāma. It is my duty to tell you what is happening. Now it is for you to decide."

Rāvaṇa stirred in his seat, his eyes darkening with anger. "I see no danger here. Rāma will never rescue Sītā. Away with you!" he roared.

After Vibhīshaṇa's departure, the demon king sank into a reverie. After some time, he decided again to call the leaders of Lankā together for a meeting. As his chariot rolled toward the royal hall, multitudes of rākshasas lined the way to greet their king. They blew conches and beat drums. Dozens of chariots, drawn by prancing steeds, followed him.

Once seated on his golden throne inlaid with lapis lazuli, Rāvaṇa said, "I have called you here once more because my brother, the brave and immeasurably strong Kumbhakarṇa, has joined the assembly at my request."

Kumbhakarṇa needed no introduction. A giant who towered three stories high, he had to enter the great hall on his knees. Immensely powerful, he could crush hundreds of men in his mammoth fingers. So destructive was he that Brahmā cursed him to sleep most of his life away, in order to stop him from destroying innocent people in his path.

Turning to face Kumbhakarṇa, who took up most of the space in the great hall, Rāvaṇa said, "As you know, I have carried Sītā, the wife of Rāma, to this fair city. I am love-struck with her. There is no other woman as beautiful, graceful, or sweet-tempered on earth. My desire is like a flame that burns me day and night. Plunged in turmoil, my days are filled with suffering, for she refuses to come to my bed. I have given her a year, out of my love for her, but now Rāma has marched to the sea and threatens to cross it. I need you to help me stop his advance and keep Sītā."

Kumbhakarṇa clearly felt irritated by his brother's weakness. "You are asking for advice too late. The time to stop the river from flowing into the ocean is when it's still on the mountain. You should have consulted your ministers before you stole Sītā. At that point there was still time to avoid calamity. As it is, you have acted recklessly and attracted enemies.

"But do not worry, I will save you from this disaster. I will fight these monkeys and tear them with my teeth. Rāma does not have a chance against me. I will drink his blood and then Sītā will be yours."

No one spoke for a while, because Rāvaṇa was visibly angered by Kumbhakarṇa's rebuke. Finally the valiant Mahāpārshva said, "Why not take Sītā by force? The one who is in the beehive and does not drink the honey is surely a fool. Once you satisfy your desire, you will surely vanquish Rāma with your prowess."

Rāvaṇa shook his ten heads. "I have to tell you a secret. I cannot take Sītā or any woman by force, due to a curse laid on me by Lord Brahmā. Once I ravished his granddaughter, and he divined it. He threatened to blow my ten heads into a thousand bits if I ever took another woman against her will. Otherwise, being mighty as the ocean and swift as the wind, I would have brought Sītā to my bed long ago. But no matter, just as I have conquered the Devas and celestials, I will destroy Rāma and his monkey army."

Then the high-souled Vibhīshaṇa stood up. The company stirred. Surely he would not dare anger the king again. "You attempt to embrace a deadly viper, my Lord. For Sītā is as dangerous to you as a serpent. Even with all your might, you and Kumbhakarṇa can no more vanquish Rāma than the clouds can vanquish the sky. Even the Devas stand in awe of the one who follows the way of Dharma."

He turned and faced the ministers. "You say you are my brother's friends, but you act as his enemies. If you want to act in his interests, restrain him from this vile deed even if you have to drag him from the hall by the hair. The path you advise is the path of destruction for us all. Persuade him to return Sītā; it is the only way to save this city and all who are dear."

Angered by his uncle's words, Indrajit burst out, "How dare you speak to my father this way? Are you such a coward that you think we will fall before those weakling princes? Have I not captured and bound Indra himself and sent the Devas running? Ho! There is nothing to fear in a mere mortal."

Vibhīshaṇa, who was himself a valiant warrior, superior even to Indrajit, responded again with wisdom and candor. "You speak the words of a child who is unable to fathom the danger that approaches. Using your power as my brother's favorite son, you boost his ego and lead him to destruction. You are speaking childish nonsense and should never have been allowed to join in this discussion. Neither you, nor I, nor Rāvaṇa, nor anyone here can withstand the arrows of Rāma. Let us give back Sītā with gifts of gold and jewels, and live our lives in peace."

Unable to control his rage any longer, Rāvaṇa shouted at Vibhīshaṇa, "It is true of all species that their worst enemy is their own kinsman. You are jealous of my success, and now you wish to disgrace me. If anyone else had spoken such treasonous words, they would now be dead!"

At these harsh and unjust words, Vibhīshaṇa sprang into the air, mace in hand. Floating high above the assembly with his four trusted ministers surrounding him, his words echoed around the hall. "I can no longer stay in your presence, my brother, for you do not follow the path of Dharma. When I try to help you, you only return my love with harsh and unjust words. Be well, fortify your city, and fight bravely. Do not worry, I will no longer plague you with unwanted advice. They say that those who are doomed do not accept the advice of their loved ones. Now I know this to be true."

With that, Vibhīshaṇa left the rākshasas and flew across the ocean to the sandy shore where Rāma was camped.

यो हि भृत्यो नियुक्तः सन्भर्त्रा कर्मणि दुष्करे ।
कुर्यात्तदनुरागेण तमाहुः पुरुषोत्तमम् ॥

They say the finest messenger completes a difficult task
with dedication, exactly as the king asks—and then does more.

—Yuddha Kāṇda 1.7

CHAPTER 41

Rāma Offers Protection to Vibhīshaṇa

To be true to Dharma,
to be kind,
to be a knower of truth,
you must give shelter
to one who begs for mercy—
even your own enemy.
Protect him
with all your power,
even with your life.

If you do not show mercy,
but allow the one to die
who has thrown himself
at your feet,
then with death he takes
all your good deeds,
leaving behind only
a stony heart.

Thus will I welcome Vibhīshaṇa,
thus would I welcome even Rāvaṇa,
thus do I welcome all
who seek refuge in me.

As Sugrīva and his guards surveyed the sea for signs of the enemy, they saw a strange light crossing the ocean. "Look out!" the guards shouted, sounding the alarm just as Vibhīshaṇa and his ministers flew into view. "These rākshasas are armed with every weapon. Give us the command and we will destroy them." To arm themselves, the monkeys grabbed boulders, uprooted trees, and driftwood logs to brandish as clubs.

Vibhīshaṇa calmly floated in the sky above the sand. That intelligent and pure-hearted warrior said to Sugrīva, "I am Vibhīshaṇa, brother of King Rāvaṇa. I have advised Rāvaṇa to abandon his evil path and return the lady Sītā to her husband. He has answered my well-considered counsel with insults and threats. Thus I have given up my home and family to come here. Please tell Rāma that I seek safety with him."

Sugrīva quickly brought the news to Rāma. "Vibhīshaṇa has surely come here to spy on us," he said, his voice agitated and shrill. "These rākshasas will use any disguise or trick to undo us. You will know what is best to do, but remember that he is the brother of Rāvaṇa. We should destroy him before he destroys us."

Rāma thanked Sugrīva courteously and turned to the monkey ministers who surrounded him. "A good king always asks the advice of his counselors. So now I ask each of you, my well-wishers, to speak. Offer me your honest thoughts about what course we should take with Vibhīshaṇa."

Everyone smiled, their hearts filled with love for Rāma. They recognized that he knew everything and had no need to ask their advice, yet he consulted them to show courtesy and love, as well as respect for the Vedic principles of enlightened rulership.

Angada spoke first. "Having come from the enemy side, he may have hidden intentions. Why not give him a test, to ascertain his true mind, before we accept and trust him?"

"Let us assign our spies to find out what Vibhīshaṇa truly wants," said the monkey commander Sharabha. "Then we can decide what to do."

Jāmbavān, the revered elder leader of the bears, spoke next. "This Vibhīshaṇa is to be suspected on all counts, for he is the brother of the evil Rāvaṇa, and he comes at the wrong time and place."

Another learned leader, Mainda, said, "Let's question him in a friendly way to see what he is really thinking."

Finally, when all had spoken, Hanumān addressed Rāma in his simple and logical way. "You are the most learned and wise judge in the three worlds. I am offering my advice now, not because I want to argue with the others, but because your courtesy and kindness inspire me to reveal my feelings.

"It seems to me that there are flaws in the suggestions that have been offered. To test his abilities and sincerity would take time, which we cannot afford. To send a spy would not be right, because the circumstances do not require a secret investigation. By our questioning him, he would only become suspicious, and we may lose a true friend. Further, it is not even possible to learn a person's inner intentions just by questioning him.

"It was said that he came here at the wrong time and place, but I feel the opposite. He did right in coming here tonight, considering that the evil Rāvaṇa is bent on destruction and that you are all-powerful. I noticed that when he spoke, there was no dishonesty or shadow on his face. Someone with hidden designs could not behave so freely and naturally. These are my thoughts, and now I leave it to you to decide for yourself."

Rāma smiled, for Hanumān had once again distinguished himself as an astute judge and brilliant speaker. With a tranquil mind Rāma addressed the entire group. "I know that every one of you has my interests at heart, so listen to my thoughts now. I cannot turn away someone who calls himself my friend, even if he hides evil intentions. The compassionate would not look upon me with favor if I refused to give help to a friend."

Sugrīva repeated his doubts even more strongly than before. "But this rākshasa, whether he has good thoughts or bad, has deserted his own brother, who is in grave danger. Whom else will he desert?"

Rāma nodded. "You reveal your deep understanding with this remark." He glanced at his dearly loved brother Lakshmaṇa and said, "Yet not all brothers are like Bharata, not all sons treat their fathers as I did, and for that matter, not all friends are like you, Sugrīva. A king has only two enemies: his kinsmen and his neighboring monarchs. We are not his kinsmen, and he does not seek to gain our kingdom. Also, from the way he spoke, it seems he fears for his life. He has already helped us by coming here, because his defection will create division among the rākshasas."

Still Sugrīva persisted. "Once welcomed, this brother of Rāvaṇa will strike you, or me or Lakshmaṇa. We must kill him now before he kills us."

"What can this rākshasa do to me, even if he is evil?" said Rāma. "If I wish, I can destroy him and the entire rākshasa army with my little finger. He has come here seeking safety; it is my Dharma to welcome him as a guest. Bring him here, give him this message from me: 'I am yours. I will defend you and anyone who comes here seeking my mercy.'"

At these words, Sugrīva finally dropped his objection and bowed to Rāma. "There is no one as compassionate as you. Concerned only with the happiness of others, adhering always to Dharma, you do only good in this world. In my heart I see now that Vibhīshaṇa is an honest being. Let us bring him here as our ally and friend."

When Vibhīshaṇa was brought before Rāma, he sank to his knees in gratitude. "I have abandoned my family and all that I love to take refuge in you. My hopes, my dreams, my life I place in your hands."

Rāma gazed at the high-souled Vibhīshaṇa with love and affection. Then he asked, "Can you tell me the strengths and weaknesses of Lankā?"

Without hesitation Vibhīshaṇa told Rāma how Indrajit possessed the power of invisibility, how Kumbhakarṇa's strength equaled Indra's, how the hundred thousand rākshasas in Rāvaṇa's army were capable of taking any form they chose.

At the end of this report, Rāma said, "Hear my vow. I swear by my three brothers that I will destroy Rāvaṇa, his sons, and his kinsmen in battle, or I will never return to Ayodhyā."

Vibhīshaṇa gravely bowed his head and said, "I will assist you with all my strength to conquer the army of Rāvaṇa and restore your beloved Sītā to you."

Embracing the high-souled Vibhīshaṇa, Rāma joyfully said to Lakshmaṇa, "Dear brother, take an urn and fill it with water from the sea. We will crown this wise leader king of Lankā today."

As the monkeys shouted, "Huzzah, huzzah!" the magnanimous Rama sprinkled the sacred seawater on Vibhīshaṇa's head, anointing him king of the rākshasas.

After the cheering subsided, Hanumān and Sugrīva questioned Vibhīshaṇa. "Do you know how we can cross this wide ocean with our entire army?"

"This ocean was hollowed out by the ancestors of Rāma," said Vibhīshaṇa. "If Rāma appeals to Sāgara, the lord of the ocean, he will help him make the crossing."

When Rāma heard this suggestion, he said to Lakshmaṇa, "Consult with Sugrīva and, between yourselves, advise me how I should proceed." Then he continued his conversation with Vibhīshaṇa, asking him penetrating questions about the fortifications inside Lankā.

As Rāma and Vibhīshaṇa talked, far above them flew one of Rāvaṇa's spies, Shārdūla. He scanned the impressive expanse of Rāma's army, spread along the shore like golden floodwaters from the sea, and quickly flew back to Rāvaṇa to report.

"Rāma's colossal army extends ten yojanas in every direction," Shārdūla told Rāvaṇa. "My advice is to send more spies. As I see it, you have three choices: return Sītā, make a treaty with the foe, or try to divide them with discord."

Rāvaṇa, who was lovesick for Sītā, decided on the last choice. He sent his minister Shuka to gather more information about the army and to try to win over Sugrīva.

Shuka, who was versed in the magical arts, took the form of a bird, crossed the ocean, and swooped over Rāma's army. Hovering above Sugrīva, he called down, "Rāvaṇa considers you as his brother. What is it to you if Rāvaṇa has stolen Rāma's wife? Why risk your army and your kingdom to fight one who has never been vanquished, even by the Devas? Go home and live happily."

"Rāvaṇa is not my brother," Sugrīva answered, "nor has he ever helped me. Through his evil deeds he has wronged my friend Rāma, and

I will destroy him, his sons, and his kingdom. Rāvaṇa has no inkling of the power and greatness of Rāma and Lakshmaṇa."

Then Sugrīva's monkey generals leapt into the air, seized Shuka by the legs, and spun him in a circle until his feathers began to fall off. They flung him to the earth.

"Save me, O Rāma!" cried out Shuka. "Tell them it is wrong to kill a messenger. If I die, the results of my bad deeds will pass to you."

Rāma heard Shuka cry out. He commanded, "Spare his life and capture him alive, for he came as a messenger. We can release him when we reach Lankā." Thus the monkeys took him into captivity as Rāma instructed, before night fell on Rāma's army as they camped by the sea.

अहत्वा रावणं संखये सपुत्रजनबान्धवम् ।
अयोध्यां न प्रवेक्ष्यामि त्रिभिस्तैर्भ्रातृभिः शपे ॥

I swear by my three brothers that I will destroy Rāvaṇa,
his sons, and his kinsmen in battle, or I will never return to Ayodhyā.

—Yuddha Kāṇda 19.21

Chapter 42

Rāma's Army Reaches Lankā

While Rāma's army camped by the sea, only one thought filled his mind: how to cross the waves and reach Sītā. He decided to take Vibhīshaṇa's advice and ask the lord of the ocean for help. To win the favor of the sea, he carefully spread a mat of sacred kusha grass on the shore. Sitting on the mat facing east, he folded his hands in a gesture of reverence. Then he closed his eyes and sat perfectly still on the grass mat for three days and three nights, patiently waiting for Sāgara, lord of the ocean, to appear.

But the ocean did not respond to Rāma's silent request, even though Rāma had shown all respect.

By the end of the third day, Rāma said to Lakshmaṇa, "I have offered all good qualities to Sāgara—tranquility, patience, sweetness—but this arrogant lord of the ocean apparently thinks these are signs of weakness. It seems impossible to win victory in this world through peaceful means, but only through force, as on the battlefield. Therefore I will churn the ocean and dry up the sea. Bring me my bow, dear Lakshmaṇa."

Lakshmaṇa did as he was asked, and then Rāma faced the sea, drew his bow, and shot fiery arrows into the waters. His eyes blazed red with anger. The sea roiled and churned, smoking with the heat of Rāma's arrows. Whales and fish by the thousands floated belly-up, and the ocean rose in giant waves.

Rāma drew his bow again and hissed through his teeth. But this time Lakshmaṇa jumped up and caught the arrow before it left the bow. "Stop," he cried.

Rāma issued his final warning to the sea. "I will dry up all your waters with my arrows, and then my army will cross to the other shore this very day. You do not know my strength."

When the sea remained silent, Rāma closed his eyes, invoked the dread weapon of Brahmā, and shot it into the ocean.

The sky darkened as if a veil had been drawn over it. The sun, moon, and stars shifted their positions until they formed a straight line across the heavens. Meteors flashed onto the waters and winds howled, snapping the tops of trees. Thunder crashed and lightning flashed, animals and birds shrieked in terror, and the ocean overran its shores.

At last the ocean king Sāgara rose slowly from the roaring waves. He shimmered with golden light, his head crowned with celestial flowers. Around his neck he wore a luminous strand of pearls, the jewels of the ocean.

"I am as boundless as the heavens and wide as the sky," he boomed. "No one can fathom my depths or freeze my churning waves into silence. Beloved Rāma, ask the monkey Nala, son of the divine architect Vishvakarman, to build a bridge, and I will hold it up. Nala has the power and engineering skill of his father. To protect your army as it passes, I will stop the crocodiles and other sea creatures from attacking them."

With that, Sāgara disappeared, and in his place rose the monkey Nala, who swelled to an immense size. "I did not want to speak of my powers because no one asked me," he said. "It is true what Lord Sāgara says. I can surely lay this bridge across the sea."

With Nala leading them, immediately the monkeys started building the bridge, merrily ripping up trees and snapping them in two, hoisting boulders as big as elephants and breaking off mountain peaks, which they piled at the edge of the sea. With Nala in the lead, they tossed all of these in the water, raising a sound like a thunderclap as the ocean roiled in giant waves. Then Nala organized the monkeys into work battalions, some holding strings to measure across the water, others carrying boulders and heaving them between the strings, and others filling in the spaces with more rocks and boughs of flowering trees on top. Thousands of monkeys splashed in the water, making the ocean swirl.

By the end of the first day, the bridge spanned fourteen yojanas. By the end of the second, it crossed twenty yojanas, by the end of the third day twenty-one more. The monkey army worked faster each day, covering more distance than the day before. On the fifth day, they laid the last stone on the opposite shore.

Never had such a feat been seen since the beginning of time. Ten yojanas wide and a hundred yojanas long, the vast, splendid bridge, strong, steadfast, and wide, separated the sparkling waters like the part of a woman's hair.

When it was complete, the army poured onto the bridge, the monkeys playfully performing backflips and leaps, shouting and jostling each other as they crossed. Some skipped along the middle, others spilled over the sides and swam in the water, while still others leapt overhead, landing here and there for an instant to catch their breath. Amid the innumerable monkeys and bears swarming over the bridge, Rāma rode on Hanumān's back, and Lakshmaṇa on Sugrīva's.

The Devas, Gandharvas, and Ṛishis watched this jubilant march across the sea with delight. When Rāma reached the other side, they sprinkled him with sacred oblations from above. "May you live long, Shrī Rāma, and triumph over your enemies!" they proclaimed.

As the first stars appeared in the sky, Rāma joyfully embraced Lakshmaṇa on the far shore. Then he said, "Let us march to Lankā now and camp outside its gates. Crows and vultures fall from the sky, a blue spot has appeared in the sun, and a red halo surrounds the moon. Evil winds are blowing, and there are many other bad omens. I fear there will soon be a bloodbath between the monkeys and the rākshasas."

Marching through the forests toward Lankā, the millions of monkeys in Rāma's massive army roared, "Victory to Rāma!" The earth shook, as if it could not bear such extreme weight. Closer to Lankā, the monkeys heard the drums and shouting of the rākshasas, which only whipped up their spirits. They roared like thunder until their throats grew hoarse.

Rāma halted the army when the fortress city of Lankā came into view, crowning the tallest peak of Mount Trikūta. At Rāvaṇa's behest, it had been restored to its previous glory by the divine architect Vishvakarman after Hanumān burned it. The city with its seven-story mansions and pleasure groves shone again like the jewel of the Devas.

"Gazing on Lankā, born of the mind of Vishvakarman, soaring to the sky, my heart stops beating and I can scarcely breathe," said Rāma. "All I can think of is my dear Sītā, locked in that city with Rāvaṇa."

Then his mind immediately focused on the task at hand. He called his army generals together and said, "We will set up our camp here, at the base of Mount Suvela, close to Lankā. Let us arrange the forces this way: the invincible Angada and my commander in chief, Nīla, at the heart of the army; the fearless Ṛishabha on the right flank; the brave Gandhamādana on the left; Jāmbavān and Susheṇa at the rear and Sugrīva's army at both sides. I will be at the head with Lakshmaṇa."

Eager to begin, the monkeys uprooted trees and toppled nearby mountain peaks to arm themselves. When the army was prepared to attack, Rāma said, "Let the messenger Shuka go free." Shuka, still in the form of a bird, flapped feebly across the sky to Rāvaṇa's palace.

When Rāvaṇa, seated on his lapis lazuli throne and waited on by beautiful women, saw the bedraggled Shuka standing before him, he couldn't refrain from laughing. "So you return at last. Did you let those monkeys clip your wings? Tell me all that you saw."

Shuka, who was still shaking from being attacked by the monkeys, said, "Those monkeys jumped on me and would have killed me if Rāma hadn't shown mercy. The monkeys are ferocious and angry—there is no use trying to negotiate with them. Sugrīva has joined forces with Rāma, and they have crossed the sea and lie waiting outside the city. You have only two choices: return Sītā or fight."

"I will never return Sītā!" Rāvaṇa roared. "I am itching to loose my arrows on that weakling Rāma. He does not know my strength."

The demon king ordered Shuka to return to Rāma's camp along with another minister, Sāraṇa. They were to disguise themselves as monkeys and gauge the strength of the monkey army and their leaders, including Rāma and Lakshmaṇa.

As they crept among the monkey troops, Shuka and Sāraṇa were amazed at the army's size and power. It stretched from the gates of Lankā to the seashore and across the bridge, as the rear of the army was only now leaving the far shore of the ocean and beginning the crossing. The two spies moved freely among the monkeys until Vibhīshaṇa recognized his fellow rākshasas and ordered the monkeys to seize them.

"These are Rāvaṇa's spies, disguised as monkeys," said Vibhīshaṇa, as the monkey guards dragged the spies to Rāma.

Shuka and Sāraṇa fell to the ground. "Spare us, for we were sent here by Rāvaṇa to find out everything there is to know about your army," they said.

Rāma laughed heartily to hear them admit openly that they were spying. Ever compassionate, the protector of all beings who ask for his protection, he said, "If you are through gathering your information, you may return safely to Rāvaṇa. If you need more time, feel free to wander about some more. Vibhīshaṇa will show you. Messengers without weapons should not be killed."

The two spies, feeling lucky to escape with their lives, flew back to Rāvaṇa without lingering. Again, Shuka advised his king to give up Sītā. "Those monkeys are crude and vicious, and it is only through Rāma's grace that we escaped. Rāma is strong enough and has the weapons to level Lankā on his own. When his strength is combined with that of Lakshmaṇa, Vibhīshaṇa, Sugrīva, and the vast monkey army, who are capable of magnificent feats and can grow to an enormous size, then even with the help of the asuras it will be impossible to defend Lankā. Our only hope is to make peace with them and give back Sītā."

Rāvaṇa bellowed, "Even if the Devas, Gandharvas, and celestials unite to fight me, I will never give up Sītā. You're just shaken from being handled roughly by those monkeys. No one can defeat me in battle."

Having ignored their advice, Rāvaṇa nevertheless summoned Shuka and Sāraṇa to a tower window that looked down on the sea of golden monkeys camped below. He ordered the spies to point out each leader and describe his strengths. Dutifully, Shuka and Sāraṇa described in detail the formidable strength of Hanumān, Sugrīva, Angada, Nīla, Nala, Susheṇa, Tāra, Ṛishabha, Gandhamādana, and the wondrous feats of all the monkeys, born of Devas and Gandharvas. They pointed out the army of bears led by Jāmbavān, the son of Brahmā, and his older brother Dhumra. And they described the supreme power of the magnanimous, blue-tinted Rāma and the unfathomable skill and determination of the golden-hued Lakshmaṇa.

"So great is this army it is impossible to count," concluded Shuka.

"There are monkey soldiers numbering at least one hundred crores," added Sāraṇa, "and each monkey is as large as a mountain and as strong as Indra."

"Enough!" roared Rāvaṇa. Recognizing his enemy's unconquerable might for the first time, Rāvaṇa felt a tremor of fear pierce his heart. But rather than admit this weakness, he covered it up by blustering to his spies, "How dare you praise the enemy in front of me? Displeasing a king brings certain death. Only the memory of your past service keeps me from ending your lives."

The two faithful ministers hung their heads, humiliated and trembling from fear. Whispering "Victory to Rāvaṇa," they slipped away, feeling lucky to escape Rāvaṇa's wrath alive.

Rāvaṇa sent yet another set of spies. "Find out what Rāma plans to do next," he ordered. "Victory is certain for the king who is informed of his enemy's intentions." But they too were apprehended by Vibhīshaṇa and roughed up by the strong monkeys before Rāma could release them. "It's not possible to spy on these monkeys," they cried to Rāvaṇa when they returned. "They are too powerful and alert. The monkey army is now camped just outside Lankā. You must give up Sītā or fight."

"I will never give up Sītā!" roared Rāvaṇa once more. But even though his ten faces looked as arrogant and proud as ever, underneath he was deeply shaken. He quickly called his council of ministers. Having received their advice, he summoned the sorcerer Vidyujjihva, who was skilled in black magic.

Together they walked to the Ashoka Grove. Before they reached Sītā, Rāvaṇa stopped in a secluded spot, hidden by trees.

"I need you to make a head that looks like Rāma's, and a bow and arrows exactly like his," whispered Rāvaṇa, rubbing his hands together in delight. The sorcerer immediately created the head. Rāvaṇa, eager to put his plan into action, strode toward Sītā, who sat on the bare ground, her head hanging in despair, guarded by dozens of fierce rākshasa women.

"Your precious husband is dead," the evil Rāvaṇa announced to Sītā. "Now you have no excuse not to become my wife. Give up your silly pride and come to my bed. Your Rāma met a most unpleasant end. Our army attacked his at midnight, and in one clean sweep our general, Prahasta, severed Rāma's head while he was sleeping. Hanumān, Sugrīva, Angada, and all the monkey leaders are slain, and Lakshmaṇa has fled for his life. Here is Vidyujjihva, who brought the head to me."

The magician placed the false head of Rāma, dripping with blood, on the ground in front of Sītā, along with Rāma's bow and arrows.

"Look on your husband," said the cruel Rāvaṇa. "What good does he do you now?"

Sītā opened her eyes, saw her husband's head, and fainted away. When she regained consciousness, she lamented, "O my beloved one, what has become of your vow to always take me with you? Now you have left your youthful and devoted wife behind. I must have done some evil deed in the past to meet this fate. Here you have come to rescue me, and because of your love for me, you have met your death. What will Kausalyā say, when she finds her son has been killed and I am in captivity? Kaikeyī will finally be happy, for she has destroyed the family at its roots. Cut off my head, Rāvaṇa, and throw it beside my husband's. That would be the kindest thing to do, for I cannot live without him." Crying and moaning, Sītā was beside herself with grief.

At that moment, Rāvaṇa was called away by Prahasta and the other ministers, who urgently needed to confer with him to plan the battle. The moment he left the Ashoka Grove, the false head of Rāma disappeared.

Sītā, like a suffering mare who rolls in the dust, did not even notice that the head was gone. Seeing her anguish, the soft-spoken rākshasī Saramā, who had become Sītā's friend, sat down beside her and began stroking her hair.

"This is only a trick of Rāvaṇa's," she said in soothing tones. "If you were not so worn down with hunger and heartache you would remember that it is not possible to vanquish the invincible Rāma. He camps outside Lankā's door with his expansive army, having crossed the bottomless ocean. Your time for rejoicing has come. Give up your tears."

And so Sītā learned that Rāma was not dead after all, but was closer to her than he had been in months.

"I could fly to Rāma this very minute and give him your good wishes, my lady of dark eyes," said the kindhearted Saramā.

"I know you could fly even to the heavens, if you wished," said Sītā sweetly. "I know you will attempt the impossible on my behalf. If you wish to help me, let me know what Rāvaṇa is planning. He has thrown my mind into turmoil with his evil threats." And so Saramā flew to Rāvaṇa's court, to listen.

She soon flew back and told Sītā, "Rāvaṇa's own mother, Kaikasī, and the elderly ministers are advising him over and over to return you to Rāma. But he is bent on destruction. Only when Rāma vanquishes him in battle will you be released. I see in my mind's eye that Rāma will soon free you, and sitting on his lap, you will return with him to Ayodhyā."

Just then they heard the beating of the drums and the shouting of the monkey army outside Lankā's gates. The earth shook with a deafening clamor, and throughout the city the rākshasas shivered in terror.

विशालः सुकृतः श्रीमान्सुभूमिः सुसमाहितः ।
अशोभत महासेतुः सीमन्त इव सागरे ॥

The vast, splendid bridge, strong, steadfast and wide, stretched across the sparkling waters like the part of a woman's hair.

—Yuddha Kāṇda 22.79–80

CHAPTER 43

The War Begins

Rāma's army of monkeys
extends as wide as the ocean,
covers the land like locusts,
and blots out the sun.
Each monkey has the strength of ten elephants,
some the power of a hundred, and some of a thousand.
The captains are stronger still.
Standing upright, they

gleefully lift fallen trees like toys,
with bared teeth as strong as a tiger's,
nails as sharp as a lion's.
Sons of Devas,
invincible as the earth,
able to change their form at will,
these monkeys fight on the side of truth.

Rāvaṇa, who made the three worlds wail, heard the tumult outside the city gates. Sitting with his chief ministers, he said with a sneer, "I see that you tremble at the sound of Rāma's army. You seem to have forgotten your own prowess."

Then Mālyavān, Rāvaṇa's maternal grandfather and the most learned of the ministers, slowly rose to speak. "A king becomes powerful when he is learned in the Vedas, follows the principles of statecraft and keeps his enemies under control—either by appeasing the strong or conquering the weak. A king should never underestimate his enemies. That is why I feel you should return Sītā to Rāma. All the Devas and Ṛishis pray for Rāma to succeed. For all these years now, you have championed *adharma*, and have shattered the yagyas of the Ṛishis. But that has only made the Ṛishis and Devas strengthen their resolve to uphold Dharma. Now they will use your own evil deeds to destroy you.

"Remember, too, that Lord Brahmā gave you immunity from death at the hand of Deva, Gandharva, yaksha, asura, or rākshasa. But you have no immunity from man or monkey. There are bad omens everywhere. Housewives dream of disasters, a red cloud drips blood over the city, and Death hovers over every home. Consider these warnings and do what you know is right."

Rāvaṇa's eyes turned red and spun in their sockets. His breath grew hot and labored, and he shouted, "This harsh advice could hardly be in my best interest. I have never been defeated, never. How could this mere man hurt me? Why should I give up Sītā out of fear of monkeys? I will destroy them all, you will see."

No one dared counter Rāvaṇa when he raged like this. So his ministers wished him victory, and the rākshasa king stomped out of the hall. Rāvaṇa's mind was now made up. There would be no more discussion with his advisors. He called his military leaders together and began preparations for war.

Meanwhile, from his camp at the foot of Mount Suvela, Rāma planned his attack on Lankā. "We must remember that this is Rāvaṇa's city," said Rāma to Lakshmaṇa, Sugrīva, and his other military chiefs. "We should take extra precautions."

At that moment, Vibhīshaṇa arrived at the war council. "I have sent my ministers, disguised as doves, into the city of Lankā," said Vibhīshaṇa. "My brother Rāvaṇa has placed Prahasta and his army at the eastern gate, Mahodara and Mahāpārshva at the southern gate, and Indrajit at the western gate. The spies Shuka and Sāraṇa, along with Rāvaṇa himself, wait at the northern gate, and Virūpākasha is stationed at the center. In all there are one thousand warriors on elephants, ten thousand on chariots, twenty thousand on horseback, and nearly one hundred thousand on foot."

With this valuable information, Rāma quickly arranged his army. "I am determined to kill Rāvaṇa myself," he said. "With Lakshmaṇa, I will penetrate the northern gate and overcome him."

Rāma gave a few prudent orders to the monkey chiefs, who had the power to appear in any form they chose. "None of us will appear as men, except Vibhīshaṇa, his four ministers, Lakshmaṇa, and me. Everyone else will retain their form as monkey or bear, and that is how we will distinguish our allies from our foes—for these rākshasas often look the same as men."

Then Rāma said, "Let us climb Mount Suvela. From there we can better see the city of that demon that carried off my wife. On account of his evil deed, his whole race will perish at my hand."

Angry at the thought of Rāvaṇa, eager for battle, Rāma strode up the path to the top of Mount Suvela. Followed first by Lakshmaṇa, ever vigilant, his bow ready to vanquish the enemy, and next by Vibhīshaṇa, Angada, Sugrīva, Hanumān, the other monkey leaders, and the entire army of monkeys and bears, Rāma reached the summit and gazed at Lankā across the valley.

Rāma and his retinue were so close that they could see Rāvaṇa himself on the palace balcony, robed in a dazzling red silken garment. They smelled the fragrance of blossoming trees wafting from Rāvaṇa's gardens, and heard the cooing of exotic birds from the thick woods surrounding the city. They saw its impregnable walls thrusting high into the clouds above Trikūta Mountain. Hordes of rākshasas guarded its gates, and drawbridges operated by machines were folded up like moths' wings, making the moat impassable.

When Sugrīva saw Rāvaṇa on the balcony of his palace, being fanned by rākshasas waving fans of white yak tails, he could not contain his wrath.

Springing into the air, that strong and powerful monkey leapt across the valley and hovered above Rāvaṇa. "I am Sugrīva, the friend and humble servant of Rāma, who rules the world with his benevolence," he cried. "I will destroy you today!" Sugrīva swooped over the dreaded Rāvaṇa's head, snatched his crown, and hurled it onto the marble terrace.

Enraged, Rāvaṇa, who made the three worlds tremble, screamed, "You were once known for your thick and powerful neck, but now I will snap it in two." Jumping up, he grabbed Sugrīva and threw him down, but like a ball Sugrīva bounced up again and threw Rāvaṇa down. The two mighty warriors, equal in strength and skill, locked arms in a fierce combat and pounded each other with their fists. When one got thrown by the other, he only sprang up and started again. Sometimes one circled like a cat; other times they locked arms and tumbled over and over. Once they lurched over the castle wall and fell toward the ground—but just before reaching it, they both shot up into the sky and landed on the terrace again, ready for a new round.

Finally, unable to vanquish Sugrīva by his own strength, Rāvaṇa decided to resort to magic. Intuiting this, Sugrīva bounded into the sky, undefeated. Having humiliated the rākshasa king in his own palace, he leapt back to Rāma, greeted by the roars and cheers of the delighted monkeys.

Rāma embraced his friend and gently chided him. "You should never do such an impulsive thing again without consulting me," he said. "Leaders of armies should not indulge in such rash feats. What would become of me if something happened to you? As I watched you, my heart was filled with misgiving."

Sugrīva, ever the faithful friend, said simply, "When I saw Rāvaṇa, who carried off your faithful wife, I could not help but avenge that insult to you, knowing my own strength."

Hearing this, Rāma praised his loyal friend, who had bravely attacked and humiliated Rāvaṇa.

After camping overnight on the mountain, Rāma said to his valiant brother Lakshmaṇa, "I see all the omens of a catastrophe. The wind blows in fierce gales, the moon is dim and encircled with a red halo, and a black patch mars the sun. See, the stars have lost their brightness, O Lakshmaṇa, foretelling and hastening the end of a *yuga*. Let us march to Lankā now."

When they reached Lankā, the commander in chief Nīla, along with his forces, took the eastern gate, Hanumān and his army the west, and Angada took the south. Rāma and Lakshmaṇa stationed themselves at the northern gate, where Rāvaṇa waited behind Lankā's walls. Thousands of monkeys clustered at each entrance with their leaders, surrounding the city and all the land to the sea, making the rākshasas within Lankā shake with fear.

Having positioned the army for combat, Rāma gathered his commanders and ministers and consulted with them once more. After listening to their advice, he said to Angada, "Go to Rāvaṇa and deliver this last warning from me: 'You have stolen my wife by trickery. Now you will suffer the consequences of a lifetime of evil deeds against Devas, Gandharvas, Ṛishis, and men. No more will you stomp the earth, making all good people tremble in your wake. I, a mere man, will destroy you and your kingdom and place the high-souled Vibhīshaṇa in your place. Take a last look around Lankā and prepare yourself for death.'"

Angada, eager to serve Rāma, flew immediately to the throne room in the palace where Rāvaṇa sat, surrounded by his ministers. Standing a short distance away, the youthful monkey prince delivered Rāma's message.

Rāvaṇa burned with rage and smoke poured from his ears. "Seize him!" he roared.

The youthful Angada, brimming with vigor and strength, allowed the four fiercely armed demon guards to catch hold of him. With them clinging to his arms, he soared high in the air and then flicked off the guards like flies, watching as they tumbled to their deaths on the marble floor beside Rāvaṇa.

As he flew out the window, Angada spied the royal crest adorning the top of Rāvaṇa's palace. He kicked it with his powerful legs, and it plummeted to the ground and smashed into bits, striking terror into the heart of Lankā. Now even Rāvaṇa could foresee dreadful things to come. Rākshasas grabbed their weapons and rushed to and fro within the city walls, as if hit by the force of a wild wind.

Greeted by cheering monkeys, Angada returned to Rāma victorious. With this auspicious act, Rāma's army, eager to fight, launched their attack on Lankā. Rāma, thinking of Sītā and her terrible suffering, entered the fray with ferocious joy.

Rāvaṇa's ministers informed him, "The enemy has begun the attack." Rāvaṇa doubled his armies at each gate and climbed to the top of his palace to survey the battle below.

There, in plain sight, he saw thousands of monkeys beating on the walls of Lankā with stones, tree trunks, and their bare fists, running and tumbling over each other in their eagerness to storm the city, shouting "Jai Shrī Rāma!" They overran the outer ramparts like an ocean in a storm. Then they choked the moat with rocks and trees, which allowed them to cross and gain a foothold inside the moat.

Rāvaṇa ordered his armies to march out to meet the foe. The city's four gates opened and hordes of fierce, dark-skinned rākshasas flooded out of the dread city of Lankā like the engulfing waters at the end of time. Screaming and howling, beating their drums and blowing a thousand conches, they were armed with maces, swords, javelins, spears, and hatchets.

Thus began the fight between the demons and the monkeys, which rivaled the war between the Devas and asuras of old. A terrific din filled the air, as elephants, horses, and chariots joined in combat. The rākshasas whirled amongst their enemies with weapons flashing. The monkeys scratched and clawed and pummeled their foes. Some jumped up on the city's wall and rained stones on the enemy below. Soon the ground was covered with blood.

As golden chariots flashed in the sun and decorated horses pranced into battle, many duels were fought all around the gates to the city. Angada fought Indrajit; Hanumān smashed Jambumālī with his bare hand; Sugrīva killed Praghasa with the trunk of an axlewood tree; and Sushеṇa vanquished Vidyunmālī. Several rākshasas together fought Rāma, who shot off their heads with his arrows.

Everywhere the fierce rākshasas were demolished by Rāma and the ferocious monkeys, and the demon army withdrew to regroup.

Having renewed their forces, the fierce rākshasas again charged the monkeys, devouring them in their fury. The monkeys responded with equal furor, pounding the demons with their powerful paws. As night fell, the battle raged on, the golden armor of the rākshasas gleaming in the gloom. The cries of the dying filled the air on that dark night of destruction, while Rāma's fiery arrows found the hearts of thousands of demons.

In the duel between Angada and Indrajit, Angada had destroyed Indrajit's chariot. Once his chariot and horses were gone, that devious son of Rāvaṇa left the battlefield. The Devas and the celestial Ṛishis, looking down from above, showered the youthful Angada with praises, as did Rāma and Lakshmaṇa. "Wonderful!" shouted the monkeys, for all knew of Indrajit's strength.

Having retreated, Indrajit, who had once bound Indra in battle, was beside himself with fury. He could not bear to be vanquished by a mere monkey. He returned to fight, determined to use magic to gain a victory.

Rāma saw clouds churning furiously and realized that Indrajit was driving his invisible chariot to the spot where Rāma stood beside Lakshmaṇa at Lankā's northern gate. Rāma said to the monkeys, "It is better if you stay behind with Sugrīva, and let Indrajit win this one battle, for the time is propitious for his victory. There is nothing I can do against his magic." Then Indrajit, who hid behind a shield of invisibility like the sun behind a cloud, struck Rāma and Lakshmaṇa on their arms, legs, and bodies with arrows that pierced deeply and made them bleed.

"I was able to vanquish Indra himself, so how did you think you could escape me?" Indrajit taunted. A group of monkeys tried to stop the son of Rāvaṇa, but they spun aimlessly about the battlefield like a whirlwind, unable to attack their invisible tormentor.

Rāma fell first, bound with serpents as thick as ropes. Seeing his brother fall, Lakshmaṇa lost heart, and soon he too was bound by Indrajit's deadly serpent-weapons. Without the ability to see the crafty Indrajit, the two sons of Dasharatha could not defend themselves and sank to the ground, fettered and senseless, bleeding profusely from their wounds.

दृश्यन्ते न यथावच्च नक्षत्राण्यभिवर्तते ।
युगान्तमिव लोकस्य पश्य लक्ष्मण शंसति ॥

See, the stars have lost their brightness, O Lakshmaṇa,
foretelling and hastening the end of an age of a yuga.

—Yuddha Kāṇḍa 41.19

Chapter 44

The War Rages

Hanumān, Angada, Sugrīva, and all the monkey chiefs gathered around Rāma and Lakshmaṇa. Seeing the heroes lying on the ground unconscious, unable to move, those valiant commanders cried out in anguish. When Vibhīshaṇa arrived, he alone, having the eyes of a rākshasa, could see Indrajit hiding in the sky.

"I have slain the brothers who disgraced my aunt Shūrpaṇakhā, who killed the immeasurably strong Dūshaṇa, and who have kept my father awake on sleepless nights," cried Indrajit. Then he rained down more arrows on Hanumān, Sugrīva, and Angada, injuring them badly before withdrawing to his father's palace to celebrate. The entire rākshasa army, seeing the brothers lying dead on the ground, whooped in victory.

Vibhīshaṇa saw the pale color and downcast eyes of Sugrīva and the other brave monkey chiefs. "Do not be distressed, Sugrīva. Sometimes a battle is lost, sometimes won. They will recover from their faint. Show your courage, and your troops will feel courageous too."

Asking that water be brought, Vibhīshaṇa chanted a prayer and bathed Sugrīva's eyes with the water. This he did twice. Then he said, "This is nothing to Rāma. He is not going to die. Let us not spend our energy in wasteful emotions, but rather in reviving him and Lakshmaṇa. Comfort your forces; do not let them lose hope. I will find out what can be done." Thus the greathearted Vibhīshaṇa saved Rāma's army from succumbing to fear.

MEANWHILE, INSIDE HIS palace, Rāvaṇa could not contain his joy. When Indrajit first told him the news, he sprang from his throne with jubilation. He embraced his son, praising him as a hero, and made Indrajit sit beside him and tell again and again how he had felled the invincible warriors Rāma and Lakshmaṇa. Conches blew, drums rolled, and the citizens spilled onto the streets of Lankā in wild jubilation. After ordering flags of victory and bright banners to be strung from all the buildings, Rāvaṇa sent for the rākshasīs who guarded Sītā.

Trijatā arrived with the others, and they bowed to their king. "Tell Sītā," said Rāvaṇa, "that her husband and his brother have been killed by Indrajit. Take my aerial car, Pushpaka, and fly Sītā over the battlefield where Rāma and Lakshmaṇa lie slain, so that she can see for herself that there is no hope of her husband ever rescuing her. Now she can abandon her pride and her obstinacy, and surrender to me adorned with every jewel."

The rākshasīs bowed to Rāvaṇa and did as they were told. When Sītā was flown over the battlefield and saw her husband and the brave Lakshmaṇa lying on the field, their limbs pierced with arrows and lying limp, she burst into tears. As sobs wracked her body, she lamented, "All the learned astrologers, who predicted that I would live a life untarnished by inauspiciousness, have been proven wrong by Rāma's death. Those who read auspicious signs, who saw these lotus markings on my feet and predicted that I would sit on a throne by my husband's side, were mistaken also. What good were all those happy predictions, when now my husband and his brother are dead? Having performed numerous brave and heroic acts, having never spoken a wrong word or thought of a wrong deed, my beloved lord has lost his life. Alas, I weep for myself, but even more for Mother Kausalyā, who waits each day for the return of her son."

Trijatā directed the flying chariot, which flew by thought alone, back to the Ashoka Grove, where Sītā collapsed under the tree, her heart broken. Sītā's sadness was so overwhelming that Trijatā sat on the ground beside her, smoothing her hair and gently drying her tears.

"Do not grieve so, my lady," Trijatā said. "For Rāma is not dead. Didn't you notice how the monkeys standing around him appeared alert and hopeful? They did not bear the signs of wild mourning, which would be fitting if their leaders were truly dead. No one in this world could kill your Rāma. Please, for your own sake, believe what I tell you, for I have never spoken an untruth. I speak only out of affection, for you have been kind to me despite all your troubles."

Sītā clasped her hands tightly together and whispered, "I pray with all my heart that these words prove true."

As Sugrīva and the other monkeys stood watch over the inert bodies of Rāma and Lakshmaṇa, Rāma opened his eyes. Still bound by poisonous serpents, his whole body bleeding and painful, he gazed at his brother Lakshmaṇa, who lay unmoving on the field. "How can I live without my brother?" Rāma cried out. "I could never find another brother such as Lakshmaṇa, who has been my trusted friend and my constant companion. If he is dead, I will take my own life. O Lakshmaṇa, you have always cheered me when I was sad. Why are you silent now? You have never said an unkind word to me; you have only brought me good. Yet you have been lured to your death on my account."

Rāma glanced at his friends and supporters. "Dear Sugrīva," he said. "You have been an ideal friend. No one could have done more for me than you. You have pleased me with your devotion. Now you must return home and leave me here to die with Lakshmaṇa."

Tears rained down the faces of the monkeys who encircled the brothers like a garland. As they stood there weeping, a fierce wind kicked up, scattering the clouds. Lightning cracked the sky, and the sea heaved mountains of water. Trees snapped and fell into the ocean. The sea creatures escaped to the still depths of the ocean.

Suddenly a giant bird swooped down upon them. At the sight of the bird, the serpents that bound Rāma and Lakshmaṇa fled to the sea for safety. Hovering over the two heroes, his feathers sparkling with white light, the mammoth bird gently brushed their bodies with his wings. At his touch, all their wounds disappeared, and they recovered from their swoon with their prowess, energy, and skill not only restored but doubled in strength.

Sitting up, his robust good health revived, Rāma said, "Who are you, great bird? I feel like embracing you as a brother or as my own father."

"O Rāma, I am Garuda, your dear friend of old, your very breath. When I heard that the serpents of Indrajit bound your limbs, I flew across the wide ocean to heal you. Now you know that these rākshasas resort to trickery; they do not fight in a straightforward way as you do."

Then Garuda, the king of the birds, who was in fact a descendant of Lord Vishṇu, reassured Rāma with encouraging words. "Do not be too curious about our friendship, Rāma. All will be revealed to you at the end of the war. Ever following your Dharma, loving even your enemies, you will be victorious over Rāvaṇa and reunite with Sītā once more."

Seeing Rāma's miraculous recovery, the monkeys cheered with joy. In their delight they danced and pounded their drums and blew their conches. They somersaulted and cartwheeled around the battlefield, playfully scaling the walls of Lankā and bounding down again.

Rāvaṇa, hearing the drums, asked his ministers, "What is this joyful noise coming from Rāma's camp?" When he was told that Rāma and Lakshmaṇa had revived and escaped their bonds, for the first time the demon king plunged into despondency. "If Rāma can free himself from Indrajit's dread serpent-weapons, given to him by the Devas, then I fear our army is doomed."

Hissing like a dragon, he bellowed, "Dhūmrāksha! Take your army and march on Rāma and his monkey troops!"

Dhūmrāksha mounted his chariot and sailed out from the city gates at the head of his army, armed for battle and thirsty for Rāma's blood. But when he crossed under the soaring arch of the city gate, a dead vulture tumbled into his chariot. Dhūmrāksha saw other portents of impending death and trembled with fear.

Gathering his courage, he plunged into the ocean of monkeys followed by his fierce demon army. A terrific struggle took place, with both sides fighting valiantly. Eventually, the monkeys gained the upper hand, and the rākshasas fled. But the powerful Dhūmrāksha himself set upon the monkeys in a fury, scattering them in all directions.

Then Hanumān dueled with the powerful rākshasa. First the Son of the Wind smashed the demon's chariot, while Dhūmrāksha rained blows on that invincible warrior's head with a spiked mace. Losing patience, Hanumān grabbed the crest of a nearby mountain and broke it off, smothering Dhūmrāksha beneath it.

When Rāvaṇa heard that his mighty warrior was slain, he could not believe the news. In a voice hoarse with rage he ordered Vajradaṁshtra to the battlefield.

Vajradaṁshtra circled his chariot with folded hands and, mounting it, led a multitude of demons in gold chariots with their elephants, camels, and horses. Thundering out of the southern gate like a dark cloud, they immediately saw fiery sticks falling from the blue sky. Jackals howled. Beset by these evil omens, even the fierce commander Vajradaṁshtra shivered. But trained to be courageous, he pressed on to the fight.

The monkeys set on those demons with tree trunks and rocks. Vajradaṁshtra and his fierce troops cut a wide swath through the monkey army. The relentless twang of the bows, crunching blows, and wild war whoops created a fearful clamor.

Seeing his monkey army being destroyed, the youthful Prince Angada felt anger boiling in his heart. The invincible Angada mowed down multitudes of rākshasas before he faced Vajradaṁshtra alone, like a tiger facing an elephant. He rushed at Vajradaṁshtra with a shāla tree trunk, screaming like Death itself.

Vajradaṁshtra shot hundreds of arrows into Angada's stomach. Not even feeling the pain, Angada cast aside the tree trunk and lifted an enormous rock and flung it at the chariot. Vajradaṁshtra nimbly leapt out before the boulder bashed the chariot to bits. Swiftly Angada broke off an entire mountain peak and crushed the valiant Vajradaṁshtra beneath it.

The demon warrior stopped breathing. Then he suddenly jumped up and clobbered Angada with his mace. That son of Bāli, strong as marble, pounced on Vajradaṁshtra and pummeled him with his paws. The fight continued with tree trunks, swords, shields, and rocks being hurled back and forth. Finally both warriors fell to their knees, exhausted by each other's blows. Suddenly Angada felt a burst of energy and, springing up, grabbed Vajradaṁshtra's sword and cut off his head.

The remaining rākshasa army, seeing their leader slain, tore through Lankā's gates and into the city streets, chased by the victorious monkeys. Surrounding Angada, the monkeys cheered and lifted up their heroic prince, honoring him as the Devas honored Indra.

And so it went. The terrifically strong rākshasa warrior Akampana sallied into the furor of battle next. A cloud of dust rose so thick that no one could see, as if the darkness of night had fallen. In that fog of war, friends killed friends and foes killed foes. Akampana, who could not be conquered even by the Devas, wreaked havoc on the monkey army.

At one point, Hanumān peered through the veil of dust, saw the monkey army scattering, and ran to rally it. Grabbing the top of a mountain, he flung it at Akampana, but the demon's half-moon arrows crumbled the mass of boulders in midair. Then Hanumān grabbed a tree trunk and cracked the warrior's head. Again the rākshasa army scurried back inside Lankā's walls, howling in terror.

Rāvaṇa, beside himself with rage, summoned Prahasta, his eldest warrior and commander in chief. "It seems that to save the city we must send you, Indrajit, or myself," said Rāvaṇa. "What do you advise?"

Prahasta bowed to Rāvaṇa and said, "When you asked my opinion earlier, I advised you to send Sītā back to save the city. Even though you did not follow my advice, you have always bestowed upon me the highest honors, and I will not fail you now. Nothing—not my life, my children nor my wealth—is as important to me as doing my duty. Let me command a multitude of rākshasas. Soon those monkeys will flee in fright. Soon they will be lying dead at my sword."

A larger force of demon warriors was assembled, and smoke filled the streets of Lankā as rākshasas prepared for battle by offering ghee to sacred fires. Drums rolled, conches trumpeted, and rākshasas screeched as Prahasta took the lead. Bursting through the eastern gate, rumbling like thunder, the demons struck fear into the hearts of all creatures.

Yet this massive army also met with evil omens. The planets reeled too close to the sun, vultures wheeled above Prahasta's chariot, and his trusted charioteer accidentally dropped his whip. Prahasta's innate courage faltered as he saw his horses stumble. But he rallied and bravely led his army into the fray, trouncing the monkeys in his path.

Seeing the rākshasa horde pour out of the eastern gate of Lankā, Rāma asked Vibhīshaṇa, "Who is this giant rākshasa who leads this attack?"

"That is Prahasta, commander in chief of the rākshasa armies. He leads the rākshasa forces and has gained victory over the Devas in battles past."

Prahasta fought valiantly, scattering the monkeys in his way. Then Nīla, son of Agni and the commander in chief of Rāma's army, spotted him. He rushed forward to attack Prahasta and soon was covered with Prahasta's arrows like a mountain covered with trees. Nīla pummeled Prahasta with rocks and trees, and snatched the rākshasa's bow. Prahasta battered the illustrious monkey's body with a club. The struggle went on for some time. Finally, Nīla raised a colossal boulder and smashed Prahasta's head under it.

Once again, the demons tucked their javelins, spears, and clubs at their sides and ran back to Lankā, their hopes scattered to the winds.

अहं सखा ते काकुत्स्थ प्रियः प्राणो बहिश्चरः ।
गरुत्मानिह सम्प्राप्तो युवयोः साह्यकारणात् ॥

O Rāma, I am Garuda, your dear friend of old,
your very breath, outward-moving, and I have come here to heal you.

—Yuddha Kāṇḍa 50.46

Chapter 45

The Rākshasas Awaken Kumbhakarṇa

When he heard the bad tidings, Rāvaṇa for once was silent. Finally he said, "It's not a good idea to make light of this foe, who has killed my commander and all his elephants. Now it is time for me to end this battle with a resounding victory."

Rāvaṇa flew out of Lankā's massive golden gates in his aerial chariot, followed by demons armed with javelins, swords, and clubs, their mouths filled with vicious, sharp teeth.

When Rāma saw Rāvaṇa, shining like a black cloud even from a distance, he said, "I can see his strength by the intense glow his body radiates. Surely he shines more brightly than Indra or the holy sages. But today I will repay him for his evil designs on Sītā."

Sugrīva rushed at Rāvaṇa first, hurling a mountain peak at Rāvaṇa's head. The demon king's arrow sliced the mountain into smithereens before it touched him. Then he shot a blazing arrow into Sugrīva's chest. The king of the monkeys fell to the ground in a faint. Other fearless monkeys rushed at the rākshasa king, but Rāvaṇa easily struck them down with his arrows.

Rāma, who was watching closely from his camp, resolved to fight. But Lakshmaṇa said, "Let me kill him."

Rāma nodded, saying, "Seek out his weak points and put forth all effort. Be vigilant, always on the alert." Lakshmaṇa embraced his older brother and bowed to him, then hastened to the battlefield.

Yet before the fearless brother of Rāma could reach that rider of the night, Hanumān faced Rāvaṇa.

"You may have gained immunity from death by a Deva, but a humble monkey such as I can destroy you," cried Hanumān.

"Strike quickly before I send you to death!" roared Rāvaṇa.

"Have you forgotten how I snuffed out the life of your son Aksha?" taunted Hanumān.

Rāvaṇa struck the fearless Hanumān on the chest in rage. Hanumān reeled and fell down. Then that sagacious monkey drew up his strength and sprang on Rāvaṇa, jolting him in the torso. Rāvaṇa staggered and swayed inside his chariot, like a mountain in an earthquake.

Seeing Rāvaṇa faltering, the Devas showered flower petals on Hanumān.

Even Rāvaṇa cried out, "Well done, monkey! I see by your strength that you are a worthy foe."

"I care nothing for this praise, for you still live," said Hanumān. "Ready yourself for Death's abode, you fool."

This made Rāvaṇa so furious that he slugged Hanumān in the chest with all his might. Hanumān collapsed in a daze. Rāvaṇa took the opportunity to shoot flaming arrows at Nīla, who quietly withstood their fiery burning and hurled a mountaintop at him. By this time Hanumān had recovered, but ever the follower of Dharma, Hanumān could not attack Rāvaṇa, since the rākshasa king was now engaged in combat with Nīla.

Nīla hurled rocks, trees, and boulders on Rāvaṇa. Then, to escape the demon's scorching arrows, Nīla shrank his body to the size of a mouse and sprang onto the flagpole of Rāvaṇa's chariot. The monkey armies burst out laughing, seeing Nīla tease the dread demon king.

The laughter enraged the proud Rāvaṇa. "You may be nimble and full of magic tricks," he said to Nīla, "but this arrow of Agni will take your life."

He shot the weapon at Nīla, who fell to his knees. Due to his own inner strength and the compassion of Agni, his father, he was not killed, only stunned. With Nīla in a swoon, Rāvaṇa turned next to Lakshmaṇa.

"Fight me rather than mere monkeys," cried Lakshmaṇa.

Incensed by the taunt, Rāvaṇa cried, "You will soon be turned to ashes by my burning arrows!"

"True warriors do not need to boast in battle," observed Lakshmaṇa coolly.

Rāvaṇa let fly seven arrows. Lakshmaṇa let fly seven more, which chopped Rāvaṇa's in two.

On it went. No matter how fast Rāvaṇa shot his arrows, Lakshmaṇa headed them off with his own. When Lakshmaṇa let loose a volley of arrows as swift as Indra's thunderbolt, Rāvaṇa stopped them. Finally Rāvaṇa sent the dread missile of Brahmā, striking Lakshmaṇa on the forehead.

Lakshmaṇa swayed, momentarily dazed. His bowstring hung slack, weakened by the blast. But the brave Lakshmaṇa summoned his strength and fired off three more arrows, which broke Rāvaṇa's bow and caused him to faint. Bathed in blood, Rāvaṇa regained consciousness and hurled the javelin of Brahmā, bestowed on him by Brahmā himself.

Lakshmaṇa speedily dispatched arrows to intercept the fearful javelin, but it still struck him near his heart, and he fell down. Before he could struggle to his feet, Rāvaṇa sprang on him and tried to heave him over his shoulder to carry him off. But the demon king, who was strong enough to carry off Mount Meru, could not lift Lakshmaṇa. For at that moment Lakshmaṇa remembered his origin in the invincible Vishṇu himself, and he could not be budged.

As he watched the fight, Hanumān became outraged that the demon king had tried to wrestle Lakshmaṇa when he was already injured. Hanumān landed a blow on Rāvaṇa's chest so powerful that it brought Rāvaṇa to his knees and he could not stand up. The monkeys, Devas, and Indra cried out in exaltation, seeing the proud rākshasa humbled.

Then the ever-devoted Hanumān gathered in his arms the princely warrior Lakshmaṇa, who allowed the faithful monkey to carry him to Rāma's side. There the invincible Lakshmaṇa regained his strength and his wounds miraculously healed. The javelin of Brahmā dissolved and returned to Rāvaṇa's chariot.

Seeing Rāvaṇa laying waste to the monkey chiefs, Rāma at last strode into the fray. Hanumān cried, "Here, ride on my shoulders."

When Rāma faced Rāvaṇa for the first time, his voice of truth rang throughout the battlefield. "Stop here, lord of the demons! Now that I have set eyes on you, you cannot escape, no matter whom you seek for safety."

Rāvaṇa rained blistering arrows on Hanumān's back, which only increased that formidable monkey's radiance. Angry that Rāvaṇa would hurt Hanumān, Rāma shot swift arrows that destroyed Rāvaṇa's chariot, his flagstaff, his horses, and banners.

Then Rāma's arrows struck Rāvaṇa himself full in the chest. Rāvaṇa reeled in pain and dropped his bow. Rāma selected a powerful half-moon arrow, and with it he struck Rāvaṇa's crown, breaking it into bits.

Rāvaṇa fell to his knees, weak and humiliated. Rāma said, "You deserve to suffer the consequences of my wrath, having done wrongs to Sītā, my warriors, and to me. But I see that you are fatigued from battle. Return tomorrow in your chariot, armed with your bow. Then you will see my true strength."

The king of the rākshasas, the terror of the world, limped back to Lankā on foot, his head hanging, his ears burning with shame. The Devas, Gandharvas, and other celestials laughed with joy.

Rāvaṇa had never before experienced defeat, much less total humiliation. Yet he had been crushed by Rāma like an eagle crushes a snake with its powerful beak. "I asked for immunity from Devas and rākshasas, but not from men," he told the assembly of ministers. "Now I see what Brahmā meant when he said, 'Know that you shall have cause to fear men.'" He slumped on his throne, his luster dimmed.

"The curses of the long-ago past have found me," he said, momentarily humbled, his eyes downcast. "The words of those Ṛishis who cursed me must prove true." He sank into silence.

"Nevertheless, we will win." Suddenly he rallied, reverting to his usual boasts. "Guard the gates with increased care. And send a division to wake up Kumbhakarṇa. He has returned to his bed to sleep for the next six months, but we need him on the battlefield. He is the strongest of us all. Even though Rāma defeated me, he will be crushed in the arms of Kumbhakarṇa. We must wake him up now and save Lankā from destruction."

Everyone knew that waking Kumbhakarṇa was easier said than done. Cursed to sleep six months of the year, he slept in a cave that was three yojanas in circumference, and his mammoth body filled most of it. Even entering the cave was tricky, for the force of Kumbhakarṇa's breath was as strong as the north wind, and it blasted the rākshasas out of the cave whenever they drew near. Finally, by timing their advances just right, they snuck into the cave while he was drawing an inward breath and quickly darted around his body, being careful to stay out of the path of his outgoing breath.

They had brought with them all kinds of scents, noisemakers, and implements to goad him awake. They waved strong aromas of burning sage under his nose, and they beat drums and blew conches in his elephant-sized ears. They poked him with long sharpened poles that looked like toothpicks next to his immense body.

The rākshasas piled up a mountain of dead animals and filled giant vats of wine near his nose, hoping to awaken him with the smell of food and drink. They covered him in flowers. They sang his praises in loud voices. They jumped on him as if he were a giant mattress.

Then the mighty rākshasas struck Kumbhakarṇa on the chest with clubs, maces, mallets, fists, and even mountaintops, but he lay fast asleep on the ground.

They assembled ten thousand rākshasas to shout and scream in his elephant ears. The din was so loud that citizens who lived far away in Lankā had to cover their ears, yet Kumbhakarṇa still snored.

Finally, they drove a herd of one thousand elephants over his body. Kumbhakarṇa stirred when he felt a slight twinge of pressure on his chest. They continued to pummel him with tree trunks and yanked his hair, pulling on it in teams of ten. At last he sat up yawning, his mouth gaping like a hole in the clouds. The warriors pointed to the mountain of animals, and he began to stuff whole antelopes, pigs, and buffaloes into his cavernous mouth. Lifting a wine vat as big as a city well, he slaked his thirst. When his hunger seemed satiated and he sat staring at his feet in a sluggish stupor, the rākshasas dared to approach him.

"Why have you awakened me? Is all well with my brother, the king? I am ready to help him if he needs it." His eyelids drooped, and the warriors thought they'd better hurry up and speak before he fell asleep again.

As soon as Kumbhakarṇa heard about the grave danger Lankā faced, he agreed to fight. First he bathed, then he gargled with vats of oil to cleanse his mouth. Finding himself thirsty again, he swallowed a few thousand pots of liquor.

Finally that sleepy, half-intoxicated giant stood up and strode through the streets of Lankā, toward the palace of Rāvaṇa. Seeing that invincible Kumbhakarṇa awake, his body adorned with gold and jewels, as befits a ruler's brother, the people of Lankā took hope and covered him with flower petals.

The ground trembled, and the monkeys in Rāma's army thought there was an earthquake. Looking toward Lankā, they saw Kumbhakarṇa moving through the city, his head and shoulders towering far above the seven-story mansions, his head almost touching the sun. The monkeys cried out in terror and ran to Rāma, seeking protection.

तं शैलशृङ्गैर्मुसलैर्गदाभिर्वक्षः
स्थले मुद्गरमुष्टिभिश्च ।
सुखप्रसुप्तं भुवि कुम्भकर्णं
रक्षांस्युदग्राणि तदा निजघ्नुः ॥

Then the mighty rākshasas struck Kumbhakarṇa on the chest with clubs, maces, mallets, fists, and even mountaintops, but he lay fast asleep on the ground.

—Yuddha Kāṇḍa 60.40

Chapter 46

Kumbhakarṇa Enters the Fray

Kumbhakarṇa reached the golden palace of Rāvaṇa and saw his brother sitting on his throne, eyes downcast. Rāvaṇa rose to greet him. After stretching out his enormous body in obeisance to his brother the king, Kumbhakarṇa sat up, straightened his giant crown, and said, "Why did you wake me up early? Is there someone you wish me to fight?" His eyes, small and hard in his mammoth body, flashed red.

Rāvaṇa, who knew his brother well, could see that he was angry. Not wishing to antagonize him further, he said, "I throw myself at your mercy. I have spent all of my strength and my wealth trying to defend Lankā, but now mostly widows and children remain. Please use your unmatchable strength to scatter these monkeys, who are as large as a mountain, as numerous as autumn leaves. Destroy this foe Rāma out of love for me and your people."

Kumbhakarṇa laughed bitterly. "You refused to listen to me or others when we told you to return Sītā. Without any thought of the consequences, you stole Sītā in a fit of lust, without consulting your ministers. Such a king brings ruin on his people. You did not consider duty or wealth, nor did you consider the proper steps of governing."

"How dare you criticize me!" roared Rāvaṇa. "If you are a true brother, you will help me in my time of need."

Seeing Rāvaṇa's anger, Kumbhakarṇa quickly tried to soothe him. "Even if you did make a mistake, I'll help you set it right. This very day, I'll swallow the entire monkey army for dinner, and then for dessert I'll crush Rāma with my powerful jaws."

Rāvaṇa was satisfied with this answer, but his other brother and minister, Mahodara, had something to say to Kumbhakarṇa. "How dare you attack the king on issues of government? You say that evil actions bring evil results, but that is not necessarily so. Our king has always done what he wanted and he has enjoyed a lifetime of luxury."

"It's precisely people like you who have sent Rāvaṇa to his ruin," shouted Kumbhakarṇa. "You tell him what he wants to hear, instead of giving him sound advice as ministers should."

Eager for his brother to fight Rāma, Rāvaṇa laughed demonically. "I know you can conquer Rāma; go and destroy him." Rāvaṇa adorned his brother's mountainous body with oversized gold earrings, bracelets, necklaces of pearls, and rings set with huge precious gems. Kumbhakarṇa looked like Mount Mandara when it was draped by the king of the serpents and made ready for the churning of the ocean.

Outside the palace, Kumbhakarṇa stretched to his full height, holding a gigantic iron club and spear, his body flashing in the sun. Lumbering to the city wall, he crossed it in one step, as if it were a child's playhouse. Evil omens assailed him, but he chose not to notice. Seeing thousands of monkeys scattering in fear, he threw back his head in a terrifying roar that rolled all the way to the sea and churned up ferocious waves that crashed against the shore.

Even Rāma was amazed at the monstrous size of Kumbhakarṇa as he lumbered toward them. He quickly rallied the monkey troops, who armed themselves with trees, rocks, and boulders.

Nīla, Nala, and Gavāksha fled before the giant, but the youthful prince Angada rallied them, saying, "How can you abandon your honor by running away? This is not really a rākshasa anyway, but merely an apparition they have concocted to frighten us."

The monkeys, their courage revived by Angada, rushed on Kumbhakarṇa, hurling logs and boulders. Kumbhakarṇa felt nothing. Rocks dissolved into powder on impact, without leaving a scratch, and giant tree trunks snapped against his massive body. He stomped into the monkey ranks, sweeping up monkeys by the armful and dashing them to their deaths on the ground. The entire monkey army fled in terror, running for their lives, and plunged into the sea.

Again the fearless Angada stopped his army's rout. "Where will you run to? You act like cowards. Stay and fight like the heroes you are!" he commanded. At that moment Kumbhakarṇa snatched seven hundred monkeys in one hand, and the monkey army kept on running.

But the heroic Nīla, Nala, and Gavāksha heard Angada and rallied around him with their troops. Angada began reciting the leaders' heroic deeds from past battles, to keep them buoyed with courage.

Other courageous monkeys attacked the rākshasa army, cracking them with trees, pummeling them with their fists, and raking them with their nails. The rākshasas fought back with swords and spears, and blood ran like a river.

Hanumān rained down arrows on Kumbhakarṇa's head from above, but Kumbhakarṇa swept them away with his club. When Kumbhakarṇa charged the monkey army, Hanumān stood in his path and thrashed him with a chunk of a mountain. His head spinning, Kumbhakarṇa stumbled and nearly collapsed. Then he recovered and stabbed Hanumān in the chest, and the valiant monkey howled and fell in a faint.

Nīla and a half-dozen monkey warriors rushed on the giant. He shook them off like fleas, smacking monkeys off his knees, arms, and head. The fearless monkeys lay in a stupor at his feet.

Now thousands of monkeys swarmed over the giant's body, punching, tearing, and pounding him. He swallowed them by the handful. The enraged demon crushed monkeys beneath his feet and in his cruel hands.

Angada attacked next. He hurled a mountain peak at Kumbhakarṇa's head, making him stumble and almost fall. Righting himself, the giant hurled a spear at Angada, who nimbly stepped aside and bashed the blubbery demon in the chest with his fist. Kumbhakarṇa fainted.

But once he revived, he again laughed his demonic laugh and struck Angada in the head, knocking him senseless.

Then Sugrīva attacked the hulking rākshasa. He, too, flung a mountain peak at Kumbhakarṇa, but it dissolved like a sugar cube on that giant demon's broad chest. Enraged by the assault, Kumbhakarṇa threw his long spear at Sugrīva. Reviving from his faint, Hanumān jumped up, swift as the wind, and grabbed the spear before it could hit the monkey king, then broke it in two over his powerful knees.

"Huzzah! Huzzah!" shouted the monkeys. They ran to Hanumān from all directions, their courage roused by his heroic deed. A tremor of fear slowly made its way over Kumbhakarṇa's face when he saw a mere monkey break his spear. In retaliation, he broke off the peak of a mountain and mashed Sugrīva with it. Then the fearsome Kumbhakarṇa snatched up Sugrīva in arms that were as big as tree trunks and carried him off the battlefield.

The monkey army milled about in turmoil. Hanumān, who saw his king lying limp in the giant's grip, reflected on the best course of action. "I could easily rescue Sugrīva and rally the monkeys, but Sugrīva is strong enough to vanquish that demon. Once he regains consciousness, he will free himself. If I do it for him, it may humiliate him and be a blight on his honor for years to come." Instead the humble and intelligent Hanumān rallied the monkeys, who had scattered in a panic.

Meanwhile, Kumbhakarṇa carried Sugrīva inside the walls of Lankā and through the streets. As the demons of Lankā cheered and showered the giant with flower petals, Sugrīva suddenly woke up. Regaining his strength, the invincible leader of the monkeys sprang from the demon's arms, climbed onto his head, and tore off his ears and nose. Then he leapt over the city wall to rejoin Rāma.

The towering giant looked like a mountain flowing with rivers of blood. Bellowing with fury, he stumbled back onto the battlefield to fight. In his bloodthirsty rampage, he snatched up hundreds of monkeys, bears, and even rākshasas and stuffed them into his mouth, consuming everything in his path like a raging fire.

Finally, Lakshmaṇa took his stand against Kumbhakarṇa. He shot hundreds of arrows, which did not seem to affect the lumbering giant much, but covered his shining gold armor until he looked like a black cloud.

"You have pleased me with your valor, courage, and strength," said Kumbhakarṇa. "Even Indra was afraid to fight me the way you have done. But now I wish to face Rāma alone. I am ready to kill him, and then my warriors can finish off your army."

Lakshmaṇa smiled politely, but his voice rang out strong and clear over the battlefield. "It is true that before this day, even Indra could not fight you. But now you face Rāma, who stands as firm as a rock."

At that moment Rāma drew his bow and pierced Kumbhakarṇa with dozens of blazing arrows. Weakened by the attack, the giant dropped his mace and other weapons. He staggered about the field, blood pouring from his body.

"Let's send all the monkeys crawling over his body; their weight will bring him down," suggested Lakshmaṇa. But the giant shook them off as a dog shakes off water.

"We must stop this demon," said Rāma, as he strode closer to the rākshasa. Rāma plucked his bowstring, sending a thunderclap resounding through the air. Kumbhakarṇa rushed at him in a fury. Then Vibhīshaṇa placed himself on the field, armed with a mace, willing to fight his own brother on behalf of Rāma.

Here Kumbhakarṇa showed his wisdom, for he said, "Even though I fight against you, I know that you are a follower of Dharma, and since you chose to side with Rāma, you will be the only one left to perpetuate our race. But I pray of you, do not stand in my path, my brother, for in this crazed state I cannot distinguish between friend and foe. As your elder brother, it is my duty to protect you."

Moved to tears by his brother's words, Vibhīshaṇa said, "No one would listen to me, so I had no choice but to save our family line by joining Rāma." Taking Kumbhakarṇa's advice, he waited out the battle far from the savage reach of his brother.

Again Kumbhakarṇa lunged for Rāma. "I am ready for you," said Rāma calmly. "Be prepared to lose your life within the hour."

Kumbhakarṇa's grim laugh rolled out from his belly like waves rolling on the ocean. "You may think I am wounded, but I cannot feel a thing. Now I will eat you up."

Rāma let loose a torrent of arrows, the same ones that had killed Bāli and pierced the seven sturdy shāla trees. Yet they barely scratched the giant. Kumbhakarṇa whirled his club in all directions. He grabbed a hilltop and slung it at Rāma, but Rāma crumbled it with his arrows before it could hit him.

Then Rāma invoked the arrow of Vāyu, the wind. It struck Kumbhakarṇa in the shoulder, cutting off the arm that held the club. Looking like a mountain without its peak, Kumbhakarṇa uprooted a tree with his other arm and rushed on Rāma—but now Rāma sliced off that arm, too. As the massive arm tumbled to the ground, it crushed hills, rivers, and rākshasas.

Still the armless giant rushed on Rāma. Unperturbed, that knower of reality coolly shot off his foe's legs, each the size of a mountain. Kumbhakarṇa, minus his arms and legs, opened his mouth to swallow Rāma. But Rāma sent a volley of arrows into that wide and cavernous mouth, filling it up so the giant could no longer breathe.

Eager to end the fight, Rāma dispatched the sharpened arrow of Indra, which resembled the rod of Brahmā and vied with the wind in speed, trailing bright rainbow feathers like a comet. It severed the head of the demon Kumbhakarṇa, which crashed onto the fortress of Lankā and demolished part of the wall. The monstrous body fell into the sea, flattening thousands of rākshasas as it fell and drowning thousands more in the surging tides of its wake.

Earth, sky, and ocean rejoiced at the demise of Kumbhakarṇa. Devas, Ṛishis, and celestials rained down flower petals and shouted with joy. Dancing in jubilation, the army of monkeys leapt to the heavens and back. Having defeated Kumbhakarṇa in battle, Rāma shone as bright as the sun that dispels the darkness of the celestial worlds after being delivered from the mouth of Rāhu.

अथाददे सूर्यमरीचिकल्पं स ब्र
ह्मदण्डान्तककालकल्पम् ।
अरिष्टमैन्द्रं निशितं सुपुङ्खं
रामः शरं मारुततुल्यवेगम् ॥

Then Rāma dispatched the sharpened arrow of Indra,
which resembled the rod of Brahmā and vied with the wind in speed,
trailing bright rainbow feathers like a comet.

—Yuddha Kāṇda 67.165

Chapter 47

Rāvaṇa Sends His Sons into Battle

How can you leave me,
you who were my right arm,
who laughed when Indra's dread thunderbolt
bounced off your vast chest?
With you I was invincible,
with you I shattered the enemy armies.
Now the Devas howl with laughter.
Now I am as good as dead.
What joy is there in Sītā now?
Or my kingdom,
when I have lost you,
my invincible brother,
destroyed in the purifying fire that is Rāma.
If only I had listened to the pious Vibhīshaṇa.
If only I had followed his sage advice,
you and the valiant Prahasta would be alive,
and all would be well.

When Rāvaṇa heard the shocking news of his brother Kumbhakarṇa's death, he slid from his throne and collapsed on the floor. Recovering only slightly, he wailed and beat his chest. "I should have listened to Vibhīshaṇa!"

"This lamenting and wailing is not fit for a great warrior like you," counseled his valiant son Trishiras. "What is there to lament? You possess the weapons bestowed on you by the Devas, including the javelin and armor of Brahmā. You have vanquished the Devas in countless battles without even wearing that flashing armor. Go now and conquer Rāma. Better yet, let me."

The other sons of Rāvaṇa—Devāntaka, Narāntaka, and Atikāya—joined in. "I will go first!" cried one. "No, I will lead!" said another.

Rāvaṇa gazed at his powerful sons, who were as strong as Indra, adept at magic, and educated in the Vedas. They, too, possessed powerful boons. The wicked Rāvaṇa, his mind bemused by pride, felt he had been given a second chance.

Rāvaṇa embraced his sons, decorated them with jewels, blessed them, and sent them off to battle.

The sons of Rāvaṇa, immense in size and strength, prostrated themselves at their father's feet and circled him with their hands folded in respect. Then they sallied forth into battle in their magnificent chariots, banners flying and gold flashing.

Of all the sons of Rāvaṇa, Atikāya was the best bowman. He towered above the others, tall as Mount Meru, wearing his golden, jeweled crown. Trishiras had three heads, Narāntaka rode a gleaming white horse draped in gold, and Devāntaka brandished an iron club set with jewels.

When the rākshasa army saw the sons of their king riding out into battle, their jeweled ornaments flashing in the sunlight, they greeted them with a tumult of ringing bells and piercing war whoops. The thunder of elephants, horses, and camels pounded the earth. The monkeys heard the din and saw the rākshasas bearing down on them like a dark storm.

The monkey army of Rāma fearlessly attacked the rākshasa hordes. They pounded them with boulders, pummeled them with fists, and tore at them with tooth and nail.

To stop their advance, Narāntaka rode his powerful horse through their midst, mowing down countless monkeys with his barbed club. Seeing his army being destroyed, the invincible Angada, armed only with his nails, teeth, and fists, bashed the skull of Narāntaka's horse and soon Rāvaṇa's son lay dead.

Narāntaka's death infuriated his brothers and Rāvaṇa's brother Mahodara, who circled around Angada, attacking the monkey chief with their clubs, arrows, and spears. Though he had to fight three terrifying rākshasas at once, Angada showed no sign of fatigue or strain. He bounded about, first raining down boulders on his enemies, then wielding an uprooted tree. When Mahodara tried to run over him with his elephant, he stepped nimbly aside and smacked the elephant with his open palm, bringing the beast tumbling down. Then he grabbed a tusk off the elephant and struck Devāntaka with it. Devāntaka swung his club and stunned Angada for a moment, but he leapt up to fight again—only to be shot by three arrows of Trishiras, which made his forehead bleed profusely but did not stop him.

Seeing Angada fending off three warriors by himself, Hanumān and Nīla rushed to his aid. Soon the mighty Hanumān flattened Devāntaka, and Nīla knocked off Mahodara's head. Enraged at his loved ones' deaths, Trishiras wheeled his chariot on Hanumān, raining down arrows. When Hanumān sprang on the backs of his horses, Trishiras let fly his blazing javelin. The Son of the Wind caught it and snapped it like a twig. Trishiras responded by plunging his sword into Hanumān's chest, which only inflamed that courageous monkey to rise up and strike Trishiras with his massive fist. As Trishiras stumbled and fell, his sword slipped from his grasp. Quick as the wind, Hanumān snatched the sword of Trishiras and cut off his three heads. The three crowns rolled in the dust.

The monkeys cried out in jubilation, and their shouts filled the air like thunder. Hearing their victory cries, Rāvaṇa's brother Mahāpārshva grabbed his mace, now crusted with the blood of his enemies, and struck the monkey chief Ṛishabha in the chest like a thunderbolt. The enormously strong Ṛishabha snatched the mace and smashed Mahāpārshva's head into pieces.

Now Atikāya saw what had happened and raced his chariot to the spot. His eyes blazing fire, his colossal form terrified the monkeys in his path, who thought he was Kumbhakarṇa resurrected.

Rāma spotted him wheeling across the battlefield and asked Vibhīshaṇa, "Who is this formidable rākshasa, who with his spears and weapons blazing reminds us of Shiva himself? Large as an elephant, his face as serene as the moon, he flames like the fire at the end of time. With four charioteers, thirty-eight quivers, and numerous shining red crossbows, his golden amulets flashing, he scatters the monkeys with his power."

"He is Atikāya, the son of Rāvaṇa," said Vibhīshaṇa. "He has all the strength and prowess of his father. He has mastered many celestial weapons, and Brahmā himself has bestowed upon him immunity from death at the hand of Deva or asura. Brahmā has also given him a set of shining armor, which makes him invincible. He has humbled the Devas in a hundred battles. Use all your strength with him, for he is not to be trifled with."

Atikāya mowed down vast numbers of monkeys with his arrows, which were made of iron. Even Nīla and other monkey chiefs were paralyzed by them. Driving fearlessly to the spot where Rāma stood, Atikāya shouted, "I will not fight just anyone. If you dare, come and fight me."

Lakshmaṇa was incensed by this cocky statement and plucked his bow. The thunderous sound looped the earth and reverberated up to the heavens, striking fear into the hearts of the rākshasas.

"You are a mere boy," said the arrogant Atikāya as he mounted his arrows on his bow. "Send me a man to fight."

"Warriors are measured by their feats in battle, not by their age," answered Lakshmaṇa. "Let me see your actions, for boastful words do not make you a hero."

In answer Atikāya let loose his powerful arrows, but Lakshmaṇa shot them down. Atikāya mounted a celestial weapon and shot Lakshmaṇa in the chest, and the mighty Lakshmaṇa reeled from the blow, bleeding heavily. Then, remembering his origin in the absolute power that was Vishṇu, Lakshmaṇa healed himself and sent a celestial arrow sizzling like a molten snake straight into Atikāya's forehead.

Staggered by the blow, Atikāya finally regained his balance and said, "I see by the force of that arrow that you are, indeed, a worthy opponent."

After that, the two warriors kept shooting weapons, but each time the other cut them down. Even when Lakshmaṇa's arrows hit Atikāya's chest, they glanced off like a ball bouncing.

"It's his armor," explained Hanumān. "He won it in a boon from Brahmā, and you can never penetrate it except with a Brahmā missile."

So Lakshmaṇa invoked the Brahmā weapon. The earth trembled, the sky quaked, and the sun, moon, and stars hid in terror. As the Brahmā weapon blazed through the sky, Atikāya shot a torrent of arrows to counteract it. Still the missile bore down on him. As it came closer and closer, he valiantly tried to fend it off with his sword and mace. At last it found its mark and sliced off his head. The rākshasa army, stunned by the defeat of their invincible leaders, fled to Lankā, wailing with fear, exhaustion, and defeat.

The monkeys surged forward, crowding around Lakshmaṇa and praising him for his miraculous strength and skill.

स पुत्रान्सम्परिष्वज्य भूषयित्वा च भूषणैः ।
आशीर्भिश्च प्रशस्ताभिः प्रेषयामास वै रणे ॥

Rāvaṇa embraced his sons, decorated them with jewels,
blessed them, and then sent them off to battle.

—Yuddha Kāṇḍa 69.15

CHAPTER 48

Hanumān and the Mountain of Herbs

HEARING OF ATIKĀYA's demise, Rāvaṇa collapsed into his throne, nearly slipping to the floor. Reviving, he sobbed, "First Dhūmrāksha, then Akampana, Prahasta, and Kumbhakarṇa. No one has ever defeated them. Now my dear sons and brothers have been killed by these giant monkeys. How endless must be the strength of Rāma and Lakshmaṇa, that they could escape the bonds of Indrajit. By whose magic, by whose power do they operate? Rāma must be Vishṇu himself, for no other being could lay my forces low."

The doomed rākshasa king managed to dispense a few orders. "Let all the gates be fortified with strong warriors and watchmen. Especially guard the entrances to the Ashoka Grove, where Sītā sleeps." Then he was again lost in grief.

Seeing his all-powerful father crushed with anguish, Indrajit said, "Do not mourn while the conqueror of Indra still lives. I will lay waste this monkey army. I swear on my honor and my strength that I will cut down Rāma and Lakshmaṇa today."

With that vow, Indrajit mounted his chariot and flew onto the battlefield, accompanied by elephants, horses, chariots, and thousands of fierce warriors armed with weapons that flashed in the sun and dazzled the eyes. They followed him joyfully, singing his praises.

Shining like the sun and moon together, the powerful rākshasa Indrajit first sat down by a sacred fire at the Nikumbhilā Grove, the secret place on the western slope of Trikūta Mountain where he performed his rituals. Wearing red shining robes, he uttered magical spells over his weapons, chariot, and bow. Next he made himself invisible. Finally, he invoked the weapon of Brahmā, making the earth shake and the sky crack.

Having secured his strength, Indrajit drove his invisible chariot into the monkey army, flanked by whooping, frenzied rākshasas. Drawing his bow, Indrajit dropped a curtain of arrows on the monkey forces. The brave monkey warriors looked up but could see nothing but a blaze of arrows. Unable to see where the arrows came from, unable to retaliate in any way, the monkeys were struck by arrows, hatchets, spears, swords, and javelins from all sides. Seven monkeys at a time were struck down by Indrajit's missiles. Many fled in terror. Those left standing showered rocks, boulders, and trees on the spot where they thought Indrajit was hiding, but they could do nothing to defend themselves against the relentless storm of arrows that glinted in the sun like a cascading waterfall of glass shards.

Soon nearly the entire monkey army was wounded, dead, or in a faint. Even the heroic monkey chiefs—Hanumān, Angada, Nīla, and Nala—were struck down, their bodies covered with hundreds of arrows. Then Indrajit increased his attack and shot hundreds of arrows at Rāma and Lakshmaṇa. The two brothers could scarcely see each other in the hail of arrows.

Rāma, who felt no pain or fatigue despite being struck, called out to Lakshmaṇa, "There is no way we can defend ourselves against Indrajit when he is invisible to us. And these missiles he is sending, which have their origin in Brahmā himself, are unfathomably powerful. Let us honor the missiles of Brahmā, and let them overcome us. Indrajit will think we are dead and go back to Lankā to celebrate."

Indeed, when he saw those two illustrious heroes lying on the ground, Indrajit shouted, "Victory is ours!" and raced his chariot back to Lankā to offer his victory at the feet of his father.

Soon after Indrajit left the battlefield, Hanumān, Nīla, Nala, and

Angada recovered, being uncommonly strong and powerful. Then they saw that Rāma and Lakshmaṇa had fallen. Confused and frightened, they did not know what to think. Vibhīshaṇa, who had not been injured, saw their confusion and said, "Do not worry, they are only showing honor to the missiles of Brahmā by allowing themselves to be struck down."

When he ransacked the Ashoka Grove, Hanumān himself had submitted to Indrajit in order to honor the missile of Brahmā. Now he suggested that the monkey leaders go to the battlefield to bring comfort to those still breathing. Picking their way among the thousands of bodies, lighting the way with torches, they came upon Sugrīva and many other mighty warriors lying prostrate on the field. Then they searched out Jāmbavān, the eldest warrior and the son of Brahmā. Vibhīshaṇa found the great bear lying with hundreds of arrows poking from his body like the quills of a porcupine.

"O brother of Rāvaṇa," said Jāmbavān in a hoarse voice, "I cannot open my eyes but I recognize your voice. Tell me, has the Son of the Wind survived?"

"It seems strange that you ask about Hanumān before inquiring after the welfare of Rāma and Lakshmaṇa and all the monkey chiefs," said Vibhīshaṇa.

"I will tell you why if you listen carefully," whispered Jāmbavān. "If Hanumān is alive, he can save us all. If he is dead, we all are as good as dead." Hearing this, Vibhīshaṇa summoned Hanumān, who bowed to the ancient bear, greeted him respectfully, and waited patiently for him to speak, hands folded in respect.

"O Hanumān, just hearing your voice makes the life force throb in me again, even though every limb of mine is wounded," said the venerable leader Jāmbavān. "For you alone can heal us all and restore Rāma and Lakshmaṇa to their full strength. Fly across the ocean to the Himālayas, and there between Mount Ṛishabha and the sacred Mount Kailāsa, you will see Mount Mahodaya, home of all medicinal herbs. O best of monkeys, you will see four luminous herbs that grow on its peak and light up the ten regions of the sky with their brilliance. One is the reviver of the dead (*mṛitasanjīvanī*), another is the healer of wounds (*vishalyakaraṇī*), the third is the restorer of the skin (*sandhānī*), and the last the restorer of the skin pigment (*suvarṇakaraṇī*). Now is the time for you to show your immeasurable valor and grant health to all the monkeys. Pluck the herbs and bring them here, son of the bearer of fragrance, and heal us all."

Hanumān felt a rush of energy and power coursing through his veins, like the ocean rising in waves, and he started to swell in size. He bounded up one of the three peaks of Trikūta Mountain, which crumbled under his weight. Trees tumbled to the earth and burst into flames. Lankā reeled and lurched as if it were dancing on hot coals, and its turrets tumbled to the ground.

From Trikūta Mountain Hanumān sprang to Malaya Mountain, covered with lotuses and lilies, waterfalls tumbling down its cliffs like strings of jasmine flowers. Landing on the mountain, Hanumān opened his mouth and let loose an earth-shattering howl. The citizens of Lankā cowered in their houses. Lifting his tail high and springing from his haunches, he leapt into the air, the force of his flight yanking trees and boulders along with him like a hurricane.

Stretching his arms out before him, he coursed through the air, fast as the wind. Hanumān crossed over forests, rivers, lakes, and cities far below. Without a twinge of fatigue he reached a distant summit in the Himālayas.

Landing on one of the snow-covered peaks, he gazed down on remote caves, pristine forests, and frothy streams cascading down cliffs. There he surveyed holy hermitages dotting the mountainsides and divine sages meditating in orange robes. He saw the mountain home of Brahmā, the silvery Mount Kailāsa where Shiva sat deep in meditation, the heavenly abode of Indra, and the luminous palace of Kubera.

Between the rocky cliffs of Kailāsa and Ṛishabha he recognized Mount Mahodaya, a mountain covered with herbs that glowed with an inner light even in the twilight. Landing on that mountain, Hanumān searched for the celestial healing herbs. But the herbs made themselves invisible, and he was unable to find them. The courageous Hanumān, who had traveled far to reach the mountain, grew angry and his eyes burned like coals.

"How could you behave this way, when Lord Rāma lies on the battlefield waiting for you to heal him?" he shouted. "Do not trifle with me or I will break you into pieces!"

Then that immensely strong monkey, out of patience, broke off the mountain peak with all its precious metals, trees, herbs, and forest animals, and hoisted it with one arm like a platter of food. Holding it high he leapt into the air and flew back to Lankā, while the Devas, Gandharvas, and Ṛishis showered him with praises and shouts of "Wonderful! Wonderful!"

Hanumān blazed like a comet as he flew across the night sky. Reaching Lankā, he set down the mountaintop in the center of Rāma's army as the monkeys cheered. Bowing his head to his commanders and other monkey chiefs, he embraced Vibhīshaṇa.

As soon as they inhaled the scent of those divine herbs, Rāma and Lakshmaṇa were revived. Soon the casualties of Rāma's army were completely healed—not only those who were wounded, but those who had perished in battle rose from the dead. In this way the entire army of monkeys was restored to life, their wounds mended. By Rāvaṇa's order the rākshasas had thrown their dead into the sea, so they could not be revived.

As soon as the herbs had done their work, Hanumān lifted the mountain peak and carried it back to the Himālayas, restoring it to the mountain like a hat on its head. Without feeling weary, he flew back to Lankā and took his place by Rāma's side.

तस्य वानरशार्दूल चतस्रो मूर्ध्नि संभवाः ।
द्रक्ष्यस्योषधयो दीप्ता दीपयन्तीर्दिशो दश ॥

O best of monkeys, you will see four luminous herbs that grow on its peak and light up the ten regions of the sky with their brilliance.

—Yuddha Kāṇḍa 74.32

Chapter 49

Indrajit Meets His Destiny

After Hanumān returned from his flight to the Himālayas, Sugrīva said, "Rāvaṇa has lost so many warriors, he will not be able to defend the city properly. Let us scramble over the walls with torches and again set fire to the city."

Monkeys swarmed through the gates and over the walls, setting fire to every house in Lankā. As the fire blazed once again through the city, jeweled turrets toppled, mansions crumbled, and demons rushed through the streets in screaming throngs, desperate to escape the heat and smoke. Multitudes of rākshasas perished in the blaze, and the burning skyline of Lankā reflected in the sea like a mirror, turning the waters crimson.

As the once-glorious mansions collapsed in molten heaps, the scent of burning aloe and sandalwood filled the air. Thousands of demon warriors, roused from their sleep, armed themselves with armor, sharp spears, javelins, clubs, and maces. They marched out of the city, ankle bracelets ringing, their grotesque rākshasa faces made more ghoulish by the flickering light and shadow of the blaze.

They rushed to meet the monkey army, and a ferocious battle took place. He who bit was bitten, he who stabbed was stabbed, and soon the field was covered with the bodies of the dead and wounded.

Seeing his city once more on fire, Rāvaṇa became a storm of fury. His anger swelled in his body and shook the four quarters of the universe.

"Kumbha and Nikumbha!" he shouted to the sons of Kumbhakarṇa. "Now is the time to join the other rākshasa warriors in battle."

They immediately followed their uncle's command, but soon the fierce Kumbha was killed by a blow from Sugrīva, and Nikumbha was beheaded by Hanumān. In a battle as ferocious as the one between the Devas and asuras at the beginning of time, monkeys and rākshasas grappled with each other on the battlefield.

Now Rāvaṇa sent the wicked Makarāksha, son of his other dead brother, Khara, to duel Rāma. All the Devas and celestials gathered to see the marvelous sight of the two superb bowmen fighting. Arrow stopped arrow as they fell like rain all around. After a terrific fight, Rāma employed the missile of Agni and shattered the evil Makarāksha's heart.

When Rāvaṇa heard of the deaths of his nephews, he exploded with rage. He again summoned his eldest and only remaining son, the invincible warrior Indrajit. "You have run off the king of the Devas, so you will easily vanquish these mere men," he said. "Go now and come back victorious."

Indrajit rolled his chariot to the Nikumbhilā Grove, where he once again performed ceremonies to gain the power of invisibility. Surrounded by monsters riding lions and tigers, he drove his magical chariot to the place where Rāma and Lakshmaṇa were dispatching their arrows into the rākshasa ranks.

Having covered himself and his chariot with a smoky veil that obliterated the four directions, Indrajit rained down arrows on Rāma,

Lakshmaṇa, and the monkeys. No one could tell where the arrows came from, for his chariot and bow made no sound, and he nimbly shot them from all directions. Soon the monkeys were wounded and fainting on the field, and soon the limbs of Rāma and Lakshmaṇa were covered with brightly feathered arrows like blossoming trees.

"Let me send the Brahmā missile, and I will obliterate the entire rākshasa race," suggested Lakshmaṇa.

"We cannot kill all rākshasas just for the sins of one," said Rāma. "It is forbidden to kill one who cannot defend himself, who hides, begs with folded hands, surrenders, runs away, or is taken unawares. We must try harder to conquer Indrajit alone. If the monkey chiefs could only see this trickster who hides behind a magical veil, they themselves could vanquish him. No matter, whether he hides in the core of the earth or the celestial heavens, he will fall when struck by my arrows." Then Rāma was quiet, as he contemplated how to bring an end to Indrajit.

Indrajit divined Rāma's intentions, and he wheeled his chariot back to Lankā to plan a different strategy. His brain sizzled with anger as he thought of his sons, brothers, cousins, and uncles who had been killed by Rāma, Lakshmaṇa, and the monkey chiefs. Feeling the pain of their deaths, he came up with a wicked plan. Using his considerable powers of sorcery, he created an illusion of Sītā and placed her in his chariot. Then he drove her toward the monkey army.

Hanumān felt his eyes fill with tears to see Sītā in such dire straits. Pale, thin, and distraught, the phantom Sītā wore a dirty garment, and her body was streaked with grime.

"What is the meaning of this outrage?" cried Hanumān as he and the other monkey forces rushed on Indrajit's chariot.

As he saw the monkeys coming, Indrajit stood up and seized Sītā by the hair. He struck her and she cried out, "Rāma, O Rāma!"

By now Hanumān was sobbing, so keenly did he feel the grief of Rāma's beloved wife. "You are doomed to the netherworld by seizing Sītā's hair," Hanumān's voice rang out. "It is known that you are a descendant of the revered Ṛishi Pulastya. How could you treat her so heartlessly, she who has been deprived of husband, kingdom, and home? You deserve to suffer along with others who murder women."

"You say that it is wrong to murder women," said Indrajit. "But it is right to do anything possible to vanquish the foe." With those words, while Hanumān and the other monkeys watched in horror, Indrajit pulled out his sword and stabbed the phantom Sītā, who crumpled to the floor of the chariot.

Laughing wickedly, he said, "Now what do you have to fight for?" He bellowed victoriously, rejoicing in his heinous deed.

Witnessing this unspeakable act, the dejected monkeys scattered like leaves in a windstorm. But even in his shock, the fearless Hanumān rallied them, saying, "It is not fitting for brave warriors to run like this. For the sake of Sītā and Rāma, gather your forces and attack!" He seized a monstrous boulder and flung it at Indrajit's chariot. The charioteer nimbly drove away, and the boulder killed a hundred rākshasas instead.

Inspired by Hanumān, the other monkeys lashed at the rākshasa army, smashing them with their open palms, and with rocks and trees. When Indrajit saw the destruction being wielded on his army, he turned his chariot on the monkeys and flung hatchets, spears, clubs, and arrows on them.

The monkeys fought fearlessly and were holding their own, but Hanumān eventually said, "We cannot win this battle. Let us withdraw and tell Rāma the dreadful news of Sītā's death."

When Indrajit saw Hanumān withdrawing the monkey army, he turned his chariot around and drove it straight to the Nikumbhilā Grove. There, in the presence of his rākshasa troops, he began a ceremony of sorcery to once again make himself invisible, making all the necessary offerings to the blazing fire according to all the proper rules.

Meanwhile Rāma had heard the din raised by Indrajit's trick and the ensuing fight, and he said, "No doubt Hanumān is performing great feats. Jāmbavān, take your army of bears to support him."

But as the bear army marched onto the battlefield, they met Hanumān and his army retreating. "Turn back," cried Hanumān. "All is lost."

When he reached Rāma, Hanumān bowed at his feet. He could barely speak, for his emotion overtook him. "O Rāma, I have come here to tell you that the wicked Indrajit has killed Sītā before our eyes as we fought him."

Rāma fainted. Lakshmaṇa knelt beside his stricken brother and cradled his head in his lap. The monkeys, seeing Rāma unconscious, ran to fetch water and sprinkled it over his face to revive him.

"You who are the knower of truth," cried the ever-devoted Lakshmaṇa, "what use was your steadfastness to Dharma? Surely, those who adhere to Dharma suffer from misfortune, for even though you have never harmed anyone, you have had your wealth, your kingdom, and your wife snatched from you. If Dharma and adharma were real, you would be enjoying all prosperity and Rāvaṇa would be in hell. Instead he laughs and enjoys his wealth. The moment you gave up the kingdom, Dharma was severed like the root of a tree. Without wealth, all streams of happiness dry up—without wealth there are no friends, no well-wishers, no pleasures, and no rest for the mind. The death of Sītā is the result of giving up your wealth and your kingdom.

"But rise up, O knower of truth," he said. "How can you forget that you are the supreme Self, *Paramātmā*? I am here to serve you, and in my wrath over Sītā's death I will level Lankā."

Lakshmaṇa choked back his own tears in order to comfort Rāma. Just then Vibhīshaṇa arrived to report to Rāma after surveying the troops. "What is this?" he asked, distressed at seeing Rāma lying on the ground. "What has happened?"

When he heard the news, he knelt beside Rāma and said with urgency, "This is nothing but a trick of Rāvaṇa's, please believe me. I know Rāvaṇa's mind like my own. He would never allow Sītā to die any more than the ocean would dry up. He is much too attached to her; he refused to give her up even to prevent his own ruin. Indrajit has used this sorcery to distract you from his real objective: to become invisible again. Shake off this gloom, Rāma, and send Lakshmaṇa to stop the spell from being completed. Once Indrajit is invisible, none can vanquish him."

Rāma opened his eyes and stared at Vibhīshaṇa in a daze. Still sunk in grief, he only vaguely understood the meaning of Vibhīshaṇa's words. Finally he said, "I need you to repeat what you just said."

Again Vibhīshaṇa, who was a masterful orator, urged Rāma to stop Indrajit before he finished the rite for invisibility.

"If he completes the rite and is able to use the invisible chariot and horses and the missile of Brahmā that he received for his austerities, we cannot defeat him. Yet Brahmā predicted his death when he said, 'The enemy who interrupts your rite at Nikumbhilā and attacks you before the battle will end your life.' So let us go and fulfill that prophecy."

Rāma said, "It is true that once the cruel Indrajit uses his witchcraft to become invisible, no one can return his arrows. Even when he fights the Devas, he makes them fall into a faint. Lakshmaṇa, go to Indrajit and fulfill his destiny. Take Hanumān, Jāmbavān, and all the monkey chiefs. Take Vibhīshaṇa, for he knows the land and the ways of the rākshasas."

Lakshmaṇa of the auspicious markings covered himself in golden armor and grabbed his sword and bow. Glowing with the radiance of the Devas, raising high his quiver, he vowed, "These arrows will soar over the treetops of Lankā and end the life of Indrajit!" He circled his brother, bowed to Rāma's feet, and joyfully joined Vibhīshaṇa and the monkey chiefs.

"See the rākshasa forces hugging that hillside like a black cloud?" asked Vibhīshaṇa. "If you disperse them, Indrajit will have to stop his ceremony to rally them."

Following Vibhīshaṇa's advice, the monkeys and bears armed themselves with trees, rocks, and boulders and attacked the rākshasas on the hillside. Lakshmaṇa blotted out the sky with his torrent of arrows. Hanumān rallied the monkey army, who loved to fight, with these words: "This is virtually the last remnant of Rāvaṇa's army. When Indrajit is killed today, there will be only one more rākshasa and his troops to conquer!" As the monkeys attacked, a ferocious din rose from the battlefield.

Just as Vibhīshaṇa had predicted, Indrajit emerged from a thick clump of trees to save his army from being destroyed. In a rage, he mounted his chariot. His eyes red and mouth fiery as a hundred torches, he looked as terrifying as Death itself. When they saw their leader, the rākshasas rallied around him.

"Take me to that monkey," cried Indrajit, pointing to Hanumān. "I will kill him before he destroys our army."

While Hanumān occupied Indrajit in fierce combat, Vibhīshaṇa spirited Lakshmaṇa away to the Nikumbhilā Grove. There they saw the fire, still burning, under a huge banyan tree.

Suddenly Indrajit appeared, having seen them heading to his private altar. "Have you no shame?" he railed. "You are my uncle, my blood, yet you show the enemy my secret shrine! You know nothing of Dharma, or you would not harm your own kin."

"Though born a rākshasa, I never agreed with my people's evil ways," Vibhīshaṇa fired back. "It is right to leave the company of the wicked. It makes one rejoice. Stealing another's wife, committing violence, and stealing another's property—these are the three evils that the righteous cannot abide. It was because your father refused to stop committing these crimes that I left him. Now you too will die for your sins at the hand of the virtuous Lakshmaṇa."

Furious, Indrajit raised his formidable bow and taunted Lakshmaṇa.

"Remember that you have fallen twice under my arrows that tear like fire. This time you will not recover from your swoon!"

"Boasts cannot save you," said Lakshmaṇa. "Without the crutch of your magic, I will triumph."

In answer to Lakshmaṇa's words, Indrajit shot a volley of fiery arrows that flashed through the air like comets. They struck Lakshmaṇa all over his body, drawing blood. Indrajit whooped in delight. "I will kill you first, next your rogue brother Rāma. Jackals will eat your entrails."

Lakshmaṇa felt no pain from Indrajit's arrows, nor was he perturbed by his verbal barbs. "Your words are empty without actions to back them up. As you will see, I will vanquish you without harsh words or boasting." He fired off five missiles that struck Indrajit in the chest, surprising him with their power.

The two warriors were equally matched. Each a master of celestial weapons, when one shot an arrow the other swiftly countered, dissolving it with another. Some of the arrows struck home, and both Lakshmaṇa and Indrajit were covered with wounds. But each was so focused on his task that neither felt any pain.

All of the Devas, Gandharvas, and Ṛishis gathered above the fray to watch the relentless barrage of arrows by the master bowmen. The two warriors strung new arrows and shot them so swiftly that it was impossible to see their hands. The thick volley of arrows darkened the sky, and the wind stopped blowing. The Ṛishis prayed, "May all be well with the three worlds!"

One of Lakshmaṇa's arrows killed Indrajit's charioteer, but Indrajit fought on, directing his horses by thought alone while he continued to shoot arrows. The host of Devas marveled at his dexterity. Lakshmaṇa, irked that Indrajit was able to continue maneuvering without a charioteer, struck the horses with his arrows. Vibhīshaṇa finished them with his mace and then fired arrows that struck Indrajit full in the chest.

Incensed at his uncle's interference, Indrajit shot the dread weapon of Yama at Vibhīshaṇa. But just as quickly, Lakshmaṇa mounted a weapon that had been given to him in a dream by Kubera. The two arrows collided head-on in the sky, and golden fragments streamed to the ground like fireworks, incensing both warriors.

Then Lakshmaṇa shot the missile of Varuṇa; Indrajit shattered it in midair with the weapon of Shiva. Indrajit fired the blazing missile of Agni; Lakshmaṇa destroyed it with the weapon of the sun.

The battle raged for three days and three nights. Finally, wishing to end the duel, the younger brother of Rāma fitted an arrow to his bow that had a rounded head, brilliant feathers, and a dazzling gold color. Lakshmaṇa slowly pulled back the arrow, deadly as a viper and smoking with heat. Closing his eyes, he made a solemn vow, "If Rāma, son of Dasharatha, is the soul of Dharma, steadfast in truth and unmatched in valor, let this arrow take the life of the son of Rāvaṇa."

The arrow shot true. It severed the head of the cruel Indrajit, and his body crashed to the ground.

Vibhīshaṇa and the multitude of monkeys raised their arms to the heavens in gratitude and jubilation. Celestial musicians filled the air with vibrant notes and the rolling of drums. The Devas, Gandharvas, and Ṛishis showered down flower petals, heaping them on the radiant Lakshmaṇa.

With the demon Indrajit gone forever, the Devas vowed, "From this day may the Brahmins perform their duties without fear."

The monkeys crowded around their hero Lakshmaṇa. Laughing and cheering, they slapped their tails on the ground in joy. "Victory to Lakshmaṇa!" they shouted.

One by one, Vibhīshaṇa, Jāmbavān, Hanumān, and the other monkey leaders embraced Lakshmaṇa and congratulated him on his stunning victory. They followed him like a parade as he walked to the place where Rāma waited, sometimes leaning on Vibhīshaṇa and Hanumān for support. Lakshmaṇa humbly stood by Rāma's elbow while Vibhīshaṇa regaled Rāma with tales of his brother's prowess in battle.

"Well done, Lakshmaṇa!" said Rāma. "I am pleased with you. With the death of Indrajit, victory is ours. You have done what no one else could have achieved. Without Indrajit, Rāvaṇa is missing his right hand. Now I will end his evil rule forever."

Smiling broadly, having honored Lakshmaṇa with these words, Rāma affectionately kissed his brother on the top of his head. Drawing him close in an embrace, he suddenly realized that Lakshmaṇa was badly wounded.

Rāma called Susheṇa, the revered grandfather of Prince Angada, to his side. "Heal the valiant Lakshmaṇa and restore him to good health. Also restore the brave Vibhīshaṇa and all the monkeys and bears who have been wounded in battle."

The highly respected commander Susheṇa then gave Lakshmaṇa a powder made of herbs. When Lakshmaṇa inhaled it, his wounds instantly disappeared, and his pain was gone. Susheṇa administered the same herb to Vibhīshaṇa, Hanumān, Jāmbavān, and all the forces of Rāma's army. Far into the night, the rejuvenated monkey army told stories of the great deeds of Rāma and Lakshmaṇa, creating a din with their merrymaking.

धर्मात्मा सत्यसन्धश्च रामो दाशरथिर्यदि ।
पौरुषे चाप्रतिद्वन्द्वस्तदैनं जहि रावणिम् ॥

If Rāma, son of Dasharatha, is the soul of Dharma, steadfast in truth and unmatched in valor, let this arrow take the life of the son of Rāvaṇa.

—Yuddha Kāṇḍa 90.69

Chapter 50

The Fall of Rāvaṇa

O Rāma,
Bow to the Sun,
Sūrya, bringer of seasons,
giver of light,
the seer who bestows life.

Bow to the Sun,
Ushas, daughter of heaven
who appears on the horizon
and fills the dawn with radiance,
shedding golden beams
that warm the earth.

Bow to the Sun,
Hiraṇyagarbha, the golden egg,
the bird that floats in the void,
and fills it with daylight.

Bow to the Sun,
Āditya, the bestower of happiness,
hidden in the cave of the heart,
ruler of the worlds,
destroyer of darkness.

Bow to the Sun,
Pūshan, the spirit of the universe,
ruler of the stars,
the luminous chariot with seven horses
that conveys the sunrise and sunset.

Bow to the Sun,
Savitṛi, the moon's consort,
who awakens the lotus,
dazzles the eye,
and dissolves the snow.

Bow to the Sun,
Prajāpati, who creates all creatures,
watches over them in sleep,
and nurtures the world with his rays.

Bow to the Sun,
Agni, the sacred fire and its fruit,
the witness in the heart of creation,
the gift of the gods,
who rejoices with rice and butter
and sweet songs of praise.

Rāvaṇa fell from the throne and lay unconscious on the floor. His beloved son Indrajit was dead. After many hours, Rāvaṇa regained awareness. Even then, he could only whisper a lament. "My child, who conquered Indra and the Devas, how could you lie dead? I hear the wailing in the women's apartments—O why have you left me and your mother and your wife?"

Then his grief turned to rage. Ever ready to flare up, his anger now consumed him. His red eyes burned, his cavernous mouth opened to howl, and his red tongue leapt out like a flame. His brow furrowed in deep creases like the waves of the ocean. Tears of wrath dropped from his eyes and coursed down his face.

"I will demolish Sītā!" he roared. "My son killed her in magic, but I will do it for real."

Arming himself with the body armor and magnificent bow that Brahmā had given him after a thousand years of penance, which neither Indra's thunderbolt nor javelin had shattered in countless battles, Rāvaṇa mounted his chariot and stormed over to the Ashoka Grove, his mind in turmoil. As he dismounted from his chariot and charged Sītā in his fury, brandishing his sword as blue as the sky, his ministers and well-wishers tried to hold him back.

Sītā saw Rāvaṇa rushing toward her, and she sobbed with fear. "Helpless as I am, he is coming to kill me because so many times I refused to marry him, being devoted to Rāma. Or perhaps Rāma and Lakshmaṇa are dead, and now he wishes to finish me off too. Fie on me that I should be the cause of their deaths! Oh, if only I had flown across the sea on Hanumān's back and avoided all this."

Seeing the pure-hearted Sītā waiting for her death, one of Rāvaṇa's high-minded and wise ministers, Supārshva, flew to Rāvaṇa's side. "You have so dutifully ruled your kingdom according to the laws of Dharma," he addressed Rāvaṇa. "Why should you commit this unforgivable sin of killing a woman? Come, win the war with Rāma, just as you have won every battle, and then Sītā will be yours."

These words, which appealed to Rāvaṇa's vanity as well as his honor, had the desired effect. Rāvaṇa directed his chariot to return to the palace. Entering the assembly hall again, he sank heavily into his throne and ordered his generals to resume the conflict at dawn.

As the epic fight began again the next day, Rāma invoked the Gandharva *astra*, a missile whose power was vested only in Rāma and Lord Shiva. Through its power he was able to multiply himself on the battlefield a thousandfold. The rākshasas sometimes saw a thousand Rāmas, sometimes just one. Sometimes they beheld a veil of destruction so dense that they couldn't see anything of Rāma at all. His attack was like the wheel of a chariot spinning. Rāma formed the hub, shooting sparks and fiery arrows. He struck down the rākshasa army with such speed that within a few hours, ten thousand swift chariots, eighteen thousand elephants, fourteen thousand horses and riders, and fifty thousand infantry were annihilated. After nearly the entire army was destroyed, the few remaining chariots, elephants, horses, and soldiers limped back to Lankā in disarray.

"Well done, Rāma!" cried the Devas, Gandharvas, and Ṛishis from above.

The women and children of Lankā passed the night sobbing and wailing for the loss of their loved ones. Women everywhere cried out for their sons, husbands, and brothers. One and all, they blamed Rāvaṇa. "Even now, he does not see that the one who takes on the fair-formed, truth-loving son of Dasharatha is headed for destruction," they moaned amongst themselves. "If only Shūrpaṇakhā hadn't insulted Rāma—if only Rāvaṇa hadn't stolen Sītā—if only our king had listened to the wise and pure-minded Vibhīshaṇa."

Hearing the pitiful wails from every home in Lankā, Rāvaṇa fell into a deep depression. But—once again—it was not long before his ferocity resurged. He summoned Virūpāksha, the last of his commanders. "Come with me into battle, where I will slay Rāma and Lakshmaṇa, and avenge the deaths of my sons and brothers," he said. "Like an elephant I will trample the monkey army under my feet. I will blacken the sky, sending forth billows of arrows from my oceanlike bow."

As the night wore on, the commanders searched the remaining buildings of Lankā, gathering what was left of Rāvaṇa's once vast army. When the sun came up Rāvaṇa donned his armor and mounted his chariot with eight steeds. His commanders followed him in their chariots. When Rāvaṇa reached the battlefield, jackals howled, darkness covered the sky like a blanket, and the clouds rained blood. But Rāvaṇa in his folly ignored the bad omens and rode on to his destiny.

The battle began. Rāvaṇa killed thousands of monkeys, and the field was covered with their bodies. Yet destiny was on the side of the good. After a ferocious fight, Sugrīva killed Virūpāksha with a blow to the chest. Seeing that brave warrior slain, the monkey army rallied and rushed on the rākshasas. Like waves crashing in a hurricane, the two armies created a frightful din.

Soon Rāvaṇa roared across the battlefield like the devourer of time. He bellowed, "I will avenge the tears of all the women of Lankā, I will chop down the tree that is Rāma, with Sītā as its fruits and flower. I will destroy these monkeys in a blaze to end the world!"

The mountains, rivers, and ocean shook as Rāvaṇa's chariot thundered to the place where Rāma stood. That wicked king released the missile of the asuras, the power of darkness. It shot across the sky like a meteor and exploded, burning the monkeys and creating chaos in Rāma's army.

As the monkeys fled the blaze, Rāvaṇa found himself face to face with Rāma. The all-powerful Rāma stood serenely on the battlefield, Lakshmaṇa at his side. Rāma, thrilled to be facing Rāvaṇa at last, plucked his bowstring, and the sound slapped the sky and tore up the earth.

First Lakshmaṇa shot his flaming arrows at Rāvaṇa. But Rāvaṇa shot his arrows to deflect them, and then, wishing to fight Rāma alone, showered that invincible warrior with arrows. Rāma swiftly cut down the arrows of Rāvaṇa with his own, and the two circled each other, blotting out the sky with a cloud of dark arrows, the sun flashing through the chinks like lightning.

Then Rāvaṇa again let loose the missile of the asuras, which took the shape of heads of deadly lions, tigers, wolves, jackals, and alligators. Rāma coolly launched the missile of Agni, and his sharp arrows shone as bright as the sun, moon, and stars. They struck down the dreadful missiles of Rāvaṇa in midair.

"Well done!" shouted Rāma's army, and that first among bowmen smiled in satisfaction.

Rāvaṇa sent the missile of the sun, which Rāma's arrows sliced into discs that lit up the four quarters. Some of Rāvaṇa's arrows struck Rāma, but that fearless warrior did not feel the pain. Rāma's arrows struck Rāvaṇa's armor, but bounced off.

Then Lakshmaṇa's arrow beheaded the charioteer, while Vibhīshaṇa smashed Rāvaṇa's horses with his mace. Rāvaṇa leapt out just before his chariot crashed to the earth. Incensed by his younger brother's blows, Rāvaṇa hoisted a javelin to kill him, but Lakshmaṇa stepped between the two brothers and fired off a volley of arrows.

Watching Lakshmaṇa protect Vibhīshaṇa, Rāvaṇa called out to him, "Your strength is worthy of praise, but now I will hurl this javelin at you with all my might and end your life."

Seeing the powerful javelin of the demon Maya sailing through the air with its eight bells, Rāma prayed, "May Lakshmaṇa live long. May this javelin fall down without hitting its mark." But the javelin struck Lakshmaṇa full in the chest, pierced him through, and pinned him to the ground, his blood spurting in all directions. Seizing the javelin in both hands, not minding the arrows from Rāvaṇa that continued to rain on him, Rāma wrenched it from his brother's body and snapped it in two.

"For this I will send Rāvaṇa to his death this very day," vowed Rāma. "I will repay him for the misery Sītā and I have suffered at his hands. This is the day I have been waiting for, like the rain cloud waiting until the right season to shower the earth. Today all the monkeys, Devas, Gandharvas, and Ṛishis will see my true power as a warrior, the unconquerable strength that makes me Rāma."

Rāma, his eyes streaming with tears, seeing his brother suffering on account of that demon, felt his rage rekindle and sent a torrent of arrows at Rāvaṇa. Unable to withstand the intensity of Rāma's onslaught, the rākshasa king fled from the battlefield to find another chariot.

His enemy routed, Rāma fell on his knees and cried out, "How can I fight when my brother lies on the ground fatally wounded? Where would I ever find such a brother as he? What use is fighting, what use is a kingdom or my life, without Lakshmaṇa?"

Susheṇa, the highly respected monkey chief and physician, reassured Rāma with well-spoken words. "You must not grieve. Your brother is not dying; he sleeps and breathes. See the bright color on his face and limbs, and his smile of satisfaction? Those are the marks of a long-lived man."

Susheṇa quickly crushed the right herb and placed it under Lakshmaṇa's nose. Smelling the medicinal herb, Lakshmaṇa immediately sat up, his wounds healed in an instant.

Rāma and the monkeys rejoiced, and Rāma embraced his brother again and again. Though still weak, Lakshmaṇa had the presence of mind to whisper, "You must not waste time thinking about me. You have made a vow to kill Rāvaṇa, and one who speaks only truth must honor his promises. No enemy has ever escaped your arrows. Now is the time to fulfill your long-held intention."

Galvanized by Lakshmaṇa's words, Rāma grabbed his bow and stood waiting for Rāvaṇa, who barreled onto the battlefield in a new chariot and hammered Rāma with arrows as rain clouds storm a mountain.

At this point, the Devas, Gandharvas, and Ṛishis who had gathered to watch remarked that it was not a fair fight—Rāma stood alone on the ground with only a bow and arrows, while Rāvaṇa had an unending supply of chariots equipped with every kind of weapon. Indra, the king of the Devas, decided to make the fight more equal.

He ordered his charioteer, Mātali, to drive to earth in his golden chariot, resplendent as the sun, decorated with jewels and hundreds of tinkling bells, and present it to Rāma. Mātali greeted Rāma with folded hands and said, "Indra asked me to offer this to you, to ensure your victory." He handed Rāma the brilliant bow of Indra, plus a long and sharp javelin. Then he said, "I will be your driver. With this chariot, bow, and javelin, you will slay the king of demons."

Rāma circled the chariot and bowed before it in reverence to Indra. He shone radiant like the sun. The Devas, Gandharvas, and Ṛishis called down from above, "Victory to Shrī Rāma!" The asuras also watched from the sky and cried, "Victory to Rāvaṇa!"

Once again Rāvaṇa attacked Rāma with the dread asura weapon, only this time the arrows became serpents. To counter that, Rāma sent the missile of Garuda, all gold and fire, and his arrows became golden eagles that frightened the snakes away.

Next Rāvaṇa shot down the flagstaff of Mātali, Indra's charioteer, and even struck the charioteer and horses of Indra with his arrows. The Devas, Gandharvas, and Ṛishis cried out, distressed to see Rāmachandra, bright like the full moon, eclipsed by Rāvaṇa, who swallowed light like Rāhu, the devourer of the moon.

Rāma roared like thunder. His eyes turned red and a terrible rage overtook him. The worlds trembled, the earth quaked, and the ocean seethed in a mass of waves.

At that moment Rāvaṇa seized his heavy spear and shouted, "I will kill you now, even though you have your brother to defend you." He hurled the spear, and it flashed across the sky, its eight bells clanging like the knell of doom.

Without wasting a moment, Rāma hurled the javelin bestowed on him by Mātali. It blazed through the sky and broke the powerful spear of Rāvaṇa. Before Rāvaṇa could recover from the shock, Rāma pulverized him with arrows, striking his chest and every limb, drawing blood. He pounded Rāvaṇa's horses with arrows as well, sending them rearing up to the clouds.

"You are no warrior!" cried Rāma in his fury. "You are merely a thief, stealing my wife when she was alone. If you had laid a finger on Sītā when I was present, I would have killed you on the spot. I will do that deed now."

Soon both warriors were covered with wounds all over their bodies, but Rāma did not feel pain even from the deepest afflictions. He seemed to grow stronger, nourished by his wrath. His mind was focused and untroubled, and whenever he thought of the weapon he needed, it immediately appeared to him.

Rāvaṇa, on the other hand, grew so agitated and fatigued that he could barely lift his bow, and the arrows he shot went awry. Seeing his king's energy flagging, Rāvaṇa's charioteer suddenly drove the chariot off the battlefield, out of reach of Rāma's arrows.

When they had withdrawn to a safe distance, Rāvaṇa suddenly recovered. But instead of thanking the charioteer for saving his life, he rebuked him, saying, "How dare you drive me away from the duel? Now I will forever be shamed by this show of cowardice. You know I love to fight and have never been afraid. Why do you act as my enemy?"

"It is the charioteer's duty to know when to drive close to the enemy and when to retreat," said the charioteer in his own defense. "It was my loyalty to you that made me turn back, when you were overcome with fatigue and your horses were sweating from overexertion. Now that you are conscious, whatever you command me to do, I will follow without question."

Pleased with this answer, Rāvaṇa said, "Turn back the chariot. Everyone knows that the great Rāvaṇa never retreats from battle."

WHILE RĀVAṆA WAS away, the wise sage Agastya had taken the opportunity to visit Rāma on the battlefield. He said, "O mighty Rāma, now I will teach you the hymn *Āditya Hṛidayam*, the Heart of the Sun. It will bring you victory over Rāvaṇa. It destroys the enemy, bestows longevity and the blessings of the divine, and banishes all cares and sorrows. If you devote your mind to Sūrya, the sun, and repeat it three times, you will win every battle."

Rāma of the devoted heart quickly learned the hymn. He repeated it three times with devotion while bowing to the sun. Sūrya gazed on the virtuous Rāma and was filled with happiness, for he knew that the evil Rāvaṇa would soon die.

Rāvaṇa charged Rāma with renewed ferocity. "Drive the chariot to Rāvaṇa," Rāma quietly directed Mātali. "Be steady and straight. I know you are Indra's charioteer and I do not need to instruct you, but I wish to kill Rāvaṇa now." The charioteer, heartened by Rāma's words, drove expertly and swiftly to Rāvaṇa.

The portents were not favorable for Rāvaṇa. Vultures landed on his chariot in a flock, the setting sun cast the city of Lankā in red, and the four directions and diagonals were enveloped in darkness. A thick shower of dust fell from the cloudless sky.

The two chariots wove around each other, darting this way and that, as Rāvaṇa and Rāma shot torrents of arrows, fifty or sixty at a time. The wind stopped blowing, the seas rose in tumultuous waves, and animals across the land cried out as the sun set.

"May all be well with cows and Brahmins, may the worlds be safe, may Rāma claim victory over Rāvaṇa," prayed the Devas and Ṛishis who were watching from above.

No one had ever seen such a fight. "There is nothing that can compare," cried the onlookers. When Rāma shot off one of the ten heads of Rāvaṇa, another sprang up in its place. When Rāma shot off one of Rāvaṇa's twenty arms, another sprouted to replace it.

"How is it that these arrows that have destroyed the other rākshasas are useless in killing Rāvaṇa?" wondered Rāma.

Yet he kept on raining arrows on his foe, as did Rāvaṇa, and the battle went on through the dark night. At an auspicious moment, Mātali said, "O Rāma, why do you keep shooting arrows only in defense, as if you do not know how to destroy him? Send the missile of Brahmā. The time for this tyrant's death has come."

The weapon of Brahmā had been made for Indra to conquer the worlds. Bestowed on Rāma by the illustrious sage Agastya, in its feathers lived the wind, in its arrowhead the sun and moon. Its body was made of space, yet it weighed as much as two mountains together. Its strength derived from the essence of all animals, it tore through whole armies with ease. Blindingly radiant, adorned with the rainbow feathers of Garuda, it appeared hard and cruel to the enemy it would destroy.

Rāma fitted the dread weapon to his bow. With his mind settled and clear, he closed his eyes and used the mantras taught to him by Agastya to invoke the weapon's celestial power. Using all of his mental and physical strength, Rāma pulled back his bow and released the missile of Brahmā.

The arrow shot in a perfect arc through the sky and pierced Rāvaṇa's heart. With one last earsplitting roar, Rāvaṇa fell, his massive body with its ten heads and twenty arms cascading to the ground. At last the demon king, who made the worlds wail, had met his end.

When the valiant Vibhīshaṇa saw his brother's body lying on the ground, he startled everyone with his anguished lament. "How can one who triumphed over the earth, a hero in all battles, be lying here, uprooted like a tree?"

Rāma gently stemmed the tide of his friend's grief. "It is not right to mourn for a warrior who exhibited such bravery, such unparalleled skill, such zeal for battle," he said quietly. "Since times of old, it has been laid down that we should not grieve for the fallen warrior. Go to his side now and attend to his parting rites."

"He was ever victorious," Vibhīshaṇa cried, his eyes filling with tears. "He could not be conquered by any but you. He performed all the proper duties of a ruler, knew the truth of the Veda, and lavished wealth on his friends and kingdom. Yet he rejoiced in evil deeds and terrified the holy ones. How can I perform his funeral ceremony with a settled heart?"

"Death quells all enmity," said the greathearted Rāma. "We have achieved our purpose. Perform his rites with honor, for he is as dear to me as he is to you."

मरणान्तानि वैराणि निवृत्तं नः प्रयोजनम् ।
क्रियतामस्य संस्कारो ममाप्येष यथा तव ॥

Death quells all enmity. We have achieved our purpose.
Perform his funeral with honor, for he is as dear to me as he is to you.

—Yuddha Kāṇḍa 109.25

Chapter 51

Sītā's Ordeal

When they heard of Rāvaṇa's death, his wives went wild with grief. They staggered out of their secluded quarters, wailing, tearing at their hair, and rolling in the dust like cows that have lost their calves. Though others tried to restrain them, they broke away and ran out of the palace, through the city gates, and onto the battlefield to search for their lord's body.

Some of the women fell on Rāvaṇa's legs, others on his arms, and still others on his chest. One wailed, "Oh, why didn't our beloved listen to his well-wishers and return Sītā? He who was always victorious, who rivaled the sun in radiance, how could he be lying in the dirt?"

Then Mandodarī, Rāvaṇa's first queen, knelt by Rāvaṇa's side and cried, "No one other than the unfathomable Vishṇu could slay you. You could never be conquered by Devas or rākshasas. How could you leave me a widow—I, who was the daughter of a celebrated warrior, the mother of the conqueror of Indra and the wife of the king of the worlds?

"If only you had listened to me and to Vibhīshaṇa. If only you had allowed Sītā to return home. For it is her purity and devotion to her husband that have been your undoing. You have proven the truth of the saying: 'The tears of women devoted to their virtuous husbands do not fall in vain.' It was only because the Devas feared you that they did not strike you down the moment you carried her away. But the consequences of evil deeds eventually catch up to wrongdoers, just as happiness comes to the good."

Then the virtuous and devoted Queen Mandodarī broke into sobs. "Oh, why didn't my heart break into a thousand pieces when you breathed your last? I cannot live without you, dearest one." Inconsolable, she collapsed on Rāvaṇa's chest.

As he witnessed the women mourning over Rāvaṇa's body, Rāma said quietly, "Now is the time to perform the rites."

Vibhīshaṇa and other surviving rākshasas bathed the slain demon king in herb-scented waters and adorned him with coral, jewels, and perfumes. They covered the body with mounds of flowers and carried it to the funeral ground on a silk and gold palanquin. Their eyes streaming with tears, the rākshasas built a pyre of fragrant sandalwood, placed Rāvaṇa on the pyre, and covered him with antelope skins. Pandits chanted Vedic hymns as Vibhīshaṇa lit the fire.

At that moment, Rāma laid down his great bow and celestial weapons. As the wind began dispersing his enemy's ashes across the land, the wrath that helped him destroy Rāvaṇa melted away, and once again a gentle smile graced his countenance.

Rāma embraced his charioteer Mātali and sent him back to Indra in his chariot with gratitude. The Devas, Gandharvas, and Ṛishis, who had watched the battle from the heavens, now returned to their celestial abodes.

Then Rāma joyfully embraced Sugrīva, and Lakshmaṇa also paid him respect. After Sugrīva returned to the monkey ranks to rest, Rāma turned to his brother. "O Lakshmaṇa, Vibhīshaṇa has been a loyal and true friend. It is my heartfelt desire to install him as King of Lankā."

"So be it," Lakshmaṇa said as he quickly placed four golden vessels in the care of four monkeys and ordered them to gather water from the four seas. Using their skill in flying, they leapt over the land and returned as quick as thought.

Vibhīshaṇa sat on high ground outside the walls of Lankā while the rākshasas and all the monkeys gathered around. Lakshmaṇa held the urn over his head and, following the customs laid down in the Vedas, anointed him with the sacred water and oil. When the auspicious moment came, Rāma placed the crown on the pious Vibhīshaṇa's head with great love and respect.

As pandits chanted the sacred mantras to install a new king, the monkeys and Vibhīshaṇa's counselors and friends were filled with happiness. The rākshasas of Lankā placed pots of curds, parched rice, sweets, roasted grains, and flowers at the feet of their new king. Ever respectful of Rāma, Vibhīshaṇa paid all honor to him and to Lakshmaṇa, and offered all his new wealth to them.

After the coronation, when he was resting in his camp at the base of Mount Suvela, Rāma summoned Hanumān, that faithful monkey who was his most trusted servant. "If the new king of Lankā approves, I wish to see Sītā," he said. "You who are the most sweet in speech, tell her that I am well, as are Lakshmaṇa and Sugrīva. Tell her in your eloquent words how Rāvaṇa came to his end. Bring her these glad tidings and report to me what she says."

With Vibhīshaṇa's blessings, Hanumān entered the city of Lankā, which he knew so well. He went directly to the Ashoka Grove, where Sītā sat desolate, alone among demon women, much the same as he had left her on his earlier mission in Lankā. Hanumān stood patiently, his head bowed in respect, until she noticed him. When her face broke into a smile, he was delighted, for then he knew she remembered him.

"Devī, I bring you glad tidings," said Hanumān. Then he told her all that had happened. "Take heart, for Rāma himself is coming to greet you."

Sītā sat for a long while, gazing on Hanumān like one dazed by the full moon.

"O graceful goddess, why do you stay silent?" asked Hanumān after a while.

Suddenly she burst into tears. "I am so happy, I could not speak. What can I offer you for bringing me this message? Gold, gems, a throne—all the riches in the world are not enough to repay you for bringing this glad news of Rāma.

"You who speak with intelligence, you are deserving of praise. Your brilliant speech expresses all good qualities: strength, skill, knowledge of the Vedas, bravery, boldness, energy, stamina, steadiness, and humility."

Hanumān humbly accepted this praise. Then he said, with his hands folded in respect, "With your permission, I'd like to kill these fearful guards who have tormented you so shamelessly."

The compassionate Sītā said, "It would be wrong to punish these women, because they are slaves who must follow the orders of their ruler, and some have been kind to me. Now that Rāvaṇa is dead, they will do me no harm. I do not blame them for all that has happened to me. It was due to some mistake in the past. Everyone reaps the consequences of their actions. No one can escape their own destiny."

Sītā went on to say, "It is never right to answer evil with evil. The jewel of the virtuous is their good conduct. The virtuous are compassionate to all, even criminals who are sentenced to death. For who is so perfect that he can say he is without fault?"

"What kind and compassionate words, fitting of one so chaste and pure," Hanumān cried. "Give me your message and I will deliver it to Rāma."

"I long to see my husband, the refuge of all," she said simply.

When the intelligent Hanumān returned to Rāma with this message, Rāma's eyes filled with tears of happiness. Yet he seemed terribly distressed. Sighing deeply, Rāma said to Vibhīshaṇa, "Dear friend, bring Sītā here after she bathes and adorns herself in gold and jewels and precious scents."

When Vibhīshaṇa flew to Sītā's side in the Ashoka Grove and relayed this message to her, she fingered her dust-covered hair and said, "I wish to see my husband as I am now."

Taken aback, Vibhīshaṇa said, "It behooves you to follow your husband's wishes. My wife's attendants will bring you fresh garments and attend to your needs."

"So be it," said Sītā, who above all was devoted to Rāma. In the royal bath, she shed her soiled garments. She bathed, washed her hair, and braided it carefully. Then she smeared her limbs with auspicious oils and scents, and dressed in the glorious silken sārī that Vibhīshaṇa's wife provided. Sītā adorned herself with precious gems and gold, and once again shone like the Devi Shrī herself. Her heart tranquil and at peace, she stepped into the royal palanquin, eager to see Rāma.

WHILE SĪTĀ WAS feeling only happiness, Rāma was consumed by joy mixed with heartbreak. There was something he had to do, even though he wished with all his heart that he could avoid it.

When Sītā's palanquin came into sight, Rāma did not rush to greet her. "Bring Sītā to me," Rāma ordered Vibhīshaṇa in a strangely harsh voice.

Vibhīshaṇa, out of respect for Sītā, dispersed the crowd of monkeys and rākshasas who were gathered, driving them away so Sītā could meet Rāma in private.

"Stop!" Rāma cried. "Why do you treat my friends like this? It is a woman's conduct that protects her, not seclusion from crowds. In times of disaster and war it is permissible for a princess to be seen by her people. Let Sītā come to me on foot."

Hearing Rāma's harsh words, Lakshmaṇa, Sugrīva, and Hanumān stared sadly at their feet. When Sītā walked toward Rāma through the army of monkeys, her face radiated love and anticipation. Though her body was thin, her purity and devotion made her appear as beautiful as the full moon in the dark sky.

She reached Rāma and waited humbly before him, her hands folded in respect.

Instead of embracing his devoted wife, Rāma spoke to Sītā loudly, so all could hear: "Today I have freed you from the demon and have obliterated the insult done to me. Today I have erased the stain of your abduction.

"I have won you back, but now there is suspicion regarding your conduct. How could I, who was born into an illustrious house, take back a wife who has sat in the lap of Rāvaṇa? Surely he could not resist your celestial and earthly beauty. With Rāvaṇa's death, I have freed myself from dishonor. Now I release you from any attachment to me. Choose another husband and go."

Sītā's eyes, large as two lotuses, flooded with tears. Rāma felt his heart breaking in two, but he stood steadfast, his face without expression. He did not rescind his shocking words.

Her voice trembling with emotion, Sītā answered his harsh words with gentle ones. Wiping away her tears, she said, "Brave hero, how can you address me as if I were a common woman? I swear to you, my conduct has been pure. If my body came in contact with Rāvaṇa when he carried me through the skies, it was against my will. I could not control that fate. But my heart, which is under my control, has never swayed from union with you. If you do not know this by now, my loss is too heavy to bear.

"Have you forgotten that in our youth we clasped hands before the sacred fire? If you meant to abandon me, why didn't you ask Hanumān to tell me earlier? I would have ended my life then and saved you all this trouble." At this, Sītā could contain her pain no longer and broke down in sobs.

Lakshmaṇa, Hanumān, Sugrīva, and all the monkeys present could not restrain their tears. When Sītā realized that Rāma would not even look at her, she lifted her chin and said in a strong voice, "Lakshmaṇa, build me a pyre. For there is no reason for me to live, now that my beloved husband has banished me from his heart."

Lakshmaṇa, clearly in agony over Sītā's words, looked to Rāma for guidance. When Rāma, stone-faced, nodded in assent, with great reluctance Lakshmaṇa built the pyre, tears streaming down his face. No one dared speak or even look up, so piercing was the pain in their hearts.

When the flames leapt high, Sītā folded her hands together and cried out to the fire, "O Agni, the witness of all, if I have always been true to Rāma, shield me from your flames! If I have always been pure in conduct, protect me from harm!"

With those words Sītā flung herself on the fire.

"Sītā, O Sītā!" lamented the women. Rākshasas and monkeys alike groaned and cried out in terror. Rāma could not stop his eyes from flooding with tears. His heart convulsed with grief.

Suddenly, a divine light filled the field. With Brahmā leading them, the Devas drove their sun-bright chariots from the heavens and landed in front of Rāma. They folded their hands together in reverence to him.

Then Indra, the king of the Devas, said, "How can you be so indifferent, when Sītā is in flames? You are the maintainer of the worlds, the self-created, the beginning, middle, and end of creation. You are acting as if you are a common man and Sītā is a common woman."

Astounded by these words, Rāma said, "But I am just a man, the son of Dasharatha. If not he, who am I really?"

Brahmā, the grandsire of the world, answered him. "You are Lord Vishṇu, the thrower of the discus, the protector of Ṛishis and men, the essence of the Veda. I am your heart and Sarasvatī your tongue. Sītā is none other than Shrī Lakshmī, your divine consort. At the request of the Devas and Ṛishis, you took this human body to kill Rāvaṇa. Your strength is infinite, your glorious feats are endless. After your time on earth, you will return to heaven in glory."

Then Brahmā himself put out the flames, and Agni delivered Sītā from the fire. She stood before Rāma untouched by the fire, her face radiant and her hair dark and curled, her lovely form adorned in a brilliant red sārī, her neck circled with fresh flower garlands. If anything, the fire had only increased her radiance, like gold burnished on an anvil.

"Behold your cherished wife, Sītā," said Agni. "She is pure and without a taint of sin. She has proven that she has never been unfaithful to you, in thought or in deed. Even though tormented by her demon guards, she never strayed in her loyalty to you. Take her now, without any reproach."

At last Rāma's heart overflowed with joy. Beaming like the full moon, that valiant warrior revealed his innermost feelings to all. "I only asked Sītā to submit to this ordeal by fire for the sake of the people. It never entered my mind that Sītā was impure, not even for a second. Rāvaṇa could not make her sway from her devotion to me any more than the ocean could dry up its infinite waters. She is to me what the light is to the sun. But I had to test her, or my subjects would have said my mind was blinded by desire. In reality I could not reject her, any more than a hero could reject his honor."

With these words Rāma, who was loved by all for his noble qualities and deeds, full of glory and deserving of happiness, took Sītā by the hand and drew her to his side with great joy, for at last he was reunited with his beloved.

Lord Shiva spoke from above. "Now you must return to Ayodhyā. There you will comfort your mothers and Bharata, and bring glory to your race and wealth to your realm."

Then Lord Shiva said something that amazed everyone even more, especially Rāma: "Welcome your father, whom I have brought from the heavenly realms to see you."

As the entire assembly watched in awe and wonder, the illustrious King Dasharatha landed his celestial chariot in their midst and alighted from it. Rāma, Sītā, and Lakshmaṇa bowed to him, their faces bathed in happy tears. Dasharatha embraced his two sons and said to Rāma, "Seeing you and Lakshmaṇa brings me more fulfillment than my stay in heaven with the Devas. I am truly blessed, for you have redeemed my honor and my soul by keeping my promise to Kaikeyī. At last I am freed from the grief that Kaikeyī's words caused me.

"Now I see that you came to earth as my son for the purpose of slaying Rāvaṇa. You may return to Ayodhyā and reign over the kingdom with justice, so your mother Kausalyā can shed tears of joy."

Rāma, ever thinking of others, pressed his palms together and said, "Dear Father, will you give your blessings to Kaikeyī and Bharata? Remember the curse you pronounced on them when you renounced your favorite queen?"

"I forgive Kaikeyī and send my blessings to her and Bharata!" Dasharatha proclaimed.

Then he again enfolded Lakshmaṇa in his arms. To that noble warrior he said, "You have attained the highest glory by serving Rāma, the inner ruler of the universe, the essence of the Veda, the adored Purusha. Your fame on earth will never fade."

To Sītā he gently said, "Do not blame Rāma for momentarily shunning you. It was for your own happiness that he proved your innocence. Having survived this ordeal, you will forever be revered above other women. I know you need no instruction, but he is the supreme lord of all."

With these words, King Dasharatha mounted his golden chariot and drove away, fading into the heavens like the crescent moon.

All was quiet for a moment as the assembled crowd took in these wondrous events. Then Indra said, "O Rāma, we are pleased with your divine deeds. Name your desire and we will fulfill it."

"I wish for all the brave monkeys and bears who have died for my sake to come back to life," Rāma said. "I wish for those who were wounded to be restored to wholeness, their energy and strength increased. I wish for all members of my army to be happily reunited with their wives and families and to live long lives in contentment and prosperity. Let waters flow pure, fruits grow in abundance, and flowers bloom wherever these monkeys and bears live."

"You have asked for a difficult boon, Rāma, but I have made a promise and I will fulfill it," Indra said.

As the monkeys and bears watched, the wounds on their limbs miraculously healed. Those who lay dead on the battlefield suddenly sat up and rose to their feet, as if awakening from a deep sleep. There was a din and a tumult as comrades embraced and all were restored to their full health and vigor. Exuberant monkeys capered over each other and joyously leapt to the sky.

The Devas, Gandharvas, and Ṛishis smiled and showered flower petals on Rāma, who cared only for the welfare of all creatures. "Now return to Ayodhyā," the Devas said in unison. "Fulfill your Dharma as the king of Ayodhyā and let the good people rejoice at last."

Then the Devas faded from sight, leaving all to rejoice at their good fortune, radiantly happy under the protection of Rāma.

इत्येदमुक्त्वा विजयी महाबलः
प्रशस्यमानः स्वकृतेन कर्मणा ।
समेत्य रामः प्रियया महायशाः
सुखं सुखार्होऽनुबभूव राघवः ॥

Rāma, who was loved by all for his noble deeds,
full of glory and deserving of happiness,
took Sītā by the hand and drew her to his side in great joy,
for at last he was reunited with his beloved.

—Yuddha Kāṇḍa 118.22

Chapter 52

Rāma Returns to Ayodhyā

In the reign of Rāma,
no woman was ever a widow,
no one suffered from sickness or disease
or old age.

In the reign of Rāma,
there were no thieves,
no calamities,
no pain in childbirth,
and no parents buried a child.

In the reign of Rāma,
people lived a thousand years.
No sorrow was known,
nor poverty, nor fear of
invasion or war.
Justice and peace
ruled the land.

In the reign of Rāma,
the seasons came on time,
the trees never ceased to flower

and bowed low with ripe fruit.
The wind was soft and playful
and clouds gave plentiful rains.

In the reign of Rāma,
birdsong filled the air,
beehives were laden with honey,
and the deer and the tiger
lived in harmony.

In the reign of Rāma,
crops clothed the land,
rivers flowed with cool water,
lotuses crowded the ponds,
and the fragrance of blossoming trees
perfumed the air.

In the reign of Rāma,
no one felt greed,
no one felt poor,
no one felt hungry,
and all were contented to do their duty,
whether their status was high or low.

In the reign of Rāma,
the people dwelled in happiness,
for they held Rāma in their hearts.
All spoke the truth,
all were beautiful to look upon,
and all were devoted to Dharma.

The next morning Vibhīshaṇa invited Rāma to the palace for a royal bath. "Attendants await you with essential oils, silken clothes, and fragrant herbs," he said.

"I think only of Bharata, who so faithfully serves me at home," Rāma said. "I cannot rest until I see him. I must set out on the journey soon, for it is a long footpath home."

"There is no need for you to wander so arduously," said Vibhīshaṇa.

"I will lend you Pushpaka, the magical flying chariot that Rāvaṇa stole from our half-brother Kubera, the god of wealth. I delayed in returning it so that I could offer it to you."

Rāma was delighted and thanked his host.

"But I do hope, since now you can return home in one day, that you will spend some time first celebrating with me here," Vibhīshaṇa said. "It would do me great honor to be able to entertain you and lavish luxuries on you and Sītā. It is the least I can do after all you have done for me."

"You have already proven your friendship by your skill in fighting and your loyalty and service to me," Rāma replied. "Now I feel I owe it to Bharata to return home as quickly as possible. My heart longs to see him and Shatrughna, my mothers Kausalyā, Sumitrā, and Kaikeyī, and all the people of Ayodhyā. My work is completed here. Please do not take offense; but you have already honored me in every possible way."

Hearing Rāma's wishes, Vibhīshaṇa summoned the majestic chariot to him. It glided through the air directed merely by thought.

As Rāma prepared to board the celestial chariot Pushpaka, Vibhīshaṇa placed his hands together in respect and said humbly, "Trusted friend, before you leave, please advise me on what I should do next."

"Reward all the monkeys and bears with gifts of precious gems, gold, and other valuables," Rāma advised. "These warriors deserve the highest honor, for they have valiantly thrown themselves into battle again and again, without fear or thought of their own lives. This will bring you glory, for all will see how magnanimous and generous you are."

After sharing other wise words of advice, Rāma bade his dear friends and noble allies farewell, praising Sugrīva, Hanumān, Jāmbavān, and Vibhīshaṇa.

Before Rāma took his leave, Vibhīshaṇa again stepped forward and humbly requested, his eyes overflowing with tears, "O compassionate one, our hearts are breaking to be parted from you so soon. It is the innermost desire of our hearts to go with you to Ayodhyā. We wish to see you crowned king and anointed with the sacred waters."

Rāma smiled. "Nothing could make me happier than to welcome all my dear friends and supporters to Ayodhyā. In this way I can honor you in some small way for the magnificent service you have given me."

Then Rāma stepped inside the chariot with Sītā and Lakshmaṇa. Taking Sītā by the hand, Rāma sat her on his lap, and she shyly accepted this exhibition of love. Vibhīshaṇa and his ministers took their seats at

Rāma's feet. Sugrīva, Hanumān, Nīla, Nala, and all the monkey chiefs, as well as Jāmbavān, his brother Dhumra, and the bear chiefs, also boarded the astonishing celestial chariot, which magically expanded so that there was ample room for everyone to sit comfortably.

Filled with Rāma and his retinue, with all the happy monkeys and bears, the chariot rose like a majestic cloud at Rāma's silent command. As they flew over the ocean to the land where he had once walked with Lakshmaṇa, Rāma pointed out the sights to Sītā. "See the bridge we built to rescue you from Rāvaṇa. And from here, the invincible Hanumān leapt across the boundless sea to deliver my message to you. There, my lotus-eyed one, is Kishkindhā, the monkey kingdom where Sugrīva fought Bāli."

When she saw Kishkindhā, Sītā said softly, "It would make me happy to invite Tārā, and all the wives of Sugrīva and the monkey chiefs, to accompany me to Ayodhyā."

And so Rāma, eager to please his tenderhearted wife, ordered the car to land in Kishkindhā. There he requested Sugrīva and the other monkey chiefs to invite their wives.

The wives, of course, were beside themselves with joy to see their husbands again. Delighted by Sītā's invitation, they adorned themselves with silks and precious ornaments. Led by Tārā of lovely limbs, they circled the celestial car and entered it.

High in the air they flew over Mount Ṛishyamūka, where Rāma and Lakshmaṇa first met Hanumān. "Here is the beautiful Lake Pampā, where I wandered desolate without you," said Rāma. "And over there is the tree where Jatāyu fought the wicked Rāvaṇa, attempting to save you. And there is Janasthāna, where I killed the fourteen thousand rākshasas, and there our charming hermitage in Panchavatī, where Rāvaṇa so hatefully carried you off.

"And look, there are the āshrams of Agastya, and Sutīkshṇa, and Sharabhanga, where we glimpsed Indra. See there the āshram of Atri, where Anasūyā gave you the celestial ornaments. And there is Chitrakūta, my dearest one, where we lived so happily. And far ahead is the spot where we met Guha so long ago.

"O Sītā! There in the distance is our beloved Sarayu River, and next to it, Ayodhyā. Let us bow down to that fair city."

The monkey chiefs could hardly keep from leaping out of the Pushpaka chariot when they saw the fabled city of Ayodhyā on the horizon, with its many-storied mansions reaching to the heavens and its crowds of elephants and horses.

But they were to wait one more day, for Rāma said, "There is Bharadvāja's āshram, where we stayed the night. Let us stop there first."

Rāma landed Pushpaka beside the hermitage. Later, after he and Sītā bowed to the great sage, Rāma asked, "What is the news of Ayodhyā? Is Bharata well and does he rule wisely? Are our mothers well?"

Ṛishi Bharadvāja smiled and addressed Rāma with love and respect. "O Rāma, your brother rules with justice and equanimity in your name, with your sandals on the throne before him. He wears the matted locks, just as you do. It makes me rejoice to see you now, returning after so many long years. By the power of my intuition, I know all that happened to you. I know that you killed the demon Rāvaṇa. Now I wish for you to spend the night here and return to Ayodhyā tomorrow, which is the last day of your fourteen years of exile. But first, I wish to grant you a boon."

Delighted, Rāma made his wish. "May all the trees growing between this holy place and Ayodhyā bear fruit year-round, and may the fruits be plentiful and sweet as honey."

"So be it," said the great sage. And at that instant, the trees from the āshram to Ayodhyā became filled with luscious fruit on every branch, and even the dead and barren ones bowed low with ripened mangoes, papayas, oranges, jackfruit, and bananas. The monkey chiefs feasted on the fruit and rejoiced as if they had landed in heaven.

As he rested at Bharadvāja's āshram, Rāma sat deep in thought. Then he said to Hanumān, "I think it would be best if you went ahead to see if everything is well at the palace. Stop first beside the River Gangā to give my greetings to Guha, a friend so dear to me that he is like my other self. He will be delighted to hear we are back.

"Then give Bharata my greetings. Tell him of all that has happened, of Sītā being stolen and the destruction of Rāvaṇa. Tell him how we met our father once again, thanks to the blessings of Lord Shiva. Tell him that I now return with powerful friends, that I have defeated my enemies, winning unparalleled glory. Watch his face carefully to see how he feels about my return. If his face blanches, or if he frowns, you will know what he is thinking. If he is enjoying his rule and wants to remain in power, then he should continue to rule as he is now."

Hanumān, ever eager to serve Rāma even when the task was difficult, took the form of a man and flew toward Ayodhyā. Swift as the king of the birds, he passed over the woods and the river and landed on his feet at Guha's kingdom.

"Your dear friend Rāma has returned," said Hanumān to the surprised forest king. "He sends his greeting. Soon you will see him and Sītā and Lakshmaṇa."

Then Hanumān rose into the air again, his hair standing on end. He passed over all the flowering trees and landed in Nandigrāma, the peaceful village outside Ayodhyā where Bharata had spent the last fourteen years. There under a banyan tree sat Bharata, his hair piled high on his head in the matted locks of an ascetic, his body thin and dusty from living outdoors and subsisting only on roots and fruits. Devoted to Dharma, he had spent the years of Rāma's exile living an austere life in Nandigrāma, just as his brother had in the forest.

Hanumān approached quietly and stood humbly before Bharata, who nodded for him to proceed.

"You will be happy to know that Shrī Rāma will soon return," said Hanumān in his simple, eloquent speech.

Bharata, whose mind had been totally absorbed in Rāma for fourteen years, collapsed in relief. When he recovered, Bharata clasped Hanumān to his breast again and again. His tears soaked Hanumān's clothing. "For these happy words, I will give you a hundred thousand cows."

After inviting Hanumān to be seated, he said, "This is the first news I have heard of Rāma since last meeting him at Chitrakūta. It is true, then, that happiness will come to every man even if he has to wait a hundred years! Now tell me all that has happened since Rāma left there."

And so Hanumān, who loved Rāma as much as Bharata did, told that faithful brother, the knower of Dharma, the remarkable tale of Rāma's feats. He told the story of the war, and how the valiant monkeys and bears had helped Rāma to win over Rāvaṇa.

"He is waiting by the River Gangā, at the hermitage of Bharadvāja," concluded Hanumān. "Once he receives word from me, he will come at once." Bharata immediately dispatched a messenger to bring his brother home.

"My heart's deepest desires are being fulfilled at last," said Bharata to Shatrughna, who was never far from his side. The two brothers embraced, overjoyed that they would soon be reunited with Rāma and Lakshmaṇa.

Thinking of the people of Ayodhyā, Bharata next asked Shatrughna to ensure that the road between Nandigrāma and Ayodhyā was smoothed and paved. Shatrughna immediately placed a thousand men on the task.

"Let the people sprinkle cool water and scatter flower petals and puffed rice," Bharata announced joyfully. "Let them decorate their homes with banners and garlands."

The next morning the three queen mothers joyously traveled from Ayodhyā to Nandigrāma to await Rāma, along with thousands of townsfolk riding in chariots or mounted on elephants and horses. The earth shook and the air roared with the boom of kettle drums and blast of conch shells. The people wore their most festive clothing and precious jewels.

Bharata walked slowly to the gates of Nandigrāma, holding his brother's sandals on his head with both hands, as the chanting of the Vedas filled the air.

"Is Rāma really coming?" Bharata suddenly asked Hanumān, so anxious was he to see his brother.

"I have heard the clamor of monkeys feasting on the fruits supplied by Bharadvāja's boon," said Hanumān. "And now here is Rāma, riding in the flowery chariot Pushpaka."

As the people of Ayodhyā watched in awe, Pushpaka, drawn by swans, appeared like the moon floating in the summer sky.

"Jai Shrī Rāma!" cried the crowd again and again, their hands folded in reverence like a thousand lotus petals. "Jai Shrī Rāma!"

The magnificent chariot gracefully came to rest, and Rāma's feet touched the earth. When Bharata prostrated himself on the ground in front of him, Rāma raised him up and embraced him. Tears of affection flowed from both brothers' eyes. Bharata bowed to Sītā and embraced Lakshmaṇa.

Then as Hanumān announced the name of each of Rāma's friends, Bharata embraced each one as his own brother and recited their praises. For he had come to know Sugrīva, Jāmbavān, Angada, Nīla, Nala, and Sushеṇa from Hanumān's stories of Rāma's journey.

"You are like a fifth brother to us now," he said to Sugrīva.

And to Vibhīshaṇa he said, "Thanks to your timely help the impossible was accomplished."

In turn, Rāma bowed to his mother, Kausalyā, and touched her feet. Grown thin through years of loneliness and longing, she raised him up and held him close as she shed tears of joy. Rāma bowed to Sumitrā, Kaikeyī, and Shatrughna, and was embraced by all.

"Welcome, the delight of Kausalyā!" cried the people of Ayodhyā.

Bharata raised high Rāma's sandals and then placed them at Rāma's feet with reverence. "My heart is fulfilled, for today I return the kingdom to you. I offer you the treasury, the grain stores, and the army, for by your grace all have increased tenfold."

Hearing Bharata's loving speech, all present wept with joy. His kingdom secured, Rāma turned to Pushpaka and said, "Return to Kubera, and may you serve him well." With those words, the marvelous car rose into the sky and flew away on white swans' wings.

Rāma walked with his family and well-wishers to the modest hut that had served as Bharata's home and the seat of his kingdom for fourteen years. There at last Rāma saw Vasishtha waiting outside. He warmly clasped the feet of his revered family guru, who was as dear to him as his own self.

"I can no more rule this kingdom than can a newborn calf," proclaimed Bharata. "Let Rāma be crowned king today. As long as the earth spins and the planets orbit the sun, he will rule over us all."

When Rāma agreed, the cheering lasted so long that his eyes filled with tears of gratitude. Immediately, the preparations for his long-awaited coronation began. Taking an auspicious seat inside the hut, Rāma granted the royal barbers permission to cut off his matted locks. The attendants gave him a royal bath, and did the same for Lakshmaṇa, Vibhīshaṇa, and Rāma's friends. In another hut the royal women took delight in attending to Sītā, and Mother Kausalyā lovingly attended to Tārā and all the wives of the army chiefs.

Later, adorned with fresh silken robes, garlands of flowers, and ornaments of gold and jewels, Rāma and Sītā took their seats in the royal chariot at the head of the royal procession. As they started on the road to Ayodhyā, Bharata held the reins, Shatrughna raised the white umbrella of the king, and Lakshmaṇa waved the white yak-tail fan. All along the way pandits chanted the Vedas while Devas, Gandharvas, and Ṛishis showered rose petals from above. The people of Ayodhyā poured out of the city to line the highway blowing conches, beating drums, ringing bells, and calling out auspicious salutations to their beloved king. Rāma repeatedly bestowed his thanks and blessings on all.

Following the royal chariot came Rāma's army chiefs, riding on elephants. Troupes of dancers and musicians performed festive songs, while Brahmins in orange robes scattered saffron rice and chanted hymns. Bards sang his praises as Rāma triumphantly entered the fabled city of his birth.

As they made their way through streets adorned with colorful flowers and banners on every balcony, Rāma said to Bharata, "Give Sugrīva my palace to live in, with its aloe and sandalwood walls and its inner garden of flowering ashoka trees."

And so Bharata brought the chariot to the gate of Rāma's palace, took Sugrīva by the hand and led him inside. Attendants greeted the other guests with traditional greetings of light, the chiming of bells, and Vedic chanting and led them to spacious rooms.

Bharata held out four golden urns inlaid with pearls and jewels. "Would the army chiefs honor us by collecting water from the four seas?" he asked Sugrīva. At Sugrīva's command, Jāmbavān brought water from the eastern sea, Gavaya delivered water from the western sea, Ṛishabha from the southern sea, and Hanumān from the north. Others carried water from the five hundred rivers.

When the water had been collected, they entered a special coronation hall with gold on all sides, and at the auspicious time Vasishtha instructed Rāma and Sītā to be seated on a throne covered with brilliant gems. With the chanting of the four Vedas reverberating throughout the hall, Vasishtha, Vāmadeva, Kashyapa, Gautama, and the other holy sages joyfully anointed the head of Rāma with fragrant oils.

Then they sprinkled the sacred waters from the four seas and the five hundred rivers on his head. Next maidens and ministers, warriors and merchants also gladly sprinkled water on Rāma's head, as was the custom from ancient times. The Devas and the guardians of the four quarters blessed Rāma with the juices of every celestial herb.

Then Vasishtha placed on Rāma's head the golden crown of his ancestors, fashioned by Brahmā for Manu, the first king of the solar dynasty. The other sages adorned Rāma with jewels. Throughout the festivities Shatrughna held the white umbrella over Rāma's head while Lakshmaṇa and Hanumān never tired of fanning Rāma with the white yak-tail fans.

Vāyu, the god of the wind, presented Rāma with a hundred golden lotuses and a necklace of pearls and precious gems. The Gandharvas sang heavenly songs, and celestial nymphs danced in delight.

To each of the Brahmins in the kingdom, Rāma distributed ten thousand horses and an equal number of cows, a hundred bulls, thirty crores of gold, costly clothing, and golden ornaments. He bestowed on Sugrīva a garland of gold and jewels that shone like a thousand suns.

To Angada he presented a pair of gold arm-bracelets set with blue sapphire, diamonds, and emeralds. To Vibhīshaṇa, Hanumān, Jāmbavān,

Nīla, Nala, and all the vānara chiefs he gave costly jewelry as well as silken clothing.

Affectionately, he adorned Sītā with a necklace of rare pearls and gems. Then Sītā, glancing at Rāma for his approval, unclasped the pearls from her own neck.

"Yes," said Rāma, seeing what she meant to do. "Give the necklace to the one who served you with strength and courage, skill and cleverness, power and intelligence."

Thus, as a token of her infinite gratitude, the dark-eyed Sītā gave Hanumān her own necklace. On his powerful chest, it looked like a halo of light circling the shining moon. Hanumān humbly bowed his head, forever the faithful servant of Rāma and Sītā.

After the jubilant day of Rāma's coronation, Rāma's friends reluctantly said their goodbyes, hearts saddened to leave Rāma, and returned to their homes in Kishkindhā and Lankā.

After their departure Rāma turned his mind to the affairs of ruling his kingdom. Grateful to Lakshmaṇa for his unfailing service over the fourteen years of exile, Rāma said, "Lakshmaṇa, you are my equal and you know Dharma. Share the kingdom with me and become the crown prince."

But Lakshmaṇa, ever modest, declined again and again. So Rāma made Bharata the prince regent of the kingdom.

Renowned for his generosity, victorious over his enemies, and famed throughout the world, Rāma ruled the kingdom with happiness and justice for ten thousand years. Like his father, Rāma performed hundreds of yagyas to gain support of nature, including one hundred ceremonies of the rare Ashvamedha Yagya. Performing so many of these auspicious yet difficult royal yagyas made him a king of kings, a ruler of the whole earth. Ever generous and magnanimous, Rāma used his power and wealth to bring peace and prosperity to all.

In the whole of Rāma's realm there was no one who suffered from bodily pains, ill fortune, or evil circumstances. Every man loved his neighbor and, contented with the state of life to which he had been born, was guided by sound morality and the teaching of scripture.

The four pillars of life—*Dharma, Artha, Kāma,* and *Moksha*—were established throughout the world. Men and women alike were devoted to worship and enjoyed the blessings of the highest heaven.

In the reign of Rāma, there was no sickness and no premature death. Everyone was fit and sound of body. No one suffered from poverty, sorrow, or distress. No one was ignorant or unlucky.

All men and women were naturally good and generous, clever and intelligent. Everyone appreciated the merits of his neighbor and was himself learned and wise. Everyone expressed gratitude for kindnesses offered to them by others. With their hearts ever one with Rāma's, they never quarreled with each other. Husbands and wives were devoted to each other and their children.

Rāma bestowed untold riches on the sages, who guided the people with wisdom, and wealth was enjoyed by all. The people of Ayodhyā found their spiritual leaders and king to be the embodiment of Dharma.

The forest was ever laden with flowers and fruit. Beasts of prey forgot their animosities and lived in harmony with one another. Honey bees softly hummed, and the cooing of birds thrilled the ear. The earth was abundant with crops and yielded jewels of every description.

Rivers flowed with an abundance of refreshing water. Lotus flowers thronged the ponds and flavored the water with sweetness. There was no fear of violent storms, and the seas remained within their bounds, casting forth pearls on their shores for all to gather. Every quarter of the world lived in happiness.

The air was mild and pleasantly cool, fragrant with flowers, and the wind felt pleasant to the touch. The sun radiated only as much heat as was comfortable, and the clouds poured forth only when desired in the days when Rāma was king.

नित्यमूला नित्यफलास्तरवस्तत्र पुष्पिताः ।
कामवर्षी च पर्जन्यः सुखस्पर्शश्च मारुतः ॥

In the reign of Rāma, the trees in the forest were ever laden with flowers and fruit. Clouds sent down rain only when desired, and the wind felt pleasant to the touch.

—Yuddha Kāṇḍa 128.103

End of the Yuddha Kāṇḍa

SEVEN

Uttara Kāṇḍa

Epilogue

Epilogue

The milky moon sets in the western sky
as the radiant sun fills the eastern quarter with warmth,
each a glorious act of creation.
Gaze on one,
and you turn from the other.
Gaze on the other,
and you turn from the one.
Such is a conflict in Dharma.
Rāma, the master of Dharma,
must choose between the Dharma of a husband
and the Dharma of a king—
a sacrifice for Sītā,
a sacrifice for Rāma,
but pleasing to Dharma.

Several years passed after Rāma and Sītā returned to Ayodhyā, and they lived happily with the support of Rāma's brothers and the able ministers of the king. Rāma built Sītā a garden next to the palace, filled with beautiful sandalwood, mango, coconut, and ashoka trees. Vines and bushes offered up fragrant flowers and fruits. Bees flocked there, as did colorful birds. Steps inlaid with sparkling gems led to ponds covered with lotus blossoms and graced by parrots, swans, cranes, and peacocks. Enclosed by flat rocks, the ponds glimmered in the sun by day and reflected the moon by night. It was as beautiful as the divine gardens of Indra and Kubera.

Each day after Rāma settled the affairs of the state, he walked with Sītā in the garden and gave her fruit drinks and other delights for her enjoyment. One day, while they were sitting in the garden, Sītā, glowing like a celestial, told Rāma that she was with child. Rāma was overjoyed and gladly offered Sītā anything her heart desired.

"I would like to visit the sages on the banks of the River Gangā once again, as we did years ago," she said.

"So be it, my lovely lady," answered Rāma. "You shall go as soon as you wish, tomorrow, if that is your desire." Then he retired to his private chambers.

Inside, Rāma, full of delight, met with his ministers. Rāma questioned them, saying, "Tell me, what do the good citizens of Ayodhyā say about me?"

One of the ministers, Bhadra, answered carefully, "They speak of your brave conquest of Rāvaṇa and of your fair hand in ruling the kingdom."

Rāma inquired further. "Tell me everything, Bhadra. Leave nothing out. Tell me the ill as well as the good, so that I may improve what needs to be improved. Tell me without fear."

And so Bhadra told Rāma what had been weighing on his heart for some time. "The people do speak well of your conquest over Rāvaṇa, but they are speaking ill words about Sītā. They say, 'Sītā sat in the lap of Rāvaṇa and lived with him for many months. Why doesn't Rāma censure her? If he accepts her behavior, then our wives will act as she has, for as is the ruler, so are the ruled.'"

Rāma's mind whirled and he felt faint. "Could my people have such short memories to have forgotten that Sītā entered the fire yet remained unharmed, because of her purity?"

Rāma turned to the other ministers. "Can this be true?" he asked. Bowing their heads to hide their distress, his trusted ministers confirmed that the people harbored doubts about Sītā and about Rāma's inability to censure her.

Rāma could scarcely believe what he was hearing. This was far worse than exile or his battle with Rāvaṇa. In those circumstances his Dharma had been clear. Now his Dharma as a husband conflicted with his Dharma as a king. How could he convince his people that he had always followed the ways of righteousness, and so, too, had Sītā? What was he to do, with suspicion and harsh words dividing the kingdom?

Sunk in despair, his face as pale as an eclipsed moon, Rāma weighed the matter in his mind and heart. Above all, he understood one of the great principles of Dharma: if he earned ill fame, he and his subjects would fall into a lower state, for dishonor was considered the worst of sins.

Having tumbled into an ocean of sorrow, Rāma determined what he had to do and called for his brothers. His face streaked with tears and his voice choking with emotion, he told them what people were saying. "I would give up my very life to save the kingdom from harm," he said. "I must take action, and I don't want you to stop me."

Then he spoke directly to Lakshmaṇa. "Tomorrow morning I want you to take Sītā across the River Gangā to the āshram of the sage Vālmīki. Once you have delivered her there, leave her and return to Ayodhyā without her. This is my command as your king." Having fulfilled his duty, Rāma retired to his chambers, overcome with sadness.

The next morning, Lakshmaṇa, agitated in mind, summoned Sumantra, who had been his father's most trusted charioteer, and asked him to prepare the chariot for Sītā. He told Sītā that Rāma had asked him to bring her to visit the sages by the River Gangā, as she had requested. Sītā was delighted, thinking that Rāma was fulfilling her wishes.

As the morning sun filled the city, Lakshmaṇa and Sītā rode out of the city and into the countryside. When they rode away, Sītā's right eye twitched, her limbs grew weak, and her mind became dizzy. She said to Lakshmaṇa, "I am greatly distressed, O Lakshmaṇa! My limbs shiver and my heart is filled with anxiety. Tell me, is all well with Rāma?"

"All is well," whispered Lakshmaṇa quietly, without looking at Sītā.

The next day they reached the banks of the River Gangā and crossing it, they rested on a grassy bank in the vicinity of Vālmīki's āshram. At this point Lakshmaṇa could contain himself no longer and fell to the ground at Sītā's feet, sobbing like a child.

"Tell me truthfully, O Lakshmaṇa, what is wrong?" asked Sītā. "Is Rāma well? I cannot be parted from him for even two days. Come, let us distribute gifts to the āshrams and return to my beloved Rāma."

Lakshmaṇa could not look at Sītā. His face pressed to the ground, he cried out, "Noble lady, Rāma has asked me to abandon you here! Rumors are afloat in the kingdom concerning your abduction by Rāvaṇa. Rāma feels that his honor has been tarnished, and that now it is his duty to uphold Dharma. His heart is breaking. Anything more I cannot tell you."

Sītā could not believe what she was hearing. "What have I done to deserve such treatment?" she sobbed. "What other wife would follow her husband to the forest for fourteen years? How could Rāma behave in this way after I entered the fire to prove my purity?"

With his whole being, Lakshmaṇa wished he could take her back to Ayodhyā, but he knew that he must follow Rāma's orders and abandon Sītā by the River Gangā. Before he turned away, he cried out to Sītā, "May Mother Earth protect you! May the canopy of stars protect you! May the gods protect you!"

Sītā gathered enough strength to console him. "Farewell, dear Lakshmaṇa. I hold nothing against you. Tell Rāma that I wish him well, that I have always been devoted to him, and will always be devoted to him for all of my days."

Lakshmaṇa ferried back across the river, and before returning to Ayodhyā, took one last look back at Sītā. She was lying on the ground, sobbing. His own heart breaking, Lakshmaṇa mounted the chariot and drove away.

After some time, the sons of sages living in Vālmīki's āshram heard Sītā crying and ran to tell Vālmīki. "She is like a goddess from heaven," they said to the sage, "and she is overcome with sorrow."

Vālmīki walked in the direction they pointed until he heard Sītā weeping in the distance. It reminded him of the cry of the krauncha bird that had lost its mate so long ago. When he reached her side, he gently said, "I know you are the daughter of King Janaka of Mithilā, the daughter-in-law of King Dasharatha of Ayodhyā, and the husband of Shrī Rāma. I also know through my ascetic practice that you are pure and have always been faithful to your husband. Come, dearest one, to my āshram, where the wives of the sages will care for you as tenderly as they would their own daughter."

Back in Ayodhyā, Lakshmaṇa told Rāma all that had happened. Paralyzed by grief, Rāma could find no words to respond to him.

The people of Ayodhyā, on the other hand, rejoiced, feeling that Dharma had been restored to their kingdom, and that Rāma had acted rightly when he placed his Dharma as a king above his Dharma as a husband. But even though separated, Rāma remained true to Sītā in his heart, and Sītā remained true to Rāma.

Many months later Sītā gave birth to twin boys. Vālmīki named them Lava and Kusha, and performed all the rites for the birth of the children.

When Sītā's handsome twins were old enough, Vālmīki taught them to recite the poem he had composed about the illustrious Rāma—his birth, his marriage to Sītā, his time in the forest, his conquest of Rāvaṇa, and his banishment of Sītā. Over the course of twelve years, the twins practiced reciting in meter until they had memorized Vālmīki's long and beautiful poem, which the revered sage called the "Journey of Rāma," the Rāmāyaṇa.

About that time, Rāma decided to hold an Ashvamedha Yagya in the Naimisha Forest. He invited all the kings from surrounding kingdoms, as well as the sages of the forest. Sugrīva arrived with his monkeys, as did people from all the near and faraway lands. Even the rākshasas of Lankā came with their virtuous king, Vibhīshaṇa.

The wise sages of the kingdom explained to Rāma that to perform such a yagya, he would need a consort, and for that he would need to marry once again. Rāma refused to even glance at another woman, and after some debate, the sages decided to build a life-size statue of Sītā, made of gold, which would be placed next to Rāma.

Vālmīki also attended the yagya, and brought with him Lava and Kusha. He instructed the boys to sing twenty verses from the story of Rāma to the sages, who sat in front of their grass huts. Everyone marveled at their extraordinary recitation. Eventually, the boys were invited to sing for Rāma himself. Rāma asked to hear the whole story, and for days the boys sang by heart the story of Rāma that they had learned from Vālmīki.

Not only did they sing with uncommon ease and charm, but they looked like Rāma himself. Without anyone noticing, Rāma moved closer to the boys, one inch at a time. Halfway through their recitation, Rāma realized that these radiant boys were his own sons. Bursting with joy at the sight of his sons, Rāma could no longer contain his love for Sītā, and asked Vālmīki to bring her to the hall the next day. Then she could prove her purity to all present.

Before dawn the next morning all were assembled, eagerly anticipating the arrival of Sītā. As the full moon set in the western sky and the sun rose in the east, Sītā walked in, her hands folded in reverence and her eyes filled with tears. After years of tapas in the forest, she looked more radiant than ever, like a celestial being. Rāma's heart swelled with affection for Sītā, and the people welcomed her with shouts of joy.

Gazing at Rāma with love and devotion, Sītā quietly asked, "May I have your permission to once again prove my devotion to you?"

Rāma nodded.

Then Sītā said loudly, for all to hear, "O Mother Earth, if you know that I have never loved any other man but Rāma, even for a moment, then open your arms and accept me now."

At that moment a chasm opened in front of Sītā and before all assembled, Mother Earth emerged and welcomed Sītā into her arms and seated her on a throne of flowers. Then the throne slowly descended and the earth closed over her head. Sītā was gone forever.

Rāma wept uncontrollably. He threatened to destroy the earth if she would not return Sītā, but Brahmā appeared to him and said, "Remember who you are, Rāma. You are Vishṇu and your consort is Lakshmī, who has appeared to you in this life as Sītā. You will be united with her in Brahma Loka, where you will live together once again for all eternity. Your separation is but a blink of the eyes in the long stretch of time."

For the rest of his life, Rāma ruled the kingdom with the golden statue of Sītā beside him. Because their king had always been faithful to Dharma, the people of his kingdom flourished. There were no diseases or premature death, the rains came in time, and everyone was happy, prosperous, and virtuous. The weather never turned violent, nor were there any fires. There was an abundance of food in the granaries and gold in the treasuries. Everyone was devoted to Rāma.

One day, many years later, while Rāma was sitting on his throne in the royal court, Kāla, the spirit of time, came to visit. He said, "O Rāma, I must speak to you alone. Please guard the doors and let no one enter, on pain of death."

Rāma asked the ever-faithful Lakshmaṇa to stand outside and guard the doors, as Kāla had requested.

Then Kāla spoke to Rāma, but Rāma already knew what he had to say. "Esteemed Rāma, now that you have lived a long and just life, true to Dharma, I have been sent by Lord Brahmā to bring you back to your heavenly abode." Rāma nodded his consent.

Just then, outside the royal court, the sage Durvāsa arrived. He was known far and wide for his ill temper. "I have come to see Lord Rāma," he demanded of Lakshmaṇa.

Lakshmaṇa answered, "I am sorry, but no one can enter the court under pain of death."

Durvāsa became angry and bellowed, "Go in and announce my presence, or I shall curse you, your brothers, and the entire kingdom of Kosala, so that no one shall live."

Lakshmaṇa thought for a minute and realized that it would be better for him to die for breaking the vow to Kāla than the entire kingdom to be cursed by Durvāsa. And so, bowing to the inevitable, he entered the hall and announced to Rāma that the sage Durvāsa wished to see him.

Rāma immediately took leave of Kāla and went to see what Durvāsa wanted. Durvāsa said that he had been fasting for a thousand years, and now he wanted to end his fast with some food. Rāma fed him with the choicest food in the land, and Durvāsa went away happily.

But then Rāma remembered Kāla and the vow that he had made. "Is this my final test?" Rāma wondered as he sank into sorrow. "Must I now kill my own brother in order to uphold my promise to Kāla?"

After a long, distressing discussion between Rāma and his ministers, Vasishtha finally rose to his feet. "Banishment is as good as death," he said.

With grief, Rāma reluctantly agreed that Lakshmaṇa should be banished from the kingdom to fulfill his vow to Kāla. After embracing Rāma, Lakshmaṇa circled his brother for the last time and bade him farewell.

Lakshmaṇa strode to the River Sarayu and, sitting on its banks, closed his eyes and sank into the unbounded Self. Soon Indra's chariot appeared before him and carried him to Brahma Loka.

Rāma could not bear to be separated from his brother after the painful years of separation from his beloved wife. He prepared to leave his mortal body, now that Lord Brahmā had beckoned him. "My time on earth has come to an end," he said to his ministers.

When Bharata and Shatrughna refused to rule the kingdom in his stead, and expressed their desire to depart with him, Rāma gave the southern half of Kosala to his son Kusha and the northern half to his son Lava and instructed them both to rule from the capital city of Ayodhyā.

Next he summoned his friend and servant Hanumān. "Wherever the name of Rāma is mentioned and wherever the story of Rāma is told, you shall be there. This story will be repeated as long as the sun and moon shine." Rāma embraced Hanumān affectionately for the last time.

As Rāma prepared to depart, the good people of Ayodhyā implored him to take them with him. Seeing their sadness, the compassionate Rāma announced to the citizens of that fabled city, "Whosoever among you wishes to join me may do so, along with your families and cows."

Walking to the banks of the River Sarayu, Rāma entered the waters along with his brothers Bharata and Shatrughna and all the people of Ayodhyā.

As the waters closed above Rāma, in his place rose the resplendent form of Lord Vishṇu, with discus, conch, mace, and lotus in his hands. To his immortal mind, only moments earlier he had closed his eyes and taken the incarnation of Shrī Rāma. Devas, Gandharvas, apsarās, and a multitude of celestials showered flower petals from above.

Arriving at Brahma Loka with all the people of Ayodhyā, he was reunited with his radiant consort, Lakshmī, who had taken the incarnation of Sītā, as well as Lakshmaṇa and the rest of his family.

Lava and Kusha remained in Ayodhyā to rule their kingdoms. Now that the story of Rāma was complete, they sang the final verses of the glorious Rāmāyaṇa, the story of Rāma.

Those who hear the Rāmāyaṇa
are freed from sin.
Those who read the Rāmāyaṇa
enjoy children, wealth,
fame, and longevity.

Women who hear the Rāmāyaṇa
are blessed with precious children
and grandchildren
who fulfill all their desires.

Those who hear these verses of Vālmīki
overcome all obstacles.
The exiled live to be reunited with their loved ones,
and the king obtains victory.

And so ends the Rāmāyaṇa.
May all good come to you.
May the strength of Vishṇu grow forever,

for Rāma is none other than he
who maintains the universe.

Those who read or hear the Rāmāyaṇa
gain blessings from nature.
Those who listen to these verses with devotion
live in heaven forever.
Whosoever recites or listens
to the story of Rāma daily
with reverence and devotion
banishes all sins
and attains a long life.

यः पठेच्छृणुयान्नित्यं चरितं राघवस्य ह ।
भक्त्या निष्कल्मषो भूत्वा दीर्घमायुरवाप्नुयात् ॥

Whosoever recites or listens to the story of Rāma daily
with reverence and devotion eliminates all sins and attains a long life.

—Uttara Kāṇda 111.19

End of the Uttara Kāṇda

End of the Rāmāyaṇa

Glossary of Sanskrit Words

āchārya	teacher
adharma	wickedness, unrighteousness
ādikavya	first poem, the Rāmāyaṇa
Āditya	sun
Agastya	illustrious Ṛishi who lived in the forest and gave Rāma celestial weapons
Agni	god of fire
Agnihotra	a particular yagya
Ahalyā	wife of Gautama, who made her invisible
Airāvata	white elephant of Indra with four tusks
Akampana	warrior in Rāvaṇa's army
Aksha	youngest son of Rāvaṇa
Alakā	capital city of Kubera, the god of wealth, located on Mount Kailāsa
āmalaka	small round fruit with a sour taste and many rejuvenating properties
Amarāvatī	city of the gods, abode of Indra
amṛitam	nectar of immortality that emerged when the asuras and Devas used Mount Mandara to churn the ocean at the beginning of time
ānanda	bliss
Anasūyā	wife of Atri, known for her yogic powers

Angada	son of Bāli and Tārā
Anjanā	beautiful apsarā; mother of Hanumān
apsarā	celestial nymph
āraṇya	forest
artha	wealth, purpose
Arundhatī	wife of Vasishtha
Ashoka Grove	grove of ashoka trees where Sītā was held captive in Lankā
āshram	Vedic school (*āshrama* in Sanskrit); the hermitage of ascetics and sages
Ashvamedha	the largest of the Vedic yagyas, performed by kings to gain dominion over other kings
Ashvapati	king of Kekaya, father of Kaikeyī
Ashvins	divine twins who symbolize sunrise and sunset; they bring treasures to men and avert misfortune and sickness (*Ashvin* in Sanskrit)
astra	missile, weapon
asura	negative force of nature
Atharva	one of the four Vedas
atibala	that which surpasses strength
Atikāya	son of Rāvaṇa
Ātmā	Self, pure consciousness, pure awareness (in Sanskrit, *Ātmā* is the nominative form of *Ātman*)
Atri	one of seven great Ṛishis who lived in the forest
Avindhya	minister of Rāvaṇa
Ayodhyā	capital city of Kosala, where King Dasharatha ruled (*Ayodhyā* means "invincible" or "unassailable")
bala	strength
bāla	boy, youth
Bālī	brother of Sugrīva, son of Indra
Bhadra	minister of Rāma
bhara	bearing back (to the Self)
Bharadvāja	great seer who was a disciple of Vālmīki
Bharata	younger brother of Rāma who ruled the kingdom in his absence

Brahmā	deity responsible for creation; the Creator; he is said to have created the universe from his mind; his consort is Sarasvatī
Brahma Loka	highest heaven, the realm of Brahmā, the Creator
Brahman	wholeness, totality
Brahmin	teacher and scholar (*brāhmaṇa* in Sanskrit)
Bṛihaspati	one of the powers of nature, the guru of the Devas
Budha	the planet Mercury
Chaitraratha	garden of Kubera, cultivated by the Gandharva Chitraratha
Chandra	moon
Chandramā	moon
chāraṇa	celestial singer
Chitrakūta	beautiful mountain in the forest where Rāma, Sītā, and Lakshmaṇa lived during the first months of exile
crore	a unit in the Indian numbering system equal to ten million
Dadhimukha	maternal uncle of Sugrīva and the guard of Madhuvana, the royal garden of Kishkindhā
Daṇḍaka	vast forest where Rāma was exiled for fourteen years
Danu	Gandharva who was freed from his rākshasa body as Kabandha
darbha	a type of grass
Dasharatha	King of Kosala and father of Rāma
Deva	positive force of nature, celestial being, a god or goddess
Devāntaka	one of Rāvaṇa's sons
Devī	positive force of nature, a goddess
Dhanvantari	physician of the Devas
Dharma	Natural Law, truth, right action, natural duty, the invincible power of nature that upholds life, maintaining evolution on every level, including personal evolution
Dhūmrāksha	general in Rāvaṇa's army

Diti	mother of the demon race (opposite of Aditi)
dundubhi	a type of earth drum formed by hollowing out the earth and covering it with the skin of an animal; deep-throated drum from ancient India
Dūshaṇa	general in Rāvaṇa's army, brother of Rāvaṇa
Ekajatā	one of the rākshasīs who taunted Sītā
Gandhamādana	one of King Sugrīva's army chiefs
Gandharva	celestial musician, celestial singer
Gandharva Veda	aspect of Sanskrit literature concerned with music
Gaṇesha	"leader of the *gaṇas*"; son of Shiva and Pārvatī; Deva who has the head of an elephant, Gaṇesha removes obstacles and brings good fortune
Gangā	River Ganges; one of the seven sacred rivers
Garuda	king of the birds; the conveyance for Lord Vishṇu
Gautama	sage and husband of Ahalyā
Gavāksha	one of King Sugrīva's monkey chiefs
Gavaya	one of King Sugrīva's monkey chiefs
Godāvarī	river in the Daṇḍaka Forest near Panchavatī; one of the seven sacred rivers
Gomatī	river near Ayodhyā
graha	planet
Guha	chief of a neighboring tribe, friend of Rāma's
guru	teacher
Guru	the planet Jupiter
Hanumān	vānara (celestial being in the form of a monkey) who was the devoted servant of Rāma and Sītā; his name means "the one with the fractured jaw"
Hemā	nymph who lived in the Ṛikshabila Cave with Svayamprabhā
Himālaya	abode of snow, the great snowcapped mountain range of northern India
Hiraṇyagarbha	golden womb of creation, the sun

Ikshvāku	family of the solar dynasty from which Rāma descended
Indra	king of the Devas
Indrajit	Rāvaṇa's eldest son who used conjuring tricks to vanquish Indra, the king of the Devas; also called "Meghnāda"
ingudī	a tree native to the Indian subcontinent having edible and medicinal uses for the bark, fruit, and seed; in English known as the soapberry tree or desert date
Itihāsa	history; the aspect of Sanskrit literature containing the two great epics, the Rāmāyaṇa and the Mahābhārata
Jāmbavān	chief of the bears, son of Lord Brahmā
Jambumālī	warrior for Rāvaṇa and son of Prahasta
Jamunā	one of the seven sacred rivers
Janaka	famous king of Videha, father of Sītā
Jānakī	Sītā, daughter of King Janaka, wife of Rāma
Janasthāna	area in the Daṇḍaka Forest where Rāma single-handedly killed fourteen thousand rākshasas
Jatāyu	ancient vulture who tried to rescue Sītā
Kabandha	giant rākshasa who was really a Gandharva named Danu
Kaikasī	Rāvaṇa's mother
Kaikeyī	favorite queen of King Dasharatha, mother of Bharata
Kailāsa	sacred mountain in the Himālayas where Shiva and Pārvatī dwell, as well as Kubera
Kalā	eldest daughter of Vibhīshaṇa
Kāla	time, a messenger of death
kalpa-vṛiksha	wish-fulfilling tree, located in Indra's garden
Kāma	pleasure, enjoyment; one of the four aims of life
kāṇda	chapter; book
Kaṇdu	sage who lived in the forest
karma	action, the result of action
Kashyapa	a great *Ṛishi*

Kausalyā	first queen of King Dasharatha, mother of Rāma (later called Kaushalyā)
Kekaya	birth kingdom of Kaikeyī
Kesarī	monkey who is the husband of Anjanā, the mother of Hanumān
Khara	general in Rāvaṇa's army, brother of Rāvaṇa
Kishkindhā	vānara (celestial monkey) kingdom ruled by Bālī and then Sugrīva
kokila	black cuckoo bird
Kosala	kingdom ruled by King Dasharatha (also called "Koshala")
krauncha	bird (*Sarus Crane*) that inspired Vālmīki to cognize the Rāmāyaṇa
Kshatriya	warrior or administrator
Kubera	god of wealth and guardian of the northerly direction, half brother of Rāvaṇa
Kumbha	son of Kumbhakarṇa
Kumbhakarṇa	Rāvaṇa's younger brother, a giant demon
kusha	sacred grass used at yagyas and other ceremonies
Kusha	son of Rāma and Sītā
Lakshmaṇa	devoted brother of Rāma
Lakshmī	the goddess responsible for good fortune, wealth, beauty, success, and charm. She is the consort of Vishṇu and incarnated as Sītā.
Lankā	"beautiful city," the island kingdom where Rāvaṇa ruled
Lava	son of Rāma and Sītā
linga	stone that signifies Shiva
madhuparka	a traditional offering of yogurt, clarified butter, honey, and coconut milk
Madhuvana	honey-sweetened royal garden of Kishkindhā
Mahābhārata	one of the two great epics of India
Mahāpārshva	Rāvaṇa's younger brother
Mahārāja	great king
Mahendra	mountain by the sea where Hanumān began his leap and returned after burning Lankā
Maheshvara	Shiva

Mahodara	brother and minister of Rāvaṇa
Mahodaya	mountain in the Himālayas with medicinal herbs
Maināka	highest mountain in the ocean, offered rest to Hanumān
Makarāksha	son of Khara, nephew of Rāvaṇa
Malaya	mountain near Lankā
Mālyavān	Rāvaṇa's maternal grandfather
Mandākinī	sacred river near Chitrakūta Mountain
Mandara	sacred mountain used for churning the ocean at the beginning of time (also called *Mandāra*)
Māṇdavī	wife of Bharata, niece of King Janaka
Mandodarī	favorite wife of Rāvaṇa
Mangala	the planet Mars
Mantharā	elderly servant of Kaikeyī who convinced her to demand Rāma's banishment
mantra	Vedic sound used to take the awareness inward to experience pure consciousness; verse from Sanskrit literature often employed in yagyas
Manu	first king of the solar dynasty; founder of the city of Ayodhyā; the progenitor of the human race
Manu Smṛiti	law book, code of conduct, also known as the "Laws of Manu"
Mārīcha	demon who could perform magic, and disguised himself as a golden deer to help Rāvaṇa abduct Sītā
Mātali	charioteer of Indra
Matanga	guru of Shabarī, also the name of the woods where he lived
Maya	demon who gave Rāvaṇa a magical javelin
Māyāvī	the asura who fought with Bāli in the cave
Meru	sacred mountain in the center of the Himālayas
Mithilā	capital city of Videha, where King Janaka ruled
Moksha	the state of enlightenment associated with complete freedom, liberation

Mount Mandara	See *Mandara*
nakshatra	star cluster
Nala	monkey who built Rāma's bridge, son of Vishvakarman
Nalasetu	the bridge built by Nala and the monkey army to span the ocean between India and Lankā
nāmakaraṇa	naming ceremony for a child
Nandana	garden in heaven that belongs to Indra
Nandigrāma	village east of Ayodhyā from which Bharata ruled the kingdom during Rāma's exile
Nārada	sage famous for traveling throughout the cosmos playing his vīṇā
Narāntaka	son of Rāvaṇa
Nikumbha	son of Kumbhakarṇa
Nikumbhilā	grove near the western gate of Lankā used for sacrificial rites by Indrajit
Nīla	chief of the monkey army, son of Agni
Nishākara	sage who lived in the Vindhya Mountains
nyagrodha	banyan tree; related to the fig tree
Pampā	lake next to Mount Ṛishyamūka
Panchavatī	grove in the forest where Rāma and Sītā lived near the end of their exile
pandit	learned scholar who performs yagyas and chants the Vedas (*paṇḍita* in Sanskrit)
Paramātmā	the supreme Self
Pārvatī	deity who is one of the consorts of Shiva; daughter of the Himālaya
pāyasa	mixture of milk, rice, and sugar that was given by Agni to King Dasharatha, who then gave it to his three wives as part of the yagya for gaining children
Praghasa	warrior in Rāvaṇa's army
Prahasta	commander in chief and eldest warrior in Rāvaṇa's army, also a minister to Rāvaṇa
Prajāpati	lord of creatures, the sun
Prasravaṇa	mountain where Rāma and Lakshmaṇa waited for Sugrīva during the rainy season
pṛithivī	earth

Pulastya	ancient Ṛishi, son of Brahmā, grandfather of Rāvaṇa
Purusha	universal Being, the unbounded Self
Pūshan	sun
Pushpaka	Rāvaṇa's aerial chariot, originally created by Vishvakarman and stolen by Rāvaṇa from his half brother Kubera, the god of wealth
rāga	melody, song
Raghu	an illustrious king of the Ikshvaku dynasty; Rāma's great-grandfather, thus Rāma is known as Rāghava
Rāhu	ascending node of the moon; known as the head of the dragon, Rāhu sometimes devours the sun or the moon, causing an eclipse
rājā	king
rākshasa	demon
rākshasī	demoness
Rāma	hero of the Rāmāyaṇa, son of King Dasharatha, husband of Sītā
Rāma Charita Mānasa	a sixteenth-century Hindi version of the Rāmāyaṇa by Goswāmi Tulsīdās
Rāmachandra	nickname for Rāma, because he was radiant like Chandra, the full moon
Rāmāyaṇa	story of Rāma, one of the two great epics of India
rāshi	sign of the zodiac
Rāvaṇa	ten-headed rākshasa who ruled Lankā and stole Sītā; son of the sage Vishravā and grandson of Ṛishi Pulastya; his mother was the rākshasa Kaikasī
Ṛik	first of the four Vedas, *Ṛik Saṁhitā*
Ṛikshabila	beautiful cave that detained Hanumān and the other monkeys
Ṛishabha	one of the monkey generals; a mountain in the Himālayas
Ṛishi	seer, sage; custodian and teacher of Vedic knowledge who guides the people
Ṛishyamūka	mountaintop where Sugrīva lived

Ṛishyashṛinga	the youthful seer who performed the Ashvamedha Yagya to bestow children on King Dasharatha
Rohiṇī	consort of the moon, the ninth constellation of stars
Rūmā	wife of Sugrīva
Sagara	an ancestor of Rāma whose sixty thousand sons hollowed out the ocean and created a home for Sāgara, the lord of the ocean
Sāgara	lord of the ocean
Sāma	one of the four Vedas
samādhi	transcendental consciousness, pure consciousness, the state of Yoga
Sampāti	vulture, the older brother of Jatāyu
Saramā	demoness who guarded Sītā and soothed her
Sāraṇa	spy for Rāvaṇa
Sarasvatī	consort of Brahmā, goddess of learning and music
Sarayu	river circling Ayodhyā in the kingdom of Kosala (later spelled *Sarayū*)
Savitṛi	sun
Shabarī	woman saint who waited years to greet Rāma and Lakshmaṇa
Shani	Saturn
Sharabhanga	sage who lived in the forest
Shārdūla	spy for Rāvaṇa
Shatabali	one of the monkey generals
Shatrughna	brother of Rāma
Shiva	known as "the auspicious one," the deity responsible for destruction and reproduction; associated with silence, kindness, and benevolence, he is traditionally represented in the form of a linga; one of his consorts is Pārvatī
shloka	meter, verse (four lines with eight syllables each)
shoka	suffering

Shrī	title of honor—as in *Shrī Rāma*; at other times refers to light, grace, beauty, and the goddess Lakshmī
Shrutakīrti	wife of Shatrughna, niece of King Janaka
Shuka	Rāvaṇa's minister and spy
Shukra	Venus
Shūrpaṇakhā	demoness, sister of Rāvaṇa
siddha	perfected being
Siṁhikā	demoness who captured her prey by first seizing its shadow
Sītā	daughter of King Janaka, wife of Rāma
soma	ambrosia of immortality, the juice used in performing a yagya; the moon
Sthūlashirā	sage who cursed the Gandharva Danu
Sugrīva	leader of the monkeys, son of the sun
Sumantra	charioteer, friend, and chief minister of King Dasharatha
Sumitrā	queen of King Dasharatha, mother of the twins Lakshmaṇa and Shatrughna
sundara	beautiful
Supārshva	minister to Rāvaṇa
Surasā	mother of the serpents, tried to stop Hanumān from crossing the ocean
Sūrya	sun
Susheṇa	grandfather of Angada, monkey general, Āyurvedic doctor
Sutīkshṇa	sage who lived in the forest
Suvela	mountain nearest to Lankā
Svayamprabhā	sage who lived with Hemā in the Ṛikshabila Cave as her guardian
svayaṁvara	a royal wedding in which the royal princess could choose her spouse; in the Rāmāyaṇa, the spouse of Sītā had to first string Shiva's bow
Tamasā	river near Vālmīki's āshram
tapas	austerity, meditation; spiritual practice
Tāra	general in the monkey army
Tārā	wife of Bāli, Sugrīva's brother

Tātakā	demoness in the Daṇḍaka Forest killed by Rāma
tilaka	colorful ornamental mark placed in the center of the forehead
Trijatā	demoness who guarded Sītā and soothed her
Trikūta	three-peaked mountain on which Lankā was built
triloka	the three worlds: heaven (*svarloka*), earth *(mṛityuloka),* and the underworld (*pātālaloka*)
Trishiras	son of Rāvaṇa
Ūrmilā	wife of Lakshmaṇa, younger sister of Sītā
Ushas	dawn
Uttara	concluding, later, following
Vajradaṁshtra	warrior in Rāvaṇa's army
Vālmīki	composer of the Rāmāyaṇa who is also a sage in the Rāmāyaṇa
Vāmadeva	Ṛishi
vānara	the race of monkeylike celestial beings inhabiting the kingdom of Kishkindhā
Vanjulaka	considered an inauspicious bird in ancient texts; in English, the black-necked grebe
Varādha	giant rākshasa who lived in the forest
Varuṇa	water, one of the powers of nature
Vasishtha	guru to Rāma and the entire kingdom of Kosala
Vāyu	wind or air, one of the powers of nature, father of Hanumān
Veda	Knowledge; traditionally Veda is not a collection of man-made texts, but is cognized within consciousness; the "Vedas" sometimes refers to the four Vedas: *Ṛik*, *Sāma*, *Yajur*, and *Atharva Veda*; and sometimes refers to the Vedic literature as a whole.
Vedānga	section of the Sanskrit literature, there are six Vedāngas: *Shikshā, Kalpa, Vyākaraṇa, Nirukta, Chhandas*, and *Jyotisha*
Vibhīshaṇa	virtuous brother and minister of Rāvaṇa
Videha	kingdom ruled by King Janaka

Vidyujjihva	demon magician
Vidyunmālī	warrior in Rāvaṇa's army
vijaya	victory, a particular hour of the day
vīṇā	stringed instrument that resembles the sitār
Vinata	general in the monkey army
vinda	particular hour of the day; hour for finding, gaining, recovering
Vindhya	low mountain range in the south of India
Virūpākasha	general in Rāvaṇa's army
Vishṇu	known as "the one who pervades all," the deity responsible for preservation, associated with dynamism; traditionally he is said to have incarnated ten times, of which one is Rāma and one is Kṛishṇa; his consort is Lakshmī
Vishravas	sage, father of Rāvaṇa, Kubera, Kumbhakarṇa, and Vibhīshaṇa
Vishvakarman	divine architect of the Devas who built Lankā
Vishvāmitra	sage who took Rāma and Lakshmaṇa to the forest
yagya	Vedic performance to gain the support of the laws of nature, and create balance in nature; a ritual performed by Vedic pandits
yagyashālā	hall for performing a yagya
Yajur	one of the four Vedas
yaksha	spirit
Yama	god of death and immortality
Yoga	union, the settled mind; also, the various practices for settling the mind, such as yoga *āsanas* and meditation
yogi	one who has attained Yoga (*yogī* in Sanskrit)
yojana	measurement of distance, said to be between four and nine miles (from the root "yuj," which shares the same root as "yoke"; thus a yojana is the distance a cart can be driven by two bullocks who are yoked together (i.e., one yoke)
yuddha	war

yuga — a long age of the world. There are four yugas: *Sat* (1,728,000 years), *Tretā* (1,296,000 years), *Dvāpara* (864,000 years), and *Kali* (432,000 years); the Rāmāyaṇa is said to have occurred at the end of Tretā Yuga

Acknowledgments

While working on this joyful project on and off for two decades, we received the support and blessings of countless people along the way, and we thank them with all our hearts. We'd especially like to appreciate Allura Adelson, Care Connet, Cheryl Fusco Johnson, and Mary Zeilbeck, who read early drafts and gave us confidence that we could do justice to the original text while making it accessible to modern readers. Thanks to Bob and Carol Markowitz, Chris and Ellen Jones, Sue Brown, Cathy Gorini, and Jim Fairchild, who shared the manuscript with their students and offered valuable feedback on early versions.

We are forever indebted to Susan Shatkin, who poured her discerning intellect and magnanimous heart into a line-by-line edit that caught inconsistencies, embarrassing errors, and breaks in logic, each identified with sophisticated and thoughtful comments that inspired us to reach higher. Fran Clark contributed a thorough proofing, making the manuscript presentable for submission. Rhoda Orme-Johnson carefully reviewed the manuscript and gave us many helpful suggestions, which we incorporated into the final manuscript, and Lark Svenson also provided important insights for revision.

We are grateful to Mitch Horowitz, our editor at TarcherPerigee, who understood the relevance of this story for today's readers, opened the door to publication, and championed our project with enthusiasm. Many thanks to the hardworking production team, who efficiently shepherded the nearly five hundred manuscript pages to publication in record time; copy editor Ian Gibbs, who patiently tackled this very complicated work involving thousands of diacritical marks and Sanskrit letters; and the talented design team who created the elegant cover.

No words can express our gratitude for our families and especially our husbands, Janardhan Reddy and Thomas Egenes, who have given unselfish support to our many collaborations and lifelong endeavors. Tom played a special role in this manuscript, contributing the original Sanskrit translations at the end of each chapter and serving as chief cheerleader, champion, and Sanskrit consultant throughout dozens of revisions.

Most of all we are indebted to the tradition of knowledge that created this beautiful story, and to Maharishi, who taught us how to see it in all its depth and wisdom.

Books by
Kumuda Reddy and Linda Egenes

All Love Flows to the Self: Eternal Stories from the Upanishads by Kumuda Reddy, MD, Thomas Egenes, PhD, and Linda Egenes

Conquering Chronic Disease Through Maharishi Vedic Medicine by Kumuda Reddy, MD, with Linda Egenes

For a Blissful Baby: Healthy and Happy Pregnancy with Maharishi Vedic Medicine by Kumuda Reddy, MD, Linda Egenes, and Margaret Mullins, MSN, FNP

Super Healthy Kids: A Parent's Guide to Maharishi Ayurveda by Kumuda Reddy, MD, and Linda Egenes

Additional Books
by Kumuda Reddy

Ayurvedic Cooking Made Easy: 100+ Recipes for a Healthy You by Kumuda Reddy, MD, Janardhan Reddy, MD, and Bonita Pederson

Forever Healthy: Introduction to Maharishi Ayur-Veda Health Care by Kumuda Reddy, MD, and Stan Kendz

Golden Transition: Menopause Made Easy Through Maharishi Vedic Medicine by Kumuda Reddy, MD, and Janardhan Reddy, MD, with Sandra Willbanks

Living Life Free from Pain: Treating Arthritis, Joint Pain, Muscle Pain, and Fibromyalgia with Maharishi Vedic Medicine by Kumuda Reddy, MD, with Cynthia Lane

Putting Chronic Fatigue to Rest: Treating Chronic Fatigue and Chronic Fatigue Syndrome with Maharishi Ayurveda by Kumuda Reddy, MD, with Paul Stokstad

The Timeless Wisdom series of children's stories by Kumuda Reddy, MD, and John Emory Pruitt, including: *The Indigo Jackal*, *The Lion and the Hare*, *The Monkey and the Crocodile*, *The Wish That Came True*, *The Female Mouse*, and *The Hares and the Elephants*

About the Authors

LINDA EGENES is the author of more than five hundred articles about the benefits of meditation, yoga, and healthy living. She is the author of *Visits with the Amish: Impressions of the Plain Life*, and with Kumuda Reddy, MD, she co-authored three books on Maharishi Ayurveda for children and families as well as *All Love Flows to the Self: Eternal Stories from the Upanishads*. A practitioner of the Transcendental Meditation technique since 1971 and a certified teacher, Linda is an adjunct associate professor of writing at Maharishi University of Management in Fairfield, Iowa, where she lives with her husband, Sanskrit scholar and author Thomas Egenes.

Linda Egenes writes, "It is a tremendous privilege and joy to dive deeply into the timeless epic of the Ramayana, which has been my faithful companion for more than three decades. The charming story of Rama, Sita, and other enlightened heroes gently leads us to understand abstract principles of natural law. The story unfolds in layers of meaning and feeling, revealing hidden values that transform us and speed us on the path of self-realization."

KUMUDA REDDY, a former faculty member and anesthesiologist at Albany Medical College, practiced Western medicine in the United States for more than twenty-five years. After receiving her training in Maharishi Ayurveda, she devoted herself to bringing this holistic, natural healthcare system to her private practice. Dr. Reddy has co-authored eight books on Maharishi Ayurveda, and the Timeless Wisdom children's series, based on traditional Indian tales that she first heard as a child. Dr. Reddy and her husband, Dr. Janardhan Reddy, divide their time between the US and India, where they continue working toward their vision of creating a disease-free society through Maharishi Ayurveda.

Kumuda Reddy writes, "The Ramayana has always been very dear to my heart. I first heard the stories of Rama and Sita from my grandmother, which made a deep impact on my life even as a child. As I grew older I realized that the Ramayana is the basis of the very life and existence for every individual. In a subtle yet powerful way, it teaches the important values of life, the nuances of harmonious behavior, the sweetness of relationships, and how to pursue goals and ambitions while staying in accord with natural law.

"Rama is the ideal human being, and so also Sita and many of the characters in the Ramayana. My grandmother told us to be like a Rama, Sita or Hanuman, and would even tell us to choose someone like Rama or Sita for a spouse, and to aspire to have children who are also like Rama and Sita. That is the power of the Ramayana. The Ramayana plants the seed in every human mind and soul to pave the way for future evolution. The Ramayana took place in a bygone era, but it remains evergreen and the guiding light for all times and for all generations. I hope all of you can enjoy."